Thirteen Theories of
Human Nature

Thirteen Theories of
Human Nature

Seventh Edition

LESLIE STEVENSON

DAVID L. HABERMAN

PETER MATTHEWS WRIGHT

CHARLOTTE WITT

New York   Oxford
OXFORD UNIVERSITY PRESS

Oxford University Press is a department of the University of Oxford.
It furthers the University's objective of excellence in research, scholarship,
and education by publishing worldwide. Oxford is a registered trade mark
of Oxford University Press in the UK and certain other countries.

Published in the United States of America by Oxford University Press
198 Madison Avenue, New York, NY 10016, United States of America.

For titles covered by Section 112 of the US Higher Education Opportunity
Act, please visit www.oup.com/us/he for the latest information about
pricing and alternate formats.

Library of Congress Cataloging-in-Publication Data

Names: Stevenson, Leslie Forster, author.
Title: Thirteen theories of human nature/Leslie Stevenson, David L.
    Haberman, Peter Matthews Wright, Charlotte Witt.
Description: Seventh Edition. | New York : Oxford University Press, 2017. |
    Previous editions include: Twelve theories of human nature / Leslie
    Stevenson (6th ed.); Ten theories of human nature / Leslie Stevenson (5th
    ed.) | Includes index.
Identifiers: LCCN 2016040847 (print) | LCCN 2017007211 (ebook) | ISBN
    9780190604721 | ISBN 9780190604738
Subjects: LCSH: Philosophical anthropology. | Religions. | Philosophy.
Classification: LCC BD450 .T547 2017 (print) | LCC BD450 (ebook) | DDC
    128--dc23
LC record available at https://lccn.loc.gov/2016040847

9 8 7 6 5 4 3 2 1
Printed by LSC Communications in the United States of America

To my daughters, Sonia and Lydia, who have,
of course, taught me much about
human nature
L. S.

To my parents, Reuben and Ruth,
in many ways the sources of my own
human nature
D. H.

To the memory of
Nasr Hamid Abu Zayd
P. W.

For my mother, Mary Fox Witt
C. W.

Contents

Preface to the Seventh Edition

From the first edition (*Seven Theories*) way back in the 1970s, this book has aimed to present a variety of classic understandings of human nature in a way that is accurate, sympathetic yet critical, and at a level that is accessible to students of many disciplines and to the general reader. The number of theories considered now increases to thirteen (we are not superstitious!).

NEW FEATURES OF THIS EDITION

- Charlotte Witt has contributed a new thirteenth chapter on feminist theories of human nature.

- I decided to omit the concluding chapter (which has not been much used), but I have incorporated discussion of ethical and religious implications of evolution as a fourth section in Chapter 12.

- We have boldfaced key terms at their first occurrence and listed them at the end of each chapter. We have provided a glossary of all key terms at the end of the book.

- We have suggested some questions for classroom discussion at the end of each chapter.

- We have taken the opportunity to make a large number of minor corrections and clarifications of wording.

Thanks to Gregory Bock, Paul Carelli, Anthony Flood, Jo Ann Hedleston, Elizabeth Jelinek, Jeff Jordan, Errol Katayama, Joshua Lott, Michelle

Maise, and Ben Miller, who supplied helpful comments and suggestions for this new edition. Thanks also to Robert Miller and Alyssa Palazzo of Oxford University Press for their initiative and guidance in producing this enlarged seventh edition.

St. Andrews   Leslie Stevenson
May 2017

Introduction: Rival Theories and Critical Assessments

This book is meant for anyone who is looking for a "philosophy of life," an understanding of human nature that gives guidance for how we should live. Such guidance is usually based on a *diagnosis* of what tends to go wrong with us and some sort of *ideal* of what we ought to be.

We are using our title phrase "theory of human nature" in a very wide sense to cover ancient religious traditions, some classic philosophical systems, and various more recent theories that claim to use the methods of science to make prescriptions for human life and society. This is to stretch the word "theory" beyond scientific theories. We could use the word "philosophy" in its classical sense of *philosophia* (love of wisdom), worldview (derived from the German term *Weltanschauung*), or ideology (the beliefs and values by which a certain society or community lives or claims to live). In our wide sense a "theory of human nature" encompasses the following:

1. a background metaphysical understanding of the universe and humanity's place in it
2. a theory of human nature in the more specific sense of a distinctive set of claims about human beings, human society, and the human condition

3. a diagnosis of some typical defect, what tends to go wrong in human life and society

4. a prescription for correcting what goes wrong and an ideal for how human life should best be lived

Only theories in this very wide sense offer us hope of solutions to the problems of humankind. For instance, the assertion that everyone tends to be selfish (i.e., to act only for his or her own self-interest) is a very brief diagnosis, but it offers no understanding of what *makes* us selfish and no suggestion as to how we might overcome it. The command that we should all love one another is an attractive yet naive ideal; but it gives no explanation of why we find that so difficult and no explanation of what *sort* of "love" of others we should aspire to, and it offers no help in achieving it. The Darwinian theory of evolution says something important about the place of human beings in the universe, but it does not offer any prescription: as a purely scientific, causal explanation of how our human species came into existence, it does not tell us anything about the purpose or meaning of our life.

This book is not a conventional introduction to academic philosophy as usually defined these days, with its divisions of logic, philosophy of language, metaphysics, epistemology, philosophy of mind, ethics, political philosophy, aesthetics, philosophy of religion, and so on. We will touch on many of those areas, but our aim is to focus on thirteen selected systems of thought that offer answers to the sorts of existential, life-relevant questions that motivate many people to study philosophy in the first place, such as "What is our place in the universe?" and "Why are we here?" But it is important to note that such questions are ambiguous between the causal sense—"What brought us into existence?"—and the purposive sense—"What are we here *for*?" (What should we aim at, and do?).

Obviously, much depends on what theory of human nature we accept: for individuals, the meaning and purpose of our lives, what we ought to do or strive for, what we may hope to achieve or to become; for societies, what vision of human community we hope to work toward, what sort of social changes we favor. Our answers to these huge questions will depend on whether we think there is some "true" or "innate" nature of human beings and some objective standards of value for human life. If so, what is it, and what are they? Are we essentially products of evolution, programmed to pursue our self-interest and to reproduce our genes and thus fulfill our biological drives? Or is there no such "essential" human nature, only a capacity to be molded by society and its changing economic, political, and cultural forces? Or is there some transcendent, objective (perhaps divine) purpose for human lives and human history?

RIVAL THEORIES

On these fundamental questions there have been, of course, a variety of views. "What is man that Thou art mindful of him . . . Thou hast made him a little lower than the angels, and hast crowned him with glory and honor," wrote the author of Psalm 8. The Bible, from the book of Genesis that opens the Hebrew scriptures to the Christian New Testament, sees human beings as created by a transcendent God in his own image, with a God-given purpose for human life. So does the Qur'an, the holy book of Islam. There are the great philosophical systems of Plato, Aristotle, and Kant, which set out objective standards of value for human lives and societies to aspire to.

On the other hand, Karl Marx wrote in the nineteenth century, "The real nature of man is the totality of social relations." Marx denied the existence of God and held that each person is a product of the particular economic stage of human society in which he or she lives. "Man is condemned to be free," said Jean-Paul Sartre, writing in occupied France during the Second World War. Sartre agreed with Marx's atheism but differed from him in holding that we are *not* determined by our society or by anything else; rather, every individual person is free to decide what he or she wants to be and do. In contrast, would-be scientific theorists of human nature such as E. O. Wilson and Richard Dawkins have treated humans as products of evolution, with biologically determined, species-specific desires and patterns of behavior.

It will not escape readers' notice that these quotations from the Bible, Marx, and Sartre all use the word "man," where the intention was surely to refer to *all* human beings, including women and children. Such usage has been criticized for contributing to questionable traditions of the social and familial dominance of men and the neglect or oppression of women. These are important issues that involve much more than linguistic usage. We will note what our selected theories have to say about commonalities and differences between men and women. We will try to avoid sexist language ourselves (but it cannot always be avoided in quotations). Feminist issues will be more explicitly addressed in the new final chapter of the book.

Different conceptions of human nature lead to different views about what we ought to do and how we can do it. If an all-powerful and supremely good God made us, then it is his purpose that defines what we can be and ought to be, and we can presumably look to him for help. If we are products of our society yet many human lives are unsatisfactory, there can be no real solution until human society is transformed. If we are radically free and can never escape the necessity for individual decision, then we have to accept this fundamental truth about ourselves and make our choices with full awareness of what we are doing. But if our biological nature predisposes us to think, feel, and act in certain ways, then we had better take realistic account of that in our individual lives and in social policy.

Rival beliefs about human nature are typically embodied in different individual ways of life and in political and economic systems. Marxist theory (in various interpretations) so dominated public life in communist-ruled countries in the twentieth century that any public questioning of it could have serious consequences. In earlier centuries Christianity occupied a similarly dominant position in Western society in belief and practice; heretics were often persecuted or even burned at the stake. The sixteenth-century Reformation resulted in multiple new differences within Christianity (which was already divided between Roman and Eastern traditions). There remains in some societies or subgroups a Christian consensus that individuals can oppose only at some social cost. Since its rapid expansion in the early Middle Ages Islam has occupied a dominating position in many countries, though it too has split into rival traditions, most notably the persisting conflict between Sunni and Shi'a. Judaism, based on ethnic identity at least as much as on theological belief, has survived the twentieth-century Holocaust and many earlier persecutions; but religious Judaism also divides into rival sects.

Yet in contemporary Western societies it is quite widely assumed that there are no objective values for human living, only subjective individual choices. Liberal democracy is enshrined in the American Declaration of Independence, with its acknowledgment of the right of each "man" (i.e., *person*) to "life, liberty and the pursuit of happiness"—usually interpreted as the right of each individual to pursue his or her own *conception* of happiness. It should be noted, however, that those who believe there *are* objective moral standards (whether religious or secular) may still defend a liberal political system if they think it unjust or unwise to try to *enforce* those standards in law and social policy. So although value-subjectivism supports political liberalism, the reverse is not the case.

Let us look a little more closely at Christianity and Marxism as rival theories of human nature and note some structural parallels between them. (Detailed examination comes in Chapters 6 and 9.) Although they are radically different in content, there are some remarkable similarities in the way the parts of each doctrine fit together and are used to justify different ways of life and practical policies.

First, each makes claims about the character of the universe as a whole. Christianity is, of course, committed to belief in God, a personal being who is omnipotent, omniscient, and perfectly good, the Creator, Ruler, and Judge of everything in this world. Marx notoriously condemned religion as "the opium of the people," that is, illusory beliefs that distract people from the real socioeconomic problems of their existence. Accordingly, Christianity and Marxism offer very different interpretations of the meaning of human history. For the Christian, God uses the events of history to work out his purposes, speaking first to his chosen people as recorded in the Old Testament (the Hebrew scriptures), then revealing himself supremely in the life and death of his incarnate son Jesus Christ, and eventually bringing human history to an end in judgment. Marx claimed to find a pattern in history that is entirely internal to it, namely, a series of stages of economic development from tribal society through ancient slavery and feudalism to capitalism, with a predicted transition to an alleged consummation in a truly communist society. Thus, both see a meaning and purpose in history, though they differ fundamentally about the moving force and the direction of travel.

Second, they give very different accounts of the essential nature of human beings. According to Christianity (along with Judaism and Islam), we are made in the image of God and our individual destinies in eternity depend on our relationships with God. Everyone is free to accept or reject God's purpose, and we will be judged according to how we exercise that freedom. Marxism denies any life after death and last judgment, holding instead that we are formed by the societies we are born and socialized into and that the nature of our lives and the progress we are able to make individually and socially depend on socioeconomic structure and change.

Third, there are different diagnoses of what is wrong with the human condition. Christianity says that our relationship with God is disrupted because we misuse our God-given freedom and are infected with sin. Marx also implied a similarly sweeping value judgment with his concept of "alienation," which suggests that we fail to meet some ideal standard; his claim is that all human beings have potentials that *ought* to be fulfilled but will be only if capitalism is replaced by communism.

Fourth, there are very different prescriptions. Christianity holds that only the power of God himself can save us from our condition of sin, and the startling cosmic claim is that in the life and death of Jesus God has acted to redeem the whole world. It is painfully obvious that the world has not been perfected yet, but the Christian demand is that we each accept what God has done for us in Christ and work it out in our lives with his help. Human society will not be redeemed until individual lives are transformed by divine grace. Marxism says the opposite: that there can be no substantial improvement in individual lives until the economic system is transformed into communism. This revolutionary change is said to be inevitable because of the laws of economic development, but individuals who realize the way history is moving can join the communist movement and help shorten the birth pangs of the new age. Each belief looks forward to a future fulfillment in which human beings and society will be redeemed, whether in life after death or in a future stage of history.

As a last point of comparison, note that for each of these total belief systems, there has been a human institution that claims the allegiance of believers and exerts its authority on belief and practice: the Church or the Communist Party. To be more accurate, there have long been rival Christian churches, and since Marx's time there has been a variety of communist or socialist parties. Notoriously, churches and revolutionaries have differed markedly (and sometimes violently) among themselves about the correct interpretation of their fundamental dogmas and how to apply them to changing social conditions.

Faith in Marxist theory and the ideal of communism was found in the early twentieth century among a few Western intellectuals and in those brought up in the Soviet system, but it is now hard to find any "true believers," except perhaps in North Korea. China is still nominally communist with a one-party state, but its practice has become increasingly capitalist and nationalist. Christian faith is still with us, in many varieties. Tragic history has eroded belief in secular schemes of salvation, but new species may emerge.

Outside the West other theories of human nature have had significant social influence. Since 1948 Judaism has been re-established in Israel, one of the few contemporary states officially based on one religion. Islam, which shares its Middle Eastern origins with Judaism and Christianity, is undergoing a resurgence as the peoples of the Muslim world reject some aspects of contemporary Western culture (we are thinking here not of the terrorism that dominates the news but of the millions of peaceful defenders of Islamic religious and cultural identity). In India Hinduism is resurgent. Buddhism, originally an Indian religion, spread into China, Japan, and elsewhere in Asia; it has gained converts in the West and has taken nationalist form in some countries. After the withering away of communism, many Russians have returned to their Orthodox Christian tradition. And as China evolves beyond Marxism, the ancient Chinese philosophy of Confucius has been looked at again.

We have selected thirteen theories (philosophies or worldviews) for detailed examination. In each case we provide some critical comments that we hope will encourage students to think for themselves, and we recommend plenty of further reading. We will not endorse any one theory as the "best buy" but leave our readers to make up their own minds. Before we begin our main business, let us review the prospects for impartial, rational assessment of these highly controversial matters.

THE CRITICAL EXAMINATION OF THEORIES

Many of these theories have been embodied in human societies and institutions. As such, they are not just intellectual constructions but ways of life, subject to historical change, growth, and decay. A system of beliefs about the world and human nature that is held by some set of people not in a purely academic or scientific way but as giving rise to their way of life has been called an "**ideology**."

When a belief is used to justify the way of life of a social group, it will be difficult for the members of that community to consider it objectively. There may be strong social pressures to conform to it. People will feel that their set of beliefs, even if perhaps open to some theoretical difficulties, contains vitally important insights, a vision of essential truths that have practical, or even inspirational, importance. For many people, to question their ideology or theory of human nature is to threaten what gives meaning, purpose, and hope to their life and to cause psychological discomfort or distress. Inertia and unwillingness to admit that one is wrong play a part here. If one has been brought up in a certain belief and its associated way of life or if one has converted to it and followed its precepts, it takes courage to question or abandon one's life commitment (sometimes a convert becomes even more strongly committed to a belief system than those born into it).

The prospects for impartial, rational, "purely philosophical" examination and evaluation may not seem bright then. In so many discussions and debates in public or in private one feels that people's positions have already been decided (by social conditioning or individual commitment) long before and that all one gets by way of "debate" is a restatement of prejudices on all sides. Thus, one finds people dogmatically defending their favored ideology or theory of human nature in the face of all intellectual and moral objections.

First, believers typically look for some way of replying to objections, but often that seems to be merely "explaining away," recycling elements of the favored ideology without dealing with the real point of an objection. For example, in response to the standard "problem of evil" a theist may say that God does not always prevent evil or answer our prayers and that what seems bad *to us* may ultimately be for the best. Human suffering under a revolution or new political regime has often been excused by its propagandists as the necessary birth pangs of a new world order. Preachers and politicians become well practiced at such justification of the ways of God and his church or of the ruling party and its leader.

Second, the believer can take the offensive by attacking the motivation of the critic. Christians may say that those who persist in raising objections are blinded by sin, that it is their own pride that prevents them from seeing the light. The Marxist may claim that those who do not recognize the truth of Marx's analysis are deluded by the "false consciousness" typical of those who benefit from capitalist society. In the case of Freudian theory (see Chapter 10) criticisms of psychoanalytic theory have sometimes been diagnosed as resistance based on unconscious emotion. In such ways, suspicion is cast on a critic's motives by analyzing them in terms of the very theory being criticized.

If a theory is defended by these two devices

1. not allowing any evidence to count against the theory, always assuming that there must be some way of explaining away putative counterevidence

2. answering criticism by analyzing the motivations of the critic in terms of the theory itself

we can say that it is being held as a "**closed system.**" However, this does not mean that all believers in a theory have to hold it in a closed-minded way.

Is it possible, then, to discuss various theories of human nature rationally and objectively, as we set out to do in this book? When such theories are embodied in ways of life, belief in them seems to go beyond reasoning: the ultimate appeal may be to faith or authority, community membership, loyalty to church or party or nation. There may be no answer offered to the questions "Why should I believe this?" or "Why should I accept this authority?" that will satisfy someone who is not already a member of the relevant group or tradition.

In the contemporary world rival traditions and ideologies are as influential as ever. Religious, cultic, political, national, racial, ethnic, therapeutic, and gender-based dogmas are asserted with various degrees of aggression or politeness, crudity or sophistication. The mass media may try to bring different cultures or traditions into discussion, but all too often the results are only confrontation rather than genuine dialogue, mutual listening, and understanding. It is obvious that many people feel the attractions of certainty, commitment, identity, and membership of a strongly defined community, notably in various forms of "fundamentalism" that appeal to what are seen, rightly or wrongly, as the *essential* themes of Christianity, Judaism, Islam, Hinduism, Marxism, "free market-ism," or nationalism.

In reaction to all this, skepticism and cynicism are tempting. Nowadays they tend to take the form of cultural relativism or **postmodernism**, according to which no particular cultural tradition or ideology or theory of human nature can have any more justification than any other. One of the most influential prophets of these contemporary trends was the nineteenth-century German philosopher Friedrich Nietzsche, who has been described as a "master of suspicion" because he was always ready (like Marx before him and Freud after him) to diagnose an unacknowledged ideological commitment or psychological need behind claims to supposedly "objective" truth or morality. If we jump to the conclusion that there can be no such thing as a true account of human nature or any rational evaluation of rival theories about it, the project of this book may seem doomed from the start.

We want to suggest, however, that such despair would be premature. For one thing, not all the theories we discuss are the ideologies of any identifiable social group, and in those cases there is less likelihood of their being defended as closed systems. But more importantly, even if a theory is held by many people in a closed-minded way, some degree of rational evaluation is still possible for those who are prepared to try it. We can always distinguish what someone says from his or her motivation for saying it. Motivation is relevant if we wish to understand the personality and social background of the speaker, but if we are concerned with the truth or falsity of what is claimed and with whether there are any good reasons for believing it, then the motives of particular speakers are irrelevant. Someone may have admirable motivation for saying something that is nevertheless false, and someone else may be saying something true even if his or her motivation for saying it is questionable. Criticism is not refuted by disparagement of the critic (the most annoying critics are those who are partly right).

So if our concern is whether a theory is true, the objections that anyone produces against it must be replied to on their merits, regardless of people's motives. And if motivations *are* considered, to analyze them in terms of the theory under discussion is to assume the truth of that theory, and thus to beg the question (i.e., to argue in a circle), to take as granted something that should not be taken for granted. An objection to a theory cannot be rationally defeated just by reasserting part of the theory. It is open to us to make the effort to discuss and evaluate on their own merits the propositions and theories that anyone asserts (with all due politeness and respect to the assertor).

As to the first feature of closed systems, we can always ask whether the attempt to "explain away" an objection is successful. It is not enough just to come up with a rhetorical flourish, a one-liner or sound bite that may surprise people in debate and convey the impression that one has successfully maintained one's position. Rational, philosophical discussion—unlike "debates" in politics and in the media—is open-ended: there are no time constraints, and it is always possible to re-examine what has been said, to see if it can stand up to further scrutiny. So any attempt at "explaining away" can be held up to careful examination, to try to decide whether it is really convincing. Many people do not have the time, patience, or willingness to engage in that kind of ongoing, open-minded debate—but that does not prevent others from trying their best to do so. The ancient Greek philosopher Socrates gave us this method of "Socratic dialogue" (see Chapter 4). Jesus also set an example of being willing to talk and argue seriously with anyone, even the socially outcast, though not so much about theological questions but with concern for their spiritual well-being.

So we say to the committed (including "fundamentalists" of any religious or political persuasion) that we are asking you not to give up your commitment but to *think* about it. You can compare it with other theories, considering how far you would agree or disagree with them. You can consider how you can best reply to objections to your own beliefs. You can think about which parts of your tradition you feel lay hold of fundamental truths and which parts are perhaps optional—historically influential but not to be imposed on everybody now. It is up to you at every stage to make up (and perhaps change) your own mind about exactly what you want to affirm.

To the uncommitted or skeptically inclined we say, everybody has to have some sort of theory of human nature or philosophy to live by: you will surely have *some* conception of what affects human well-being and some views about what is worth aiming for, at least your own long-term happiness—and what does that consist in? We invite you to consider our selected systems of thought, to compare your present view (however minimal or relativist it may be) with them, and to try to rationally evaluate the differences. No human being who lives at a more than animal level can completely opt out of offering reasons for his or her beliefs and actions.

SOME BASIC PHILOSOPHICAL TOOLS

If we are in the business of serious rational evaluation of beliefs, theories, and ideologies, we need to make distinctions between various different kinds of statements or claims, to see what kind of consideration or justification is appropriate to each. What follows is part of any basic philosophical tool kit.

Value Judgments

First, a statement may be a **value judgment**", saying what ought (or ought not) to happen, rather than a factual statement about what is actually the case. Claims about human nature are especially subject to ambiguity on this. For example, is it "natural" for human beings to drink cows' milk, to tunnel into the earth for minerals, or to fly about in planes? Is it "natural" for us to be selfish or compassionate, peaceful or aggressive, well balanced or obsessive? The words "natural," "unnatural," and "nature" should be regarded as danger signals here, indicating possible confusion. If someone says "Human beings are naturally X," we should ask them, "Do you mean that all (or most) humans are X?" or "Human beings ought to be X?" or "We have an innate tendency to X?" (and should that tendency be encouraged or resisted?) or perhaps "Humans beings were X before civilization?" (and what is civilization, anyway?).

To take a controversial case about which there are deeply held beliefs and attitudes on all sides, it is often said that homosexuality is unnatural, and it is usually implied that that makes it wrong. Homosexuality has been known in almost every human society, but the reply will be that it is practiced only by a minority in each. Yet there are plenty of activities that are minority pursuits without being wrong (e.g., stamp collecting, playing tennis, or having your head shaved). Conversely, in ancient Greece perhaps a majority of men engaged in homosexual as well as heterosexual relations, but someone can still assert that that was wrong. Clearly, the sociological facts about who, or how many, go in for a practice do not decide its rightness or wrongness. Obviously, homosexual acts are unnatural in the sense that they cannot result in conception, so two cohabiting gays or lesbians cannot have a family to which both have contributed their genes. But these biological facts do not decide the relevant questions of value: whether everybody should have children, whether artificial ("unnatural?") means of conception by insemination are wrong, and whether the *only* right way of bringing up children is in the traditional ("nuclear") family. And, of course, the *historical* fact that an authority (a sacred text, cultural or tribal tradition, or legal statute) has outlawed homosexuality does not make it wrong for everyone, everywhere. But we are not here trying to *decide* this emotive issue—we are merely using it as a vivid example of the need to distinguish factual assertions from value judgments (confusion between the two is called the **naturalistic fallacy**). Another example involves the concept of **person**, which is crucial for so much of our ethical thought. Who or what counts as a person? Much of the controversy about abortion revolves around the question of whether a human fetus is a person. Does a person come into existence at the very moment of conception when sperm meets egg, at some stage of pregnancy (which stage?), or perhaps not until birth? What about a human who is brain-dead or so brain-damaged or demented as to be permanently incapable of all communication? Is he or she still a person? Or are there perhaps *degrees* of personhood: can it come into existence in stages or fade away gradually? If intelligent and friendly aliens from another planet get to communicate with us, would they count as persons? So can there be humans who are not persons and persons who are not human?

These questions may sound as if they are about a matter of fact, as if there is some esoteric, hard-to-discern truth about who or what is really a person that might be decided by further scientific research or for some people might be resolved in a different way by the authority of a moral or religious or legal tradition. But we suggest that the word "person" is a value term, meaning a being that has some degree of rationality, free will, and moral responsibility and accordingly deserves fundamental respect and should be accorded rights and duties. "Human being" is often used synonymously with "person," but it helps clarity of thought to keep it as a factual, biological term for the species *Homo sapiens.* If we make that distinction, there may be radically defective members of our species (for example, the brain-dead) who do not merit the value term "person," and for all we know there may be intelligent nonhuman species in the universe who should count as persons.

The human nature we discuss in this book is the nature of our biological species, but most, if not quite all, members of the human species have sufficient rationality, free will, and responsibility to count as persons. It is typical for us to manifest those distinctive mental capacities; they develop gradually in infancy and childhood, but they are deficient in those who are severely mentally handicapped and can fade away in mental illness or dementia. At the edges, therefore, personhood would seem to be a matter of degree.

Scientific Theories

Value judgments cannot be proved or disproved merely by finding out facts in the world, though some facts about human nature may be very relevant to them, for example, the fact that human infants and children need long-term loving care to develop well. If a statement *can* be proved or disproved by investigation of the relevant facts, involving perception through our human senses, sometimes aided by instruments, it is called an **empirical statement**.

Science depends crucially on empirical reports of observable facts, often in experimentally controlled situations (though meteorologists can't control the weather and astronomers can't perform experiments on the stars). But science is much more than the recording of individual observations; it typically involves the search for general statements ("laws of nature") that hold true universally throughout space and time. Scientific theorizing now extends to millions of years of the prehistory of the earth and earlier forms of life on earth and to the furthest reaches of the universe, thus to regions of space and time that we cannot directly perceive. It also tells us about the DNA in every living cell, the chemical elements and their laws of combination, the atomic structure of the elements themselves, and the still smaller entities that mysteriously obey the probabilistic laws of quantum mechanics. None of this is observable by our human senses; rather, these theories are evidenced by our *interpretation* of what we can observe, such as the ways in which stuffs chemically interact, the outputs of radio telescopes, X-ray crystallography, or experiments in elaborate and expensive particle accelerators. The testing of scientific theories typically involves assumptions about how the relevant pieces of kit and measuring devices work. The connection with human observations is indirect but real.

The twentieth-century philosopher of science Karl Popper put the emphasis on **falsifiability** as a criterion for scientific status. He pointed out that scientific theories can never be completely and conclusively verified, for their laws have implications for what happens *anywhere* and, obviously, we can never check out the contents of the whole universe throughout all time. However, it is an elementary truth of logic that if we come across even a single genuine counterexample to a putative law of nature, that decisively proves it false. Popper treated the practice of science as a two-step process of thinking up (creatively and imaginatively) general theories as hypotheses to try to explain the facts observed so far and then devising crucial tests for these hypotheses (often in cunningly designed experimental setups) to find out whether they hold true in those conditions. There are plenty of instances in the history of science when a previously accepted theory has been found to be false or to apply only within a more limited class of cases than previously thought. But that should not diminish our confidence in those fundamental theories that have been confirmed over and over again in a huge variety of conditions, such as the laws of gravitation, chemical combination, and natural selection as a mechanism of biological evolution (see Chapter 12). Although the *logical* possibility of finding counterexamples to these theories always remains, they can be said to be known beyond all reasonable doubt, for they apply without exception to everything that has been observed so far.

Falsifiability can thus be used as a criterion to distinguish scientific theories from metaphysical claims. But "scientific" here does not imply *true*, only that the theory has the crucial empirical status that some logically possible observations could count as evidence against it. In other words, candidates for scientific truth have to submit themselves to the test of observation, a test that they may either fail or live on to fight another day, perhaps passing further tests, and thereby earn the status of (at least provisional) knowledge.

Metaphysical Theories

"**Metaphysics**" is a word that has had many uses, some of them honorific, many of them not. Metaphysical statements or theories make some very general and fundamental claim about the nature of everything that exists, typically going beyond scientific evidence – hence the term "metaphysics." According to Popper, they are not scientific unless they are capable, in principle, of some sort of empirical test. The eighteenth-century German philosopher Immanuel Kant presented a famous trio of metaphysical claims—the existence of God, the immortality of the soul, and the freedom of the will—which he said cannot be empirically proved or disproved, though he argued that we need to believe them on other grounds connected with our moral lives (see Chapter 8).

A traditional metaphysical claim about human nature is **dualism**, the view that we have immortal souls or, rather, that we essentially *are* immaterial souls (as Plato and Descartes argued, see Chapter 4 and the Historical Interlude between Chapters 7 and 8). Usually, a **soul** is understood as a nonmaterial, nonobservable substance that persists through time, carrying personal identity, so that we can continue to exist as the same person after death. Could the existence of such souls be confirmed, and more crucially could it be *falsified* by any possible observation? In this life our states of consciousness, our thoughts and emotions and even perhaps our spiritual states, can be expressed through what we say and do; and human speech and actions are readily observable. But that truism is common to both dualist and materialist metaphysics of human nature, and cannot be deployed to the advantage of either since **materialism** says that all our mental states are somehow embodied in our brain states.

"Spiritualists" who believe that the dead can communicate with us claim that their seances provide evidence from "the other side," but their alleged evidence is not usually submitted to independent scrutiny. If the medium comes up with factual details that he or she could not have come to know in any normal way, the hypothesis of telepathic knowledge is simpler than the claim of communication from a deceased person. So if no observable evidence can count for or against dualism, it is not a scientific but a metaphysical theory. But the same is true of materialism since all observable evidence can presumably be interpreted within a materialist scheme and so could not falsify it.

This example strongly suggests the inadequacy of some philosophers' attempts to dismiss metaphysical statements as meaningless. David Hume in the eighteenth century (see the Historical Interlude), Comte in the nineteenth, and Schlick and Ayer in the twentieth (the so-called logical positivists) argued that any statement that is neither true by definition nor empirical is meaningless. (They also treated value judgments as not really statements but recommendations to action, a kind of disguised imperative.) But it is now generally agreed that this was too short a way with metaphysical theories. They are not nonsense like "The mome raths outgrabe" (Lewis Carroll), or in a different way "Colorless green ideas sleep furiously" (Noam Chomsky), nor are they self-contradictory like "Death is the end of life, but people live on after death." However, the challenge remains that any statement that is neither a value judgment nor true by mere definition (an **analytic statement**), nor testable by observation, has a problematic status. The examples considered above suggest that some of the most interesting and controversial claims about human nature may not be empirically testable. This need not condemn them outright, but it is important to establish this, for they cannot then claim the epistemological status of being scientific truths that are justified by objective observation plus rational, culture-neutral argument. Perhaps metaphysical statements can have some other legitimate function, but we had better inquire carefully what that might be in each case.

Courses in moral philosophy, theory of knowledge (**epistemology**), philosophy of science, and metaphysics consider these issues. But the aim of this book is to examine specific theories of human nature in detail. We begin with religious traditions that are much older than science, usually based on the inspired teachings or example of a charismatic founder (or set of founders). The philosophies of Plato and Aristotle were based more on rational argument, with some appeal to well-known empirical facts (the beginnings of science can be found among the ancient Greeks). Kant, writing a century after modern science got going, was explicit about the difference between his philosophy and science, as was Sartre.

Marx and Freud presented their views as scientific theories, but as we will see, it is questionable whether they measure up to that standard. Darwin and his successors in twentieth-century biology were certainly in the business of the scientific study of human nature, but as we will see, especially in Chapter 12, it is highly debatable whether science alone can support judgments of value and social policy.

KEY TERMS

analytic statement	materialism
closed system	metaphysics
dualism	naturalistic fallacy
empirical statement	person
epistemology	postmodernism
falsifiability	soul
ideology	value judgment

1

Confucianism: The Way of the Sages

No other single figure has had more influence on Chinese thought and civilization than Confucius (551–479 B.C.E.). Little is known for certain about this important figure who came to be regarded as "the teacher" in many periods of Chinese history. He was born into the aristocratic yet poor K'ung family in the state of Lu, now part of the province of Shantung. We are told that as a youth he was orphaned early and was very fond of learning. Later in his life he left his home state of Lu and traveled throughout several regions of China offering his service as an adviser to feudal lords; however, he was never successful at obtaining a position that would allow him to put his ideas into practice and so returned to Lu to devote the remainder of his life to teaching. It is useful to keep this failure in mind while considering certain aspects of his teachings. Confucius became honored in Chinese chronicles as the Great Master K'ung or K'ung Fu-tzu (or Kongfuzi), better known in the West in the Latinized form "Confucius."

By all accounts, the text known as *Lun Yu*—usually rendered into English as *The Analects*—is the most reliable source of Confucius's ideas. It consists of scattered sayings of the master that were compiled by his disciples after his death. It is a matter of scholarly debate whether any or all of the *Analects* can be regarded as the actual words of Confucius, and many will argue that some of the chapters are later additions. Although Confucianism is a complex tradition with a long history of development, the *Analects* gives voice to early and central Confucian ideas that came to define the tradition for many centuries and continue to do so. Therefore, for the purposes of this introduction, we focus exclusively on the *Analects*, treating the text as a whole, and use the name "Confucius" to refer to the source of the sayings recorded in it. Two later developments within Confucianism that pertain to theories of human nature are explored toward the end of this chapter.

THEORY OF THE UNIVERSE

The main emphasis in the *Analects* is on humanism, not metaphysics. That is, Confucius was concerned primarily with basic human welfare and spoke little about the ultimate nature of the world in which we live. When once asked about worship of gods and spirits, Confucius replied, "You are not able even to serve man. How can you serve the spirits?" (XI.12). And when asked about death, he said, "You do not understand even life. How can you understand death?" (XI.12). Avoiding metaphysical speculation, Confucius instead advocated good government that would promote the well-being of the common people and would bring about harmonious relations among citizens. Confucius did, however, recognize that there are forces in the universe that determine our lives. He characterized these by employing two related meanings of the term *ming*: the **Decree of Heaven** (*t'ien ming*) and **destiny** (*ming*).

Confucius insisted that we live in a moral world. Morality is part of the very fabric of the universe; for Confucius, there is something ultimate and transcendent about ethical conduct. He once remarked, "Heaven is author of the virtue that is in me" (VII.23). The concept of the Decree of Heaven was widely accepted in China during Confucius's day. The Decree of Heaven was generally understood to mean a moral imperative for governance, based on the belief that heaven cares profoundly about the welfare of the common people. Heaven would support an emperor only so long as he ruled for this higher purpose and not for his own benefit. Confucius added to this doctrine by extending the realm of the heavenly mandate to include every person; now everyone—not just the emperor—was subject to the universal law that obliged one to act morally in order to be in harmony with the Decree of Heaven. Ultimate perfection, then, for Confucius, has to do with cultivating a transcendent morality authored by heaven. It is possible, however, to resist or disobey the Decree of Heaven.

Nevertheless, there are certain dimensions of life that are beyond human control, areas in which human effort has no effect whatsoever. This indeterminate dimension of human life falls under the heading of "destiny," that aspect of heaven's design that is beyond human comprehension. One's place in life, social success, wealth, and longevity are all due to destiny. No amount of struggle will make any difference in their outcome; these things are simply determined by one's fate. Whereas the Decree of Heaven can be understood—although with great difficulty—destiny is beyond comprehension. The distinction between the Decree of Heaven (to which humans can conform or not) and destiny (which is beyond human agency) is fundamental for Confucius, for if one understands that the material comforts of life are due to destiny, one will recognize the futility of pursuing them and will devote all one's effort to the pursuit of heaven's morality. Morality, then—which has nothing to do with social success—is the only worthy pursuit in life. Confucius argued that it is necessary to understand the nature of both the Decree of Heaven (II.4) and destiny (XX.3) but for different reasons. The Decree of Heaven is the true object of ultimate concern, whereas destiny is simply to be accepted courageously.

Before we move on to look at Confucius's views of human nature, it is useful to examine another of his concepts: the **Way** (*dao*). Although the term *Dao* did come to be used in China as an abstract metaphysical principle (especially by the Daoists), for Confucius it primarily meant the "Way of the **sages**," those ancient rulers of earlier ideal times. The Confucian concept of the Way is linked intimately to the concept of heaven in that it involves the path of proper conduct. Although it is difficult to discern, the Way of heaven can be known through the previous actions of the sages. Regarding the sage Yao, Confucius is recorded as saying, "Great indeed was Yao as a ruler! How lofty! It is Heaven that is great and it was Yao who modeled himself upon it. He was so boundless that the common people were not able to put a name to his virtues" (VIII.19). Accordingly, the ancient sages—who modeled themselves on heaven—become models of the Way to human perfection in the present, the Way to be followed by all people (VI.17). In the end, three related things warrant reverence according to Confucius. He is recorded as saying, "The **gentleman** stands in awe of three things. He is in awe of the Decree of Heaven. He is in awe of great men. He is in awe of the words of the sages" (XVI.8).

THEORY OF HUMAN NATURE

Confucius seems to have been very optimistic about potential human accomplishments. In fact, the goal of much of Chinese philosophy is to help people become sages. Confucius's remark that "Heaven is author of the virtue that is in me" demonstrates his conviction that human beings have access to the ultimate reality of heaven's morality. For Confucius, every person is potentially a sage, defined as one who acts with extreme benevolence (VI.30). That is, all human beings have the capacity to cultivate virtue and bring themselves into harmony with the Decree of Heaven. Confucius indicates that the result of following the Way of heaven is the subjective experience of joy. Optimism regarding human potential, however, is not the same as optimism about the *actual* state of human affairs. The truth is, Confucius went on to attest, that a sage is a very rare being: "I have no hopes of meeting a sage" (VII.26). Although all human beings are potential sages, in reality this is an uncommon occurrence. Most human beings exist in a dreadful state.

What is it that enables potential sages to be so misled? Confucius said very little directly about human nature, causing his disciple Tzu-kung to remark, "One can get to hear about the Master's accomplishments, but one cannot get to hear his views on human nature and the Way of Heaven" (V.13). His dearth of statements on human nature allowed widely divergent theories to develop in later Confucianism. Despite his lack of explicit statements about human nature, however, it is clear from Confucius's sayings that in certain areas of life human beings exercise a freedom of will. Although we have no control over our destiny—we cannot, for example, determine our social status or longevity—we are free to reject or pursue morality and proper conduct. That is, we have the ability to resist or conform to the Decree of Heaven, the very source of virtue. While acknowledging that human beings have no significant choice as to the circumstances of the life they live, Confucius stressed that we do have a choice as to *how* we live in any given situation.

While he did not define human nature in any detail, Confucius insisted that all human beings are fundamentally the same. We simply become differentiated due to our different ways of being. "Men are close to one another by nature. They diverge as a result of repeated practice" (XVII.2). What this means, among other things, is that human beings are extremely malleable. We can become almost anything. We are unfinished, impressible, and in need of constant molding to achieve our ultimate end of moral perfection. In accord with modern sociologists and psychologists, Confucius seems to be suggesting that our environment and ways of being significantly determine our character, thus his great concern with paradigmatic figures—the sages—and the role they play in shaping the ideal human life. Human life without carefully crafted culture produces disastrous results. The subsequent state of problematic social conditions is taken up in the next section.

Two additional matters are worth mentioning in regard to Confucius's views of human nature. First, the ideal moral figure for Confucius is the "gentleman" (*junzi*). This term is decidedly masculine. While the term might be applied in a manner that includes both genders, it is clear that Confucius used the term in an exclusive way. He has little to say about women, and when he does speak of them he frequently does so in unflattering terms. On one occasion, for example, he lumps them together with "small men" and warns that in one's household both are "difficult to deal with" (XVII.25).

Second, although Confucius informs us that human nature is fundamentally uniform, he does not clarify whether this is a good nature that needs to be guarded carefully or a bad nature that stands in need of serious reform. His lack of specificity on this issue spawned much heated debate in later Confucianism. We will see what two major thinkers in the Confucian tradition have had to say about this important issue in the last section of this chapter.

DIAGNOSIS

Although the sayings of Confucius are predominantly prescriptive, they give a clear indication of what is wrong with human life. Generally speaking, the human condition is one of social discord caused by selfishness and ignorance of the past. Stated perhaps more succinctly, human beings are out of accord with the Decree of Heaven. Consequently, human interaction is marred by strife, rulers govern with attention only to personal gain, common people suffer under unjust burdens, and social behavior in general is determined by egoism and greed. Such is the dismal state of human beings.

What are the reasons for these distressing circumstances? At least five causes can be discerned in the *Analects*: (1) people are attached to **profit**, (2) society lacks the respect of **filial piety**, (3) the connection between word and action cannot be trusted, (4) ignorance regarding the Way of the sages prevails, and (5) benevolence is absent from human affairs. Let us examine these causes one by one.

Confucius said, "If one is guided by profit in one's actions, one will incur much ill will" (IV.12). One of the central tenets in Confucian thought is the opposition between rightness and profit. "The gentleman understands what is moral. The small man understands what is profitable" (IV.16). Ordinary human behavior is driven by a strong concern for the outcome of a particular action with regard to the self. That is, people typically ask, "What will I get out of this action?" The common aim in action, then, is a selfish one. Actions are generally performed to increase one's wealth or power. This is what Confucius means by action guided by profit. Even if a person does what is right, if the motivation is a nonmoral purpose—say, to gain rank—that person is still guided by profit. Confucius warns, "It is shameful to make salary your sole object" (XIV.1). Since he believed that morality should be the sole guide for all action, Confucius contended that action guided by profit leads to immoral circumstances and social disharmony wherein all people are selfishly looking out for themselves alone. Material benefits derived from invested labor are not in themselves bad, but the means by which they are obtained is of critical importance to Confucius. "Wealth and rank attained through immoral means have as much to do with me as passing clouds" (VII.16).

Selfish conduct motivated by personal profit implies a lack of true respect for others in a given society. For Confucius, this lack of respect reveals improper relationships within families, which in turn demonstrates a lack of self-discipline. This occurs because individuals have lost their grounding in morality, leading to problems in the family, which is the very basis of a good society. In this sense, Confucianism is very much a tradition of family values, and relationships are at the center of a well-lived life. A son who does not know how to treat his father respectfully will be a very poor citizen. Corrupt individuals, then, who have not cultivated the personal virtue necessary for proper familial relationships spread ill will throughout society. On the other hand, "It is rare for a man whose character is such that he is good as a son and obedient as a young man to have the inclination to transgress against his superiors" (I.2). Becoming a moral person—a "gentleman" (*junzi*)—therefore depends upon giving attention to one's own individual duty, and filial piety or respect for one's elders has much to do with this.

Another problem noted by Confucius is the fact that there is often a difference between what is said and what is done: "I used to take on trust a man's deeds after having listened to his words. Now having listened to a man's words I go on to observe his deeds" (V.10). Confucius recognizes that people are often untrustworthy. Without a direct connection between word and deed there is no basis for trust since trust rests on the premise that what is said will be done. Without this basic trust, individuals lose the ability to represent themselves sincerely and to rely on others with any degree of confidence. Accordingly, society loses its footing.

Ignorance of the past is also a major cause of the troublesome human condition. What Confucius means specifically by this is an unfamiliarity with the Way of the sages. It was pointed out earlier that the sages model their lives on heaven, thereby establishing a paradigm for the path to moral perfection. Without knowledge of the Way of the sages, people are cut off from the moral insight of the past. In such a state they become morally adrift and prone to wrong action. Confucius had so much faith in the Way of the sages that he remarked, "He has not lived in vain who dies the day he is told about the Way" (IV.8). The most important virtue that a human being can possess for Confucius is benevolence, or *ren*. To embody benevolence is to achieve moral perfection. This central Confucian idea is represented by a Chinese character that has been explained pictographically as consisting of two parts: the component for "human" and the component for "two." That is, it represents two people standing together in harmony. Essentially, benevolence has to do with human relationships. Several scholars have argued that *ren* is better translated into English as "human-heartedness" or "humaneness." Regardless, *ren* is a wide-ranging moral term that represents the very pinnacle of human excellence for Confucius. And, according to him, it is definitely within the reach of human beings: "The Master said, 'Is benevolence really far away? No sooner do I desire it than it is here'" (VII.30). The core of a perfected human being, then, is a benevolent heart. Unfortunately, Confucius observes, this virtue is all too rare in the world: "I have never met a man who finds benevolence attractive" (IV.6). Consequently, potential social harmony is replaced with strife.

PRESCRIPTION

The Confucian prescription for the ills of human existence is based on self-discipline. When questioned about the perfect man, Confucius said, "He cultivates himself and thereby brings peace and security to the people" (XIV.42). The ideal ruler for Confucius rules by personal moral example. But just what does self-cultivation mean in this context? The answer to this question can be found by exploring the proposed solutions to the five ills outlined in the preceding section.

To overcome the human tendency to act out of a concern for profit, Confucius proposed "doing for nothing." Specifically, this involves doing what is right simply because it is morally right and not for any other reason. For Confucius, the moral struggle is an end in itself; through it, one achieves a union of will with the Decree of Heaven. Acting in order to do what is right, rather than what is profitable, can serve also as a shield against life's disappointments. The state of benevolence is characterized by an inner serenity and equanimity and an indifference to matters of fortune and misfortune over which one has no direct control. Righteousness is its own reward, a joyous reward that transcends any particular social situation. Even if all one's efforts go unrecognized, by following the principle of "doing for nothing" one is never discontented. "Is it not gentlemanly not to take offence when others fail to appreciate your abilities?" (I.1).

Furthermore, this principle motivates one to keep working for righteousness in a world that has little appreciation for it. Confucius himself is described as one "who keeps working towards a goal the realization of which he knows to be hopeless" (XIV.38). Faith in the Way of heaven does not depend on results within the social world of rank and recognition. Remember that Confucius himself failed to secure a political position that would have provided him recognition and allowed him to put his ideas into practice. He says in the *Analects* that a man should strive to enter politics simply because he knows this to be right, even when he is well aware that his principles cannot prevail (XVIII.7). This relates to the notion of destiny discussed in the first section of this chapter. Social success is a matter of destiny; Confucius therefore concludes that it is futile to pursue it. Moral integrity, however, is within one's control, and in truth it is the only thing in life worth pursuing. One can struggle to understand the ways of heaven, but it is clear that one should act humanely whatever heaven sends. Again, it is the cultivation of self that is important, not social recognition. "The gentleman is troubled by his own lack of ability, not the failure of others to appreciate him" (XV.19).

The cultivation of self as a good family member is another of Confucius's prescriptions for a harmonious society. He believed that being a good family member had tremendous influence beyond the boundary of one's immediate family. "Simply by being a good son and friendly to his brothers a man can exert an influence upon government" (II.21). The transformation of society begins with the cultivation of the self within the environment of the family; it then spreads out like ripples caused from throwing a pebble in a still pond. The rules and relationships that govern the family are to be extended to include all of society. Benevolence toward people outside one's family should be an extension of the love one feels for members of one's own family. The most important relationship of all for Confucius is the one between a son and his father. When questioned about filial piety, Confucius advised, "Never fail to comply" (II.5). If, however, the son truly feels the father is wrong or his orders are contrary to *ren*, Confucius advises the son to remonstrate with him gently (IV.18). The manner in which a good son honors a father is by following his ways. "If [after his father's death], for three years, a man makes no changes to his father's ways, he can be said to be a good son" (I.11). This depends, of course, on the virtuous qualities of the father. Confucius is adamant that the father of the family, or by extension the emperor of the state, must rule by moral example: "If you set an example by being correct, who would dare to remain incorrect?" (XII.17).

Confucius was once asked what would be the first thing he would do if he were put in charge of the administration of a state. He replied, "If something has to be put first, it is, perhaps, the rectification of names" (XIII.3). The rectification of names means that there is an agreement between name and actuality. This correction is necessary because without the agreement between name and actuality, or between word and deed, much is lost. For Confucius, a name carries certain implications that constitute the very essence of the named object. For example, when asked by a duke about good government, Confucius responded, "Let the ruler be a ruler, the subject a subject, the father a father, the son a son" (XII.11). The concept of "father," for example, as we have just seen, is more than a biological designation. The name implies certain attitudes and responsibilities essential to harmonious existence. Moreover, without the connection between word and actuality there is no genuine trust. This is the definition of a lie. After hearing Confucius's remark on good government, the duke exclaimed, "Splendid! Truly, if the ruler be not a ruler, the subject not a subject, the father not a father, the son not a son, then even if there be grain, would I get to eat it?" That is, the word "grain" and the availability of grain are two different things. If there is no connection between them, then one may go hungry because of a locked, or perhaps even empty, granary. Words are easy to produce; if a person or government uses them to conceal the truth, then social chaos ensues. Trust is a critical ingredient of all dependable social interaction. Therefore, the self-cultivating gentleman is "trustworthy in what he says" (I.7) and "puts his words into actions" (II.13).

The antidote for the ignorance of the past referred to in the preceding section is **study**. Confucianism is a scholarly tradition. In China it is known as the Ru School—the term *ru* means "scholar"—and is recorded in Chinese sources as the school that delights in study of the Six **Classics**. From this it is evident that Confucius placed great emphasis on learning. He advised, "Have the firm faith to devote yourself to learning, and abide to the death in the good way" (VII.13). But what is the content of this learning that allows one to abide in the good way? It is clear from the representation of Confucianism just mentioned that the content of Confucian learning is the Classics, a collection of books that constitutes the cultural legacy of the past. Most important for Confucius, the Classics give expression to the Way of the sages and thus grant access to the exemplary conduct that leads to moral perfection. Because of this, study of the Classics is understood to be a vital element in achieving excellence and a sacred enterprise that expands one's nature. It is also an important aspect of good government: "When a student finds that he can more than cope with his studies, then he takes office" (XIX.13).

Excellence is defined by the Confucian tradition primarily as the embodiment of benevolence (*ren*). The manner in which one comes to embody benevolence constitutes the last of the five solutions being explored. This process really involves three elements: clinging to benevolence at all times while following the "golden rule" and observing the "**rites**."

Confucius said, "The gentleman never deserts benevolence, not even for as long as it takes to eat a meal" (IV.5). That is, one is to be ever mindful of benevolence in everything one does. The Confucian goal is to let benevolence determine all aspects of life since it is the perfect virtue that denotes the Decree of Heaven. Confucius himself is described in the *Analects* as one who maintained correctness and benevolence at all times (VII.4). But how is one to know what constitutes benevolence?

The practice of benevolence consists in balanced consideration for others and oneself. One measure of the consideration for others is determined by the treatment one desires for oneself. Confucius says, "A benevolent man helps others to take their stand in so far as he himself wishes to take his stand" (VI.30). In other words, this is the golden rule: "Do unto others what you would have done to yourself." Confucius also states this rule in negative form. When asked to define benevolence, he said, "Do not impose on others what you yourself do not desire" (XII.2). In a general sense, then, one's own self becomes a measure of decent conduct. However, Confucius has more to say about the measure of excellent conduct than this. Even if a person's heart is in the right place, it is possible to offend others because of a lack of knowledge about what is appropriate conduct in a particular situation. Knowledge is a key component to ethical action. Specifically for Confucius, this means knowing ritually correct behavior, or the rites (*li*). These consist of regulations governing action in every aspect of life, as well as ceremonial propriety, such as in making offerings to the ancestors. The rites are designed to teach individuals how to act well and are therefore a critical component in moral education. Knowledge of the rites functions as a guide for action beyond the general decency derived from using one's own self as a measure of conduct. Self-interest must finally be harnessed to the rites in order to achieve moral perfection. "To return to the observance of the rites through overcoming the self constitutes benevolence" (XII.1). Observing these rules, a person transcends self-interest. The rites are a body of rules culled from past moral insights and guide action toward perfection. What are the rites based on, and how does one come to know about them? They are based on the Classics, and one comes to know of them through study. Thus, the interconnectedness of Confucius's ideas comes into focus. Moral perfection, or benevolence, is achieved by following the rites, which are known by studying the Classics, which give expression to the Way of heaven as embodied by the sages.

Perhaps the most significant passage of all those recorded in the *Analects* is one that gives a summary indication of the path to perfection as it is understood in early Confucianism: "The Master said, 'At fifteen I set my heart on learning; at thirty I took my stand; at forty I came to be free from doubts; at fifty I understood the Decree of Heaven; at sixty my ear was atuned; at seventy I followed my heart's desire without overstepping the line'" (II.4). Here, Confucius is saying that at fifteen he took up serious study of the Classics. This gave him access to knowledge of the Way of the sages and, therefore, an awareness of the rites, the institutional form of their perfect demeanor. At age thirty he was able to take a stand in the rites or to put the proper conduct of the rites into practice. By practicing the rites, he moved at age forty from mere observation of the rites to true understanding of the rites. This led to a concomitant understanding of the Decree of Heaven by age fifty. At sixty Confucius experienced a union of wills with the Decree of Heaven so that by age seventy he could follow his own desire—now in harmony with the Decree of Heaven—with the result that he spontaneously acted with perfect benevolence.

Indicated here is the salvific path of paradigmatic action. As perfect beings, the sages naturally act with benevolence. Their benevolence is the external expression of a perfected inner state. As such, their benevolent actions become models of and for perfection for Confucians who desire to achieve the accomplished state of a sage. Again, the Way of the sages is available in the Classics, thus the great attention paid to study in the Confucian tradition. What the sages perform naturally becomes the model for the conscious self-discipline that leads to moral perfection. Proper disciplined action is represented in the Confucian tradition as the rites (*li*). From an outsider's perspective, the natural benevolent actions of a sage and of a self-disciplined person who follows the rites appear the same, but the internal motive is different. The sage's behavior is the natural expression of an inner perfected state, whereas the disciplined person's behavior consists of studied actions—the rites—that are modeled on the benevolence of the sages. The goal of disciplined action, however, is to achieve a state wherein perfect moral action becomes natural and spontaneous. This is the state of the "gentleman," and this is what is said to have happened to Confucius toward the end of his life. The sages express moral perfection naturally, whereas the gentleman has achieved perfection by intentionally modeling his life on the behavior of the sages. The actions of a gentleman and a disciplined Confucian student may also appear the same from the outside, just as a master musician and a disciplined student appear to be making the same moves. But once again, the motives are different in both cases. The master musician has so internalized the fingering chart of the instrument she is playing that she is no longer conscious of it, whereas the student is still consciously following the fingering chart. Likewise, the gentleman has so internalized the Way of the sages that he now acts spontaneously, whereas the Confucian student who "stands in the rites" consciously follows the proper conduct that the rites represent. In either case, by following the rites, both the gentleman and the diligent student have embodied benevolence, the very zenith of moral perfection.

As a paradigmatic tradition, Confucianism produces a chain of perfected moral action that makes the benevolent Way of the sages present for the common people and creates moral examples for those who are not involved in the elite tradition of textual study. It should be clear by now that moral perfection for the Confucian tradition is represented by the sages and that, as the ideal of human perfection, the gentleman has achieved moral perfection by studying the Classics and internalizing the Way of the sages. The Confucian practitioner is ideally moving along this same path. Direct observation of present-day human practitioners takes the place of textual study for those unable to read. To the degree that a practitioner can embody benevolence by following the Confucian rites, the Way of the sages is then present for all of society to observe and to follow. In this way, a line of moral perfection reaches back from the time of the sages and continues into the very present. If all people would follow this Way, Confucius believed, individuals would achieve perfection, society would be radically transformed, and benevolence would rule.

LATER DEVELOPMENTS

Because Confucius did not spell out his views on human nature in any detail, a major debate arose within the tradition soon after his death regarding this question: Is human nature originally good or evil? Opposing answers were supplied by two leading figures in the Confucian tradition. Representing the "idealistic wing," Mencius (or Mengzi, 371–289 B.C.E.) contended that human nature is originally good; representing the "realistic wing," Hsun-tzu (or Xunzi, ca. 298–238 b.c.e.) argued that human nature is originally evil. Although we cannot possibly do justice to the entire Confucian tradition here, a brief examination of this debate gives further indication of the complexity of this tradition and adds to our overall consideration of human nature.

The writings and ideas of Mencius rank second in the tradition only to those of Confucius, and, above all, his name is associated with his theory of the original goodness of human nature. In a collection of his sayings recorded in a book that bears his name, Mencius articulates his position on the controversy over human nature that came to be regarded as orthodox for the Confucian tradition and normative for much of Chinese culture.

In the *Mencius*, Mencius refutes a philosopher named Kao-tzu, who argues that human nature is intrinsically neither good nor bad and that morality therefore is something that has to be added artificially from the outside. "Human nature," Kao-tzu maintains, "is like whirling water. Give it an outlet in the east and it will flow east; give it an outlet in the west and it will flow west. Human nature does not show any preference for either good or bad just as water does not show any preference for either east or west." Mencius, however, is insistent that human nature is innately good. He counters Kao-tzu by explaining, "It certainly is the case that water does not show any preference for either east or west, but does it show the same indifference to high and low? Human nature is good just as water seeks low ground. There is no man who is not good; there is no water that does not flow downwards" (VI.A.2).

The core of Mencius's theory about innate human nature relates to his understanding of the human heart. For Mencius, the thinking, compassionate heart is a gift from heaven (VI.A.15). This is what defines our essential humanness and sets us apart from animals. Specifically, the heart is a receptacle of four incipient tendencies, or "seeds," as Mencius calls them. He maintains that "Man has these four germs just as he has four limbs" (II.A.6). If unobstructed and nurtured carefully, these seeds sprout into the four virtues so greatly prized by the Confucian tradition, as lofty trees grow naturally from small seeds. The four seeds of compassion, shame, courtesy, and sense of right and wrong develop respectively into the four virtues of benevolence, dutifulness, observance of the rites, and wisdom (II.A.6). And Mencius insists that these four seeds "are not welded on to me from the outside; they are in me originally" (VI.6). For Mencius, our original heart identifies us all as potential sages.

Mencius, however, agrees with many of the philosophers of his time that human beings are creatures of desire. He acknowledges that moral development can be hindered when a person fails to engage the compassionate heart and pursues egoistic ends. Selfish desire in particular threatens to overwhelm the four seeds that define the source of our higher moral nature. The heavenly gift of the thinking heart is therefore recognized to be fragile and can be lost if not used and cultivated. This, of course, is the norm. Mencius says, "Heaven has not sent down men whose endowment differs so greatly. The difference is due to what ensnares their hearts" (VI.A.7). The ensnarement of the human heart, for Mencius, is the source of all evil, thus the great concern for carefully nurturing its innate qualities. "Given the right nourishment there is nothing that will not grow, and deprived of it there is nothing that will not wither away" (VI.8).

All hope for humanity, according to Mencius, lies in the human heart. Our desiring nature is something we share with all animals, but it is our thinking heart—that special gift from Heaven—that sets us up to be benevolent sages. Mencius offers a proof for the innate goodness of all people:

> My reason for saying that no man is devoid of a heart sensitive to the suffering of others is this. Suppose a man were, all of a sudden, to see a young child on the verge of falling into a well. He would certainly be moved to compassion, not because he wanted to get in the good graces of the parents, nor because he wished to win the praise of his fellow villagers or friends, nor yet because he disliked the cry of the child (II.A.6).

What Mencius seems to be saying here is that every person in this situation would have an immediate, spontaneous, and unreflective urge to save the child. This reveals a pure impulse for righteousness over selfish profit. Mencius says nothing about the ensuing action. It may be the case that the man involved would, upon any reflection following the "all of a sudden," engage in calculating thoughts of self-interest. Regardless of what follows, however, the momentary urge indicated in this statement is all Mencius needs to demonstrate what he refers to as the seed of compassion. For him, this proves that human nature is innately good and has thus the solid potential for benevolence.

Mencius's strongest opponent was Hsun-tzu, an important Confucian writer who was born toward the end of Mencius's life. Hsun-tzu held that our interior world is dominated by dynamic impulses of desire. The basic human problem for Hsun-tzu is that human libidinous urges have no clear limit. Nature has given us unlimited desires in a world with limited resources; hence, social strife arises among necessarily competitive human beings. In a text he composed himself, Hsun-tzu writes, "Man is born with desires. If desires are not satisfied for him, he cannot but seek some means to satisfy them himself. If there are no limits and degrees to his seeking, then he will inevitably fall to wrangling with other men" (section 19, p. 89). This view caused him to formulate a position on human nature diametrically opposed to that of Mencius: "Man's nature is evil; goodness is the result of conscious activity" (section 23, p. 157). Hsun-tzu was well aware of Mencius's ideas but insisted that they were wrong. "Mencius states that man's nature is good, and that evil arises because he loses his original nature. Such a view, I believe, is erroneous" (p. 158). Hsun-tzu replaces Mencius's theory of the four seeds with his own theory of four incipient tendencies for profit, envy, hatred, and desire, which if left in their natural state give rise to the four evils of strife, violence, crime, and wantonness. These, he insists, are innate in all humans so that the path that follows our own nature leads only to evil. "Any man who follows his nature and indulges his emotions will inevitably become involved in wrangling and strife, will violate the forms and rules of society, and will end as a criminal" (p. 157).

Hsun-tzu goes on to compare the criminal-like human being to a warped piece of wood. "A warped piece of wood must wait until it has been laid against the straightening board, steamed, and forced into shape before it can become straight, because by nature it is warped" (p. 164). Surprisingly, Hsun-tzu is rather optimistic about potential human accomplishments, for he too believed that with the proper education and training all people could become sages. "The man in the street can become a Yu [a sage]" (p. 166). What is it, we might ask, that transforms the warped pieces of wood that are human beings into the straight boards of sages, or at least proper citizens? That is, what constitutes the straightening board for human beings? After his statement about warped wood, Hsun-tzu writes, "Similarly, since man's nature is evil, he must wait for the ordering power of the sage kings and the transforming power of ritual principles; only then can he achieve order and conform to goodness" (p. 164). Hsun-tzu here confirms the absolute value of a fundamental Confucian idea; the straightening board consists of the rites (*li*) or what is here translated as "ritual principles." For him, the rites are the products of the sheer intellectual activity of the sages and were designed to curb and channel the boundless desires of human beings. When Hsun-tzu says that "goodness is the result of conscious activity," he means a conscious effort to transform oneself by diligently applying oneself to the rites, those guiding principles created and embodied by past sages. Hsun-tzu is clearly an advocate for culture over nature, for the rites are not an essential part of human nature. Everything that is good is a product of conscious human effort. The fact that we have two arms is natural, but virtue comes only with assiduous human effort. For him, the attentive application of the unnatural rites is the key to achieving human perfection. "In respect to human nature the sage is the same as all other men and does not surpass them; it is only in his conscious activity that he differs from and surpasses other men" (p. 161). The sage, then, for Hsun-tzu, is a human being whose nature has been radically transformed by the Confucian rites.

The contrast between Mencius and Hsun-tzu is dramatic. Mencius believed that morality is naturally present in our hearts, whereas Hsun-tzu believed that it is something artificially instilled from the outside. Nevertheless, we observe an agreement in the ideas of Hsun-tzu and Mencius that identifies them both as Confucians. They agree that human beings commonly make a mess of things and that the path to sagehood comprises the Confucian rites, those proper modes of action based on the paradigmatic behavior of past sages. For Hsun-tzu the rites function as a straightening board to transform warped human beings into straight and benevolent citizens, whereas for Mencius they function more like a racket press designed to keep a stored wooden tennis racket from warping—although innately present, the heart of compassion can become twisted if not reinforced with the constant observance of the rites. Although the two philosophers disagree sharply in theory, they are in complete agreement regarding practice. Human perfection is achieved through a process of careful study and following the paradigmatic actions and insights of past sages.

CRITICAL DISCUSSION

We may conclude this introduction to Confucianism with a few comments designed to bring into sharper focus some possible criticisms already hinted at in our discussion. Besides being a system that is rooted in the common decency of the golden rule, Confucianism is a tradition that teaches obedience to superiors. The relevant superiors are the father of the family, the ruler of the state, and the Confucian scholar who makes accessible the Way of the sages. If the heads of the family and state are just men, then all is well. But if such men are unjust, then the entire system is undermined. Confucius himself was aware of this problem and therefore insistent on the moral character of leaders. Nonetheless, his system gives a great deal of power to a few individuals and leaves the majority in a subordinate position.

Confucianism is also a fairly conservative tradition that looks to the past for guidance. This may be seen as an attitude that restricts the creativity of individuals in the present. This made Confucianism a primary target of attack during the Chinese Cultural Revolution of the late 1960s and early 1970s. Furthermore, it is a system dependent on an elite of literati, the Confucian scholars. We might ask, "Do scholars have access to the past in a manner that is free of their own ideological agendas?" Confucianism, it has been shown, is based largely on a transcendent view of morality. It may be argued that such a view is simply a way for a certain group to give special privilege to its own view of morality. We might then ask, "Whose view of the past and whose view of morality is Confucianism based on?" Most historians today contend that no view of the past is completely neutral or apolitical. All historical representations involve issues of power.

Many people seem to be excluded from the Confucian enterprise. The common people are represented as an undifferentiated and generally inept mass, another problem from the perspective of communist China. Women in particular do not seem to be included in Confucius's educational system. His view of human perfection is decidedly masculine, and all in all he has little to say about the potential of women for self-cultivation. When Confucius does speak about women, he does so in derogatory terms, suggesting that they are generally unruly and resistant to legitimate authority. Although the Confucian path to perfection may be expanded by its advocates to include both genders, the *Analects* poses a problem for readers who believe in the equality of the sexes.

Finally, the pragmatic nature of Confucianism has been criticized by other Chinese philosophers, such as the more metaphysically minded Daoists. The Daoist philosopher Chuang-tzu (or Zhuangzi), for example, criticized the Confucians for their reduction of reality to only that which concerns human social affairs. Chuang-tzu reversed Hsun-tzu's assessment of what is valuable by advocating nature over culture. As a nature mystic aware of the immensity of life in all its forms, Chuang-tzu believed that the Confucians occupied a tragically small world. He also characterized Confucians as people overly concerned with utilitarian matters and countered this preoccupation with a celebration of the usefulness of uselessness. Daoists also suggested that the Confucian emphasis on rules often generates opposition and encourages prohibited behavior. Over the course of time, however, Confucianism has proven to be a much more attractive system to Chinese thinkers for establishing virtuous human society than the more abstract metaphysical thought of Daoism.

Although Confucianism was discredited in China in the early twentieth century by the collapse of the imperial system and was a primary target of the Cultural Revolution (which identified it with everything that had been wrong with the older system), it has experienced somewhat of a revival, especially since the death of Mao Zedong in 1976. The revival, known as New Confucianism, has been carried out by a group of scholars who aim to modernize Confucianism rather than abandon it altogether. The modernization involves a process of weeding out those aspects of the older Confucian culture that are deemed problematic from a modern perspective, such as the subordination of women. An exemplary figure of this new movement is Tu Weiming, a professor currently at Peking University and Harvard University who has explored Confucian thought for its application to the contemporary quest for more socially just and ecologically harmonious ways of living. He sees Confucianism as a positive resource for thinking about ways to overcome the destructive side of modernization that threatens both human communities and the natural world. In this new form, Confucianism is once again making significant contributions concerning the big questions of the day.

FOR FURTHER READING

Basic text: *The Analects* (many translations and editions). We have quoted from the excellent translation by D. C. Lau, *Confucius: The Analects* (London: Penguin, 1979). This is a very readable and reliable text that includes a valuable introduction. Another readily available translation is that by Arthur Waley, *The Analects of Confucius* (New York: Macmillan, 1938; New York: Vintage, 1989).

Mencius: We have quoted from the translation by D. C. Lau, *Mencius* (London: Penguin, 1970). This edition also includes an excellent introduction.

Hsun-tzu: We have quoted from the translation by Burton Watson, *Hsun Tzu: Basic Writings* (New York: Columbia University Press, 1963).

For more on Confucianism, see Xinzhong Yao, *An Introduction to Confucianism* (Cambridge: Cambridge University Press, 2000); and Paul Goldin, *Confucianism* (Berkeley: University of California Press, 2011).

To gain a better understanding of the place of Confucianism in Chinese philosophy, see A. C. Graham, *Disputers of the Tao* (Lasalle, IL: Open Court, 1989); Benjamin I. Schwartz, *The World of Thought in Ancient China* (Cambridge, MA: Harvard University Press, 1985); and Philip J. Ivanhoe, *Confucian Moral Self-Cultivation*, 2nd ed. (Cambridge, MA: Hackett, 2000).

For more on New Confucianism, see Tu Weiming, *Confucian Thought: Selfhood as Creative Transformation* (Albany: State University of New York Press, 1985); and Stephen C. Angle, *Sagehood: The Contemporary Significance of Neo-Confucian Philosophy* (New York: Oxford University Press, 2009).

KEY TERMS

Classics	*ren*
Decree Of Heaven	**rites**
destiny	sages
filial piety	study
gentleman	way
profit	

QUESTIONS FOR DISCUSSION

1. What are human ideals based on for Confucius? What do you see as the strengths and weaknesses of this approach to morality?
2. If everyone is potentially a "sage," why is it that sages are so rare in the world according to Confucians?
3. What does Confucius mean by "doing for nothing"? What are the advantages of this for the individual and society?
4. What is the salvific path of paradigmatic action for the Confucian tradition? What are its various components, and how does it work? Can you think of other examples of such paradigmatic action?
5. Mencius and Hsun-tzu give different accounts of innate human nature. Which do you think is more accurate, and why?

2

Upanishadic Hinduism: Quest for Ultimate Knowledge

An introductory examination of Hinduism can be very challenging since there is no founder, no clear historical beginning point, and no central text, as we find in most other religious traditions. Hinduism is an extremely diverse tradition that consists of a wide range of practices and beliefs, making the task of generalization nearly impossible. The term "Hinduism" itself is largely a Western construct designed simply to refer to the dominant religion of the majority of the people who inhabit the south Asian subcontinent. Therefore, in many ways, it is absurd to attempt to represent Hinduism with a single text, for no particular text is accepted as authoritative by all people who might identify themselves as Hindus and many think of their religion as being grounded in a way of action, rather than a written text. Nevertheless, if one were to seek a "foundational text" to represent significant tenets of Hindu philosophy, a good selection would be one of the principal Upanishads. The collection of texts known as the Upanishads has played a decisive role throughout Hindu religious history; they have defined central philosophical issues in India for centuries and continue to be a major source of inspiration and guidance within the Hindu world today. One of the objectives of this chapter is to give a sense of the wide range of interpretive possibilities that emerge from early

Hindu texts, demonstrating specifically how practices as diverse as world **renunciation** and forms of worship that embrace the world itself as divine are justified by the same texts. The earliest Upanishads were composed in northern India in the seventh or eighth century B.C.E. The term "Upanishad" means literally to "sit near" but has come to mean "esoteric teaching," for these texts represent secret teachings passed on to groups of close disciples by forest-dwelling meditation masters. The Upanishads, which contain highly speculative thought about the ultimate nature of reality, are among the greatest intellectual creations of the world. Although the Upanishads do not present a single philosophical system but rather give voice to exploratory and often contradictory reflections, their overall theme is one of ontological unity, the belief that everything is radically interconnected. The oldest and largest of the Upanishads is the *Brihad Aranyaka Upanishad* ("The Great and Secret Teachings of the Forest"). This text is not the product of a single author but a compilation of a number of conversations between teachers and students. The *Brihad Aranyaka Upanishad* has a great deal to say about the ultimate nature of the world and the true identity of human beings and, thus, provides a good starting point for exploring important issues within Hindu philosophy.

THEORY OF THE UNIVERSE

We observe in the *Brihad Aranyaka Upanishad* an ardent metaphysical search for the absolute ground of all being. One of the central philosophical tenets of the Upanishads is that there is a single, unifying principle underlying the entire universe. At the level of ultimate realization, the world of multiplicity is revealed to be one of interconnected unity. The attempt to identify that unifying principle can be seen in a famous passage involving the philosopher Gargi Vacaknavi and the great sage Yajnavalkya (3.6). Gargi opens an inquiry into the ultimate nature of the world, challenging Yajnavalkya to identify the very foundation of all existence. She asks the sage, "Since this whole world is woven back and forth on water, on what, then, is water woven back and forth?" Yajnavalkya responds initially, "On air, Gargi." But Gargi is not satisfied with this answer: "On what, then, is air woven back and forth?" Yajnavalkya supplies another answer, and then another, and still another as Gargi presses him to identify increasingly fundamental layers of reality. Finally, the sage reveals to her that the entire universe is woven back and forth on what he calls "***brahman***." At this point he claims that he can go no further; *brahman* is declared to be the end of Gargi's search.

Although other entities were suggested as the possible foundation of all being (e.g., space [4.1.1] and water [5.5.1]), these were rejected as the one ultimate reality and absolute ground of all being came to be identified as *brahman*. *Brahman* was declared to be the highest aim of all metaphysical inquiry: "All the vedic learning that has been acquired is subsumed under '*brahman*'" (1.5.17).

The term "*brahman*" is derived from a Sanskrit root that means to "grow," "expand," or "increase." Although in early usage it was associated with sacred utterances, over the course of time it came to be identified with the very force that sustains the world. During the time of the Upanishads, it settled into its principal meaning of "ultimate reality," the primary cause of existence, or the absolute ground of being. Brahman was identified as the fine essence that pervades the entire universe. It is the totality of all reality, both manifest and unmanifest. Another famous passage from the *Brihad Aranyaka Upanishad* portrays the metaphysical quest for the unitary ground of being that ends in *brahman* (3.9). Since this passage yields keen insight into Hindu theology, we quote it in full.

The passage opens with the searcher Vidagdha Shakalya questioning the sage Yajnavalkya about the number of gods in existence. "How many gods are there?" he asks. Yajnavalkya responds first, "Three and three hundred, and three and three thousand." Not satisfied with this answer, Vidagdha continues.

"Yes, of course," he said, "but really, Yajnavalkya, how many gods are there?"
"Thirty-three."
"Yes, of course," he said, "but really, Yajnavalkya, how many gods are there?"
"Six."
"Yes, of course," he said, "but really, Yajnavalkya, how many gods are there?"
"Three."
"Yes, of course," he said, "but really, Yajnavalkya, how many gods are there?"
"Two."
"Yes, of course," he said, "but really, Yajnavalkya, how many gods are there?"
"One and a half."
"Yes, of course," he said, "but really, Yajnavalkya, how many gods are there?"
"One."

When asked by Vidagdha to identify this "one god," Yajnavalkya concludes, "He is called '*brahman*.'"

Although divinity expresses itself in multiple forms, ultimately it is One. Here again, we witness philosophical inquiry into the ultimate nature of reality that ends with the discovery of the single unifying principle called *brahman*. But if reality is One, how—and why—did it become many? Creation stories maintained by any tradition tell us much about that tradition. We find in the *Brihad Aranyaka Upanishad* an account of creation that provides answers to these questions and serves as a model for much Hindu thought.

"In the beginning there was nothing" (1.2.1). Yet a great deal can come from nothing, for much of the Hindu tradition holds that the entire universe came out of this original nothingness. Like the modern Big Bang theory, this text describes an expansion from an original dimensionless point of infinite unity; yet, unlike the Big Bang theory, this account of creation tells us *why* the expansion occurred.

In the beginning there was nothing but the single unitary principle, *brahman*. However, because it was alone, it was lonely and "found no pleasure at all" (1.4.2). In this state of loneliness, it desired another and so divided itself into two parts, a male and a female. Departing from the original state of abstract neutrality, the male and female pair began to interact sexually, and from this was born the entire universe of diverse forms. Thus, the original point of undifferentiated unity divided itself and, exploding outward, produced the phenomenal world of multiple forms. The *Brihad Aranyaka Upanishad* calls this "*brahman*'s super-creation" (1.4.6). This account of creation expresses the true nature of reality and the ultimate aim of beings within that reality. We will have occasion to refer to this story later, but the important point is to realize that it accounts for the multiplicity of the world, while recognizing in a fundamental way the radical interconnectedness of the world. The original unity is never lost; it simply takes on the appearance of multiple forms.

This theory of the origin of the universe recognizes the simultaneity of unity and diversity. The one reality differentiates itself through what the text calls "name and visible appearance" (1.4.7). The world we experience with our senses, then, is a single reality, though it is clothed with a variety of names and appearances. This is aptly expressed in the following verse:

> The world there is full;
> The world here is full;
> Fullness from fullness proceeds.
> After taking fully from the full,
> It still remains completely full. (5.1.1)

Here we have a portrait of divinity that is simultaneously immanent and transcendent. *Brahman* is not only *in* the world, it *is* the world; there is also a dimension of *brahman* that is completely beyond the world of multiple forms. This is asserted in the *Brihad Aranyaka Upanishad* as a teaching about the two aspects (*rupa*) of *brahman* as the form and the formless: "the one has a fixed shape (*murta*), and the other is without a fixed shape (*amurta*)" (2.3.1). *Brahman* as all forms is everything that is solid and transitory, whereas *brahman* as the formless is ethereal and unchanging. A good way to approach this philosophy is to reflect on the double meaning of the phrase "Nothing ever remains the same." The world of concrete things is in constant flux and always changing; things never remain the same. On the other hand, the no-thingness from which all comes is eternal and unchanging; it ever remains the same. It is important to remember, however, that these are not two separate realities but the same reality seen from different perspectives. The world of forms is pervaded by the unified *brahman* as salt pervades the water in which it is dissolved: "It is like this. When a chunk of salt is thrown in water, it dissolves into that very water, and it cannot be picked up in any way. Yet, from whichever place one may take a sip, the salt is there! In the same way this Immense Being has no limit or boundary and is a single mass of perception" (2.4.12).

Before we move on to examine what the *Brihad Aranyaka Upanishad* has to say about human nature, one additional important point should be mentioned. Several passages insist that *brahman* is inexpressible and therefore impossible to define. We are told, for example, that

> it is neither coarse nor fine; it is neither short nor long; it has neither blood nor fat; it is without shadow or darkness; it is without air or space; it is without contact; it has no taste or smell; it is without sight or hearing; it is without speech or mind; it is without energy, breath, or mouth, it is beyond measure; it has nothing within or outside of it; it does not eat anything; and no one eats it. (3.8.8)

That is, *brahman* is completely beyond the world we experience with our senses. This is often expressed in the text by saying that *brahman* is "not this, not that (*neti neti*)."

On the other hand, there are passages that identify *brahman* with everything we experience with our senses:

> Clearly, this self is *brahman*—this self that is made of perception, made of mind, made of sight, made of breath, made of hearing, made of earth, made of water, made of wind, made of space, made of light and the lightless, made of desire and the desireless, made of anger and the angerless, made of righteous and the unrighteous; this self is made of everything. (4.4.5)

In direct contrast to the "not this, not that" view, this passage continues: "He's made of this. He's made of that." These two different ways of describing *brahman* led to divergent understandings of the world and the self, which in turn resulted in significant differences in religious practice. Two of the most important interpretations of the Upanishads are explored in the final section of this chapter.

THEORY OF HUMAN NATURE

The recognition that all of life is interconnected has clear implications for a theory of human nature. According to the *Brihad Aranyaka Upanishad*, our kin are not only fellow human beings but all other beings as well. This text teaches that the essential self of a human being is radically connected to all beings: "The self within all is this self of yours" (3.5.1). The ultimate self—referred to in the Upanishads by the term *"atman"*—is not, therefore, an autonomous unit operating independently of other beings but rather a part of this larger interrelated network of reality. "This very self [*atman*] is the lord and king of all beings. As all the spokes are fastened to the hub and the rim of a wheel, so to one's self are fastened all beings, all the gods, all the worlds, all the breaths, and all these bodies" (2.5.15). The text makes it very clear that the true self not only animates all beings but is inseparable from the whole of reality (2.5.1–14). The self is all, and all is the self.

The Upanishads certainly recognize a self that is transitory and separate from other selves. That is, the self as ego (*ahamkara*) is identified with the body and its social environment. This is the self we immediately think of when someone asks us who we are. This is also the self we ordinarily invest with great meaning and strive to preserve. This, however, is neither the ultimate self nor the true identity of a human being. The essential self is defined as the *atman*. Our ordinary self is simply a finite, conditioned mask covering our true and infinite nature.

Some passages in the *Brihad Aranyaka Upanishad* suggest that the *atman* is undefinable; it is not to be identified with anything: "About this self (*atman*), one can only say 'not—, not—.' He is ungraspable, for he cannot be grasped. He is undecaying, for he is not subject to decay. He has nothing sticking to him, for he does not stick to anything. He is not bound; yet he neither trembles in fear nor suffers injury" (3.9.28). Other passages, however, identify the *atman* with everything: "Clearly, this self is *brahman*—this self that is made of perception, made of mind, made of sight, made of breath, made of hearing, made of earth, made of water, made of wind, made of space, made of light and the lightless, made of desire and the desireless; this self is made of everything. Hence there is this saying: 'He's made of this. He's made of that'" (4.4.5). Note the seemingly contradictory nature of these two statements, which might be used to support very different notions of the self and the world. In either case, the text goes on to define the *atman* as the immortal, unchanging self; it "is beyond hunger and thirst, sorrow and delusion, old age and death" (3.5.1). A central teaching of the Upanishads is that the true self, or *atman*, is that eternal dimension of reality that is somehow not different from the highest reality of *brahman*: "And this is the immense and unborn self, un-ageing, undying, immortal, free from fear—the *brahman*" (4.4.24). Since the *atman* is identified with *brahman*, it too is defined as the very source of all life, the root of all existence: "As a spider sends forth its thread, and as tiny sparks spring forth from a fire, so indeed do all the vital functions, all the worlds, all the gods, and all beings spring from this self [*atman*]. Its hidden name is: 'The real behind the real,' for the real consists of the vital functions, and the self is the real behind the vital functions" (2.1.19). In sum, the *Brihad Aranyaka Upanishad* teaches that one's essential self transcends individuality, limitation, suffering, and death.

Another common designation we find for the *atman* is that it is the "inner controller" of all life (3.7.2–23). This designation is connected to perhaps the most notable characterization of the *atman* we find in the *Brihad Aranyaka Upanishad*. The *atman* is not an ordinary object of consciousness but rather the subject of consciousness or the silent witness of consciousness. The *atman* is the knower of all knowledge or the "perceiver of perception."

> When, however, the Whole has become one's very self [*atman*], then who is there for one to smell and by what means? Who is there for one to see and by what means? Who is there for one to hear and by what means? Who is there for one to greet and by what means? Who is there for one to think of and by what means? Who is there for one to perceive and by what means? By what means can one perceive him by means of whom one perceives this whole world? Look—by what means can one perceive the perceiver? (2.4.14)

As the perceiver of perception, the *atman* is not an object of consciousness and therefore cannot be known in any ordinary way, for it is declared to be consciousness itself. Although there is a great deal of similarity between Upanishadic Hinduism and early Buddhism, many Buddhists tend to reject the idea that consciousness is identical to an essential self. Nonetheless, the Upanishads identify our true self as that which enables us to be conscious beings, namely, all-pervasive consciousness. The primary aim of the Upanishads is to bring about a shift in identity from the transient ego self associated with the body to the eternal and infinite self that is not different from the All. In other words, the goal is to realize that the *atman* is *brahman*, although the task of delineating the details of this equation was left to later writers.

·   According to the Upanishads, our present life is just one in a long, long
series of death and rebirth. When our present life ends, we are reborn in a
new body. "It is like this. As a caterpillar, when it comes to the tip of a blade
of grass, reaches out to a new foothold and draws itself onto it, so the self
[*atman*], after it has knocked down this body and rendered it unconscious,
reaches out to a new foothold and draws itself onto it" (4.3.3). That is, as
a caterpillar moves from one blade of grass to another, so we move from
one body to another. Although some later philosophers insisted that it is
a different type of self that constitutes the individual self that undergoes
reincarnation, reincarnation seems to have been assumed in the Upanishads.

Informed by this assumption, two paths are outlined in the *Brihad Aranyaka Upanishad* as possible postdeath experiences (6.2.15–16). The first
option is the path of return to this life. After death, people's bodies are
placed on the cremation fire. Those who performed religious sacrifices designed to enhance worldly life pass into the smoke. From the smoke, they
pass into the night and eventually end up in the world of the ancestors.
From there they pass into the moon, where they are turned into the rain,
by which they return to the earth. Reaching the earth, they become food.
The food is eaten by a man and then offered in the fire of a woman, where
people take birth once again. This is the ongoing cycle of death and rebirth
that defines life for most people. Enjoyment of the cycles of existence is
presented here in a positive light.

There is another path, however, for the forest-dwelling meditation masters who have achieved the highest knowledge. After death, these are placed
on the cremation fire and pass into the flames. From the flames, they pass
into the day and eventually reach the world of the gods. From there they pass
into the sun. The sun in much Hindu mythology represents the doorway out
of this world, and, indeed, we are told that those who achieve the highest
knowledge go on from the sun to reach the world of *brahman*, from which
they never return to worldly life. This is one of the earliest representations
of *moksha*, or "liberation" from the ongoing cycle of death and rebirth. Although these two paths are presented simply as the two postdeath possibilities in the *Brihad Aranyaka Upanishad*, some later Upanishads insist that the
path of no return is far superior to the path of return. According to the more
ascetic Upanishads, return to this world is an indication of one's failure to
achieve ultimate knowledge of one's self. A very special kind of knowledge,
then, is declared to be the culmination of a successful human life.

DIAGNOSIS

The main problem with human existence is that we are ignorant of the
true nature of reality. "Pitiful is the man, Gargi, who departs from this

world without knowing this imperishable" (3.8.10). We see from this statement that all success rests on knowing the imperishable *brahman*, of which we are a part. It is extremely difficult to know, however, since it is that "which sees but can't be seen; which hears but can't be heard; which thinks but can't be thought of; which perceives but can't be perceived. Besides this imperishable, there is no one that sees, no one that hears, no one that thinks, and no one that perceives" (3.8.11). Without knowledge of the unified and infinite *brahman*, one perceives only the ordinary objects of consciousness and therefore suffers the fate of identifying completely with the dying world of fragmentary and transitory forms. "With the mind alone must one behold it—there is here nothing diverse at all! From death to death he goes who sees here any kind of diversity" (4.4.19).

Ignorance of the true nature of reality is tantamount to ignorance of the true nature of our own selves. Or, stated in different terms, the human predicament consists of a severe identity problem: we don't know who we really are. We identify ourselves with the fragmented, seemingly disconnected phenomenal world of diversity, instead of with the One *brahman*. We are creatures of infinity stuck in highly conditioned and finite personalities. While in reality we are kin to the immense universe, we spend our lives overwhelmed and blinded by the limited projects of our own ego. The result of this is alienation: from others, from the very source of life, from the One, and even from our own true self. The human condition is thus an ongoing experience of fragmentation, isolation, and loneliness. Consequently, our social worlds are riddled with crime and hostile conflict, informed by belief in our own individuality, and we are plagued with existential anxiety, rooted in an investment in the disconnected, transitory self.

The life of the lone individual is anything but free, according to the Upanishads. Life grounded in the belief in a separate self is heavily conditioned and determined. The determining factors are identified as **karma** in the *Brihad Aranyaka Upanishad*, the first text to mention this concept so important to later Hindu thought. The sage Yajnavalkya talks about karma in this way: "What a man turns out to be depends on how he acts and on how he conducts himself. If his actions are good, he will turn into something good. If his actions are bad, he will turn into something bad. A man turns into something good by good action and into something bad by bad action" (4.4.5). Ordinary human life, informed by the belief in an autonomous self, is revealed to be highly contingent, conditioned by forces determined by previous actions. Yajnavalkya continues, "A man resolves in accordance with his desire, acts in accordance with his resolve, and turns out to be in accordance with his action." What this means is that we are psychologically programmed in such a way that under normal circumstances free action is impossible. We act out of desire, which itself is the result of some prior action recorded in the unconscious mind. That desire manifests itself as a resolve for action. The subsequent action leaves an impression in the mind, which then goes on to determine the nature of another desire, the root of future action. Here, then, is a picture of the human predicament as a cycle of psychological bondage. A great deal of Hindu yoga and meditation aims to free us from this limited and conditioned state of existence.

PRESCRIPTION

The Upanishads are generally optimistic about the possibility of attaining ultimate freedom from conditioned existence, called *moksha*. The *Brihad Aranyaka Upanishad*, however, does not outline a single prescriptive path. A major task of later systematic writers was to articulate a coherent interpretation of this and other Upanishads and to delineate a specific path leading to the ultimate state that those texts describe. As we shall see, the divergent interpretations that emerged differed greatly about the nature of the world and the self.

Generally speaking, the Upanishadic path to freedom involves acquiring a special kind of knowledge. Ordinary knowledge will not cut the chains of our bondage. "Into blind darkness they enter, people who worship ignorance; And into still blinder darkness, people who delight in learning" (4.4.10). The Upanishadic texts do not disparage all learning but rather sound a note of caution about the limits of conventional knowledge. What this passage seems to be saying is that it is dangerous to rely too heavily on ordinary knowledge. Ordinary information is fine for operating in the conventional world of multiple forms; however, it is worthless for knowing the ultimate nature of reality and the self.

The *Brihad Aranyaka Upanishad* makes it clear that one must finally let go of any attachment to ordinary ways of knowing. The text tells us that one "should stop being a pundit and try to live like a child. When he has stopped living like a child or a pundit, he becomes a sage" (3.5.1). That is, after gaining significant exposure to the scriptures and becoming an expert in the scholarly sense, one should abandon any reliance on learning and try to return to the simple and spontaneous state of a child. This still, however, does not give a clear indication of how one is to achieve ultimate knowledge and freedom. Only in very general terms does the *Brihad Aranyaka Upanishad* recommend a path of withdrawing from ordinary ways of being and meditating continually on the *atman*. This vagueness is characteristic not only of this text but of other Upanishads as well. It remained for later commentators to spell out in detail exactly what the final state involves and how it can be attained.

DIVERGENT INTERPRETATIONS

One of the greatest disagreements within Hinduism occurs between those who view ultimate reality as an impersonal absolute and those who emphasize a personal relationship with ultimate reality. (A concomitant question is, "Is the world ultimately real or not?") Not surprisingly, these two radically different stances have led to widely divergent interpretations of the *Brihad Aranyaka Upanishad*. A complete introduction to later Hinduism would involve a description of an expansive array of religious practices, including domestic rites, temple rituals, pilgrimages, yogic discipline, and so forth, as well as the beliefs that inform these diverse practices. Although such a task is impossible within the limitations of this chapter, the ideas of two leading philosophical figures from the Hindu tradition, Shankara and Ramanuja, are examined to indicate the wide range of practices and beliefs that are included under the rubric of Hinduism. Both are identified as Vedanta philosophers, where "Vedanta" means literally the "end of the Vedas," that is, the culmination of the revealed books of wisdom known as the Vedas. This term is taken primarily to refer to the teachings of the Upanishads but also includes the Bhagavad Gita and the *Brahma Sutra*. Although there are also schools of Hindu philosophy that are not Vedanta, Shankara and Ramanuja represent two of the most influential schools of Hindu thought and practice. Since both Shankara and Ramanuja wrote commentaries on the *Brahma Sutra*, a text that further investigates the concept of *brahman* introduced in the Upanishads, we can use these two works to explore their fundamental divergence in interpretation.

Shankara's Advaita Vedanta

Shankara (c. 788–820) is one of the best-known Hindu philosophers in India and in the West. Although his philosophical system of Advaita ("nondualism") informs the activities of only a small minority of Hindus and has tended to overly dominate Western understandings of Hinduism, it represents an important philosophical position within the Hindu world and constitutes one of the most popular rationalizations for the act of religious renunciation.

What does it mean to know *brahman*? Perhaps the most pressing question that remained from Upanishadic speculation was, "What is the relationship between the ultimate reality of *brahman* and the world of multiplicity we experience with our senses?" A concomitant question arose: "What is the status of a personal God and the individual soul?" Shankara was one of the first Indian philosophers to formulate a consistent and singular viewpoint based on the Upanishads that addressed these important questions. His is a philosophy of unity that ultimately devalues all diversity. For Shankara, *brahman* is the only truth, the world is ultimately unreal, and the distinction between God and the individual soul is only an illusion.

Brahman, for Shankara, is the sole reality. It is the absolute undifferentiated reality, one without a second (*advaita*) and devoid of any specific qualities (*nirguna*). Since he understands the highest realization of *brahman* to be a state in which all distinctions between subject and object are obliterated, he concludes that the world of diversity must finally be false. Shankara recognizes that the Upanishads speak of two aspects of *brahman*, one with qualities (*saguna*) and one without (*nirguna*); but he maintains that the former is simply the result of perception conditioned by limiting factors. "Brahman is known in two aspects—one as possessed of the limiting adjunct constituted by the diversities of the universe which is a modification of name and form, and the other devoid of all conditioning factors and opposed to the earlier" (1.1.12). In fact, Shankara claims that all apparent distinctions within *brahman* are the result of the superimposition of the frames of reference of the viewer. This brings us to one of the most important concepts in his philosophy: the theory of illusion, or "**maya**." *Maya* is the process by which the world of multiplicity comes into being; it is the force by which the formless takes form. *Maya* both conceals and distorts the true reality of *brahman* and is manifest epistemologically as ignorance (*avidya*). Its workings cannot be explained in words since language itself is a product of *maya*. Since all diversity is finally false for Shankara, *maya* is the major obstacle to the highest realization of ultimate knowledge.

What this means is that the world we experience with our senses is not *brahman* and therefore not ultimately real: "The senses naturally comprehend objects, and not Brahman" (1.1.2). By this Shankara certainly does not mean that the world is a figment of our imagination. He was a staunch opponent of subjective idealism. For him the world has an apparent reality; that is, it is existentially real: "It cannot be asserted that external things do not exist. Why? Because they are perceived. As a matter of fact such things as a pillar, a wall, a pot, a cloth, are perceived along with each act of cognition. And it cannot be that the very thing perceived is non-existent" (2.2.28). Shankara does recognize the category of the nonexistent and gives as a stock example "the son of a barren woman." Our world, on the other hand, has an apparent reality and, in this sense, "exists." However, since the experience of the world is devalued by the ultimate experience of *brahman* in which all distinctions are obliterated, it cannot be the absolute reality. Just as the contents of a dream are devalued upon waking, so too the experience of the world is devalued upon the waking of ultimate enlightenment. The stock example used to explain this is the snake and the rope. A person erroneously perceives a rope to be a snake in dim light. The fear that the person subsequently feels is real enough, existentially. However, when the light of knowledge illuminates the "snake," it is discovered to be a rope all along. The snake was merely superimposed onto the rope, giving the snake an apparent reality. So too—as the illustration is applied—the world and *brahman*. The world of multiplicity is ordinarily superimposed onto the nondual *brahman*, with the result that we live in an illusory world. The experience of the world, however, is revealed to be false in the ultimate knowledge of *brahman*. This theory allows philosophers to disassociate the problematic world from the true reality, just as reflections of the moon in various pots of water are finally disassociated from the moon.

The same argument is applied to two other important differentiated entities: the personal God and the individual soul. Shankara defines the personal God as *brahman* with attributes. But since all attributes are the product of the limiting factors of ignorance, God, too, is finally declared to be an illusion. Worship of the personal God, however, is highly beneficial, for although God is not the highest reality, it is the highest reality conceivable for creatures still enmeshed in the cosmic illusion of *maya*. That is, the personal God is a necessary component of spiritual experience since it provides a transition between the world and *brahman* for those who are still attached to the world. In the end, however, one must give up this sense of separateness and reintegrate all gods back into one's self.

A related concept for Shankara is the individual soul (*jiva*). By now it should be clear that all diversity for Shankara is considered to be the result of illusory perception, so it will come as no surprise to learn that he ultimately rejects the individual soul as illusory. Although the *jiva*, or individual soul, involves a higher level of realization than the ego-identity associated with the body, in the final analysis it, too, is unreal. The true self for Shankara is the *atman*, defined as pure consciousness. Like the world and God, the individual soul is merely an apparent reality, whose appearance is the result of viewing the self through the limiting factors of ignorance. He writes that the self "is endowed with eternal consciousness . . . it is only the supreme Brahman Itself, which while remaining immutable, appears to exist as an individual soul owing to association with limiting adjuncts" (2.3.18). Though in everyday experiences we feel ourselves to be agents of our own actions, this, too, is an illusion. This means that the true self is eternally free from the conditioning effects of karma; to be free one needs only to realize that bondage is a mental construct. Shankara also maintains that the self is beyond all experience since this involves a difference between the experiencer and that which is experienced. Therefore, at the highest level of realization, the individual soul, the subject of all experience, disappears as an illusion; the true self is declared to be identical with *brahman*, the absolute unified ground of being. The goal of all spiritual endeavor for Shankara is the realization of this ultimate fact. The highest level of the knowledge of *brahman* involves the obliteration of all distinctions between the knowing subject and all known objects in the state of absolute identity. A favored metaphor for the ultimate experience so conceived is the reemergence of all drops of water back into the single undifferentiated ocean. This is how Shankara interprets the Upanishadic quest for ultimate knowledge.

But what are the essential components of a path designed to accomplish this ultimate feat? In the first section of this chapter we encountered the *Brihad Aranyaka Upanishad*'s creation myth, which recounts how the world of multiple forms came into being out of desire, a desire for another. The essential element in the story for Shankara is the unity that precedes the diversity produced by desire. Since desire is associated with the creative force that divides the original oneness, eradicating desire is a necessary step toward the process of reunification. This brings us to the idea of renunciation. The highest spiritual path, according to Shankara, consists of a meditative practice designed to lead one to the insightful realization that "I am *brahman*." He calls the practice of meditating on and realizing the true self "*samadhi*." An important prerequisite to this practice, however, is a withdrawal from ordinary social and domestic activities and a retreat from our ordinary investment in the data of the senses. That is, one of the most prominent consequences of Shankara's theory is the move toward the practice of world renunciation. Shankara is credited with founding an important order of renouncers (*sannyasi*) known as the Dashanamis. These are men who embark on the path of ultimate realization by performing their own funeral rite, thereby indicating the end of their former identity and the beginning of full-time participation in a celibate religious community and meditation on *brahman* as the impersonal absolute.

Ramanuja's Vishishta Advaita Vedanta

Diametrically opposed to the views of Shankara is the perspective of those Hindus—especially the Vaishnavas (worshippers of God in the form of Lord Vishnu)—for whom the personal nature of the divine is an ultimate attitude and not an illusion to be transcended. One of Shankara's most determined and well-known opponents was Ramanuja (c. 1017–1137), an important theologian and chief interpreter of Vedanta for the southern Indian devotional movement known as Shri Vaishnavism. His philosophical system is designated Vishishta Advaita ("nondualism of the differentiated") since it takes differentiated entities to be real and understands them to be attributes of a nondual reality. Ramanuja's philosophy values both unity and multiplicity, a stance that results in a very different view of the nature of God, the world, and the self.

In his commentary on the *Brahma Sutra*, Ramanuja criticizes Shankara for his refusal to acknowledge any qualities or distinctions in the nondual reality of *brahman*. Like Shankara, Ramanuja accepts the Upanishadic assertion that *brahman* is the sole reality; however, for him, *brahman* means God, who is endowed with innumerable excellent qualities. "The word 'Brahman' primarily denotes that supreme Person who is the abode of all auspicious qualities to an infinite degree and is free from all worldly taint. This supreme Person is the only Being the knowledge of whose real nature results in liberation" (1.1.1, p. 1). Thus, Ramanuja does not make a distinction between *brahman* and God, as does Shankara. Rather, Ramanuja interprets Upanishadic descriptions of *brahman* as "without qualities" to mean the absence of certain kinds of qualities: qualities that are negative or binding. In effect, he reverses Shankara's privileging of *brahman* without qualities (*nirguna*), arguing that *brahman* with qualities (*saguna*) is the higher form. Specifically, Ramanuja resists Shankara's conceptualization of *brahman* as pure undifferentiated consciousness, contending that if this were true, any knowledge of *brahman* would be impossible since all knowledge depends on a differentiated "object." "Brahman cannot be, as the Advaitins say, non-differentiated pure Consciousness, for no proof can be adduced to establish non-differentiated objects" (1.1.1, pp. 19–20).

The particular kind of experience for which we should aim, according to Ramanuja, is a blissful knowledge of *brahman* as the Lord with infinite and amazing qualities or, stated more simply, the love of God. But for this relationship to be possible, there must be a distinction between the knowing subject or the one who loves (the individual soul) and the known object or the beloved (the Lord). Many of the devotional theologians within Hinduism remark that they do not want to become sugar (Shankara's goal); instead, they want the blissful experience of tasting sugar (Ramanuja's goal). For this to occur there has to be a difference between the tasting tongue and the sugar (while simultaneously realizing that even the tongue is essentially sugar). This means that difference must be taken seriously, and this implies a very different picture of the world of sense experience from the one we encountered in Shankara's Advaita system.

The world is real, for Ramanuja, and was created out of God's desire to become manifold. That is, the world is the result of a real transformation of *brahman*. The stock example used to explain this viewpoint is the transformation of curds from milk. Curds that are produced from processing milk are both different and nondifferent from their source. This view is more widely accepted by Hindus than is Shankara's view that the world is ultimately an illusion. It implies that the creative process that resulted in multiplicity is not finally to be overcome but rather is to be appreciated for what it truly is, the product of God's creative activity. Like Shankara, Ramanuja connects the desire of the one to become many with the concept of *maya*; but instead of conceptualizing *maya* as "illusion," as does Shankara, Ramanuja takes it to be the "creative power" of God. "The word Maya does not mean unreal or false but that power which is capable of producing wonderful effects" (1.1.1, p. 73). The world, then, is viewed in a much more positive light, and in fact Ramanuja goes on to characterize it as the "body of God." He maintains that *brahman* "is the creator, preserver, and destroyer of this universe, which It pervades and of which It is the inner Ruler. The entire world, sentient and insentient, forms its body" (1.1.1, p. 55). That is, the conditioned and transitory world is an attribute of the unconditioned and eternal God, as the transitory body is an attribute of the eternal soul. The world is therefore different from God, yet it is also inseparably connected to God, as an attribute is connected to its substance.

This is also the case with the individual soul (*jiva*). It, too, is considered to be part of the body of God, and it is in this manner that Ramanuja interprets the Upanishadic identity of *brahman* and the true self. Whereas Shankara ultimately characterized the individual soul as a false illusion, for in his view all distinction is obliterated in the final experience of *brahman*, Ramanuja maintains that it is real and eternal. As a part of *brahman*, the soul is both different and nondifferent from the whole (2.3.42, p. 298). The world of matter and individual souls enters into God at the time of dissolution and separates from God at the time of creation. Rejecting Shankara's claim that the true self is pure consciousness beyond all experience, Ramanuja maintains that the true self is a special enjoyer of experience (2.3.20, p. 285). In its highest state, it is the eternal, blissful knower of *brahman*.

The path to freedom and the blissful experience of *brahman* is well represented in the following passage.

> This bondage can be destroyed only through Knowledge, i.e., through the Knowledge that Brahman is the inner ruler different from souls and matter. This Knowledge is attained through the Grace of the Lord pleased by the due performance of the daily duties prescribed for different castes and stages of life, duties performed not with the idea of attaining any results but with the idea of propitiating the Lord. (1.1.1, p. 80)

Far from renouncing the world of action, a very particular way of acting is indicated here that is linked to the karma-yoga of the Bhagavad Gita, the other major Vedanta text. Bhagavad Gita 2.47 states that one in pursuit of ultimate liberation should act in a manner that avoids both an attachment to the results of action and the abandonment of action. That is, as a path of action, karma-yoga is situated between two modes of behavior current in Hindu religion. On the one hand, the path of Vedic sacrifice—and ordinary action, for that matter—is a mode of action wherein the act is performed with a controlling concern for the outcome of the action. Why, after all, do we do anything if it is not for the result we expect to achieve by performing the act? Much religious activity follows the same logic; a religious act such as Vedic sacrifice is performed to obtain some desired result. In accord with the Bhagavad Gita, however, Ramanuja holds that such action reveals a fundamental ignorance and serves only to bind us further. Life, according to Ramanuja, is a cosmic play (*lila*), wherein God is the ultimate playwright (2.1.33, p. 237). The ordinary human urge to control the outcome of all our actions is tantamount to an effort to usurp the role of the playwright. Moreover, insisting on a particular outcome of action in a world ever abundant as *brahman* is like walking into an extraordinary store filled with an amazing assortment of candies with a fixed desire for a certain kind of candy bar, one that, as it turns out, happens not to be there. The result is suffering and bondage in a potentially wonderful situation. What, then, to do? The answer certainly does not lie in abandoning all action, for that is the other mode of behavior to be avoided. Following the Bhagavad Gita, Ramanuja insists that one should engage in the action that comes to one according to one's own life situation. World renunciation is simply another attempt to establish control and cannot lead us to the state of blissful enjoyment. Instead, Ramanuja advises us to surrender completely to God, for only then are we free to enjoy the marvelous show that is the world. Whereas Shankara renounces the world, Ramanuja demonstrates how to live in it freely.

Although Ramanuja has little to say about the worship of concrete forms of God in his commentary on the *Brahma Sutra*, he belongs to a devotional community in which this type of meditation is the central religious practice. Acts directed to pleasing the Lord instead of one's egoistic self are often enacted in the context of worship of concrete forms or bodies of God, either in a temple or at a home shrine. Informed by such texts as the *Brihad Aranyaka Upanishad*'s conversation wherein Vidagdha asked Yajnavalkya how many gods there are, these concrete forms are considered to be multiple forms of a single, nondual divinity. *Brahman* is understood to be fully present in these special bodies, which are limited forms of the infinite that God compassionately assumes for the purpose of granting accessibility to embodied human beings with ordinary senses. The limited forms are like the defining frame placed around certain works of art that serves to allow focused perception of something that might have otherwise been missed. A great deal of Hindu practice involves the loving service of such concrete forms of God. Whereas Shankara saw these acts as preliminary to the higher business of *samadhi* meditation, for Ramanuja, loving acts directed toward God are supreme. Loving devotion implies a very different attitude toward human emotions from that observed in Shankara. Since the world is real for Ramanuja, everything in it—including human emotions—can be used as fuel for the spiritual life. The goal of such devotional acts is a kind of union with God, wherein the liberated soul lives in the loving presence of the Lord but does not dissolve into undifferentiated oneness with him. This is often conceived of in Vaishnavism as an eternal and blissful existence in God's heavenly abode of Vaikuntha. Here "the released self abides as an enjoyer of the supreme Brahman" (4.4.20, p. 493).

We observe, then, two radically different religious sensibilities arising from—or at least being justified by—the same Upanishadic texts. For Shankara, the nondualism of the *Brihad Aranyaka Upanishad* means that the world of multiplicity and everything connected with it is, in the final analysis, an illusion. With the dawn of true consciousness, the world, the individual self, and even God are revealed to be unreal. Participation in the ordinary world, then, is viewed as a hindrance to the highest spiritual life. The consequence of this view is a religious life that values world renunciation and is suspicious of anything based on ordinary human senses. Ramanuja, on the other hand, interpreted the nondualism of the *Brihad Aranyaka Upanishad* to mean that there is a single cause to everything but that the multiple effects of that single cause are real. Ultimate reality is understood to be God as the inner controller of the manifold world and the individual soul. The consequence of this position is a religious life of devotional activity that views the world positively and uses the ordinary senses to pursue a blissful experience of the differentiated *brahman*. Although world-renouncers can still be found in almost all religious centers in India today, devotional practices in temples and home shrines dominate the Hindu tradition.

CRITICAL DISCUSSION

The Vedanta philosophy represented by Shankara and Ramanuja is a textual tradition. What this means specifically is that Vedanta philosophers—though they insist that the final proof of anything must be experience—rely heavily on scriptures such as the *Brihad Aranyaka Upanishad*, which they take to be authoritative. Many philosophers today would not accept scripture as a reliable source of truth. Moreover, Vedanta philosophy rests on the transcendental claims of the Upanishads, represented by the concept of *brahman*. Obviously, this too makes it suspect for secular philosophers, for whom the idea of transcendence is highly problematic. This is, after all, what makes Vedanta a "religious" philosophy. The philosophical traditions of India differ from many of those in the West on this exact point, for much of Hindu philosophy is intended to be of practical assistance to spiritual experience.

In contrast to many of the other theories represented in this book, Vedanta philosophy appears to have little to say about social and political struggles and reforms or about practical morality. Although some recent defenders of Vedanta philosophy have denied this accusation, it holds a certain amount of truth. The writings of Vedanta philosophers are preoccupied with achieving a higher knowledge and freedom and with metaphysical concerns regarding the nature of ultimate reality, the world, and the self. *Brahman* for Shankara, for example, has little to do with the ordinary world and transcends all normative distinctions, and the true self is beyond the categories of good and evil. It should be pointed out, however, that Shankara insists that there are moral consequences of all actions for people living in the conditioned world of *maya*. Selfless, compassionate acts erode false boundaries and lead to higher realization, whereas egoistic, violent acts reinforce false boundaries and lead to further bondage. Moreover, although in theory Ramanuja's system values the world, sometimes in practice it is the case that worldly particulars are valued only so far as they lead to the knowledge of God and not in themselves.

Although women participate actively in the metaphysical discussions of the *Brihad Aranyaka Upanishad* and there is no textual evidence to suggest that they were in any way excluded from the higher goals expressed in that text, women are excluded from Shankara's order of renouncers and are never allowed to serve as temple priests in Ramanuja's tradition of Shri Vaishnavism. Although Ramanuja opened his tradition to women and the lower classes, Vedanta philosophy in general, and Shankara's school in particular, tends to be very elitist. It requires a knowledgeable religious practitioner who is well educated in scripture, at least in its expectations for the highest realization. In classical Indian society, this deters all but those who occupy the upper classes. Those denied such preparation by birth are likewise often denied the opportunity for the highest achievement—at least in this lifetime.

FOR FURTHER READING

Basic text: *Brihad Aranyaka Upanishad* (many translations and editions). All quotations are from the translation by Patrick Olivelle, *Upanisads* (New York: Oxford University Press, 1996). This is a very readable and reliable text that includes a valuable introduction. Other readily available translations are those by Robert E.

Hume, *The Thirteen Principal Upanishads* (New York: Oxford University Press, 1971), and by R. C. Zaehner in *Hindu Scriptures* (New York: Knopf, 1966).

Shankara's commentary on the *Brahma Sutra*: Few reliable translations exist. We have quoted from one of the most available English translations: Swami Gambhirananda, *Brahma-Sutra-Bhasya of Sri Shankaracarya* (Calcutta, India: Advaita Ashrama, 1977).

Ramanuja's commentary on the *Brahma Sutra*: Few reliable translations exist. We have quoted from one of the most available English translations: Swami Vireswarananda and Swami Adidevananda, *Brahma-Sutras, Sri Bhasya* (Calcutta, India: Advaita Ashrama, 1978).

For an overall introduction to Indian philosophy, see M. Hiriyanna, *Outlines of Indian Philosophy* (Bombay, India: George Allen & Unwin, 1973). For an introduction to Hinduism, see Gavin Flood, *An Introduction to Hinduism* (Cambridge: Cambridge University Press, 1996).

For more on the philosophy of the Upanishads, see Paul Deussen, *The Philosophy of the Upanishads* (New York: Dover, 1966).

For more on the *Brahma Sutra*, see S. Radhakrishnan, *The Brahma Sutra: The Philosophy of Spiritual Life* (London: George Allen & Unwin, 1960).

For more on Shankara's Advaita Vedanta, see Eliot Deutsch, *Advaita Vedanta: A Philosophical Reconstruction* (Honolulu: University Press of Hawaii, 1969), and Natalia Isayeva, *Shankara and Indian Philosophy* (Albany: State University of New York Press, 1993).

For more on Ramanuja's Vishishta Advaita Vedanta, see John Carman, *The Theology of Ramanuja* (New Haven, CT: Yale University Press, 1974), and C. J. Bartley, *The Theology of Ramanuja: Realism and Religion* (London: Routledge Curzon, 2002).

For more on the worship of concrete forms of divinity within Hinduism, see Diana Eck, *Darsan: Seeing the Divine Image in India* (New York: Columbia University Press, 1998), and Joanne Punzo Waghorne and Norman Cutler, eds., *Gods of Flesh, Gods of Stone: The Embodiment of Divinity in India* (New York: Columbia University Press, 1996).

KEY TERMS

ahamkara	**karma**
atman	*maya*
brahman	*moksha*
jiva	**renunciation**

QUESTIONS FOR DISCUSSION

1. Think about the conversation between the Upanishadic sage Yajnavalkya and Vidagdha Shakalya regarding the number of gods. What does this tell you about Hindu theism? Would you say this is a polytheistic tradition or a monotheistic one? Or does it indicate some other conceptual option?

2. What would be some implications of the radically interconnected conception of self (*atman*)?

3. What is the human predicament according to the *Brihad Aranyaka Upanishad*, and how does one overcome it?

4. What is the ultimate state according to Upanishadic thought, and what is the primary stumbling block to achieving it?

5. What would you say are some of the main issues at stake in the divergent interpretations of Shankara and Ramanuja?

3

Buddhism: In the Footsteps of the Buddha

Buddhism is a multifaceted religious tradition that includes a variety of teachings and conceptions of the **Buddha** as well as many different pathways to the ultimate goal. Most Buddhists, however, regard their tradition as a way of following the Buddha to the goal of nirvana or Buddhahood. Although Buddhism arose on the Gangetic plain of northern India in the fifth century B.C.E., it soon spread to become a very prominent form of religion through most of Asia. Sometime after its establishment, Buddhism split into two major divisions. One branch eventually developed into Theravada, or the "Way of the Elders," which became the dominant type of Buddhism in southeast Asia, and the other developed into Mahayana, or the "Great Vehicle," which became the dominant type of Buddhism in central and east Asia. A third offshoot, Vajrayana, or the "Diamond Vehicle," developed further into a distinctive form of Mahayana and became prominent in Tibet. Although there is much variety within the Buddhisms of the world, for the limited purposes of this chapter we will focus on some of the main teachings of and differences between Theravada and Mahayana Buddhism. This will be achieved primarily by comparing several aspects of south and southeast Asian Theravada Buddhism as represented in the Pali Canon with aspects of Mahayana Buddhism as represented in the *Lotus Sutra*, a text of enormous importance in east Asian Buddhism.

The Pali scripture of Theravada Buddhism has much to say about how we are to understand Buddhist teachings. Imagine that you find yourself before a great being, a master, a being who knows it all. This is a chance of a lifetime, your opportunity to ask any questions for which you ever wanted an answer. What might you ask? Is the world eternal, or does it have an end? Does a person continue to exist after death or not? Is there a soul separate from the body or not? What might the answers be? There is a story of such an experience found in the Pali Canon. Here we meet a monk by the name of Malunkyaputta who comes before the Buddha asking these very questions. Furthermore, he tells the Buddha that if he receives satisfactory answers to these questions, he will continue to live a religious life under the guidance of the Buddha. But if he does not receive acceptable answers to these questions, he will abandon the monastic life. The Buddha informs him that he does not intend to answer his questions, for he reminds Malunkyaputta that he never promised to answer such questions and insists that "the religious life does not depend on dogma" (PC 121). He says that anyone waiting for such answers from the Buddha will die before he ever receives them all.

> It is as if, Malunkyaputta, a man had been wounded by an arrow thickly smeared with poison, and his friends and companions, his relatives and kins-folk, were to procure for him a physician or surgeon; and the sick man were to say, "I will not have this arrow taken out until I have learnt whether the man who wounded me belonged to the warrior caste, or to the Brahman caste, or to the agricultural caste, or to the menial caste. . . . I will not have this arrow taken out until I have learnt whether the bow which wounded me was a cupa, or a kodanda. . . . I will not have this arrow taken out until I have learnt whether the shaft which wounded me was feathered from the wings of a vulture, or of a heron, or of a falcon, or of a peacock, or of a sithalahanu. . . . [The man's long list of questions goes on and on.]" That man would die, Malunkyaputta, without ever having learnt this. (PC 120–21)

What is the problem with the kinds of questions Malunkyaputta puts before the Buddha? If we examine them closely, we see that they take something for granted that the Buddha did not share; they assume something about the nature of reality not held by the Buddha. Any answer, therefore, would result in affirming something that the Buddha did not want to affirm. In a sense, such metaphysical questions establish their own parameter and limit the range of possibilities. Moreover, the kinds of questions Malunkyaputta brought to the Buddha lock one into a dualistic, two-value logic. In effect they are inquiring, "Is reality this or that?" They are like the problematic question, "Did you stop beating your wife; yes or no?" Such questions make clear assumptions that may not fit the case. Built into the metaphysical questions Malunkyaputta put to the Buddha were ideas and a whole baggage of presuppositions that the Buddha did not care to confirm. Thus, he refuses to answer such questions. In effect, the Buddha of the Pali Canon is saying, "If you come to me with a load of presuppositions, we cannot hope to communicate. In a sense you have already answered your question. And has it gotten you anywhere? Is reality really such that it can be grasped with two-value logic?" The Buddha as a practical physician also seems to be asking, "And what good does a rational picture of reality do for you? If I told you, for example, that the world is eternal, would it alleviate your suffering and enable you to achieve peace?" The Buddha of the Pali scriptures avoids metaphysical sidetracks and establishes a direct path to teachings that are designed to achieve ultimate goals. He says, "And why, Mulunkyaputta, have I not elucidated this? Because, Malunkyaputta, this profits not, nor has to do with the fundamentals of religion, nor tends to aversion, absence of passion, cessation, quiescence, the supernatural faculties, supreme wisdom, and Nirvana; therefore have I not elucidated it" (PC 122).

The pointlessness of metaphysical inquiry is illustrated with the story of the poisoned arrow; surely, this man will die without ever knowing the answers to his many questions. What difference do the answers make anyway? "The Tathagata [a title for the Buddha]," the Buddha informs another questioner, "is free from all theories" (PC 125). Rather than constructing yet more seductive theories, the Buddha clears the way of distracting speculations in order to remove the very arrow causing all suffering and to cure all illness. Early Buddhist teachings, then, are often said to be regarded as a raft that is to be discarded once one has crossed over the ocean of suffering or like medicine that is to be dispensed with once one has gained full health. The Buddha of the Pali Canon proceeds as a wise physician by dispensing the medicine of the **dharma**, practical teachings designed to remove the arrow of human suffering; these concern the nature of suffering, the origin of suffering, the cessation of suffering, and the path leading to the cessation of suffering. This is what the Buddhist tradition calls the **Four Noble Truths**. Before examining these, let us look briefly at the life of the remarkable figure who set forth these truths about the nature of human existence.

LIFE OF BUDDHA

The story of the life of the Buddha is a major cornerstone of Buddhism. But how are we to read this story? An attempt was made in much of the scholarship of the nineteenth and twentieth centuries to separate mythology from history in the story of the life of the Buddha and to expunge the story of the former in an attempt to bring the real facts of the story to light. Presumably this effort would result in a clearer picture of who the Buddha really was. This approach, however, totally compromises the authors of the texts that portray the life of the Buddha and undermines their sense of reality. The only accounts we have of the life of the Buddha are the stories as they are told. What we today find incredible may have been completely believable to Buddhist authors and vice versa. Our aim should not be to fit these stories into our contemporary sense of reality but rather to strive to understand the meaning expressed in the stories themselves. We suggest that the story of the life of the Buddha be read as the sacred property of the Buddhist community that accounts for how the Buddhist spiritual path came into being and establishes an ideal pattern for life. Furthermore, it is a story that expresses an existential message concerning the nature of human life. Many have claimed that an understanding of Buddhism depends upon comprehending this existential message.

The story of the life of the Buddha does not begin with a single birth, for Buddhism shares a belief in reincarnation with other south Asian religious traditions. Buddhists trace a long sequence of virtuous past lives of the Buddha in a series of texts known as the Jatakas ("Birth Stories") as he gradually advances toward the culmination of awakening in his last life. In this final life, the Buddha was born of royal parents as a privileged prince. His name was to be Siddhartha, and his birth was not an ordinary one. His mother, Maya, conceived him while dreaming of a white elephant, and he was born immaculate without pain from his mother's side in the wooded grove of Lumbini in the vicinity of the town of Kapilavastu located in the Himalayan foothills near modern Nepal. Upon birth the infant Siddhartha took seven steps, declaring that he would be enlightened in this very life. The unusual birth of the Buddha identifies him as a special, even superhuman being, making him a worthy exemplary figure. But if the future Buddha were too superhuman, it would not be possible for humans to emulate him. Accordingly, the humanness of Prince Siddhartha must be established, and the story is explicit in making the struggles of the future Buddha very human.

After his birth, a prophetic seer predicted that if he took constant pleasure in household affairs, he would become a universal monarch; but if he renounced worldly pleasures, he would become instead a great religious leader. Prince Siddhartha grew up in a social context perfect by conventional standards, a world of great wealth in which all his physical desires were more than fulfilled. Furthermore, no signs of suffering or unpleasantries were allowed within the palace walls. The prince's seductively comfortable world was created and carefully controlled by his father, King Suddhodana, who feared that any exposure to suffering would cause his young son to question a future as a powerful, wealthy political leader.

And yet, even in this seemingly perfect world something was amiss—and this something forced Prince Siddhartha to seek a goal higher than that of conventional definition. What was it that shattered the ideal world of the palace? Is it really possible to avoid suffering in human life?

One day Prince Siddhartha desired to go for a chariot ride in a nearby royal park. During this outing he came upon something that he had never previously seen: an old man. Never having encountered such a being before, he assumed that this man was a unique individual and asked his chariot driver what kind of person this was. His driver stunned him by revealing to him that the condition of old age is the future of everyone—the young prince included. Greatly agitated by this realization, Prince Siddhartha hurried back to the palace. King Suddhodana was informed about what had happened and immediately set about trying to take his son's mind away from the inevitability of aging by arranging sensual entertainment for him. Although the king redoubled his efforts to protect his son from any exposure to suffering, on another day Prince Siddhartha ventured again into the park in his stately chariot. This time he came across a man who was gravely ill. Once more he asked his chariot driver whether this was a particular kind of man or whether sickness could strike anyone, and again the driver disturbed the prince's world of childlike innocence by telling him the truth. The prince returned to the palace even more distraught. Even though the king once more tried his best to distract his son and keep him busy with sensual enjoyment, the prince journeyed to the park again. This time he encountered a sight that disturbed him even more and shattered the last shred of his youthful ignorance: he saw a dead man. The words of his chariot driver made it clear to him that death would be the end of him too, for death is inevitable for all beings. Though his father tried his best, there was no consoling Prince Siddhartha. On his final excursion to the park, the privileged prince saw a simple monk who had renounced the world and sensed that this man showed a possible way out of the world of suffering. From this moment on, although he was married to a beautiful princess who had just given birth to their son, Prince Siddhartha was determined to renounce the life of the palace.

Pressing through the resistance of his father and the heavy gates of the palace, Siddhartha left the royal city to take up a life of ascetic practice in the forest to search for a way out of suffering. Once free of the city he cut off his majestic topknot of hair and sent all his jewelry and fine clothes back to the palace with his favorite horseman. He then embarked on a six-year experimentation with ascetic practices, going from teacher to teacher to learn and master the different meditative techniques each had to offer. None of these, however, satisfied him. He then met five ascetics with whom he practiced severe types of austerities and nearly starved himself to death by extreme fasting. This too he found unsatisfactory.

Realizing that the austere practices of the forest were just as fruitless as the life in the palace, the former prince left this way of life too by accepting a bowl of sweet milk rice pudding from a cowherd woman. With this action he discovered the "Middle Way," situated between the decadently opulent life of the palace and the harshly ascetic life of the forest. His five companions were so scandalized by his behavior that they abandoned him, assuming that he had fallen from the true path. Soon after, the future Buddha sat beneath a bodhi tree, determined not to rise until he had pierced through the problem of suffering. Fearing he was slipping beyond control, Mara, the god of egoistic desire, attacked him with great force, horrific demons, and seductive nymphs to drive him from his power spot previously occupied by preceding Buddhas. Mara's efforts, however, were in vain, for Siddhartha would not budge. Mara then demanded of the former prince, "Who is witness to your great merit?" In a gesture that is celebrated in much Buddhist sculpture, Siddhartha reached down with his right hand to touch the Earth, which quaked an affirmative response. At this point Siddhartha's success was assured; entering into deep meditation, he contemplated the nature of existence and achieved enlightenment that very night. He became the Buddha, "the Awakened One."

The Buddha passed seven days sitting under the bodhi tree experiencing the bliss of profound freedom or **nirvana**. Then, after deciding to teach others what he had realized, he got up and traveled to a deer park located near the famous holy city of Benares, where he found the five ascetics he had practiced with formerly. Here he turned the "wheel of dharma" for the first time and taught them the core of his realization in the form of the Four Noble Truths. Laying out the basic principles of his teachings, he established through his own life the rules for a monastic existence and a model of discipline for future monks to follow. After a long teaching career and upon reaching the age of eighty, the Buddha traveled to a grove of trees near the city of Kushinagara. There he lay down on his right side, and after urging his followers to recognize the transitory nature of everything and work toward enlightenment with diligence, he remained completely mindful and passed into what is called *Maha-Pari-Nirvana*, "the Great and Complete Emancipation." The Pali Canon of Theravada Buddhism suggests strongly that the only lasting influence of the Buddha is the dharma—his teachings—and the **Vinaya**—the monastic discipline. Buddha himself passes beyond all influence, leaving only a model for how one can achieve supreme enlightenment and nirvana oneself.

A very different view of the Buddha, however, is presented in the *Lotus Sutra*. Without actually denying the more personal and historical view of the Buddha expressed in the Pali scriptures, the Mahayana view of the *Lotus Sutra* states that the Buddha who lived on Earth in a particular span of time appeared in a "phantom body," or in a body self-created by a being who is cosmic and eternal. That is, his human form was a particular skillful means (*upaya*) to assist those who needed the Buddha in this form. Mahayana Buddhism later developed the notion of the three bodies of the Buddha. The historical Buddha is regarded as the *Nirmana-kaya*, or "emanation body" manifested for the spiritual development of certain kinds of people. The *Sambhoga-kaya*, or "enjoyment body," is a celestial body in which Buddha appears to bodhisattvas, followers of Mahayana, in pure celestial Buddha worlds and is enjoyed in visions. But the most important of the three bodies is the *Dharma-kaya*, which is a cosmic body encompassing the totality of all reality. It is paradoxically nonexistent, and yet all existence depends on it. It is unconditioned because it is not conditioned by karma and desire but not unconditioned because it has the capacity to manifest itself as something conditioned. It is infinite, immutable, simultaneously immanent and transcendent, eternally present, and spread throughout all places in the universe. Furthermore, the teachings of the Buddha are not limited to a particular time and place but rather are ongoing, infinite, and multifaceted. In the Mahayana language of the *Lotus Sutra*, Buddhists are not orphans after the passing away of the historical Buddha but rather the children of a compassionate father who is directly involved in the world, working tirelessly to edify human beings and develop them toward the ultimate realization of their own Buddhahood. The Buddha of the *Lotus Sutra* is a powerful and actively engaged savior who thinks, "I am the father of all creatures and I must snatch them from suffering and give them the bliss of the infinite, boundless Buddha-wisdom" (LS 88). This unified cosmic Buddha is able to take many different forms in the world appropriate for saving particular types of people. "The present buddhas in the universe, whose number is as the sands of the Ganges . . . appear in the world for the relief of all creatures" (LS 71). As we will see, this perspective on the Buddha opens up the possibility for many other expressions of religiosity besides monastic discipline. In this context, for example, worship of the Buddha and other devotional practices find a welcome home.

THEORY OF EXISTENCE

What was it that the Buddha taught about existence? Answers to this question are varied, but almost all Buddhists recognize a core of the Buddha's teaching that includes an articulation of the three marks or characteristics of existence. That is, the Buddha explained that human reality is characterized by impermanence (*anitya*), lack of a solid self (*anatma*), and unsatisfactoriness (*dukkha*). A major Buddhist insight—well represented in the story of the four signs Prince Siddhartha encountered in the royal park—is that all things are subject to change. *Anitya*, the first of the three marks of existence, tells us much about the nature of the world in which we live—namely, that it is transitory or fleeting. There is nothing solid or autonomous in the world. Everything that is born dies; no thing, being, idea, plan, or state of mind endures. This leads to a great deal of anxiety for human beings, who are always striving after something lasting and secure. But nothing is permanent in the world. Theravada Buddhists do not normally recognize any creator god, ground of being, or "unmoved mover" behind the continual movement of the world. The distinctive way Buddhists express insight into the nature of existence is to say that everything that arises does so in a manner that is dependent upon something else. Moreover, not only are all things continually changing but their changes also effect subsequent changes in other things.

That nothing is solid or autonomous is best understood by the teaching of **dependent origination**, which illustrates the radical interconnectedness of all things and interrelatedness of all beings by demonstrating that everything that exists is contingent on something else. Theravada tradition maintains that while he was meditating under the bodhi tree the future Buddha comprehended the interdependent nature of states of being in terms of a twelvefold chain of causation. Human ignorance leads to mental formations, which lead to individual consciousness, which leads to the formation of a personal mind and body, which leads to the six senses, which lead to sensorial contact, which leads to sensations, which lead to cravings, which lead to clinging, which leads to the desire for further becoming, which leads to rebirth, which leads to aging and dying, which in turn leads to more ignorance. The twelvefold chain of causation explains the arising of all things, beings, and states. In effect, it functions like a creation myth in other religious traditions. Since the twelvefold chain of dependent origination has no clear beginning, it is often depicted in Buddhist art as a twelve-spoked wheel. Tibetan Buddhist artists, for example, portray the twelvefold chain of dependent origination as the wheel of existence, wherein each of the twelve conditions is illustrated with a picture. The hub of the wheel is driven by hatred, delusion, and desire, usually depicted as a snake, pig, and cock, respectively; and the entire wheel is held in the jaws and claws of Mara, the demonic ruler of conditioned existence who fights to keep all from achieving liberation. Buddhist teachings aim to dissolve this chain of radically conditioned existence by freeing one from the snare of ignorance (particularly through the Four Noble Truths), for once this link is broken, the entire chain unravels.

According to Buddhist notions of reincarnation, our present life is but one in a long successive series of lives. One's place in the current world is determined by one's own karma. That is, one's birth in the world is not the result of an accident, nor is it decided by a rewarding or punishing god; rather, it is the consequence of one's own intentional past actions, good and bad. Again, there is no creator god in Buddhism; karma alone is understood to be sufficient to propel the universe along its course. Buddhists conceive of many different realms that one might be born into as a result of the quality of one's karmic action. The Tibetan wheel of life just referred to often depicts the many possible worlds one can be reborn into; besides the human realm, these include both heavenly and hellish realms.

A somewhat different view of the world from what is found in the Pali Canon of Theravada Buddhism is suggested in the Mahayana Buddhism of east Asia. Although it is difficult to make general statements about Mahayana Buddhist conceptions of the nature of the world, the notion of the *Dharma-kaya* of the Buddha, a form that is cosmic, eternal, omnipresent, and intensely involved in the world, implies that there may be something unconditioned and unchanging in or behind the world. The Buddha of the *Lotus Sutra* certainly is a powerful and substantial presence who is very much in charge of the world. Nonetheless, even this text stops short of defining the Buddha as a creator god; and in the end, Mahayana Buddhism affirms the insubstantiality of the world.

THEORY OF HUMAN NATURE

The teaching that there is nothing solid in the world also applies to the self. The second mark of existence teaches that there is no self (*anatma*). A story in the Pali Canon about an encounter between one king, Milinda, and a wise monk by the name of Nagasena expresses Buddhist notions of human nature. After establishing that he is free from political retribution for any comment he might make, Nagasena inquires about the mode of transportation by which the king has arrived at their meeting. Upon learning that the king has come in a chariot, the wise monk questions him about the nature of his chariot (PC 131–32). He asks, "Is the axle the chariot?" The king answers that it is not. "Are the wheels the chariot?" Again, the king denies this is so. The conversation continues with Nagasena moving through the entire chariot, identifying the individual parts and asking whether any particular part is the chariot. The king persists in rejecting the idea that any of the individual constituents of the chariot are the chariot itself. The monk comes to his main point:

> "Your majesty, although I question you very closely, I fail to discover any chariot. Verily now, your majesty, the word chariot is a mere empty sound. What chariot is there here? Your majesty, you speak a falsehood, a lie: there is no chariot. . . . Just as the word 'chariot' is but a mode of expression for axle, wheels, chariot-body, pole, and other constituent members, placed in a

certain relation to each other . . . in exactly the same way the words 'living entity' and 'Ego' (autonomous self) are but a mode of expression for the presence of the five attachment groups, but when we come to examine the elements of being one by one, we discover that in the absolute sense there is no living entity there to form a basis for such figments as 'I am,' or 'I'" (PC 132–34).

Nagasena insists that a person's name is "but a way of counting, a term, an appellation, a convenient designation, a mere name; for there is no Ego (autonomous self) here to be found" (PC 129). His point is that the claim that a person consists of a permanent, unchanging, autonomous self is false. No basis can be found for its reality.

The "five attachment groups" mentioned in the quotation above refer to the five *skandhas*, alternatively translated as the five "aggregates" or "components" that make up a person. Before examining these five components of a person, we need to understand that for Buddhists just as there is no chariot separate from its individual parts, likewise, there is no "person" apart from these five components. The teaching of the five aggregates is a way of accounting for an entire person without resorting to the idea of a "self." Once the five aggregates are examined and analyzed, one discovers that there is nothing behind them that can be taken as a substantial center or permanent "I." Buddhist practice aims to dismantle the unexamined (and false) belief in separate individuality or the idea of the self. Any concept of an ego, self, or soul as an everlasting, independent, and absolute entity, an unchanging substance behind the changing phenomenal world, is strongly denied any authentic existence. According to the teachings of the Buddha, the idea of a self is an imaginary belief corresponding to no veracity.

This means not that there is no sense of self-reference, continuity of memory, or relative individuality but that there is no permanence underlying being. Rather than a permanent being, the human is a mind, body, and sense of self that consist of sequences of passing moments. In this sense, a human "being" is really more of a human "becoming." Furthermore, the idea of a separate self, which leads to selfishness and egoism, not only is false but produces many harmful effects; it is the root of all existential suffering (especially regarding death) and social problems, such as theft, poverty, and violence—all of which assume separate selves in competition with one another. The realization of the absence of a separate self, on the other hand, can lead to a state of selfless loving-kindness and compassion for others. Thus, great effort is made in Buddhist teachings to erode and eventually eliminate the idea of one's own permanent individuality.

The first of the five *skandhas*, "components" or "aggregates" of a person, is "form" (*rupa*), the material aspect of a thing or person. It is matter, or the stuff of the world, itself made up of ever-changing atoms. In the context of a person, the first aggregate of "form" is the body, including the six sense organs (the mind is included in the list of senses in Buddhism), as well as their corresponding objects in the external world. The second *skandha* is the aggregate of "sensations" (*vedana*), the physiological process resulting from contact of form with form, of the senses with their corresponding objects. Sensations are the feelings produced as the eye comes in contact with visible forms, the ear with sounds, the tongue with tastes, the nose with odor, the body with tangible objects, and the mind with mental objects, such as thoughts. These are said to be of three kinds: pleasant, unpleasant, and neutral. The third aggregate is "perception" (*samjna*). When the six sense organs come in contact with their corresponding objects, sensations are produced that then lead to recognition of objects. When one touches a table with the hands and eyes, for example, not only are sensations produced but the result is a detection of the object as "table." Perception also occurs in contact with mental objects. Perceptions, then, are the six types of mental discriminations resulting from the six types of sensations. The fourth *skandha* is the aggregate of "mental formations" (*sanskara*). The mental formations include our predispositions, impulses, attitudes, and tendencies that make up the unique character of our own personality. What is known as "karma" is also included in the aggregate of mental formations. Sensations and perceptions alone do not produce karmic effects, but mental formations are tied to volitional activities in thought, word, or deed, both good and bad, such as wisdom or conceit. Mental formations play a key role in the creation of our ongoing conditioned existence and need to be looked at again after examining the fifth aggregate, which is "consciousness" (*vijnana*). Consciousness is comprised of moments of awareness: not only does one sense and perceive a table, to return to the example above, but one is now aware of the table. Although some Asian schools of religious thought look to consciousness itself as being the core of a permanent self, the Buddha of the Pali Canon taught that consciousness arises only when one of the six sense organs experiences a sense object. Consciousness is dependent upon the conditions in which it arises and, therefore, is neither independent nor permanent but as conditioned as the other four aggregates.

A second look at the fourth *skandha* is instructive for better understanding the way the five aggregates relate to one another. When the arising and passing moments of form, sensations, perceptions, and consciousness interact they create karmic residue or latent impressions called *sanskaras*, or mental formations. These in turn are the predispositions that generate and condition the continual arising and passing away of additional combinations of the four other aggregates. One's consciousness, then, is deeply conditioned by mental formations. A romantic affair that goes sour, for example, very often affects one's next love affair, even though in theory the two are completely separate relationships. Something is carried over that shapes and influences the next experience. Driven and conditioned by unconscious latent impressions, the combinations of form, sensations, perceptions, and consciousness are both ongoing and self-perpetuating. Again, there is no unmoved mover behind the movement; there is only movement, only change. One thing disappears, conditioning the appearance of the next in a series of causes and effects. The mental formations, however, which include both conscious and unconscious memories, provide a connection between the arising and passing moments of the unique combinations of the aggregates.

What this means is that a human life is, in effect, very short. "Strictly speaking, the duration of the life of a living being is exceedingly brief, lasting only while a thought lasts. Just as a chariot-wheel in rolling rolls only at one point of the tire, and in resting rests only at one point; in exactly the same way, the life of a living being lasts only for the period of one thought" (PC 150). Rebirth or reincarnation, then, is happening rapidly and constantly each moment of our lives. As contemporary biology, psychology, and physics confirm, our bodies and minds are changing incessantly. Buddhists explain the concept of the simultaneity of continuity and discontinuity in the process of reincarnation with the aid of a candle. During further conversations, the wise monk Nagasena asks King Milinda whether he is the same person he was as a young boy. "Nay, verily bhante. The young, tender, weakly infant lying on its back was one person, and my present grown-up self is another person" (PC 148). Here, discontinuity is emphasized. But Nagasena presses the king on this point and gets him to see it also in the case of a person. "It was I, your majesty, who was a young, tender, weakly infant lying on my back, and it is I who am now grown up" (PC 148–49). Now continuity is stressed. How can both of these statements be true? Buddhists use the metaphor of a flame to illustrate this point. If you were to light a candle and then come back an hour later, would you see a different flame or the same flame? Nagasena questions the king:

> "It is as if, your majesty, a man were to light a light; would it shine all night?"
> "Assuredly, bhante, it would shine all night."
> "Pray, your majesty, is the flame of the first watch the same as the flame of the middle watch?"
> "Nay, verily, bhante."
> "Is the flame of the middle watch the same as the flame of the last watch?"
> "Nay, verily, bhante."

"Pray, then, your majesty, was there one light in the first watch, another light in the middle watch, and a third light in the last watch?"

"Nay, verily, bhante. Through connection with that first light there was light all night."

"In exactly the same way, your majesty, do the elements of being join one another in serial succession: one element perishes, another arises, succeeding each other as it were instantaneously. Therefore, neither as the same nor as a different person do you arrive at your latest aggregation of consciousness." (PC 149)

Nagasena's point is that just as the flame one witnesses upon lighting a candle and the flame one witnesses upon returning an hour later are both a different flame and the same flame, so too a person now and that person ten years earlier are both a different person and the same person. The difference is due to the fact that a person is continually changing (the aggregates of form, sensations, perceptions, and consciousness comprise moments that arise and pass away), and the sameness is due to the connecting memories, predispositions, unconscious impressions, and karmic links of the aggregate of the mental formations. By extending the metaphor of the candle to include the fresh lighting of one candle with another candle—just as the latter is about to go out—an explanatory illustration is provided for rebirth or reincarnation following the death of the physical body with the persisting karmic connections that determine and condition the next life.

So what are we to conclude about Buddhist conceptions of human nature? Clearly, the Buddha labored hard to dismantle the idea of a permanent, autonomous self. But are we to understand the teaching of no self as a firm and absolute doctrine? When the Buddha was asked directly whether a soul does or does not exist, he remained silent. Let me close this section with a statement from the Pali Canon that complicates any simplistic view of the Buddhist notion of the self. After a section that lays out the teaching of the five aggregates and confirms that there is no basis of an "I" here, we read,

He, however, who abandons this knowledge of the truth and believes in a living entity must assume either that this living entity will perish or that it will not perish. If he assumes that it will not perish, he falls into the heresy of the persistence of existences; or if he assume that it will perish, he falls into that of the annihilation of existences. . . . To say: "The living entity persists," is to fall short of the truth; to say, "It is annihilated," is to outrun the truth. (134)

This statement, to say the least, challenges one to think deeply about the very nature of existence.

DIAGNOSIS

What is the basic problem of human existence according to Buddhist teachings? This question brings us to the Four Noble Truths, the very core of Buddhist dharma, the subject of Buddha's first sermon delivered to the five ascetics in the deer park near Benares, and the key to shattering the twelvefold chain of causation at the point of ignorance. The First Noble Truth states that life is *dukkha*; this is also the third mark of existence. The word *dukkha* is often translated as "suffering" but is perhaps more accurately translated as "dissatisfactory." As we saw in the story of the life of the Buddha, this is also true for a privileged prince who has it all. *Dukkha* includes feelings such as insecurity, uncertainty, lack, and loss. It refers to a state of basic existential anxiety about life, that things are imperfect, always flawed. It is also a response to impermanence; good things never last. Human beings are uneasy, anxious, vulnerable, frustrated, and disappointed in a world in which everything—including one's own self—is constantly changing and cannot be held onto in any lasting way. As with other Buddhist teachings, the claim that life is suffering is not to be taken as an ultimate doctrinal statement about the nature of reality but rather as a statement about the experiential reality of human beings. The Buddha did not claim that life is ultimately *dukkha* and nothing but *dukkha* but rather that we experience it as *dukkha*. In the role of a wise physician (rather than a metaphysician) the Buddha diagnoses the human predicament as *dukkha* and proceeds from there.

Three kinds of *dukkha* are recognized in Buddhist literature. First, there is ordinary suffering, such as aging, sickness, and death. Ordinary suffering also includes such experiences as encountering unpleasant conditions, separation from loved ones, not getting what one wants, and sadness. The second type of suffering is *dukkha* produced by change. Even the experience of ordinary happiness eventually yields a form of suffering produced by change. The Buddha is not saying that there is no happiness in human life, but rather he highlights the fact that happiness—like everything else—does not last and therefore is not fully satisfactory. When happiness disappears, unhappiness arises. The last type of suffering is *dukkha* as conditioned states, primary among them being the troublous state created by a false sense of self. The emphasis on *dukkha* does not make Buddhism a pessimistic religion; Buddhism simply stresses the necessity of first facing a realistic assessment of the ordinary human condition as characterized by suffering in an effort to move beyond it.

After diagnosing the human condition as *dukkha*, the Buddha as an effective physician moves on to identify the cause of our disease. The Second Noble Truth asserts that the cause of our suffering is "craving" or "grasping" (*tanha*). Our problem is that we try to hold onto things and experiences that by nature cannot be held onto. *Dukkha* is caused by an ever-changing self trying desperately to cling to a world in continual flux; it is the result of a nonexistent self trying to possess things that by definition cannot permanently be possessed. The essence of life is change, while the essence of grasping is to prevent change. Importantly, this grasping must be seen as a selfish kind of craving. Craving is a willful act that is motivated by the idea of a separate and permanent self. It is the expression of an intense desire to perpetuate the self. It is a thirst for the will to be, to exist, to become more and more, to grow more and more, to accumulate more and more, to have more and more. And all of this leads to continual and conditioned suffering.

PRESCRIPTION

What then are we to do about the human condition of suffering according to Buddhist thought? Is it possible to escape from the experience of *dukkha*, and if so, what is the means to do so? These questions lead us to the Third and Fourth Noble Truths. The Buddha does not leave his followers in a hopeless state. Far from it: he claims that there is a healthy state beyond the existential anxiety of *dukkha*. The Third Noble Truth asserts that there is a cessation of *dukkha*, which, of course, involves the end of craving. The Third Noble Truth, in effect, negates the First Noble Truth, thus the importance of seeing Buddhist teachings as useful only so long as they are applicable.

The ultimate state in Buddhism is referred to as "nirvana." The word "nirvana" literally means "blowing out" or "extinguishing," as in the blowing out of a fire. In the present context, the reference is to the blowing out of *dukkha* by means of extinguishing the fire of craving (*tanha*). This leads to the blessed state of nirvana. When craving becomes extinct, *dukkha* is gone, and the result is nirvana. This is the highest goal of Buddhist practice, and perhaps this is all that can be said about nirvana. Buddhist scriptures warn again and again that nirvana can never be completely defined by words. Describing nirvana to one who has not experienced it is said to be like a turtle trying to describe to a fish what it is like to walk on dry land. There is nothing in the fish's experience that enables it to understand land conceptually. So too with nirvana, which is wholly beyond ordinary experience. Despite the warnings, however, attempts have been made to define nirvana. It is perhaps best defined as absolute freedom but has also been referred to as the "unconditioned," "truth," "bliss," or "ultimate reality." It is the freedom to see things as they really are, emancipated from the limiting distortions of self-projections. It is a tranquil liberation from the tormenting existential anxieties of life, such as those that drove young Prince Siddhartha out of his palace. Far from the pessimistic self-annihilation of nihilism, nirvana is said to be a blissful and dynamic state in which all hatred, delusion, and desire have been annihilated. Nirvana is a sublime religious state that can be experienced in this very life, as is demonstrated in the sacred biographies of the Buddha by the fact that the Buddha lived for more than forty years after achieving the awakening of nirvana under the bodhi tree.

We now come to the Fourth Noble Truth, the prescription to end the disease of *dukkha,* the medicine that allows one to achieve the supremely healthy state of nirvana: the **Eightfold Path**. This path is also known as the "Middle Way" since it is situated between the two extremes of a life dedicated to satisfying ordinary pleasures, as exemplified by the palace in the story of the life of the Buddha, and the excessive asceticism exemplified by the harsh routine the future Buddha practiced with the five ascetics in the forest. Some spiritual paths that originate in India—such as the eight-limbed practices of classical yoga—are meant to be followed successively, as one climbs a ladder rung by rung; but the Eightfold Path is comprised of eight practices that are to be followed simultaneously, as one might follow the spokes of an eight-spoked wheel concurrently to its central hub. The Eightfold Path addresses three major concerns: ethical conduct (*sila*), which is based on the concept of universal love and compassion for all living beings; mental discipline (*samadhi*), which culminates in the meditative realization of the true nature of the self and the world; and wisdom (*prajna*), which has to do with establishing correct knowledge about reality and is fulfilled in Enlightenment. In general, it may be said that the Eightfold Path aims at cultivating behavior not motivated by the idea of the self.

Ethical conduct includes three practices of the path: *Right Speech* means that one should speak in a manner that benefits all beings. One should speak at the right time and place and abstain from lying, harsh or harmful speech, and useless speech. If one has nothing worthy to say, one should maintain a "noble silence." *Right Action* involves the cultivation of moral, honorable, and peaceful conduct in oneself and others. It avoids killing, stealing, cheating, engaging in illicit sex, and consuming intoxicants. *Right Livelihood* denotes making a living or profit that does not involve harming other beings or come at the expense of the welfare of others. Examples of wrong livelihood are the manufacture and sales of weapons, the slaughter of animals, and the production of intoxicants and poisons.

Mental discipline is comprised of the following three practices: *Right Effort* entails applying oneself energetically to the generation and cultivation of wholesome states of mind. Overcoming unwholesome states, one should channel one's energy to the development of all aspects of the Buddhist life.

Right Mindfulness is a meditative practice in which one aspires to be diligently aware of one's body, feelings, mind, and thoughts. It is often considered to be the most critical aspect of the path. Mindfulness meditation usually involves giving attention to breathing as one seeks deeper and deeper insight into the nature of reality as marked by dissatisfaction, impermanence, and lack of a solid self. All of Buddhist practice might be summed up as, Be ever mindful! *Right Concentration* differs from mindfulness meditative practices in that it involves the cultivation of meditative states through the technique of calming the mind and concentrating it on a single point. There are, then, two types of meditative practice referred to in Buddhist scripture. One involves withdrawing the senses from ordinary sensory experience and narrowing awareness from its usual wide spectrum in order to achieve one-pointed concentration. Rather than narrowing awareness or shutting down awareness, the other aims to open awareness completely so that one becomes fully aware of reality as it really is and achieves deep insight into the nature of the world and self. If a balloon were popped behind a person in an ordinary state of being, that person would most likely jump. If a series of balloons were popped, the person would typically react less and less as the series went on until that person became used to the sound. If a balloon were popped behind a person in deep concentrative meditation, there would presumably be no reaction since that person's senses and awareness are withdrawn. If, however, a balloon were popped behind a person engaged in mindfulness meditation, the person would react and, not only that, would go on reacting to the entire series of poppings, experiencing each as a new and unique event.

Wisdom includes Right Thought and Right Understanding. Right Thought involves thoughts of selfless detachment, thoughts that transcend the idea of the self, or simply, loving thoughts. *Right Understanding* means understanding things as they really are. It connotes harmonizing one's mind with the ultimate nature of reality characterized by the three marks of existence. Most important, this means understanding the Four Noble Truths, for it is this teaching that explains things as they really are. Thus, there is something wonderfully circular about Buddhist teachings: the Fourth Noble Truth is the Eightfold Path, and the eighth aspect of this path consists of understanding the Four Noble Truths, the main subject of the Buddha's first sermon.

DIFFERENT PATHS

In addition to understanding the complexity of Buddhist practice in terms of the Eightfold Path, it is important to appreciate the great variety found within Buddhism. Within Theravada Buddhism alone there exist two very different ways of being Buddhist: one for the monks and another for the laity. Buddhist monastic discipline is defined primarily by the Vinaya, namely, 227 rules that govern the monk's life. Although the word "discipline" may have negative connotations in some contexts, here it comes to mean a way of acting that is not motivated by personal desire or self-concern. Discipline is concerned with volition and volitional acts, that is, with karma. Whereas ordinary action is self-directed and produces conditioning karma, disciplined action—action performed without the burden of self—will not produce further conditioned action or karma. Detached actions that are not motivated by personal desire do not produce further attachments or bondage; they are thus a path to freedom. Put simply, the studied actions of monastic discipline lead to selfless action—action minus the self. Buddhist monks are not so concerned with acting in a pragmatic way but in a way that is in harmony with the highest reality. Moreover, Buddhist monks strive not just for freedom but for a particular experience represented by the Buddha's enlightenment. This means that Buddhist discipline aims to follow in the footsteps of the Buddha as carefully as possible, for the perfected way of life expressed spontaneously by the awakened Buddha is understood to be the very model for monastic discipline. That is, the Buddha's way of being and the monastic way of life are two sides of the same coin; the difference is in the motivation. The Buddha's actions are the natural expression of a disciplined mind, whereas the monk's actions are intentional means to create a disciplined mind; but in either case, the actions are ideally the same.

Pursuit of a perfected way of being, however, requires the controlled environment of the monastery and the support of a nonmonastic laity. The Buddhist laity is comprised of those who have accepted the five Buddhist precepts but do not aim for the higher goal of nirvana in this lifetime; rather, they strive to improve their karmic lot in this life and the next by generating good karmic merit. There are, then, really two goals in Buddhist society: nirvana is actively pursued by the monks, while the laity occupy themselves with laying the foundation for its attainment in a future life by amassing beneficial merit. The relationship between the monks and the laity is one that is to be mutually supportive. The laity supply the monks with food and clothing in exchange for at least three important returns: the monks teach the Buddha's dharma, exemplify a model life, and provide a productive field for merit-making. Buddhist monasteries in Sri Lanka and southeast Asia are often located near settlements to facilitate the daily round of the monks' begging for food. The monastery is regularly opened to the laity so that they can listen to the monks chant Buddhist texts, hear a sermon on the life and teachings of the Buddha, and receive the five precepts: not to kill, steal, lie, consume intoxicants, or engage in illicit sex. In this way the monks actively influence the lifestyle of the lay Buddhist society in their role as active teachers. In addition to this, to the degree that the Buddhist monks maintain the Vinaya or monastic discipline, they lay claim to being the legitimate bearers of the spiritual path articulated by the Buddha. As they express this publicly through a range of rituals, the monks formally declare the eternal presence of the Buddha's dharma and affirm their role as the successors to the Buddha's authority in matters of spirituality. The result is that the monks provide a model of perfection for their greater society and establish themselves as legitimate fields for merit. As the monks follow in the footsteps of the Buddha and imitate his way of being in the world, they establish a concrete and empirically available model for the laity who interact with them. The devout laity in turn provide another kind of model for those members of their society who have not taken the five precepts. In this way a paradigmatic line can be observed that stretches back to the Buddha through the monks and to a lesser extent through the laity. Furthermore, giving gifts of food, clothing, and shelter to the monastic community, which is considered to be a rich and fruitful field for making good karmic merit, becomes a promising occasion for the laity to develop themselves spiritually as they prepare to better themselves in this life and the next.

The considerable variety within Buddhism can be even better appreciated when we examine a Mahayana text such as the *Lotus Sutra*. Mahayana Buddhists consider their approach "greater" for several reasons. It is open to all, involves an all-embracing compassion, and has a greater goal. The Mahayana Buddhism of the *Lotus Sutra* differs greatly from Theravada Buddhism. We have already seen that Mahayana Buddhists have a different view of the Buddha: whereas Theravada Buddhism is oriented to a historical understanding of the Buddha, without actually denying this understanding, the *Lotus Sutra* asserts that if the Buddha had lived on earth in a particular span of time, it was in an "emanation body" by a being who is cosmic and eternal but can manifest in numerous forms. There are further differences. The Theravada ideal of human perfection is the accomplished monk, or *arhat*, who worked diligently for his own enlightenment, while the Mahayana ideal of human perfection is the bodhisattva, literally an "enlightenment-being." The bodhisattva is one who takes a double vow: to realize Buddhahood but not to enter final nirvana before all beings have been liberated. Rather than disappearing from worldly existence at the end of life as do the *arhats*, bodhisattvas pursue various perfections (*paramitas*) and dedicate their bodhisattva lifetimes and subsequent lives as Buddhas to the compassionate act of helping others attain the liberation of enlightenment.

Important among the perfections pursued by a bodhisattva is the perfection of wisdom. Specifically, this refers to achieving insight into the "**emptiness**" (*sunyata*) of all factors of existence. Mahayana Buddhists claim that all aspects of existence are "empty of own-being" (*svabhava*); this is another way of saying that all things are radically interdependent and interconnected. The *Heart Sutra* claims that the aggregate of "form is emptiness and emptiness is form." This is true for all of the five aggregates that make up a person. In a sense, the bodhisattva looks simultaneously through two seemingly contradictory lenses: through the lens of wisdom the bodhisattva sees that there are no independent beings; through the lens of compassion the bodhisattva resolves to save all beings. The teaching that form is emptiness does not mean that matter does not exist, but rather it tells us something about the nature of matter. Emptiness is not an ultimate reality that transcends all forms of existence, but rather all forms of existence are themselves empty. Emptiness regarded in this nondualistic way ultimately affirms the value of this world and all beings. This is the insightful wisdom of the bodhisattva that supports magnificent compassion for all beings. The greatly compassionate and vastly wise bodhisattva is often contrasted in Mahayana literature with the *arhat*, who is characterized in this context as a haughty, cold, and self-centered monk.

Furthermore, the concept of the dharma, or the Buddha's teachings, is expanded. If the Buddha existed only in northern India during the sixth century B.C.E., then his teachings would be finite and complete upon his death. On the other hand, if the Buddha exists at all times, his teachings are infinite in form and continue at all times. Consequently, dharma would be the ongoing teachings of an omnipresent being. Many Mahayana sutras claim to present a teaching that is given only when the time and place are right for the revelation of advanced wisdom. The *Lotus Sutra* regards the dharma as "infinite, boundless, unprecedented" (LS 52), and considerably varied in a manner suitable to the great variety of human dispositions. Additionally, whereas the highest goal of Theravada Buddhism is a final passing out of this world, Mahayana Buddhist texts often speak of realizing "Buddha nature." But even when the term "nirvana" is used, it is understood quite differently.

One of the astounding claims of Mahayana Buddhism is that the supreme goal of nirvana and ordinary existence (*samsara*) are the same. The *Lotus Sutra* puts it this way: "All existence, from the beginning, is ever of the nirvana-nature" (LS 66). Some schools of Mahayana Buddhism, consequently, hold a view of consciousness somewhat different from that presented in Theravada scriptures. These schools maintain that prior to being affected by the conditioning and distorting influences of mental formations and defilements, consciousness exists in its true essence as a pure and enlightened luminosity that is the basis for Buddhahood. The aim, then, is to uncover what is already there. Nirvana is said to be unattainable for at least two reasons. First, it is unattainable because it is not some objective thing or concrete goal that can be attained. Second, it cannot be attained because it already is. Striving for nirvana or Buddhahood elsewhere is compared in east Asian Buddhism to the process of searching for an ox while riding an ox. The implications of this for Buddhist practice are immense.

A story is told in the *Lotus Sutra* about a man who went to visit a friend and while with him got so drunk that he fell asleep. The man's friend had to leave on official business, but before he left he sewed a priceless jewel inside the man's jacket as a gift. When the man awoke he set out on a journey to a foreign land seeking his livelihood by working extremely hard just to make ends meet. Sometime later he once again met his friend, who was horrified to learn that the man had been laboring so hard when all the while he had a priceless jewel sewn in his jacket.

> Tut! Sir, how is it you have come to this for the sake of food and clothing? Wishing you to be in comfort and able to satisfy all your five senses, I formerly in such a year and month and on such a day tied a priceless jewel within your garment. Now as of old it is present there and you in ignorance are slaving and worrying to keep yourself alive. How very stupid! Go you now and exchange that jewel for what you need and do whatever you will, free from all poverty and shortage. (LS 177)

The text makes it clear that the priceless jewel is eligibility for Buddhahood and that the pittance the man had earned from his hard labor is the lesser goal achieved through short-sighted monastic discipline. If he had only known the truth, the man would not have had to work for a daily wage as he had an infinitely precious and free gift with him all the time. In fact, his labors kept him from realizing what was there with him all along. A similar story is found in the *Lotus Sutra* about a king and his young son, who ran away, forgot his origins, and fell into a life of poverty. The wayward son too labored hard for a meager wage (i.e., the *arhat's* nirvana) until the day he found his way back home and realized that as son of the king he already possessed infinite wealth (i.e., Buddha nature) (LS 110–15). Both of these stories make the same point: that one does not have to work to achieve Buddha nature, but rather one merely needs to realize what already is. The *arhats* of the *Lotus Sutra* come to understand, "From of old we are really sons of the Buddha, but only have taken pleasure in minor matters" (LS 115). From a Mahayana perspective, the goal-oriented activity of monastic discipline that seeks nirvana elsewhere steals attention away from the here and now and blocks acceptance of what truly is. To the degree that a conception of nirvana posits a perfect world outside of the present one, it creates dissatisfaction with present existence and, therefore, can in its most radical form be seen as a cause of *dukkha*. A motto of Theravada Buddhism might be "Be on constant guard," while a motto of Mahayana Buddhism might be "Be on friendly terms with whatever comes."

Whereas the path to perfection within Theravada Buddhism is understood to be singular, as defined by the Vinaya, the Mahayana Buddhism of the *Lotus Sutra* recognizes countless ways to realize Buddha nature. In addition to strict monastic practice, this opens up a world of devotional surrender to Buddha as a savior and to various forms of temple worship. Included among the countless ways to achieve the ultimate, the *Lotus Sutra* claims,

> Even anyone who, with distracted mind, with but a single flower has paid homage to the painted images shall gradually see countless buddhas. Or those who have offered worship, were it by merely folding the hands, or even raising a hand, or by slightly bending the head, by paying homage to the images gradually see innumerable buddhas, attain the supreme Way. . . . If any, even with distracted mind, enter a stupa or temple and cry but once 'Namah Buddha,' they have attained the Buddha-way. (LS 69)

Alongside of those forms of Buddhism that rely on self-effort in realizing enlightenment, then, we find various forms of Buddhism that understand the spiritual path to be one of reliance on an all-powerful and saving Buddha. Within Japanese Buddhism, these two approaches are called, respectively, *jiriki* ("by the power of oneself") and *tariki* ("by the power of another").

WOMEN IN BUDDHISM

Buddhism, like all the great world religions, is comprised of enormous variety. It would therefore be difficult to marshal a critique of Buddhism as a whole since any remark made would most likely be contradicted by some form of Buddhism. Instead, we will end this chapter with a few comments on the position of women in Buddhism as represented in the Pali Canon and the *Lotus Sutra*. Overall, Western feminists have pointed out that in traditional forms of monastic Buddhism women have been viewed as spiritually inferior to and as temptresses for male monks. Women in monastic literature have been depicted as being sensually unrestrained and having animalistic tendencies not found in men. The Buddha of the Pali scriptures advises men to avoid women as much as possible. A segment of the Pali Canon well illustrates the somewhat ambiguous view of women situated with a monastic perspective. In a section of the text that addresses the admission of women into the monastic order, a maternal aunt of the Buddha named Gotamid asked the Awakened One if she could retire from the household life to pursue a monastic life. The Buddha replied, "Enough, O Gotamid, do not ask that women retire from household life to the houseless one, under the Doctrine and Discipline announced by The Tathagata" (PC 441). Seeing her in a sad and dejected state, the Buddha's close disciple Ananda intervened on Gotamid's behalf and approached the Buddha himself. At first the Buddha repeated his refusal to let women into the order, but Ananda changed his tactic and inquired about the competency of women for achieving the higher states, including the ultimate state of an *arhat* (here translated as "saintship"). To this the Buddha replied, "Women are competent, Ananda, if they retire from household life to the houseless one, under the Doctrine and Discipline announced by The Tathagata, to attain to the fruit of conversion, to attain to the fruit of once returning, to attain to the fruit of never returning, to attain to saintship" (PC 444). After admitting this, the Buddha agrees to allow women into the monastic order under the condition that they accept eight additional rules, all designed to keep them distant from and subordinate to men. We learn from this, then, that women were allowed into the monastic order according to the Pali scriptures and, furthermore, were considered to be capable of achieving the highest spiritual goal. However, this comes at a cost. The Buddha explains to Ananda that if women had never been allowed into the order, Buddhist dharma would have lasted fully intact for one thousand years, but since they were allowed into the order, Buddhist dharma would last for only five hundred years. "Just as Ananda, when the disease called mildew falls upon a flourishing field of rice, that field of rice does not long endure, in exactly the same way, Ananda, when women retire from household life to the houseless one, under doctrine and discipline, that religion does not long endure" (PC 447). Although we must be careful not to conflate the representation of women in Buddhist literature with any on-the-ground social reality, there is obviously much that is problematic from a modern perspective about the viewpoint expressed above. Much of it appears to be male projectionism. On the other hand, many Theravada Buddhists point out that the Buddha created the women's order in a way that kept them independent of the men's order to assure their freedom from male domination, and the texts refer to many holy women and good daughters of the Buddha.

The *Lotus Sutra* fares somewhat better in its attitudes toward women. This text advocates an all-inclusive universal salvation, which clearly includes women. Virtuous women are recognized in the *Lotus Sutra* as "good daughters" and regarded as skilled teachers and potential bodhisattvas, although there may still be a residual sense that they do best under the guidance of a male "good son." Nonetheless, the Buddha of the *Lotus Sutra* acknowledges the place of virtuous women alongside virtuous men: "If there be any people who ask what sort of living being will become Buddhas in the future, you should show them. . . . If good sons and good daughters receive and keep, read and recite, expound, copy even a single word of the Law-Flower Sutra . . . these people will be looked up to by all the worlds; and as you pay homage to tathagathas, so should you pay homage to them" (LS 187). Today, as Buddhism continues to establish itself in new countries and cultures around the world, women are carving out novel places for themselves in a tradition that has been largely dominated by men.

FOR FURTHER READING

The Pali Canon (PC) is available in different forms and translations. All quotations and references are from the selections in Henry Clarke Warren, *Buddhism in Translations* (New York: Antheneum, 1974), since this paperback edition is still readily available through a number of publishers.

Several translations of the *Lotus Sutra* (LS) exist. Quotations and references are from Bunno Kato, Yoshiro Tamura, and Kojiro Miyasaka, trans., *The Threefold Lotus Sutra* (New York: Weatherhill, 1984).

For an overview of Buddhism, see Donald W. Mitchell, *Buddhism: Introducing the Buddhist Experience* (New York: Oxford University Press, 2008); Richard H. Robinson, Willard L. Johnson, and Thanissaro Bhikkhu, *Buddhist Religions: A Historical Introduction*, 5th ed. (Florence, KY: Wadsworth/Thomson, 2004); and Peter Harvey, *An Introduction to Buddhism: Teachings, History and Practices* (Cambridge: Cambridge University Press, 1990).

For more on Theravada Buddhism, see Robert C. Lester, *Theravada Buddhism in Southeast Asia* (Ann Arbor: University of Michigan Press, 1973); Walpola Rahula, *What the Buddha Taught* (New York: Grove Press, 1974; many other editions are available, including an online edition); and Kate Crosby, *Theravada Buddhism: Continuity, Diversity, and Identity* (Hoboken, NJ: Wiley-Blackwell, 2013).

For more on Mahayana Buddhism, see Paul Williams, *Mahayana Buddhism: The Doctrinal Foundations* (London: Routledge & Kegan Paul, 1989).

For more on women in Buddhist literature, see Diana Y. Paul, *Women in Buddhism* (Berkeley: University of California Press, 1985); and Jose Ignacio Cabezon, ed., *Buddhism, Sexuality, and Gender* (Albany: State University of New York Press, 1992).

KEY TERMS

anatma
anitya
Buddha
dependent origination
dharma
dukkha
Eightfold Path

emptiness
Four Noble Truths
karma
nirvana
skandhas
Vinaya

QUESTIONS FOR DISCUSSION

1. Since Buddhist teachings are claimed not to be dogma, what are they and why is the distinction necessary?
2. What role does the life story of the Buddha play in Buddhist philosophy?
3. What are some of the major dissimilarities between the Theravada and Mahayana understandings of the Buddha, and what are some of the chief implications of this difference?
4. What do Buddhists mean by the interrelatedness of all beings, and what does this tell us about the Buddhist conception of self?
5. What advantages do you see to the Buddhist teaching of no-self (*anatma*) over the notion of a permanently autonomous self?
6. What is the cause and nature of our limiting conditionedness according to Buddhists? What is the way out of this?

4

Plato: The Rule of Reason

Let us start our examination of Western theories of human nature by considering the philosophy of Plato (c. 429–347 B.C.E.). Although it dates back two and a half millennia, Plato's pioneering thought has been enormously influential down the centuries and is still of contemporary relevance. He is one of the first and greatest philosophers, appealing to the systematic use of our reason to show us the best way to live. But he was not a purely rational philosopher, for in some of his stylish, artfully constructed dialogues he suggests that we need to be inspired by a vision of goodness and beauty beyond ourselves. A clear conception of virtue, based on a true understanding of human nature and its problems, is in Plato's view the only way to individual happiness and social stability. His thought has influenced Christian theology via Plotinus and St. Augustine (see our Historical Interlude).

LIFE AND WORK

Plato was born into a high-class family in the ancient Greek city state (*polis*) of Athens, which in the fourth century B.C.E. enjoyed economic prosperity through empire and trade and at one stage developed the first experiment in citizens' direct democracy. We remember ancient Athens

as a center of unprecedented advances in the arts and intellectual inqui-
ries, including sculpture, drama, history, mathematics, science, and philosophy. One of its greatest figures was the ethical philosopher Socrates,
whose charismatic example deeply impressed the young Plato. But these
thinkers lived through a disturbed period: the Peloponnesian War ended in
disastrous defeat for Athens, and a period of tyranny ensued. When a new
faction came to power, Socrates became politically suspect and was condemned to death in 399 B.C.E. on a charge of subverting the state religion
and corrupting the young.

Socrates's method of arguing and teaching was akin to that of the
so-called Sophists, self-styled experts who offered (for a fee) to impart
certain kinds of skill, in particular the art of rhetoric (i.e., persuasion by
public speaking), which was important for political advancement. They
might be described as the public relations consultants of their time, but
they also touched on ethical and political issues. Athenians were aware of
the variety of beliefs and practices in various cultures around the Mediterranean, so they were confronted with the question of whether there is any
criterion of truth in such matters. The Sophists often expressed skepticism about whether moral and political values were anything more than
arbitrary conventions. What we now call **relativism** was thus already a
tempting option at this early stage of thought.

Unlike the Sophists, Socrates charged no fees and concerned himself
with fundamental philosophical and ethical questions rather than mere
rhetoric. His great inspiring idea was that we may come to know the
truth on these matters, and hence the right way to live, if only we use
our reason carefully and systematically. He has been called "the founder
of philosophy," not so much for any particular conclusions he reached
but for pioneering the use of rational argument and inquiry in an open-
minded, nondogmatic way; but he left no written records. Plato's early
dialogues (especially the *Apology*) portray Socrates showing his interlocutors by persistent logical questioning that they did not really know what
they claimed to know. As represented by Plato (we have scant other evidence), Socrates claimed superiority to other people only in that he was
aware of his own ignorance about philosophical matters. One of the most
famous sayings attributed to him is that "the unexamined life is not worth
living," and he made his fellow Athenians think about their lives in ways
they might not otherwise have done. Socrates felt called, with a kind of
religious intensity, thus to disturb people's complacency; so it is perhaps
not surprising that he found himself a focus of hostility, even to the point
of death. (Comparisons have been made with Jesus.)

In all this Socrates deeply influenced Plato, who was shocked at the
execution of the inspirational teacher. Although disillusioned with

contemporary politics, Plato retained Socrates's faith in rational inquiry; he was convinced that it was possible to attain knowledge of deep-laid truths about the world and about human nature and to apply this knowledge for the benefit of human society. He sometimes expressed skepticism about the value of books, tending to agree with Socrates that actual dialogue was the best way to get people to think for themselves and perhaps change their minds and their approach to life. Yet Plato himself wrote extensively, often with great literary skill; and his works are the first major treatises in philosophy. They are in conversational form, typically with Socrates taking the leading part. Most scholars think that in the early dialogues, such as *Apology*, *Crito*, *Euthyphro*, and *Meno*, Plato was mainly expounding Socrates's ideas, whereas in later works (which tend to be longer and more technical) he was expressing his own distinctive theories. He founded the Athenian Academy, which can be described as the world's first university.

One of the most famous and widely studied of Plato's texts is the *Republic*, a lengthy, complex, and closely argued debate between several speakers; though traditionally divided into ten "books," these do not always make natural divisions of the argument. As the title suggests, one main theme is an outline of an ideal human society, but a central theme is the problems and fulfillment of individual human beings. In this major work Plato touches on many topics, including metaphysics, epistemology, human psychology, morals, politics, social classes, the family, education, and the arts. We will concentrate on the *Republic*, with occasional reference to other dialogues (using the traditional page numbering for Plato's texts, references are to the *Republic* unless otherwise stated).

METAPHYSICAL BACKGROUND:
THE THEORY OF FORMS

Although Plato talks of God, or gods in the plural, at various places, it is not clear how literally he means this. He was hardly a believer in the rampant polytheism of Greek popular religion, but neither does he have the Judeo–Christian–Islamic conception of a personal God who communicates with individual people and intervenes in human history. Plato has a more abstract ideal of God as the ultimate reason (*logos*) in or behind the universe. (The prologue of the Gospel of John, "In the beginning was the word [*logos*]" shows the influence of this idea.) In the *Timaeus* Plato presents a creation story in which "divine wisdom" organizes the world out of preexisting matter and can only do the best it can with recalcitrant material; this is different from the biblical doctrine of God's creation out of nothing.

What is most distinctive of Plato's metaphysics is his theory of **forms** (the Greek word is *eidos*). But it is not easy to say what this amounts to, for he rarely presents it as an explicit theory; it is mentioned or assumed at crucial points in various dialogues, and to his credit he wrestles with difficulties for it in the *Parmenides*. We must remember that he was a pioneer in philosophy, struggling to express fundamental ideas for the first time in human thought.

Plato's grand **metaphysical** theory is that beyond the world of changeable and destructible material things and creatures there is another realm containing the unchanging eternal forms. The things we can perceive through our senses are only distantly related to these ultimate realities, as Plato suggested by his haunting image of the human condition as being like prisoners inside a cave, chained up facing the inner wall so that all they can see are mere shadows cast on the wall and all that they can hear are echoes (514–17). In this allegory, the shadows can be interpreted as the changing material things we normally occupy ourselves with, while not knowing about the real unchanging forms. (If Plato were alive today, he would surely point out how well his image applies to so many of us who rely for our supposed "knowledge" of reality on watching television, movies, and computer screens.) Plato elaborates on his cave story to make it fit the fourfold **epistemology** that he develops in the preceding passage known as "the divided line" (508–14), where he subdivides the perceptible and the intelligible realms and distinguishes four increasing degrees of human thinking: imagination, belief, thought, and understanding. Elsewhere he acknowledges that human perceptual knowledge is not mere passive observation: in the *Theaetetus* he realizes that we actively interpret the stimulations we receive through our sense organs, applying concepts to classify what we perceive (as in Kant's epistemology, see Chapter 8).

There are four main aspects of the Platonic forms: *semantic* (meanings and concepts), *metaphysical* (what is ultimately real), *epistemological* (what we can know), and *moral or political* (how we ought to live). The logical or semantic aspect is their role as concepts or principles of classification that constitute the meaning of general terms. What justifies our application of one word or concept such as "bird" or "table" to many particular birds or tables? At 596, part of Plato's point is that craftspeople who make things must have a concept of what they are trying to make. But the "one over many" structure applies to any concept; we recognize species of animal and plant and various kinds of metals, rocks, and liquids. Even with simple sensory qualities such as redness or heat there are many things that are red and many that are hot (and some that are both), but there is only one concept of each quality. At 507 Plato distinguishes the many different good things and beautiful things from the single forms of Goodness and Beauty.

The **nominalist** view of universals is that there is nothing that all instances of a concept literally have in common—there are only *similarities* between them. But **Platonic realism** is the view that what makes particular things count as *F*s is their resemblance to, or "participation in," the form or idea of *F* understood as an abstract entity, something existing in its own right and different from the individual instances. At 596 Plato's view seems to be that for every general term there is a form, but elsewhere he suggests that only *some* words, those that pick out what we would now call "natural kinds", express a form. He is reluctant to accept that there are forms corresponding to the terms "mud," "dirt," or "barbarian" (the latter was applied to all non-Greeks, like our word "foreigner") presumably on the ground that instances of these terms have nothing significant in common.

The metaphysical aspect of the forms is that they are *more* real than material things, in that they do not come into existence, change, decay, or cease to exist. Physical objects get damaged and destroyed, and creatures are born, live, and die; but the Forms are not in space or time; they are not knowable by the senses, only by the human intellect or reason (485, 507, 526–27). The allegory of the cave illustrates this conception vividly.

In Plato's view most people are concerned only with mere "shadows" and remain ignorant of true reality, but he thought that by a process of education it is possible for human minds (at least, the more able of them) to attain rational knowledge of the world of forms. The epistemological aspect of his theory is that only this intellectual understanding properly counts as *knowledge*. In the *Republic* he is explicit that only what fully and really exists can be fully or really known: perception of impermanent objects and events in the physical world is only "belief" or "opinion," not knowledge (476–78). A clear application of the theory of forms comes from the geometrical reasoning which Euclid was to systematize later. In geometry we think about lines, circles, and squares, although no material object or diagram is *perfectly* straight, circular, or equal-sided. What we call straight or equal for practical purposes will not be so by a more precise standard, for irregularities can always be found if things are examined closely enough, perhaps by a microscope. Yet we can prove theorems concerning idealized geometrical concepts—straight lines without thickness, perfect circles, lines of exactly equal length (*Phaedo* 74)—usually with the help of diagrams (imperfectly drawn) such as marks on paper or lines in the sand. Similarly we know truths of arithmetic that are quite independent of the vagueness or impermanence of the material things we count (for example, $1 + 1 = 2$ is not disproved by the merging of two water droplets). We thus attain knowledge of exactly defined, unchangeable mathematical objects or structures. Like many philosophers since, Plato was impressed by the certainty and precision of mathematical knowledge; and he took it as an ideal to which all human knowledge should approximate.

He therefore recommended the teaching of mathematics as a vital way of detaching our minds from gross perceptible objects.

However, it is the moral application of the theory of forms that plays the most important role in Plato's conception of human nature and society. We distinguish particular courageous actions or just dealings from the general concepts (forms) of Courage and Justice. In the early dialogues Plato depicts Socrates seeking general definitions of the virtues, and never being satisfied with mere examples of them. Moral ideals are distinct from the complex and messy reality of human beings in real-life situations: sometimes an action may be right, just, or admirable in one way but not in others (doing one's best for *one* person may involve neglecting another). But Plato holds that the ethical forms set absolute standards of value for us (472–73). Just as no material object is perfectly square, no human being or society is perfectly good. And for Plato the form of Goodness is preeminent in the world of forms: it plays an almost God-like role, as the source of all reality, truth, and goodness—but it is not a person, with consciousness, desires, and will. He compares its role in the world of the forms to that of the sun as the source of all light in the world of material things (508–9). Plato's twin images of sun and cave—the source of light and the coming to "see the light"—give us memorable pictures of his theory.

It is crucial to Plato's moral and political philosophy that by the proper use of our reason we can come to *know* what is good, and actually *become* good. In this he was following the lead of Socrates. Some of the early dialogues (*Protagoras* and *Meno*) portray Socrates arguing for what seems to have been the historical Socrates's own doctrine, that to *be* virtuous it is enough to *know* what virtue is. All the virtues are said to be identical at root, in that one cannot possess any one of them without having the others; and this unique human goodness is identified with knowledge in the wide sense of wisdom, not mere store of information, or intellectual virtuosity. But if Socrates was committed to the doctrine that nobody knowingly or willingly does what he or she thinks to be wrong, this seems to conflict with the obvious facts that we often know what we ought to do, yet somehow we don't get around to doing it—indeed we may find ourselves unwilling to do it. We shall see later how Plato attempts to cope with this difficulty.

The theory of forms is Plato's answer to the intellectual and moral skepticism or relativism of his time. It is one of the first and greatest expressions of the hope that we can attain reliable knowledge both about the world as a whole, and about the proper conduct of human life and society. Yet we may suspect that he has overintellectualized the role of reason and knowledge. He makes a strong case that we all need to exercise rational self-control, moderating our emotions and desires and their expression in actions. But in the central metaphysical sections of the *Republic*

(Books V–VII) Plato insists on a highly theoretical conception of reason as consisting in a knowledge of the forms that seems to be open only to a highly trained intellectual elite. We should ask ourselves whether such specialized philosophical thinking is necessary or sufficient for human virtue (and whether Plato really meant to say so).

THEORY OF HUMAN NATURE: THE TRIPARTITE STRUCTURE OF THE SOUL

Plato is one of the main sources for the **dualist** view according to which the human soul or mind (using these terms synonymously here) is a non-material entity that can exist apart from the body. One of his most remarkable doctrines is that the soul exists *before birth* as well as eternally after death. In the *Meno* he tries to prove this preexistence of the soul, arguing that what we call learning is really a kind of "recollection" of the knowledge our souls supposedly had with the forms before birth (this is a version of the doctrine of reincarnation in Eastern religions—see Chapters 2 and 3). People of average intelligence, like the slave boy who Socrates induces to prove a geometrical theorem at *Meno* 82-5, can be brought to realize why some simple mathematical propositions must be true by having their attention called to the steps of a proof. It is plausible that such mental ability to recognize the validity of the inferences and the conclusion must be innate, for to learn anything one must already have the *ability* to learn. But then Plato makes the much more disputable claim that the innateness of such abilities can be explained only by the human soul's knowledge of the forms in a previous life. We would presumably prefer evolutionary explanations of innate human abilities (see Chapter 12), but it is worth noting that these also appeal to something predating an individual, namely the evolution of the species.

In the *Phaedo* Plato presents a number of arguments that the human **soul** must persist after the death of the body. He tries to disprove the **materialist** theory of the earlier Greek atomists such as Democritus, that the human soul is composed of tiny particles that dissipate into the air at death. He also argues against the conception (which Aristotle later elaborated—see Chapter 5) that the soul is a kind of "harmony" of the living human body and brain, like the music made by an instrument when tuned and played. Plato's arguments sometimes seem like mere logic-chopping, but we can learn a lot by trying to specify where they go wrong.

As represented by Plato, Socrates held that it is the soul, not the body, that attains knowledge of the forms. The soul is seen as in some way divine, being rational, immortal, indissoluble, and unchangeable; it is the higher element in human nature, and the body is the lower. The preoccupation of the philosopher or wise person should be the care of his or her soul; and since the soul is immortal, this is a preparation for the life after death. In the famous scene at the end of the *Phaedo* depicting Socrates's last conversation in prison before drinking the fatal hemlock, Plato presents his hero as looking forward to the release of his soul from all bodily cares and limitations. The doctrines of the immateriality and immortality of the soul appear at the end of the *Republic* in "the myth of Er" in Book X (608–20). This has seemed to many readers an ill-fitting mythological appendix to a philosophical work, but Plato resorts at certain points to more literary language, which is ironic, given his stated suspicion of the rhetorical, non-rational power of poetry.

What is central to Plato's moral discussion in the *Republic* is his theory of the three parts of the soul (435–41). Although this is expressed in terms of "the soul," we need not interpret it as involving metaphysical dualism: we can read it as a distinction between three different aspects of our human nature. We can all recognize the existence of conflicting tendencies in ourselves, even if we take a materialist evolutionary view of human beings as animals with well-developed brains. (We will concentrate here on Plato's tripartite theory, but we should note that in the *Philebus* and *Laws* he presents human nature as divided in *two* ways, between reason and pleasure; and he says more about pleasure in the *Gorgias* and *Protagoras*.) Echoes of his threefold distinction can be found in many thinkers (notably in Freud—see Chapter 10). Here we can see Plato acknowledging the implausibility of the Socratic doctrine that nobody willingly (clear-sightedly or wholeheartedly) does what he or she believes to be wrong. He wrestles with both the theoretical question of how such inner conflict is possible and the practical problem of how one can achieve inner harmony. Let us first examine his arguments for the tripartite structure.

Consider an example of mental conflict or inhibition, such as when someone is hungry but does not eat the available food because he or she suspects it is poisoned, or because of a religious fast (we do not immediately gratify all our bodily urges). Conversely, we sometimes find ourselves giving way to the temptations of a second cream cake, a third glass of wine, or a seductive charmer, even though we know that the consequences are likely to be bad for us. Habits can notoriously become addictive: gluttony or anorexia, alcoholism, drug dependence, search for new sexual partners. Plato argues that where there is any kind of internal conflict there must be two different elements with contradictory tendencies. In the case of the hungry person, there must be one part that makes him or her want to eat, and a second that forbids it; the first Plato calls **appetite** (under which he intends to include all the physical urges such as hunger, thirst, and sexual desire), and the second he calls **reason**.

So far Plato is on familiar ground. But he also argues for the existence of a *third* element in our nature by examining some other cases of mental conflict. His first example is rather weird: a story of someone who felt a fascinated desire to look at a pile of corpses and yet was disgusted with himself for having such a desire (440). Plato claims that to explain cases like this we need to recognize the existence in ourselves of a third element that he calls **spirit** or passion. His argument for this is not very explicit, but it seems to be that because there is an *emotion* of self-disgust involved, not just an intellectual recognition of the irrationality or undesirability of the desire, spirit must be distinct from reason.

We surely have to agree that emotion is different both from bodily desires and from rational or moral judgment. Love is not the same as lust, but it is more than an intellectual judgment about the admirable qualities of a person. Anger, indignation, ambition, aggression, and the desire for power are not *bodily* desires; but neither are they mere judgments about the value or disvalue of things, although they involve such **value judgments**. Plato goes on to remark that children (and even animals) show spirit before they display reason; anyone who has dealt with children can confirm this from experience of their high spirits, delights and frustrations, stubbornness, and (sometimes) aggression and bullying.

Plato asserts that spirit is usually on the side of reason when inner conflict occurs. But if it is a genuinely distinct element in the mind, there must presumably be cases where it can conflict with reason. He quotes a line of Homer in confirmation of this: "He smote his breast, and thus rebuked his heart." And we can add examples from our own experience: occasions when we have felt emotions of anger, jealousy, or attraction that we may nevertheless judge as unreasonable, undesirable, or even immoral. Perhaps there can even be cases in which one is pulled in *three* directions, for example, by lust, romantic love, and reasoned judgment about who would be the best partner!

Plato presents his threefold theory in some more vivid images. In the *Phaedrus* at 253–54 (a dialogue mainly about love) he compares the soul to a chariot, pulled by a white horse (spirit) and a dark horse (appetite), driven by a charioteer (reason) who struggles to keep control. At *Republic* 588 he describes a person as composed of a little man, a lion, and a many-headed beast. This obviously involves an infinite regression (a person within a person, and so on), but Plato is too good a philosopher not to notice this, he is surely offering the picture only as an image.

Is this tripartite anatomy of the soul adequate? It is surely and interesting first approximation, distinguishing some elements in human nature that can conflict with each other. But it is hardly a rigorous or exhaustive division, even if one redescribes the parts in modern terms as intellect, emotion, and bodily desire. In particular it is not clear what Plato's middle element of spirit amounts to. Emotions are part of our nature, of course; but Plato seems also to have had in mind desires or drives that are not bodily but not exactly emotions either, such as self-assertion, ambition, and desire for money, status, or power. Does he accept that it is one thing to recognize or judge (with one's reason) what one ought to do and another to do it, or does he believe that rational judgment about what is good already implies willingness to act accordingly? A different tripartite distinction of mental faculties that has emerged since the advent of Christianity is reason, emotion, and will (see Augustine in the Historical Interlude, Kant in Chapter 8, and Sartre in Chapter 11). Perhaps we will need to distinguish at least five factors in human nature: reason, will, non-bodily motivations, emotions, and bodily appetites.

Much of Plato's discussion seems to be conducted with men rather than women in mind, but he had views about gender that were strikingly original in his time. In ancient Greek society, women played almost no part in public life and were usually confined to their reproductive role and household duties. The discussions of love (*eros*) in the Platonic dialogues are about male homosexual love, which was socially accepted then as part of the education of teenage boys (rather different from contemporary gay relationships). At 449–61 Plato argues that although men and women have different bodies, they have similar souls (454) and there is no role that need be restricted to either sex. He allows that some women are athletic, musical, philosophical, and even "high-spirited" (by which he meant courageous and suitable for military service). He still assumes that men are on average better than women at everything, but he thinks that the only absolute distinction is the biological one and that other differences are matters of degree. He was therefore prepared to admit women of appropriate talent to the ruling class.

One more crucial feature of Plato's understanding of human nature should be emphasized: that we are social creatures, living in society is natural to us (unlike some species of animals that live almost entirely solitary lives). Human individuals are not self-sufficient; we each have many needs that we cannot meet by ourselves—food, shelter, and clothing can hardly be obtained without the help of others (these economic facts are emphasized by Marx—see Chapter 9). A desert island individual would struggle for survival and would miss out on the distinctively human activities of family, friendship, play, art, politics, and reasoning. People have different aptitudes and interests; there are farmers, craftspeople, soldiers, administrators, scholars, and so on, each fitted by ability, training, and experience to specialize in one kind of task; division of labor is essential in society (369–70).

DIAGNOSIS: DISHARMONY
IN SOUL AND SOCIETY

Reason, spirit, and appetite are present to some degree in every person. Depending on which element is dominant, Plato distinguishes three kinds of person. The main desire of each type is knowledge, reputation, or material gain: they can be described as philosophical, victory-loving, or profit-loving (581). He has a very clear view about which of the three elements should rule: it is our reason that ought to control both spirit and appetite (590). But each has its proper role to play, and there should ideally be harmonious agreement between the three aspects of our nature, with reason in overall command. Plato expresses this in an eloquent passage at 443:

> Justice . . . isn't concerned with external actions, but with a man's inward self. The just man will not allow the three elements which make up his inward self to trespass on each other's functions or interfere with each other, but by keeping all three in tune, like the notes of a scale . . . will in the truest sense set his house in order, and be his own lord and master, and at peace with himself. When he has bound these elements into a single controlled and orderly whole, and so unified himself, he will be ready for action of any kind.

And in human societies those people with the most highly developed "reason" (which includes moral wisdom) ought to rule, in the best interests of everyone. A well-ordered, "just" society will be one in which each class of person plays its distinctive role, in harmony with each other (434). Plato describes this ideal condition of human beings and society by the Greek word *dikaiosune*, which has traditionally been translated as **justice**. When applied to individuals, this does not have its modern legal or political connotations. There is no exact English translation: "virtue," "morality," "proper functioning," "well-being," or even "mental health" may help convey what Plato had in mind. At 444 he says that virtue is a kind of mental health or beauty or fitness, and vice a sort of illness or deformity or weakness. His fundamental point is that what is good or bad for us depends on our common human nature, the complex of factors in our psychological makeup.

The theory of the parts of the soul (with the background theory of forms as objects of knowledge) thus defines Plato's ideals for individual and social well-being; and when he looked at the facts of his own day, he found they were very far from ideal. One wonders whether his judgment of our present condition would be any different. Many people still do not show much "inward harmony" or controlled coordination of their desires and mental powers, and many societies do not manifest the orderliness and stability that Plato sought.

The problems of human individuals that Plato diagnoses are intimately related to the defects in human societies. One cannot simply attribute to him either the conservative or right-wing view that social problems are due to individual wrongdoing or the liberal or left-wing view that individual vices can be blamed on faults in the social order. Plato would say that the two are interdependent: an imperfect society tends to produce flawed individuals, and troubled or badly brought-up individuals contribute to social problems.

Book VIII of the *Republic* (543–76) offer a systematic classification of five kinds of society, beginning with the ideal of "aristocracy" (meaning a meritocracy, an aristocracy of talent rather than birth), and going on to diagnose four types of imperfect society called "timarchy," "oligarchy," "democracy," and "tyranny," along with a kind of defective individual typical of each society. Plato describes how each political stage can arise by degeneration from its predecessor, and how each individual character may be formed as a result of problems in the previous generation (concentrating on relations between fathers and sons).

In a "timarchic" society such as that of ancient Sparta, honor and fame especially in warfare and hunting, are valued above all. Reason and philosophical understanding are neglected, and "spirit" plays the dominant role in society and in members of the ruling class (545–49). Something similar presumably applied in primitive societies, and perhaps in feudalism.

In an "oligarchy" the older class divisions break down, money-making becomes the dominant activity, and political power comes to lie with the wealthy. Plato expresses disgust for the resulting type of character, who

> establishes his appetitive and money-making part on the throne, setting it up as a king within himself . . . and makes the rational and spirited parts sit on the ground beneath appetite, one on either side, reducing them to slaves. . . . He won't allow the first to reason about or examine anything except how a little money can be made into great wealth. And he won't allow the second to value or admire anything but wealth and wealthy people or to have any ambition other than the acquisition of wealth or whatever might contribute to getting it. (553)

Presumably Plato would not approve of the free-for-all competition and gross inequalities of contemporary capitalism.

"Democracy" may arise by the impoverished majority seizing power. Plato takes a very jaundiced view of democracy as he understood it, influenced no doubt by his experience of the instability of Athenian democracy, in which every adult male citizen (though not women or slaves) could vote in the meetings that decided policy, and government positions were often filled by lot (555–57). Plato thinks it absurd to give every person an equal say, when most people do not know what is best. He criticizes the "democratic" type of person as lacking in discipline, pursuing mere pleasures of the moment, indulging "unnecessary spendthrift" desires (whereas the *successful* moneymaker at least has to exert some self-discipline):

> A young man . . . associates with wild and dangerous creatures who can provide every variety of multicolored pleasure in every sort of way.
> . . . seeing the citadel of the young man's soul empty of knowledge, fine ways of living, and words of truth . . . [these desires] finally occupy that citadel themselves. . . . and he doesn't admit any word of truth into the guardhouse, for if someone tells him that some pleasures belong to fine and good desires and others to evil ones and that he must pursue and value the former and restrain and enslave the latter, he denies all this and declares that all pleasures are equal and must be valued equally. (559–61)

Anarchy is the natural sequel to the chaotic and unbridled liberty of democracy: permissiveness spreads, and fathers and teachers lose authority (Plato is horrified at the idea of liberating slaves). There arises a desire for order, and usually some forceful, unscrupulous individual wins absolute power and becomes a tyrant (565–69). The tyrannical character, in Plato's diagnosis, is not so much the tyrant himself or herself (who has to exercise some degree of intelligence and self-control to gain and maintain power), but the person who is completely dominated by his or her own appetites or addictions. He or she will sacrifice possessions and money, family relations, and friends in the frenzied pursuit of his or her lusts (572–76).

In this series of social diagnoses and character sketches one may feel that the analogies between individual and society are overplayed. But each sketch shows notable sociological and psychological insight, and their contemporary applications are obvious. Plato concludes that each type of person and society departs further from the ideal, reaching a deeper level of degradation and unhappiness. He is clear that the money-making, pleasure-seeking, and lust-dominated people are far from happy, which is why "justice" or "morality" is in the interests of the individual.

PRESCRIPTION: HARMONY OF SOUL THROUGH EDUCATION AND GOVERNMENT BY THE PHILOSOPHER KINGS

Plato has said that justice (*dikaiosune*) is essentially the same thing in both the individual and society, namely, a smooth working together of the parts within the soul, or the classes in the state (435); and the lack of such harmony is injustice. But there is some ambiguity about whether individuals can change themselves without institutional reforms, or whether social change must precede individual improvement (a problem that is still with us). One purpose of Plato is to answer the challenge of the cynical Thrasymachus in Book I of the *Republic* that what is called "justice" is only what is in the interests of the powerful (336–47), by showing that it really is in the long-term interest of the individual to be just or moral. Plato does this by reconceptualizing what justice is, insisting that, since it is a harmony of the three elements in our souls (Book IV), it is bound to make each one of us a happier, more fulfilled human being (Book IX).

But how can such harmony be attained? Plato remarks at 444 that virtue and vice are the result of one's actions, so it seems that what we make of ourselves is up to us (an existentialist theme—see Chapter 11). In Socrates' famous speech in the *Symposium* (200–12) Plato outlines a route by which our desires can be gradually transformed from erotic lust for beautiful bodies, through admiration for beauty of soul, and eventually to love of "absolute" or divine Beauty, the form of Beauty itself. But this presupposes "instruction in the things of love," and who can provide that?

Here the social element comes into Plato's story: he lays great stress on appropriate education as the most important way to produce virtuous, harmonious, well-balanced, "just" people (376–412, 521–41). He was one of the first to see education as the key to constructing a better society, and he does not mean just formal schooling but *all* the social influences on someone's development. In some places (377, 424–25) he anticipates Freud's emphasis on the importance of early childhood (see Chapter 10). He goes into considerable detail about the kind of education he envisages; formal academic study is by no means at the center but is reserved for an elite group at a more mature age. Plato sees as vital for everyone the training of the whole person—reason, spirit, and appetite together. He therefore recommends gymnastics, poetry, and music as elements of the common curriculum. We may find the details of his educational scheme amusingly archaic, but his recognition that the "character-forming" foundations are at least as important as academic superstructures remains very realistic.

But how is education to be instituted? It requires a clear conception of the goal, a whole theory of human nature and human knowledge, and it needs elaborate social organization and resources. That is why in the *Republic* Plato offers a prescription that is radically political:

> There will be no end to the troubles of states, or of humanity itself, till philosophers become kings in this world, or till those we now call kings and rulers really and truly become philosophers, and political power and philosophy thus come into the same hands. (473)

He is well aware that this sounds absurdly unrealistic, but given his understanding of the forms, human knowledge, and human nature, we can see his rationale for it. If there is such a thing as the truth about how we ought to live, then those who have this important knowledge are the only people who are properly qualified to govern society. Philosophers are, in Plato's conception, those who have come to know the ultimate realities, including the true standards of all value, so if *they* were to govern society, the problems of human nature could be solved.

To produce lovers of wisdom who are fit to be philosopher kings or **guardians**, the higher stages of education will be open only to those with sufficient mental abilities. At an appropriate age, they are to study mathematics and then philosophy, the disciplines that lead the mind toward knowledge of the forms and a love of truth for its own sake. The elite thus produced will prefer to continue with their intellectual studies, but Plato expects them to respond to the call of duty and apply their expertise to the running of society. After experience in subordinate offices, some of them will be ready for supreme power. Plato assumes that such lovers of wisdom and truth will be impervious to the temptations to misuse power, for they will value the happiness of a right and rational life more than material riches or power for its own sake (521).

The way of life of these guardians is to be spartan, in the modern sense of the word (Plato derived some of his ideas from the ancient Greek state of Sparta, which had a very military ethos). They are to have no personal property and no family life. The state is to select which guardians are suitable for breeding, and organizes "mating festivals." The resulting children are to be brought up communally by nurses, with precautions to ensure that no parent recognizes his or her own child (457–61). But here Plato goes flatly against the psychological need for strong emotional bonds between children and the carers who bring them up (normally their parents). As a high-born Greek male, he obviously had no experience of childcare.

Plato's view that these highly educated guardians will be such lovers of truth and goodness that they will never misuse their power seems naively optimistic. He goes against the adage that power corrupts, and absolute power corrupts absolutely. There is surely a need for constitutional checks and balances to guard against exploitation or tyranny. Plato asks, "Who is qualified to wield absolute power?" But should we not rather ask, "How can we ensure that nobody has absolute power, and that any government can be peacefully changed?"

What if well-educated, supposedly knowledgeable people disagree about questions of morals and politics (as they often do)? Is there any way of showing who is right? Plato hopes to use rational argument, and he is one of the great philosophical pioneers in doing so. But when people think they *know* the ultimate truth about such questions of value and policy, they may be intolerant of anyone who disagrees and may feel justified in forcing their view on others (as the history of religious and political controversies bears multiple witness).

What of the rest of society, the nonelite? There are many different economic and social functions that need to be performed, and a division of labor is the natural and efficient way of organizing this. Plato makes a threefold division of society (412–27), parallel to his theory of the soul. Besides the guardians there is to be a class called the "auxiliaries" who play the roles of soldiers, police, and civil servants, to put the directions of the guardians into effect. The third class would contain the workers: farmers, craftspeople, traders, and all those who produce and distribute the material necessities of life. The division between these three classes will be very strict; Plato says that the justice of the society depends on each person performing his or her own proper function and not interfering with others (432–34):

> The object of our legislation is not the welfare of any particular class, but of the whole community. It uses persuasion or force to unite all citizens and make them share together the benefits which each individually can confer on the community; and its purpose in fostering the attitude is not to enable everyone to please himself, but to make each man a link in the unity of the whole. (519–20)

Plato thus seems more concerned with the harmony and stability of the whole society than with the well-being of the individuals in it. We may be in favor of "community spirit" and of each person contributing something to the well-being of society, but Plato requires a strict class division and that each person fulfill his or her allotted function and that alone. This is what he calls justice in the state, but it is plainly not what *we* mean by the term, which implies equality before the law and usually some degree of social justice or fair shares for all. If a worker is not content to be a worker, to accept a strictly limited share of economic goods and have no say in politics, then Plato's ideal state would compel him or her to remain in his or her station. But what is the point of such a rigidly organized society unless it serves the interests of the individuals in it?

Plato's republic has an authoritarian, even totalitarian, character. He has no compunction about censorship, for he proposes to exclude poets and other artists from his ideal society on the grounds that they appeal to the lower, nonrational parts of our nature (605). His hostility to poetry may be more understandable when we realize that until his time Homer was almost the only source of conceptions of ethics, whereas Plato was contending for the Socratic appeal to reason. He would surely be horrified at the pervasive and almost unregulated influence of the media and the entertainment and advertising industries on everyone in contemporary society, from early childhood onward. We may not like Plato's solution of state censorship, but he calls our attention to the continuing problem of how truth and goodness can be presented amid a welter of competing cultural and economic interests and influences.

In the *Republic* Plato dismisses democratic constitutions rather quickly, and we may think unfairly. But he was thinking of every citizen having a vote on major decisions. Even if electronic voting systems make this technically feasible nowadays, it would surely result in unstable government, subject to the changing whims of an enormous population easily influenced by collective emotion and "rhetoric" or clever advertising, which was Plato's criticism of Athenian democracy. However, the crucial feature of democracies—that a government must submit itself for reelection within a fixed period of time—provides a means for peaceful change that is absent from the *Republic* (even if modern election campaigns are not noted for their rationality). It should be noted, however, that in later works, the *Statesman* and *Laws*, Plato advocated the rule of law, and endorsed democracy for all its imperfections as the best kind of constitution, given human nature as it is.

The *Republic* is one of the most influential books of all time. We have concentrated on this one work, but Plato wrote much else, developing and changing his views over time. Socrates and Plato started a tradition of rational inquiry into how we should live. Nothing would please them more than to know that some of us still carry this on.

FOR FURTHER READING

Basic text: Plato's *Republic*. There are many translations, but the one that has recently earned most praise for readability and liveliness is by G. M. A. Grube, revised by C. D. C. Reeve (Indianapolis, IN: Hackett, 1992). It is included in *Plato: Complete Works* (Indianapolis, IN: Hackett, 1997).

The *Republic* is a lengthy and complex work; some readers may prefer to approach Plato via his shorter dialogues, the *Euthyphro, Apology, Crito, Phaedo, Meno*, and *Protagoras*.

There is an excellent thematic introduction to ancient philosophy in Julia Annas's volume in the Very Short Introduction series (Oxford University Press, 2000).

For a short introduction to Plato, see R. M. Hare, *Plato* (Oxford: Oxford University Press, 1982). This is available as the first part of *Founders of Thought*

(Oxford: Oxford University Press, 1991), which also contains introductions to Aristotle and Augustine.

There is deeper philosophical discussion of the *Republic* in Julia Annas, *An Introduction to Plato's Republic* (Oxford: Oxford University Press, 1981). This combines scholarship with clear-sighted attention to the main moral argument, its foundation in claims about human nature, and its continuing contemporary relevance (see the summing up in chapter 13). More recently there is Nickolas Pappas, *The Routledge Guidebook to Plato's Republic* (London: Routledge, 2013).

Popper's classic attack on Plato's political program is in K. R. Popper, *The Open Society and Its Enemies*, 5th ed. (London: Routledge, 1966).

For a very scholarly treatment, see Terence Irwin, *Plato's Ethics* (New York: Oxford University Press, 1995).

KEY TERMS

appetite	**nominalism**
dualism	**Platonic realism**
epistemology	**reason**
forms	**relativism**
guardians	**soul**
justice	**spirit**
materialism	**value judgment**
metaphysics	

QUESTIONS FOR DISCUSSION

1. How is Plato's cave a good image of the human condition? (Perhaps discuss with reference to the details of the text at *Republic* 514a–18d, which are somewhat glossed over above.)
2. Is mathematics the ideal for all human knowledge?
3. How adequate is Plato's three-part distinction between appetite, spirit, and reason as an account of human nature? (Perhaps discuss with reference to *Republic* 435c–42d.)
4. Can you identify contemporary versions of Plato's five types of society and individual? (Perhaps discuss with reference to *Republic* 544c–80a.)
5. Is it a good idea for society to be ruled by experts—including those who have attained philosophical wisdom?

5

Aristotle: The Ideal of Human Fulfillment

LIFE AND WORK

Aristotle (384–322 B.C.E.) lived in the generation after Plato, he also spent most of his life in Athens, so the historical background sketched in Chapter 4 applies to him too. He joined Plato's Academy at the age of seventeen, and the influence of Plato on his thought is obvious. Though deeply influenced by the views of his great predecessor, Aristotle criticized them on important points (which is the ideal relationship between philosophical teacher and pupil). For a few years he was tutor to the teenager who grew up to be Alexander the Great, the world conqueror. Coming from a medical family, Aristotle did extensive research on the structure of animals and plants. This experience of empirical scientific work shows in his writings, which display a more this-worldly spirit compared with Plato's yearning for transcendence (the contrast between their styles of thought is suggested in Raphael's famous painting *The School of Athens*). Aristotle founded the Lyceum, which carried on the tradition of systematic intellectual inquiry started by Plato; but in the last year of his life political disputes forced him out of Athens.

The corpus of Aristotelian texts that have come down to us covers an amazing range—logic, metaphysics, physics, meteorology, biology, psychology, ethics, politics, "poetics" (aesthetics)—and in many of these he was a pioneer. There was no clear distinction between philosophy and science in those days, and Aristotle inquired into fundamental concepts and principles in many areas, including what we now recognize as the sciences of astronomy, physics, biology, and psychology, laying down foundations that remained largely unquestioned until the seventeenth century. Apparently, many of his writings have not survived: the talents and energy of the man were prodigious. The texts that we do have tend to be lecture notes, unlike Plato's polished, elegant dialogues. Aristotle's writing is abstract, technical, and systematic: he is a philosophers' philosopher.

However, the *Nicomachean Ethics*, one of the main works in which he discusses human life, its ideals and its vicissitudes, is relatively accessible. Our references will be to this text (using the standard numbering, prefaced by "NE"), unless otherwise indicated. It is not easy reading (no substantial philosophy is), but like Plato's *Republic* it deals with profound issues of life; it is reasonably well organized and rises occasionally to a sort of eloquence. The *de Anima* is a shorter work that is crucial for Aristotle's view of human nature.

METAPHYSICAL BACKGROUND: FORMS AS PROPERTIES AND THE FOUR CAUSES

Aristotle sometimes talks of God or gods, but (like Plato) he does not mean the biblical concept of a personal being who reveals himself to particular people. Though he seems to pay outward respect to traditional Greek polytheism (Zeus, Hera, Athena, and the rest of the gang) at *Metaphysics* XII.8, 1074b1 ff., Aristotle views these as anthropomorphic myths for the common people. He has a quasi-scientific conception of a single supreme power in or behind the universe, for in *Physics* Book VII he argues that there must be an "unmoved mover," a changeless cause of all the changes we can observe. (Thomas Aquinas adapted this in his "Five Ways" of proving the existence of the Christian God—see the Historical Interlude.) Aristotle declared that "it is the function of what is divine to think and use its intellect" (*Parts of Animals* IV.10, 686a29), but the kind of thought he attributed to his god is intellectual contemplation, not *care* about human affairs. His unmoved mover is a concept of metaphysics rather than an object of worship or obedience.

Aristotle was influenced by Plato's theory of forms but severely critical of it. We saw in Chapter 4 how Plato proposed that what makes particular things count as *F*s is their "participation in" the form of *F*, understood as an abstract entity existing apart from all the instances of it. Aristotle opposes this "separation" of the forms and rejects Plato's metaphysical picture of another intelligible world beyond the world of perceptible material things. His **Aristotelian realist** view is that there *is* something in common to all things to which a general concept of *F* can correctly be applied, namely the property (or "Aristotelian form") *F*—but this property exists *in the things that have it*, not separately in another world. Thus, he would say that all oak trees and all samples of gold share a common form (in the light of modern science we can say what that form or nature is, namely, a certain kind of DNA or atomic structure). In Aristotle's view of our epistemological situation, our need is not to find a way out of Plato's cave into a transcendent world, but rather to understand better what is already before our eyes.

This talk of forms as properties *in* things rather than as separate entities seems to be robust common sense, but when probed philosophically it can become puzzling. For example, how is the same form or property in all dogs (which differ so dramatically among themselves)? If we use a *noun* like "property" or "form," a word with a singular and a plural, we seem to be verbally committed to thinking of the property as a mysterious kind of "thing" which is completely present in many different things at the same time—and that seems paradoxical. Aristotle realizes that we need to distinguish different "categories", or fundamental kinds of concept, with which we think and classify everything—for example, things or substances are categorically different from properties or qualities.

Do we find the same one–many structure in the use of *all* general terms, or is the detail different in various cases? Aristotle notices that we often use words in extended ways that do not carry exactly the same meaning in every context. One of his examples is the adjective "healthy": we talk of healthy people, food, exercise, climate or complexion, or of having a healthy respect for something; but we do not mean to say that all these things are healthy in the literal or primary sense of having well-functioning bodies that are likely to live long.

Aristotle applied this lesson to value judgments, especially to that most general of value terms "good." He recognized that different subject matters require different methods of study and degrees of precision, so ethics differs from mathematics in its methods and results (NE 1094b12–29). Accordingly, he questions whether all good things are good in some unitary sense, involving a single Platonic form of the Good. At NE 1096a12–97a14, he offers a salvo of arguments against the Platonic view (introduced by a declaration that friendship with Plato is dear, but the truth is even dearer). One of his most important points is that we recognize *several* things as good in themselves, as worth having or pursuing for their own sake, such as pleasure, honor, and wisdom; but when we ask what makes these different things all *good*, there is no general answer we can give, for wisdom is surely good in an irreducibly different way from the way in which fame or pleasure is good. That seems to rule out an Aristotelian form of goodness, a single property that all good things possess.

Another important conception that Aristotle bequeathed to us is traditionally called the **Four Causes** (though only the third is what we now usually call a cause). In *Physics* 194b16 he distinguishes four questions we can ask about anything, with their corresponding answers:

1. What is it made of?—its matter ("the material cause")
2. What is it?—its form, the sort of thing it is ("the formal cause")
3. What brought it into existence?—its cause, in the modern sense of the word ("the efficient cause")
4. What is it for?—its purpose or function ("the final cause")

It is easy to apply this scheme to human artifacts, such as Plato's example of a bed, made of wood and nails: it has the shape or form of a bed (a horizontal framework long enough for a human body), it was made by a carpenter, and it is intended for sleeping on. However, Aristotle seems to have assumed that all four questions *always* have an answer in every case. Artifacts like tables, telephones, and computers obviously have purposes for which they were constructed; and the parts or organs of plants and animals, such as roots, leaves, hearts and eyes, have functions, as Aristotle well understood from his biological studies, though those functions are not intended by anyone (unless you believe God designed them). As for *whole* animals and plants, it is odd to speak of them existing for some purpose (unless you bring in theology), but we have some idea of what counts as a mature, flourishing specimen of each species (and this applies to ourselves). But we do not now think of inanimate natural objects—rocks, mountains, rivers, glaciers, beaches, clouds, moon, planets, stars, and galaxies—as existing for a purpose, nor do we think there is some mature or best state of these things (unless we believe in a divine intention behind every detail of the world). Yet Aristotle seems to have assumed a **teleological** view of the whole universe, according to which everything has a definite purpose or function, a goal that it serves or somehow strives toward. This was Christianized in the medieval, prescientific worldview and poetically expressed by Dante.

Aristotle teaches us not just to latch onto any idea that occurs to us or the first theory we hear of (the lazy way of philosophizing), but to think carefully, to examine a wide variety of cases, to take the trouble to recognize the complexity of the world and of our ways of thinking and talking about it, and to be open-minded, without factional spirit, in our consideration of general theories. He can be honored as an ancestor of the "analytical" style of philosophy exemplified in the later thought of Ludwig Wittgenstein in the mid-twentieth century.

HUMAN NATURE: THE SOUL AS A SET OF FACULTIES

Plato argued for the dualist view that the human **soul** is an immaterial substance that can exist apart from the body after death, but Aristotle undermines this whole way of thinking in a subtle way. Here his biological research made a vital contribution to philosophy. He sees human beings as one kind of animal, but a very special kind, uniquely capable of rational thought. And he sees animals (mammals, reptiles, birds, insects, crustaceans, etc.) as one main kind of life, plants being the other. We classify all living things in a hierarchy of orders, genera, and species; and in the nineteenth century Darwin explained how that structure is due to a family tree of evolution through deep past time (Chapter 12).

Aristotle outlines his biological approach in his groundbreaking treatise traditionally known by its Latin name *de Anima* (*Of the Soul*), which can be described as the first book on psychology. But straightaway we should be aware of the problems in using the word "soul" to translate the Greek *psyche*, for "soul" has for many of us strong religious connotations of piety and immortality, deriving from Plato and Christianity. But Aristotle offers an entirely different conception of *psyche*. We can substitute the word "mind" for "soul," but that only replaces one four-letter noun by another, whereas the crucial difference in the Aristotelian conception is that the soul or mind is not thought of as a thing or substance at all, not even an immaterial substance. We can understand Aristotle's *psyche* as a "principle (or form) of life", and interpret his assertion that living things have different kinds of soul as meaning that they have distinctive ways of living and functioning.

Aristotle applies his general distinction of matter and form to this case and says that the soul is the "form" of a living thing. But "form" here does not mean Platonic Form, nor does it mean shape; rather, it is what makes something the fundamental sort of thing it is (the "formal cause"). What makes something alive? This question is not meant in the sense of what brought it into being (the "efficient" cause) but, rather, what is it for something to *be* alive, what criteria does anything have to satisfy to count as a living thing? Since plants as well as animals are alive, the criteria are metabolism (maintenance of the individual by nutrition) and reproduction (generating new members of the species). Aristotle talked of "self-nourishment, growth, and decay" or "the nutritive faculty" (*de Anima* 412a13, 414a32), and he also mentions reproduction (415a22). What then distinguishes animal from plants? Unlike plants, they have the faculties of sense perception, desire (412a33), and self-movement (414b18).

What then do human beings have, over and above all this? Aristotle's answer is the faculty of "thought and intellect" (*de Anima* 414b19), but it may not be immediately clear what he means. It is something that other animals do not have, namely, thoughts that can be expressed in language, beliefs that something is true or that something should be done, for which reasons for and against can be given: these involve universals, general concepts that animals do not have, according to Aristotle. So the human soul or mind should thus be understood not as a thing but as a cluster of faculties labelled **reason** that are fundamental to the distinctively human way of living and functioning. Aristotle writes (408b15), "it is surely better not to say that the soul pities, learns, or thinks, but that the man does these with his soul". We might suggest, in the spirit of this approach, that it is better still to say that the **person** pities, learns, and thinks, using his or her mental faculties.

So the human being lives, acts, and functions in a human way—and that "way" can be analyzed as a set of faculties or ways of functioning that normally go together (though some can be absent, e.g., when somebody loses memory or an infant has not yet learned to speak). On this conception it is difficult to make sense of talk of a soul or mind existing without a body, for if there is no living body, there is no *way* the body is functioning. Aristotle draws this conclusion at *de Anima* 414a19: the soul cannot exist without a body (contrary to Plato), not because it is itself a kind of body (contrary to the earlier Greek materialists, who had suggested that the soul is like a whiff of gas—material but composed of very fine particles), but because the soul is *not a thing* of any kind; rather, it is a complex property of living bodies. (On this conception, the only way a person could survive death is by resurrection of the body.)

However, Aristotle made a puzzling qualification to his position when he suggested that there is something metaphysically different about the intellect, our faculty for purely theoretical thought (which he calls "contemplation," though he seems to have mathematics and physics in mind rather than aesthetic or religious contemplation). He voices the intriguing suggestion that *this* faculty, which does not have any obvious organ (the Greeks knew little about the brain), *can* exist separately from the body, "as the everlasting can from the perishable" (*de Anima*, 413b26). It looks as if Aristotle could not bring himself completely to reject his Platonic heritage, and on this point he appears to qualify the main logic of his own argument. But can we conceive of mathematical thought going on without there being a living, embodied mathematician? These days it will be suggested that a computer can do mathematics, but even if we allow that this can count as "thought" it has to involve a complex arrangement of electrodes with currents pulsing through them—a material basis, though not a *living* body. Can we make sense of the idea of mental states that are not embodied in any way? As we will see in the Historical Interlude, some of Aristotle's Islamic and Christian successors were happy to exploit this ambiguity in his position.

Aristotle was aware of Plato's tripartite theory of the soul, but he reconceptualized it. A part of an Aristotelean soul would have to be understood as one *capacity* of the person, distinct from other capacities. One might expect him to follow Plato's lead by distinguishing reasoning, emotion, and desire; but he does not exactly follow this tripartite division. He usually contrasts two elements, one possessing reason in the full sense and the other only in the weaker sense that it can obey reason, though it can also be disobedient (NE 1098a5). Elsewhere he talks of rational and nonrational aspects of the soul (NE 1192a28ff.). It seems his main distinction is between Plato's reason on the one hand, and spirit and appetite together on the other; both emotion and desire being supposedly obedient to reason, since how one feels and what one wants can be affected by one's considered judgment about what is best (though notoriously this does not always happen). Later, Aristotle makes a distinction *within* our rational part, between our capacities for reasoning about necessary propositions in mathematics and science and for deliberating about what to do (NE 1139a5). This distinction between theoretical and practical reason was taken up by Kant (see Chapter 8).

Another crucial aspect of Aristotle's understanding of human nature, like Plato's, is that we are ineradicably social beings. "Man is a political animal," he wrote (NE 1097b11 and *Politics* 1252a24), where his word *politikon* could also be rendered as "civic" or "social." Elsewhere he said, "social animals are those which have some single activity common to them all (which is not true of all gregarious animals); such are men, bees, wasps, ants, cranes" (*History of Animals* I.1, 488a8). This is a striking anticipation of the sociobiological approach which we will mention in Chapter 12. But Aristotle recognized that what is distinctive of human social life is our awareness of justice and injustice (*Politics* 1253a15). He believed that our human nature reaches its full development only when we live as members of an organized society, and his paradigm was the *polis*, the Greek city state with a population of only 100,000 or so.

But who are qualified to take part in public life and politics? Aristotle's use of the masculine gender is no accident, for like most ancient Greeks he assumes without argument that women are innately different in mental capacity from men and less fitted for rational thought, so they should stick to their reproductive and domestic roles. Rebarbatively to most modern ears, he writes, "the relation of male to female is naturally that of the superior to the inferior—of the ruling to the ruled" (*Politics* I.V.7) and "the male is naturally fitter to command than the female, except where there is some departure from nature" (*Politics* I.XII). These appeals to "nature" do not seem to be based on any empirical study of the abilities of women; rather, like many other uses of the very slippery term "nature," they are the "common sense" of the time, which may be only the expression of prejudice and perceived self-interest. With respect to women, Aristotle was conservative where Plato appears ahead of his time. For Aristotle the difference of male and female bodies implied a difference of soul (i.e., of psychology), whereas for Plato the body is only an accidental feature of the real person (i.e., the immaterial soul). (This argument has run and run!)

He also assumes that there are innate differences between individuals in their ability to think and reason. He frequently talks of "good birth," and like Plato he takes it for granted that there will be social classes based on the division of labor, with large numbers of workers (farmers, traders, craftspeople, and soldiers) who will not for the most part be capable of higher forms of thought. He also displays some prejudice against the old and the young. Moreover, Aristotle saw no objection in principle to slavery, saying that some humans are "slaves by nature":

> all men who differ from others much as the body differs from the soul, or an animal from a man (and this is the case with all whose function is bodily service, and who produce their best when they supply such service)—all such are by nature slaves, and it is better for them . . . to be ruled by a master. (*Politics* I.V.8)

However, he admits that "the contrary of nature's intention often happens" so that slaves sometimes have the bodies and upright carriage of freemen (I.V.10); and if he were more open to an unprejudiced examination of the facts, he would have to allow that some slaves have mental capacities at least equal to their masters. His discussion of slavery is nuanced, for he makes a distinction between "justified" slaveholding in cases where there is a "natural" mental difference between master and slave, yet a community of interest and a relation of friendship between them, and unjust enslavement based only on legal sanction and superior power (I.VI.10). He also assumed a "natural" distinction between Greeks and "barbarians." At *Politics* I.II.4 he implies that all barbarians are slaves by nature and quotes a saying that barbarous people should be governed by the Greeks. At NE 1154a30 he lets slip the racist remark that, although the "brutish" (animal-like) type of human being is rare, it is more common among those who are not Greek.

Aristotle's assumptions of patriarchy, slavery, and imperialism are shocking to our contemporary sensibilities. One can imagine empire builders such as the British colonial administrators of old (with their classical education) finding him sympathetic. But this should not prejudice us against the rest of his thinking: we can accept an Aristotelian analysis of mind as a set of capacities of the living human person, and a corresponding ideal of human fulfillment (see below), while insisting that rational capacities are, on average, equally present in every person (irrespective of sex, class, race, and nationality) and that human needs, aspirations, and rights are correspondingly universal.

IDEAL AND DIAGNOSIS: HUMAN FULFILLMENT, VIRTUES, AND VICES

Aristotle accentuates the positive. Rather than diagnosing some fundamental fault in the human condition and prescribing a remedy for it, as in religious emphasis on sin, he first gives us an account of the purpose or meaning of human life, then suggests how it can be put into practice and how failures to live up to the ideal might be avoided or remedied. Whereas religions (and Plato, to some extent) tend to offer an otherworldly kind of redemption or salvation, Aristotle has a much more this-worldly account of human fulfillment. In that respect his approach is more like Confucianism (Chapter 1) than the other Eastern theories we have considered so far.

Whether one presents a theory in terms of diagnosis and prescription— the framework we use in this book—or in terms of ideal and realization, as in Aristotle's approach, is a matter of emphasis and style of presentation. A diagnosis of what is wrong in human life presupposes a value judgment about how we should ideally be; conversely an ideal sets a standard that many people fail to achieve.

Aristotle begins the *Nicomachean Ethics* by asking whether there is one end or aim that we seek, for its own sake, in all our actions and projects (NE 1094a1–b12). We can all agree that there is such an end, called **happiness**, but we may disagree about what happiness really consists in (NE 1095a17). Caution is needed here about the use of "happiness" to translate Aristotle's word *eudaimonia*. The etymology of the Greek word connects it with the notion of having a good guardian spirit or "genius" (*daimon*). In Aristotle's usage it does not carry any such supernatural connotation, but it does imply meeting an objective ethical standard, whereas "happiness" in contemporary English does not. We might say of a mentally disabled adult that he is happy with his toys, or of a drug addict that she is happy when she has a source of supply and no side effects, or of a rapist or pedophile that he is happy as long as he can find victims and not get caught, but Aristotle would emphatically deny that such people are living an *admirable* life. "Fulfillment" might be a better translation, "flourishing" is an alternative, and "blessedness" might do, if divested of religious connotations. (Spinoza used the latter term for his ideal—see the Historical Interlude—a rationally contemplative state of mind, as Aristotle's own ideal turns out to be.)

Can we say anything more substantial about this state of ideal human fulfillment, the meaning or purpose of life? Aristotle applies his understanding of human nature as involving a uniquely rational capacity, and comes up with a formula that puts a bit more content into his very abstract notion of *eudaimonia*:

> if all this is so, and a human being's function we posit as being a kind of life, and this life as being activity of soul and actions accompanied by reason, and it belongs to a good man to perform these well and finely, and each thing is completed well when it possesses its proper excellence; if all this is so, the human good turns out to be activity of soul in accordance with excellence (and if there are more excellences than one, in accordance with the best and most complete). But furthermore it will be this in a complete life. For a single swallow does not make spring, nor does a single day; in the same way, neither does a single day, or a short time, make a man blessed and happy. (NE 1098a1)

The reader may be aghast to learn that this is one of the more eloquent passages in Aristotle! He is a very serious philosopher, careful to put in all the qualifications that he sees as needed, however much they clog up his sentences. The message that emerges here is a valuable one, however: (1) human fulfillment consists in *activity*, namely, the exercise of our faculties, not mere passive enjoyment or pleasure; (2) it involves the use of our distinctively human *rational* capacity; (3) this activity should be conducted "well and finely," displaying the best, most complete kind of **excellence** or *virtue*; and (4) it should last over a lifetime.

This formula obviously invites further explanation of the nature of human "excellences." The Greek word *arete* has been translated as "virtue," but for Aristotle inanimate things can have *arete*: for example, an axe has *arete* or "excellence" if it functions well in chopping (in English, we say it is a *good* axe—but not a *virtuous* one). Corresponding to the reason-giving and reason-obeying parts of the soul mentioned earlier, Aristotle distinguishes excellences of intellect and excellences of character (NE 1103a15), and divides the former into theoretical and practical. Theoretical excellences are *sophia*, intellectual accomplishment, and *episteme*, knowledge (what we would now call academic excellences). Practical excellences are *phronesis*, practical wisdom—being good at deliberating about what to do in real-life situations and reaching wise decisions about them—and *techne*, practical expertise (Aristotle displays his prejudice by not valuing the latter so highly).

Plato made no such distinction between *sophia* and *phronesis*, holding that theoretical knowledge of the forms was necessary and sufficient for correct practice. Aristotle made an important new contribution by emphasizing the independence of practical wisdom; for him, knowing a theory about the Good does not automatically make one good. As he puts it at NE 1139a21,

> What affirmation and denial are in the case of thought, pursuit and avoidance are with desire; so that, since excellence of character is a disposition issuing in decisions, and decision is a desire informed by deliberation, in consequence both what issues from reason must be true and the desire must be correct for the decision to be a good one, and reason must assert and desire pursue the same things. This, then, is thought, and truth, of a practical sort.

Aristotle holds that practical wisdom does not consist in knowing and applying a set of commandments or prohibitions, for he thinks it is impossible to formulate any set of general rules that can settle every choice that we meet in life: "the agents themselves have to consider the circumstances relating to the occasion" (1104a9). The wise person, the *phronemos*, learns from practical experience and must be trusted to make appropriate decisions in new cases.

Aristotle's inquiry in the *Nicomachean Ethics* is practical in intent; it is undertaken to help people to become good (NE 1103b27, 1179b1). His concern is not to display philosophical virtuosity and make an academic reputation, but to help promote virtue. It has to be admitted, though, that the demanding intellectual effort needed to understand his intricate analysis is unlikely to make anyone virtuous who is not already well disposed. Aristotle was well aware that there is no substitute for a good upbringing, an education in virtuous habits from childhood; but his hope, like Plato's in the *Republic*, was that his laborious elucidation of human virtues may help social theorists and legislators ("political experts," as he calls them) in their thinking about how to organize society so as to promote human fulfillment (NE I.3).

The central books of the *Nicomachean Ethics* discuss particular virtues in considerable detail, inviting comparison with the Confucian tradition in ancient China (see Chapter 1). As well as practical wisdom ("prudence"), three other virtues were traditionally recognized in Greek philosophy: temperance, courage, and justice. But Aristotle extends the list considerably, and offers a new analysis of virtues as a mean between two extremes. Courage is the right balance between cowardliness and rashness; temperance is the mean between overindulgence and asceticism; "open-handedness" about money is the right balance between being spendthrift or miserly; "mildness" (in one's display of anger) is the mean between irascibility and meekness (NE III.6–V). It is a relief to find Aristotle admitting that "life also includes relaxation, and relaxation includes amusement of a playful sort" (IV.8, 1127b35), though even here he does not relax his intellectual grip but offers an analysis of wit as the appropriate mean between buffoonery and boorishness.

Aristotle adds some virtues that may seem more peculiar to ancient Athens, such as "greatness of soul" (being worthy of great things and conscious of it) and "munificence" (tasteful spending on public projects). The former, a suitable sense of one's own worth and honor, can be represented as a mean between conceitedness and "littleness of soul" (NE IV.3). (Nietzsche fiercely rejected Christian humility and recommended something like Aristotelian great-souledness instead.)

The virtue of justice (in the modern rather than the Platonic sense) does not fit into the pattern of a mean between two extremes. There is the corresponding vice of injustice or unfairness, of course; but there does not seem to be such a thing as being too just (though it is possible to be overly scrupulous about things that do not matter). Justice crucially involves other people, not just those to whom one is related by ties of family or friendship or contractual obligation, but potentially everyone in one's society (for Aristotle it would be the city state, the *polis*). He was aware of the importance of equality before the law for commercial transactions and for the solidarity of society: "it is reciprocal action governed by proportion that keeps the city together" (NE 1131b35).

This examination of virtues outlines positive ideals for human life. But things go wrong when human actions, characters, and lives do not measure up to these ideals. Aristotle does not offer any all-embracing diagnosis of why; he is aware that there are many different ways of falling short of fulfillment (NE 1106b31). For most of the virtues there are two corresponding vices, by deficiency or by excess. The various possibilities arise from our mixed nature, as animals with bodily instincts but also with strong social susceptibilities and rational capacities. We can be tempted away from temperance by pleasure and from courage by fear. We can be moved to rashness by ambition and to injustice by selfishness.

There is a further twist to Aristotle's diagnosis when he distinguishes three kinds of undesirable states: badness, lack of self-control, and brutishness (NE 1145a16). The first is vice, the opposite of virtue, a settled disposition to do the wrong thing, not innately from birth but formed through some combination of bad training and wrong choices. The third is an incurable disposition to act in ways that are "inhuman," whether harmful to others or just weird (e.g., psychopaths or congenital idiots). The second is the most interesting to Aristotle, and he gives a subtle analysis of self-control and the lack of it in Book VII. As we saw in Chapter 4, Socrates held that nobody willingly does what he or she knows to be wrong, but this conflicts with the fact of human experience that St. Paul reports: The good which I want to do, I fail to do: but what I do is the wrong which is against my will" (Romans 7:19). Plato distinguished conflicting parts of the soul and asked how we can achieve inner harmony. One of Aristotle's important contributions is to point out that the person who lacks self-control is significantly different from the person who is simply bad or vicious, for the latter typically has no awareness of how bad he or she is, whereas the former may be painfully conscious of the gap between his or her aspirations and deeds (NE 1150b36). There is more hope of improving the former, but we should not give up on the latter, for maybe such people can be *made* aware of the wrongness of what they do.

On the positive side there is a corresponding distinction between the person who does the right thing, but only after exercising self-control to master his or her inappropriate desires, and the person who is sufficiently advanced in virtue (inner harmony, enlightenment, or the spiritual life) as not to *feel* inappropriate desires (or, at least, not so strongly as to experience inner conflict) so that he or she does the right thing easily and gracefully. Aristotle puts this ideal of *sophrosune* before us ("moderation" and "temperance" are rather pale words to express it, "gracefulness" is perhaps better).

PRESCRIPTION: POLITICAL EXPERTISE AND INTELLECTUAL CONTEMPLATION

How can human fulfillment be achieved? Aristotle holds that virtue and vice are formed by "habituation": our character is a result of our past actions, so it seems that we can be held responsible for what we have made of ourselves, at least to some extent. Exhortation, praise, and blame can have some effect in promoting appropriate action; but Aristotle ruefully acknowledges that "most people are not of the sort to be guided by a sense of shame but by fear" (NE 1179b11), and he is well aware that "it is not possible, or not easy, for words to dislodge what has long since been absorbed into one's character-traits" (NE 1179b18).

Because appropriate upbringing is the crucial ingredient in character formation, and upbringing and education presuppose a preexisting human

society, Aristotle is led to inquire into how society should best be organized. The *Nicomachean Ethics* is concerned with setting forth an ideal of
individual human fulfillment, but as early as the second page he points out
that putting it into practice is a matter of "political expertise":

> For even if the good is the same for a single person and for a city, the good
> of the city is a greater and more complete thing both to achieve and to pre-
> serve; for while to do so for one person on his own is satisfactory enough, to
> do it for a nation or for cities is finer and more godlike. So our inquiry seeks
> these things, being a political inquiry in a way. (NE 1094b8)

And the book ends by setting out a program for another inquiry into constitutions, legislation, and good government (NE 1181b13).

The detail of Aristotle's social prescription is set out in his *Politics*,
which, like Plato's *Republic*, covers a much wider range than its title suggests. It deals with marriage, parenthood, slavery, and household manage-
ment (Book I); population, territory, town planning, nursery education,
and the training of youth (Books VII and VIII); as well as citizenship and
constitutions, revolution and reform (Books II–VI). He is more humane
and realistic than Plato in allowing for family life and private property,
thus he recognizes some limits to state power. But in other ways his ideal
polis is still somewhat totalitarian, for he regards the upbringing of children and youth as so crucial for their moral development, and thus for the
moral health of society, that "their upbringing and patterns of behavior
must be ordered by the state" (NE 1179b35). It sounds as if the state must
take control over the lives of children from a very young age, but in fact
modern states do legislate for education. (It has been remarked that Aristotle's *polis* is like Calvin's Geneva in the sixteenth century in its power
over the morals of its citizens.) It is common these days to make a distinction between public law and "private" morality, but Aristotle's view
challenges us to consider whether any society or nation can survive and
flourish without some measure of agreement about how human life should
be lived and children brought up.

Before leaving Aristotle, we should return to his notion of the ideal
of happiness, and consider the prescription that he himself favors in the
last book of his *Nicomachean Ethics* (X.6–9). There he argues that of the
three conceptions of fulfilled life he mentioned in I.5 (namely, lives devoted to pleasure, to political success and honor, or to intellectual inquiry
and reflection), the third is the best. He quickly dismisses the hedonistic
life (X.6), he finds political activity second best (X.8, 1178a9 ff.), and
he awards the prize to the life of reflection (X.7–8). He argues that the
best kind of happiness will be activity of the "highest" element within
human nature, that which has "awareness of fine things and divine ones",

i.e. reflective activity (NE 1177a13). This is the most self-sufficient kind of human mental activity, requiring only modest resources. Aristotle claims that it is the only sort of activity that is done for its own sake (NE 1177b1)—thereby inviting the wrath of musicians, golfers, lovers, and anyone who enjoys a country walk!

At this point a comparison with "the gods" enters into Aristotle's argument (though one wonders how literally he takes them):

> If, then, intelligence is something divine as compared to a human being, so too a life in accordance with this will be divine as compared to a human life. One should not follow the advice of those who say "Human you are, think human thoughts," and "Mortals you are, think mortal ones," but instead, so far as is possible, assimilate to the immortals and do everything with the aim of living in accordance with what is highest of the things in us; for even if it is small in bulk, the degree to which it surpasses everything in power and dignity is far greater. (NE 1177b31ff.)

He goes on to say that it is absurd to attribute practical doings to the gods, although we believe they are blessed and happy in the highest degree, and we conceive of them as alive and active in *some* way—which can only be the reflective way, the highest kind of activity (1178b8 ff.). Moreover, if the gods care at all about humanity, Aristotle imagines that they delight in what has the greatest affinity to themselves, namely, our human exercise of intelligence (1179a25).

This argument rates intellectual activity as the supreme kind of human happiness. But why must there be a first prize here, picking out one kind of fulfillment as higher than all others? Aristotle himself pursued the life of the mind as very few others have done; he became famous for it and must have derived immense satisfaction from it. But that does not commit him (or us) to treating other pursuits as inferior. Why can't they just be good in different ways, as Aristotle himself encouraged us to think? "Intellectual activity" can include the creative arts as well as the sciences. We can admire less exalted ways of life, such as those of craftspeople, farmers, engineers, athletes, teachers, and housewives or househusbands who devote much of their time to their families. And we can admire a politician who does not pursue power for its own sake, but in order to promote peace, prosperity, and social justice. Many lives are devoted to *many* purposes (e.g., career, family, church, political commitment, music, sports), and there is no need for everyone to have a single or permanent highest priority (this theme comes up in Sartre—see Chapter 11).

If we subtract from Aristotle that overvaluation of the intellectual, and replace it with a multiple set of ideals (things worth doing for their own sake), we have a more attractive conception of human flourishing that conforms to his formula (in NE I.7) of activity using our rational capacities, conducted "well and finely" over a lifetime, where "rational" includes practical as well as theoretical rationality. There is a basis here for a human-centered ethics.

But is there something missing? We may have qualms when we reflect that people in a fortunate class or nation might live very fulfilled lives by this sort of criterion—enjoying careers, family and friends, the arts and sciences, sports and hobbies, in whatever mix suits each individual—while many other people in their own society or elsewhere have little or no opportunity for such fulfillments. In Aristotle's and Plato's society, slaves and barbarians had few rights, if any, and even among male citizens, only high-born aristocrats could aspire to intellectual or political careers. In our own time in our so-called liberal, freedom-loving, and prosperous democracies, it is painfully obvious that not everyone has the same opportunities for human fulfillment, let alone everyone in the wider world.

It may be salutary, then, to compare the modified Aristotelian humanist ethic just outlined with Jesus's summary of the commandments: "You must love the Lord your God with all your heart, with all your soul, with and all your soul, and with all your strength . . . You must love your neighbor as yourself" (Mark 12:30–31). If we factor out the metaphysical question of the *existence* of the Judeo–Christian or Aristotelian God, the ideals involved are still importantly different. Aristotle's gods are purely intellectual beings, and if they care at all about human affairs he represents them as caring only that humans—presumably only the cleverest of us—should emulate their intellectual insight. But the biblical God is a God of *love* as well as knowledge, who cares about his people collectively and individually, and demands social justice (e.g., for the poor and the orphaned), and this God is capable of forgiveness (see Chapter 6).

Aristotle is not ignorant of human love, for he devotes Books VIII and IX to the topic of friendship. (These are some of the most readable sections of the *Nicomachean Ethics* and can be read almost independently of the rest.) He notes that there is a sense in which one should love oneself, i.e. want the very best (in every sense) for oneself (NE 1168b30). But in Aristotle's conception friendship (*philia*) seems only possible for a few, it can really exist only between *good* people. But the New Testament conception of love (*agape*) is universal and unconditional. It involves more than Aristotle's "good will" (NE 1166b30); the ideal it puts before us is first, that we should be loving, i.e. compassionate, to *all* our fellow human beings regardless of sex, race, class, ethnicity, or nationality, and second, that our attitude should not depend on individual talents or good behavior, for a change of heart and forgiveness should always be seen as possible.

This ideal is almost impossibly demanding on our frail human nature. But we may feel that there is something missing from an ethic that does not set it before us.

FOR FURTHER READING

Basic text: Aristotle's *Nicomachean Ethics*. Book I alone gives the flavor of his thought. A recent scholarly translation is by Sarah Broadie and Christopher Rowe, *Aristotle: Nicomachean Ethics* (Oxford: Oxford University Press, 2002). Broadie provides an excellent introduction to the philosophical issues and a detailed argumentative commentary. J. O. Urmson gave an easier introduction in *Aristotle's Ethics* (Oxford: Blackwell, 1988).

Ernest Barker, trans., *The Politics of Aristotle*, revised with introduction and notes by R. F. Stalley (Oxford: Oxford University Press, 2009).

T. Irwin and G. Fine, eds., *Aristotle: Selections* (Indianapolis, IN: Hackett, 1995), is a useful representative selection from the whole of Aristotle's work.

J. L. Ackrill, *Aristotle the Philosopher* (Oxford: Oxford University Press, 1981), relates Aristotle to contemporary philosophy; Jonathan Barnes contributed a masterful "Very Short Introduction" in the Oxford University Press series.

KEY TERMS

Aristotelian realism	**person**
excellence	**reason**
Four Causes	**soul**
happiness	**teleology**

QUESTIONS FOR DISCUSSION

1. How widely can Aristotle's scheme of "Four Causes" be applied?
2. Is Aristotle's conception of the human soul an improvement on Plato's?
3. Does Aristotle give an adequate account of human happiness? (Perhaps discuss this with reference to *Nicomachean Ethics*, Book I, 1094a1–8a20.)
4. Compare Socrates, Plato, and Aristotle on the possibility of doing what one realizes is wrong or unwise.
5. Is Aristotle's conception of the ideal society more acceptable than Plato's?

6

The Bible: Humanity in Relation to God

The Hebrew scriptures, known to Jews as the Tanakh and to Christians as the Old Testament, contain a great variety of writings: creation stories; histories of the ancient Jewish people and their relation to God, their laws, leaders, victories and defeats; the Psalms and wisdom literature; individual human stories such as Ruth; and the later prophetic writings. They date from about the eleventh to the second centuries B.C.E. The much shorter New Testament from the first century C.E. is distinctive of Christianity and is not accepted by Judaism. We will treat these separately (with quotations from the Revised English Bible). There was a historical process by which certain writings became recognized as revelatory of God, but there has also been disagreement about exactly which texts should be included in the canon.

Judaism as it exists *today* has developed from the post-Christian Rabbinic period that produced the Talmud and other influential writings from the second century C.E. onward, after the destruction of the Jerusalem Temple by the Romans in 70 C.E. when Jews were expelled from their ancestral land and had to maintain their religion in exile. We will review only *ancient* Judaism here.

Christianity has had a continuous and complex history of development over two millennia, starting with informal groups of early followers of Christ, through persecution under the Roman Empire until the official recognition of Christianity by Emperor Constantine in the early fourth century, when it entered into the power structure with church councils settling theological disputes and formulating the Christian creeds. Then came the vicissitudes of the medieval papacy, the schism between Roman Catholicism and Eastern Orthodoxy in the eleventh century, the Protestant Reformation in the sixteenth century, the Catholic Counter-Reformation, and many more developments and divergences since. Some early forms of Christianity survive in the Coptic churches of the Middle East, Africa, and India. But we cannot deal with all that, we will concentrate on the New Testament.

The third great monotheistic world religion is Islam, which originated quite suddenly in the Arabian peninsula in the seventh century. Islam recognizes as forebears Abraham and the patriarchs and prophets leading up to Jesus, but asserts that Muhammad is the last of the prophets and the Qur'an is the uniquely authoritative message he received from God. We treat this in Chapter 7.

There are many problems in assessing ideas from the Bible. On the one hand, believers (of various stripes) treat it as sacred text that reveals the nature and purpose of God himself; some regard every sentence as infallible, and many appeal to it for guidance for contemporary ethics. Judaism and Christianity are not just theories. but living and changing traditions that inspire the lives of their adherents (like Hinduism and Buddhism— see Chapters 2 and 3). They are not attributable to a single founder. Abraham is a very distant, shadowy figure from prehistory, and Moses is not now believed by scholars to be the author of the Pentateuch (the first five books of the Hebrew scriptures). Jesus is central to Christianity of course, but like Socrates he did not leave any writings of his own; the gospels were compiled after his death.

On the other hand there has grown up a body of academic expertise in the ancient languages of Hebrew, Aramaic and Greek, and in the archaeology and history of the various communities that produced the Biblical texts, so there is now a large scholarly industry of studies and interpretations. The Hebrew texts and the Christian Testament are of various dates, produced for different purposes, written and edited by various hands. Moreover they have been used by theologians down the centuries to support different theological positions. Most historians are in little doubt that there was such a person as Jesus, but it seems impossible to know whether he himself said the many things attributed to him in the gospels (especially those lengthy discourses in the gospel of John): the quest for the real historical person behind the stories runs mysteriously into the sand. Scholars reckon that the gospels were compiled *later* than the epistles of St. Paul which form the basis of most Christian doctrine.

To say there is a Judeo–Christian belief in *X*, a Hebrew conception of *Y*, or a New Testament view of *Z* is to risk prejudice, controversy, or oversimplification. It is impossible to please everyone—the believers with their rival versions of faith, and the scholars with their academic controversies. There can be no such thing as an objective, neutral approach to the Bible, innocent of all preconceptions. In this chapter we are not committed to any particular version of Judaism or Christianity, but we cannot pretend not to have been influenced, especially by the latter. We propose the following approach: to examine first the **metaphysics** that is common to Judaism and Christianity (and Islam)—the monotheist conception of God. We can hardly avoid this eternally debated topic, but we offer only a brief review of it. The main agenda is the Hebrew and Christian conceptions of human nature, which we will examine in turn under our usual headings of "theory," "diagnosis," and "prescription."

THE JUDEO–CHRISTIAN CONCEPTION OF GOD

The opening three chapters of Genesis tell of the divine creation of the whole world, including human beings. The story continues with the descendants of Adam (Chapters 4–5), the flood and Noah's ark (6–9), and Noah's descendants and the Tower of Babel (10–11). So far, this is presented as *universal* human history, the origin of the whole of humanity. God's call of Abram to become the ancestor (renamed Abraham) of His chosen people begins at Chapter 12, and all the rest of the Hebrew Bible relates to the history of "the children of Israel."

Let us consider how God is represented in those first universal chapters. In 1–2:3 the Hebrew word is *Elohim*, a plural form, and the translation might be "In the beginning the gods [or divine powers] created the heavens and the earth." But in the second version of the creation story, in 2:4ff., God is referred to as "JHWH," a formula of consonants only, presumably because the name of God was thought too holy to write out in full, but which was later pronounced as "Jahweh," a singular name. So it looks as if the book of Genesis was put together by ancient editors from at least two different sources. In the short fragment 6:1–4 there is a mysterious reference to a time when "the Nephelim" (a race of giants) were on the earth and "the sons of the gods" had intercourse with human women; this also suggests that the text is a compilation of several stories. Whatever people may believe about its ultimately divine inspiration, the text we have is surely a result of human processes.

In Genesis 1 God does not seem to need to *do* anything to create—He just gives commands, and the results follow. In the traditional interpretation, He creates *ex nihilo* ("out of nothing"), He does not work on preexisting material like Plato's "demiurge" but brings *everything* into existence in the first place. This Hebrew God is a language-user: He has conceptions of things before they exist, and He names everything (calling the dry land earth, etc.). At each stage of creation He "saw that it was good": He makes value judgments, not arbitrarily choosing what is to be called good, but recognizing an objective standard of value. At the end of the sixth "day" of creation God "saw all that He had made, and it was very good" (1:31). There is a fundamental point made here about the intrinsic goodness of all that exists, including human beings before the Fall.

However, things soon go wrong. In Genesis 3 we are told of the first human disobedience by Eve and Adam, in 4 Cain murders his brother, and in 6:5–7 God bitterly regrets his creation of human beings because of their great wickedness. He angrily resolves to wipe out not just humans but all living things—until Noah finds favor in His eyes and is allowed to save his family and pairs of animals (6:8–9:19). God is here represented as moodily changing his mind, first about the value of the whole business of creation and then again about His intention to extinguish the human race (6:7)—which hardly fits with later theological conceptions of omnipotence, omniscience, and perfect benevolence.

In subsequent books God is repeatedly represented as *speaking* to individual people—to Adam and Eve (Genesis 2–3); to Noah (6:13); to Abraham (12:1ff., 22:1ff.); to Jacob (31:3); many times to Moses, notably from the burning bush (Exodus 3:4ff.) and when delivering the Ten Commandments on Mount Sinai (Exodus 31, 34); to Joshua (Joshua 1:1ff.); to Samuel (1 Samuel 3:4 ff.); to Elijah (1 Kings 17:2ff., 19:13); and to Job (Job 38:1). Moses is depicted as having a particularly intimate relationship with God, talking with Him face to face as one man speaks to another (Exodus 33:11), yet he was afraid to look at God (3:6) and was not allowed to see His face (33:20). If these passages are taken literally, God has a visible body and a face, but usually He is represented as having a *voice* but not a body or a spatial presence, though Job is said to see God with his own eyes (Job 42:5).

The Psalms are a collection of vivid, heartfelt prayers that echo down the ages. They are poetic in form, and some of what they say about God obviously has to be taken as metaphorical: for example, "You, Lord, are a shield to cover me" (Psalm 3:3), "the heavens, the work of your fingers" (8:3), "the Lord's throne is in heaven" (11:4), "the Lord is my lofty crag, my fortress, my champion" (18:2), "Smoke went up from his nostrils . . . He flew on the back of a cherub . . . He loosed arrows"

(18:8–14), "The Lord is my shepherd" (23:1ff). But with other talk of God it is not so clear whether we should take it metaphorically or literally: for example, "His anger flares up in a moment" (Psalm 2:12), "He answers from his holy mountain" (3:4), "the Lord has heard my weeping" (6:8), "the Lord passes sentence on the nations" (7:8), "it is God who girds me with strength" (18:32), "He revives my spirit; for His name's sake He guides me in the right paths" (23:3).

By the time of the prophets (Isaiah, Jeremiah, and the others that follow), God is represented as usually speaking through an intermediary— the prophet who has a vision (Isaiah 1:1), or who receives the word of the Lord (Jeremiah 1:4ff.), and then delivers the message to the people, using the authoritative phrase "Thus says the Lord." Typically, the prophets interpret the events of human history—past, present, and future—in terms of God's will. Predictions of invasion and destruction, of enslavement and exile, and of return, rebuilding, and restitution are expressed in terms of God's purposes, whether punishment for disobedience or merciful **forgiveness**.

In the so-called wisdom literature (Proverbs, Ecclesiastes, and the Wisdom of Solomon—the latter is in the Apocrypha, writings whose place in the Bible has been disputed) there is less explicit talk of God. Some scholars detect Egyptian or Greek influences in these writings. "The fear of the Lord is the foundation of knowledge," says Proverbs 1:7, yet the rest of the book hardly mentions Him. In the Wisdom of Solomon wisdom is personified and almost deified—and in *female* gender: "The spirit of wisdom is kindly towards mortals . . ." (1:6), "Like a fine mist she rises from the power of God . . . She is but one, yet can do all things . . . age after age, she enters into holy souls" (7:25–27). This is personification, like Aphrodite as the goddess of love in Greek myth, or Virtue represented as a female person in poetry and paintings. But is the talk of *God* also personification, a mere figure of speech? Put the other way around, is wisdom any less real than God? It is often conspicuous by its absence, but it can be recognized in some people.

The Bible surely does not treat God as a mere metaphor or symbol; much of its writing may be poetry, parable, allegory, or myth, but not God himself, who is conceived of as the supreme reality. But where should we draw the line between symbolic, metaphorical talk of God and realistic, literal talk of Him? Although God is described in the Psalms as having a face, nostrils, breath, arms, hands, and fingers, most believers say that He does not have a body. The ancient Greek writer Xenophanes remarked that each culture described the divine in its own image: the gods of the Ethiopians are flat-nosed and dark, whereas the gods of the Thracians are blue-eyed and red-haired. Stained glass and the art of Michelangelo or William

Blake have depicted God as a bearded white man of a certain age; but we are warned that those are mere pictorial images and that anyone who thinks *that* is the God of the Judeo–Christian tradition is missing the point. We may feel some sympathy with the forbidding of images at Exodus 20:4 and the Islamic ban on representational art.

Theologians have insisted that God does not have a material body, that He is not one object among others in the universe, and that He does not occupy a position in space or last for a certain length of time. Nor is He to be identified with the whole universe, the sum total of everything that exists—that is Spinoza's **pantheism**, not orthodox theism (see the Historical Interlude). God is traditionally said to be transcendent as well as immanent: although in some sense present everywhere and at all times, He is beyond the world of things in space and time (Psalm 90:2, Romans 1:20). He is not like the unobservable entities (atoms, electrons, quarks, superstrings) that scientific theory invokes to explain what we observe: He is not a scientific postulate. The existence and nature of God do not constitute **empirical statements** to be tested by observation and experiment.

Yet God is surely not a mere abstraction like numbers and shapes and the objects of mathematics. In the Bible He is conceived of as a personal being who created us, loves us, gives us guidance, enters into covenants with individuals or nations, judges us, and may redeem us from our sinfulness. Though lacking a body, He is usually conceived of as a **person**, a superhuman cosmic mind endowed with intelligence, knowledge, desires and purposes, and capable of righteous anger, love, and forgiveness, of intentions and actions in the world whether by "speaking" to people or more directly by miraculously changing the course of events. His significance is at least as much moral as cosmological: belief in him is supposed to affect how we conceive of ourselves and how we ought to live.

Much thought and debate, both popular and at more intellectual levels, has assumed that talk of God has to be interpreted realistically, as implying the existence of a superhuman person. If He does not have a body we have to think of Him as a *dis*embodied person, presumably without gender even if we continue to use the masculine pronoun, with the traditional superhuman properties of omniscience, omnipotence, and total benevolence. This is a conception of something greater than anything else we can conceive of, as Anselm put it in the eleventh century.

This may avoid **falsification**, but at the cost of conceptual and metaphysical obscurity. Can we really make any sense of the notion of a disembodied person—especially one with those idealized superlative properties? Of course we can utter the relevant words, and we *seem* to understand something by them. But what is the status of the claim that there exists such a supernormal person? It is hardly an empirical hypothesis that might even yet be confirmed or falsified by some new esoteric scientific evidence (though some people take it that way). What, then, is the point of asserting this metaphysical claim?

This is not a book about the philosophy of religion; the main business of this chapter is the Biblical account of human nature. We leave the reader with the question whether there may be a less naively realist way of interpreting the biblical talk of God, taking it as an overarching picture, a recipe for generating many metaphors. It has provided a scheme of interpretation of human life that many people have found helpful or inspiring in the effort to understand and express their experience of life: its ups and downs, its delights and disasters, its loves and hates, its failures and guilt, its illuminations and new possibilities—and *how* helpful it is can be a matter of debate and degree. Science and religion do not have to be seen as competitors, for they fulfill different purposes. Some radical interpretations of religions argue that their life-redeeming and life-affirming functions do not need any metaphysical foundation.

THE HEBREW VIEW OF HUMAN NATURE

The Biblical conception of humanity sees us as existing primarily in relation to God, who created us to occupy a special position in the universe, saying "Let us make human beings in our image, after our likeness, to have dominion over the fish in the sea, the birds of the air, the cattle, all wild animals on land, and everything that creeps on the earth" (Genesis 1:26). The question immediately arises whether we should read this story literally as describing a primal event that occurred at some specific time in the distant past, or as mythology that may poetically express important truths about the human condition, but is not history or science. Probably the original writers, editors, readers, and listeners did not make any such distinction, but it is a question we cannot avoid now.

Two large difficulties face any attempt to see literal truth here. The first is that the text displays inconsistencies, for as already mentioned there are *two* creation stories in Genesis, which give different accounts at several points, notably on the creation of woman. The first story has God creating men and women in the plural at 1:27, whereas the second has God creating a single man at 2:7, then fashioning a woman out of his rib at 2:22 (these verses can be used to support different views about the status of women). The other difficulty is the inconsistency of the literal text with the results of cosmology, geology, and evolutionary biology. Science has given us its own accounts of cosmic origins in the Big Bang, the formation of galaxies, stars, and the solar system, the formation of seas and continents, and the evolution of humans from lower forms of life. There is even a contradiction with common sense, for how did the sons of Adam and Eve find wives (4:17) if *all* humans were descended from that first couple? It is now widely accepted that these stories are myths that express deep truths about human nature, so there need be no quarrel with science. To assert the existence of one primal pair as the ancestors of all humanity is surely to insist on an overly literal interpretation of scripture.

What then can it mean to say that we are made in the image of God? The believer will say that human beings are uniquely different from other animals in that we have something of the rationality and personhood of God. But that statement can be turned around to say that our conception of God is an idealization from our own imperfect rationality and morality (see the mention of Feuerbach in Chapter 9). Whether or not we use God language, we can agree that we are (imperfectly) rational beings with self-consciousness, freedom of choice, and the capacity for loving personal relationships—though also for stupidity, hatred, and vice. What can it mean to say that human beings are made to have dominion over the rest of creation? Human beings have obviously acquired, for better or for worse, a certain degree of power over nature; people in the Middle East had already passed beyond the hunter–gatherer stage and had agriculture and livestock, which is the socioeconomic setting of the Hebrew scriptures.

But although human beings are seen as having a special role, we are also seen as *continuous* with the rest of creation. Adam was made of "dust from the ground" (Genesis 2:7), of the same matter that composes the rest of the world, and God "breathed into his nostrils the breath of life". But what does that mean? The Hebrew word *ruach* (sometimes translated as "spirit") means wind or breath, and need not be interpreted as a separable Platonic soul but perhaps more like Aristotle's conception of the soul as principle of life (see Chapters 4 and 5). We are so influenced by the dualism we have inherited from Plato and Descartes that we tend to read it into the Bible. According to the biblical conception, we are *persons* different from inanimate matter and from other animals, but our personhood need not consist in the possession of an immaterial entity that can survive the body. There is no firm expectation of life after death in the Hebrew Bible: the Jews did not develop any belief in an afterlife until the time of Jesus, and they did not agree about it (Matthew 22:22 says that the Sadducees denied the **resurrection**).

The relation of women to men in the Hebrew scheme of things is somewhat ambiguous from the start. One creation story suggests equality of the sexes, but the other implies that the male is the primary form of humanity. In the story of the Fall it is the woman who is represented as first giving in to temptation, then persuading her husband to follow (Genesis 3:6). There has long been an unfortunate tendency to see women as somehow more subject to sin, and as tempting men to sin. And the story started an association of sexuality with sin, because as soon as Adam and Eve disobey God's prohibition "the eyes of both of them were opened, and they knew that they were naked; so they stitched fig-leaves together and made themselves loincloths" (3:7). God then decrees that the wife will desire her husband (why should that be a punishment?) and that he will be "master" of her (3:16). In the stories of Abraham and his descendants there is tremendous emphasis on producing *male* heirs (typical of many cultures). And God Himself is typically described in masculine terms. For some religious cultures there is unfinished business to do with the equality of the sexes.

Probably the most crucial point in the Biblical understanding of human nature is the notion of freedom, conceived of as the choice between obedience to God's will, faith in Him, love for Him—or disobedience, faithlessness, and pride. The necessity for choice is presented in Genesis 2:16–17, where God forbids Adam to eat from the tree of knowledge of good and evil. But why should knowledge of good and evil be a *bad* thing, one wonders? Isn't it what one would expect of human maturity? The underlying thought may be that there is a primeval stage of innocence before moral distinctions and choices are understood, in early childhood and perhaps also in primeval society (though if conscious choice is absent, could that stage be *human* rather than apelike?).

Greek thought puts great store on the intellect, on our ability to attain knowledge of truth, including moral truth; we have seen in Chapters 4 and 5 how the highest fulfillment of human life was thought by Plato and Aristotle to be open only to those who are able to gain such rational knowledge. The Judeo–Christian tradition, in contrast, puts the emphasis on human goodness, a matter of basic attitude—of "heart" or will rather than mind or intellect—which is something open to all, independent of intellectual ability.

There is thus a democratic impetus, an ideal of the equality of all human beings before God, implicit in the Bible (though it can be questioned how well Jews and Christians have lived up to this ideal). The concern with human goodness is not just with right *action*: it is at least as much with the foundation in human character and personality from which such actions flow. It goes beyond the conceptions of human virtue offered by the Greek philosophers, for the Biblical writers see the only firm foundation for human goodness as faith in the transcendent yet personal God. The idea is that God created us for fellowship with himself, so we fulfill the purpose of our life only when we love and serve our Creator.

There are various dramatic exemplifications in the Old Testament of this ultimate requirement of obedient submission to God rather than reliance on our own judgments about truth and morality. A melodramatic case is the story of Abraham being commanded by God to sacrifice his only son, Isaac (Genesis 22). He obediently makes ready to do the deed, but God spares Isaac at the last moment, and praises Abraham for being a "God-fearing" man ready to give up even his own child in response to divine requirement; God then promises that he will be the patriarch of innumerable descendants. A different response to this story is to reject any such sacrifice of an innocent child as immoral and to conclude that such a "command" could not really come from a loving God. Even if it was only a "a test of faith," what sort of God would play such a trick? An anthropological interpretation is that the story shows early Judaism rejecting the practice of child sacrifice in neighboring cultures.

Another famous case of faith being preferred to reason is in the book of Job, where Job and his interlocutors struggle with the problem of undeserved suffering. Job is introduced as a blameless and God-fearing man, but Satan persuades God to test him by letting him be subjected to a series of catastrophic losses and afflictions (Job 1–2). Despite the long-winded theological efforts of Job's comforters, no satisfactory explanation of his suffering is found (3–37). In the end God Himself appears and asserts His power and authority, and Job meekly submits (38–42). The moral is apparently that we should we be humble before God (or fate, or the accidents of nature) rather than seek intellectual insight into reasons for suffering.

DIAGNOSIS: HUMAN DISOBEDIENCE

Given this picture of humanity as created by God, the diagnosis of what is wrong with us follows. We misuse our God-given free will, we choose evil rather than good, we are infected with **sin**, and we disrupt our relationship to God (Isaiah 59:2). And as argued above, the story of Adam and Eve eating the forbidden fruit can be read as a symbol of the fatal flaw in our nature: we are all liable to sinful misuse of our freedom, and we suffer from the consequences.

Genesis 3:14–19 represents familiar features of human life as punishments imposed by God for our disobedience—the necessity to work for our food, the pain of childbirth, even death itself. We can all fantasize about a life in which these things are not necessary, a primeval Eden or a heavenly paradise in which there is no tension between inclination and necessity, desire and duty, no work, no pain, no death. It seems odd, however, to conceive of these fundamental biological and inevitable features of human life as punishment for our moral failings.

Condemnations of human sinfulness recur throughout the Hebrew scriptures. The sons of Adam and Eve begin the fratricidal history of humanity when Cain murders his brother. In Genesis 6:5–7 God regrets his creation of humankind, until Noah finds favor with him. In 11:1–9 He splits up the supposed original single language because humankind was growing proud and had tried to build the Tower of Babel up to the heavens (perhaps this expressed disapproval of Mesopotamian pyramids). Throughout the subsequent history of Israel there are repeated prophetic denunciations of unfaithfulness to God, pride, sinfulness, selfishness, and injustice (Exodus 32, Numbers 25, 1 Samuel 19, Isaiah, Jeremiah, Amos). The story of David's seduction of Bathsheba, the wife of his soldier (2 Samuel 11), is remarkable for its frank depiction of wrongdoing by Israel's hero.

GOD'S COVENANTS AND REDEMPTION

The Hebrew prescription is also based on God. If God has made us for fellowship with himself yet we have broken our relationship to him, then we need God to forgive us and restore the relationship. Hence we have the idea of **salvation**, a regeneration of humanity made possible by the mercy, forgiveness, and love of God. In the Tanakh there is the recurring theme of **covenant**, a quasi-legal agreement like that between a powerful conqueror and a subject state, but made between God and his chosen people. One covenant was with Noah (Genesis 9:1–17), another was with Abraham (Ch 17), and the most important one was with the "children of Israel" led by Moses, in which God redeems them from their bondage in Egypt and promises that they will be His people if they keep his commandments (Exodus 19).

But these covenants are far from totally effective: sin does not disappear from the face of the earth (nor has it still, we may add). There is even a danger of spiritual pride, if members of any group conceive of themselves as God's chosen people and feel justified in conquering or oppressing their neighbors. The Bible frankly records genocide by the children of Israel as they took over the Promised Land, and in Joshua 8–11 God is even represented as sanctioning it. There is a tension between the exclusive tribalism—worshipping Jahweh as the God *of Israel* as opposed to the gods of other peoples—that characterizes these early stories (the deliverance from Egypt and conquest of Canaan) and the later universal tendency—worshipping the God of *all* humankind—that appears in the prophetic writings such as Isaiah 49:8, "I have formed you, and destined you to be a light for peoples."

When the Israelites failed to obey God's commandments and laws, there arose the prophetic idea of God using the events of history, especially defeat by neighboring empires, to punish the people for their sin. But there was also a promise of God's merciful forgiveness, and his **redemption** of not just the people of Israel but the whole of creation. In particular, the author of the second section of the composite book of Isaiah uses ecstatic language (unforgettably set to music in Handel's *Messiah*) to express this vision of God's forgiveness, redemption, and new creation: "Then will the glory of the Lord be revealed, and all mankind together will see it" (40:5); "You will go out with joy and be led forth in peace, before you mountains and hills will break into cries of joy" (55:12); "See, I am creating new heavens and a new earth!" (65:17). The hope arose for the coming of a God-appointed savior, the Messiah, which Christians later identified as Jesus—in fact, Christianity began as a sect within first-century Judaism. But mainstream Judaism repudiated that radical new movement, and many Jews still maintain hope for a Messiah yet to come.

THE NEW TESTAMENT

The Jewish rabbi or religious teacher Jesus of Nazareth did not leave any writings (none that we know of, anyway). But he exerted a charismatic influence on his disciples and those who met him, and an enormous influence down the centuries since, through the writings of the New Testament, and the Christian churches. There are partial parallels with Confucius, the Buddha, and Socrates, who also started traditions that persist to the present day (see Chapters 1, 3, and 4). The new world religion of Christianity developed rapidly out of the early reactions to Jesus's life, teachings, crucifixion, and reported resurrection. The earliest documents were letters ("epistles") from St. Paul and others, which scholars reckon predate the four gospel narratives of Jesus's life and death, compiled between about 70 and 100 C.E.

For Christians the coming of Jesus changed their conceptions both of God and of human nature. The God of the Old Testament became for them God the Father, and Jesus was seen as embodying or instantiating divinity, being so united with God (John 10:38) that he was described as "God the Son." The distinctively threefold Christian conception of the Trinity then developed from the recognition of God the Holy Spirit acting inspirationally within Christian believers. The Spirit was powerfully experienced by the apostles on the day of Pentecost according to Acts 2:1–5 (and in retrospect could be identified as far back as Genesis 1:2). Church councils later summed this up in the paradoxical formula of "three persons in one God."

Because of the enormous influence of Christianity in Western civilization down to our own time, the word "Christian" has often been used in honorific ways: until quite recently it was shocking to declare oneself *not* a Christian (in some circles, it still is). But what criteria must one satisfy to count as a Christian? And why is this question regarded as important? It is surely because of our cultural inheritance that has long characterized the West: the assumption that "we" are Christian and we distinguish ourselves from others—Jews, Muslims, pagans, atheists, and so on. (Notoriously, further divisions have grown up when various brands of Christianity differentiated themselves from rivals.)

Whatever extra connotations the term "Christian" has come to have, it at least involves some theological claim about Jesus. To be a Christian, it is hardly enough to say that Jesus was a very good man or a person of great spiritual insight, for atheists and members of other faiths might agree. The central Christian claim is that there was a decisive revelation of God in this particular historical figure who ministered, preached and was crucified in Roman-occupied Palestine around 30 C.E. This has been traditionally expressed in the doctrine of **incarnation**: that Jesus was both human and divine, the eternal Word of God made flesh (John 1:1–18). The later credal formulations of this in obscure Greek philosophical terms (e.g., "two natures in one substance") are perhaps optional, but the idea that God was *uniquely* present in Jesus seems basic to Christianity.

Yet even here there may be some shading at the edges. If we press the question in what respect Jesus is believed to be different in kind from other great spiritual figures of history such as the Buddha or Socrates or Muhammad (or more recent inspirational figures), the orthodox thing to say is that he was the Son of God, the divine Word incarnate in human form. Yet in the famous prologue of John's Gospel he is said to have given, to those who received him, the power to become sons of God themselves (John 1:12). Can we *all* become sons (and daughters) of God, then? What does that mysterious term "Son of God" mean, anyway? Not that God the Father literally impregnated a woman and produced a son, as some of the Greek polytheistic gods were said to do. (The Qu'ran dismisses such a thing as far beneath God's dignity.) Interpreting the concept of "Son of God" takes us into controversial and eternally debated theology. But one can be impressed and inspired by the life and teaching of Jesus as represented in the gospels—perhaps more than by any other figure—without having to take a stand on a metaphysical theory of incarnation.

THE NEW TESTAMENT VIEW OF HUMAN NATURE

The coming of Jesus expanded the conception of human nature for Christians by showing that in some sense human nature can become divine (see John 1:12 again). Eastern Orthodoxy has a concept of deification of believers. But what can that mean? In Romans 8:1–12, Paul makes a contrast between the **spirit** and the **flesh**. The latter term was the traditional translation in the Authorized Version; but the Revised English Bible has "our old nature," and the Jerusalem Bible has "human nature." A similar distinction is attributed to Jesus in John 3:5–7 (and 6:63):

> In very truth I tell you, no one can enter the kingdom of God without being born from water and spirit. Flesh can give birth only to flesh; it is spirit that gives birth to spirit. You ought not to be astonished when I say, "You must all be born again."

Being "born again" is obviously a metaphor for spiritual change: not even the most fundamentalist of Bible interpreters thinks we can literally be born twice. There is a tendency for us to interpret the change in metaphysically dualist terms, involving a contrast of incorporeal soul with physical body. But Paul's distinction seems to be not between mind and matter, or between our spiritual nature and our human nature (which would suggest that human nature is intrinsically bad, contrary to the idea of humanity being made in the image of God), but rather between regenerate and unregenerate humanity, redeemed and unredeemed human nature. The fundamental contrast is between two ways of living: "Those who live on the level of the old nature have their outlook formed by it, and that spells death; but those who live on the level of the spirit have the spiritual outlook, and that is life and peace" (Romans 8:5–6). Of course, it is tempting to identify the flesh with our biological nature—our bodily desires, especially our sexuality (remember Plato's conflict between appetite and the higher parts of the soul in Chapter 4). But it is a misinterpretation of the Christian conception of human nature to identify the distinction between good and evil with that between our mental and physical natures. Desires for wealth or fame or power are more mental than physical, but Jesus's teaching condemns these desires as worldly, not spiritual (see the Sermon on the Mount in Matthew 5–7). And for Paul, too, they are surely part of "living on the level of the old nature."

It has to be admitted, however, that the ascetic view that our sexual desires are intrinsically bad has had a strong influence in the history of Christianity. We find this tendency in Paul when he describes marriage as second best to celibacy (1 Corinthians 7), and it became more influential with the writings of Augustine. Paul was scathing about homosexuality (Romans 1:27), but it is not clear that this view is essential to Christianity rather than a cultural attitude of the time. It is notable that Paul does not condemn slavery (1 Corinthians 7:20–24) but tells slaves and their masters to make the best of it. Christians (and Jews and Muslims) have to ask themselves which bits of their scriptures reflect elements of ancestral human culture that are not compulsory now, and which parts express eternal spiritual insight.

On the relation between the sexes we should note that in gospel stories Jesus treats women with great respect, and several women were close to him, especially around his death and reported resurrection. But he did not choose any women among his officially recognized twelve disciples: in that respect he was presumably a man of his time. Paul wrote in one place that in Christ there is no such thing as Jew and Greek, slave and free-man, male and female (Galatians 3:28); yet he said that wives must be subject to their husbands (Ephesians 5:22). In 1 Corinthians 11:8–9 he refers back to the second creation story in Genesis which made women an afterthought, and he required women to cover their hair in church. Much Christian thought has found women theologically problematic—witness the continuing controversies about the ordination of women.

Is the distinction between living on the level of the old nature and living on the level of the spirit to be made purely in this life, or does it also involve life after death? Here there is a divergence between a purely spiritual inter-pretation of Christianity and an **eschatological** version involving the end of the world. Jesus is said to have proclaimed the coming of "the Kingdom of Heaven" or "the Kingdom of God" (Matthew 4:17, 23; Mark 1:15). But does this mean a psychological change, a cataclysmic event bringing history to an end, or life after death? It seems that was not clear to Jesus's followers. "Eternal" or "everlasting life" is mentioned in the fourth gospel, where Jesus is represented as offering eternal life to whoever will believe in him (John 3:16). But we need not jump to the conclusion that this means the continuation of human life after death: it might mean a new and better way of living in *this* life, embodying eternal truths and values.

Some of Paul's writing can be interpreted in this way. Consider this vivid passage in Galatians 5:16–25:

> What I mean is this: be guided by the Spirit and you will not gratify the desires of your unspiritual nature . . .
>
> Anyone can see the behavior that belongs to the unspiritual nature: fornication, indecency, and debauchery; idolatry and sorcery; quarrels, a contentious temper, envy, fits of rage, selfish ambitions, dissensions, party intrigues, and jealousies; drinking bouts, orgies, and the like . . .
>
> But the harvest of the Spirit is love, joy, peace, patience, kindness, good-ness, fidelity, gentleness, and self-control. Against such things there is no law. Those who belong to Christ Jesus have crucified the old nature with its passions and desires. If the Spirit is the source of our life, let the Spirit also direct its course.

This confirms that the old unspiritual nature is the source of worldly pas-sions as well as carnal debaucheries. It is more specific than Paul's oft-quoted hymn to love in 1 Corinthians 13, which is easily sentimentalized.

We are not merely reminded of right and wrong here; we are promised a fundamental transformation of mind from which ethical behavior will flow.

In the New Testament, love of God and life according to his will is open to all regardless of intellectual ability (1 Corinthians 1:20). Jesus famously summed up the Judaic law in two injunctions: "Love the Lord your God with all your heart, and with all your soul, and with all your strength, and with all your mind . . . Love your neighbor as yourself" (Matthew 22:34–40, Mark 12:28–31, Luke 10:25–28; with anticipations in Deuteronomy 6:5 and Leviticus 19:18). The "love of neighbor" (**agape**) that is meant here is different from mere human affection; it is divine in nature, as 1 John 4:7–8 makes clear: "Let us love one another, because the source of love is God. Everyone who loves is a child of God and knows God, but the unloving know nothing of God, for God is love."

"Eternal life" implies *at least* a spirit-inspired, divinely loving life in this world; but we cannot ignore the fact that some passages in the New Testament lay great stress on resurrection, a last judgment, eternal punishment for the wicked, and everlasting life for all believers (Matthew 7:21–23, 13:36–43, 24–25). Traditionally, the resurrection of Jesus after his death on the cross has been proclaimed as God's guarantee that there is a life after death—at least for "the saved." We are offered hope of a regenerate, spiritual life: "For anyone united to Christ, there is a new creation" (2 Corinthians 5:17). This is seen as a lifelong process, which needs life after death for its completion (Philippians 3:12–14). The Christian expectation of resurrection for all, or at least for all believers, is made explicit in 1 Corinthians 15.

THE NEW TESTAMENT DIAGNOSIS OF SIN

Judaism had plenty of occasion to record human wrongdoing down the centuries, but Christianity has developed a doctrine of "original" sin, the innate tendency of humankind toward sinfulness. That need not imply that we are totally depraved, as some medieval versions had it; but it does mean that nothing we do can be *perfect* by God's standards: "All alike have sinned, and are deprived of the divine glory" (Romans 3:23). We find ourselves in inner conflict. We often recognize what we ought to do, but somehow we fail to do it. St. Paul famously expresses this at Romans 7:14ff.; he even personifies sin (rather like the Freudian unconscious or *id*, see Chapter 10) saying, "It is no longer I who perform the action, but sin that dwells in me" (7:17). That might seem to excuse the sinner from responsibility, which was surely not Paul's intention. The fourth gospel also contrasts "slavery to sin" with being set free by knowing the truth in Jesus (John 8:31–36).

Sin is not intrinsically bodily in nature, and sexuality has its rightful place. The true nature of sin is mental or spiritual: it consists in pride, in the preference for our own selfish will against God's will and our consequent alienation from him. But this surely does not mean that all self-assertion is sinful. (Nietzsche condemned Christianity as "slave morality," praising meekness and self-abasement and discouraging vigorous human self-assertion and living life to the fullest.) A superficial reading of the beatitudes (Matthew 5) may suggest this in the line "blessed are the poor in spirit," but it is not so obvious how we are to understand those mysterious words. Some of the stories of Jesus such as his expulsion of the moneychangers from the Temple, and the vehemence of Paul's preaching, suggest no inhibition on clear moral judgment, righteous anger, and resolute action.

The Fall of humanity into sin is seen as somehow involving the whole creation (Romans 8:22): everything falls short of the glory of God. But one wonders if it is necessary to personify evil in the concept of Satan or other demonic powers—though those notions do appear in the New Testament (Matthew 4:1–11, Mark 5:1–13, Acts 5:3, 2 Thessalonians 2:3–9, Revelation 12:9). The ancient religion of Manicheism believed in twin and equal powers of good and evil: but for Jew and Christian alike, God is ultimately in control of all that happens, despite the manifold appearances of evil in the world. That provokes, of course, the well-known "problem of evil"—why does God cause or permit so much of it?

GOD'S SALVATION IN CHRIST

Scholars and theologians have debated what Jesus's conception of himself was. In the gospels he is represented as making dramatic theological claims about himself, especially in the fourth, where he claims to be the Messiah (John 4:25–26), the Son of God (5:16–47), the bread that comes down from heaven (6:30–58), and even to have existed before Abraham was born (8:58). But the gospels were compiled after Jesus's death, by writers who were already believers in his divine status. We cannot be sure that Jesus himself made any such claims. It is in the writings of Paul that we find the earliest written formulations of the Christian theory of incarnation and salvation. The central claim is that God was uniquely present in Jesus of Nazareth and uses his life, death, and resurrection to restore us to a right relationship with Himself:

As the result of one misdeed [Adam's Fall] was condemnation for all people, so the result of one righteous act [i.e., Jesus's death on the cross] is acquittal and life for all. For as through the disobedience of one man many were made sinners, so through the obedience of one man many will be made righteous. (Romans 5:18–19)

Paul writes with great eloquence and conviction, and his language has acquired enormous authority; but if we stop to think about what he is saying here, it seems to run counter to our ordinary convictions about responsibility and blame, if taken literally. How can it be just to blame all humanity for a misdeed of one man long ago? (And what about Eve? Has she been forgotten?) How can God acquit or "justify" or "make righteous" the whole of sinful humanity because of the obedience of another individual (Jesus)? There is a controversial theological theory of **atonement** here, that the historical life and death of Jesus are the means by which God reconciles the whole of creation to himself (Romans 5:6–10, 2 Corinthians 5:18–21).

For most Christians it is not enough to say that Jesus provides an inspiring example of someone being prepared to suffer death rather than go against his most fundamental values. Socrates and other historical figures (including the Christian martyrs) are not divinized in the same way. Paul and the writer of Hebrews 10 were thinking in terms of Old Testament ideas of sacrifice, but not so many theologians are now prepared to interpret Christ's "saving work" as a propitiatory sacrifice—as if, very crudely, God requires blood to be shed (any blood, even that of the innocent?) before he will be prepared to forgive sins. But how is the crucifixion of a Jewish religious teacher under the Roman governor Pontius Pilate in Jerusalem about 30 C.E. supposed to effect a redemption of the whole world from sin? This is one of the great theological mysteries (or stumbling blocks) of the Christian faith.

The Christian prescription is not complete with this "saving work" of Jesus Christ. It needs to be accepted by each individual person and to be spread throughout the world by the church. But what is required from individuals to be "saved"? Baptism became the traditional ritual for becoming a Christian, but it can only be an outward and visible sign of an inward and spiritual change. There are familiar phrases for the latter: being "born again," "believing in Christ," having "faith in Christ," "accepting Jesus as one's savior," "being justified by faith alone." But what do these pious phrases mean? Do they require a theological belief in incarnation: that Jesus is the Son of God? And in atonement: that his death atones for the sins of the world? Or do they mean a personal relationship of trust in Jesus as a religious authority, a "guru," a revealer of God, a guide to life, a source of spiritual life? But how can people who have never met him in the flesh have a personal relationship with him? What can that mean other than treating him—or rather the written representations of him that we are left with—as a supremely inspiring example of selfless living, life "in the spirit"?

A long-standing problem arises over the parts played by human beings and God in the drama of salvation. The fundamental conception is that redemption can come only from God, through his offering of himself in

Christ. We are "justified" in the sight of God not by our own good works but by faith (Romans 3:1–28), by our mere acceptance of what God does for us, his forgiveness and redemption. We are saved by this free **grace** of God, not by anything that we can do ourselves (Ephesians 2:8). Yet our will remains crucially free, for it can only be by our own choice that we accept God's salvation and allow his regeneration to transform our lives. The New Testament is full of exhortations to repent and believe (e.g., Acts 3:19) and to live the life of the Spirit. There is thus a tension between the insistence that salvation is due to God's grace and that it depends on our free response (see Augustine and Pelagius in the Historical Interlude).

SPIRITUAL OR METAPHYSICAL
VERSIONS OF CHRISTIANITY

The doctrines of incarnation, atonement, resurrection, and the end of the world challenge contemporary secular rationality; and their formulation has provoked much internal debate within Christian tradition. How can one human being be a member of the transcendent, eternal Godhead? How can his death save the world? The doctrine of the Trinity—three persons in one God—multiplies the conceptual problems. (The idea of the virgin birth has been much revered, manifesting again the tendency to divorce divinity from sexuality; but perhaps it is less essential.) A common response is that these are mysteries rather than contradictions, human reason cannot be expected to understand God's nature and operation, and we must be content to accept what He has reveal to us. But such statements from within the perspective of faith do little to answer the difficulties of the unbeliever or the puzzled.

Unlike ancient Judaism, Christianity developed a firm expectation of life after death. But this is not the Greek idea of the survival of our incorporeal soul, though many believers have taken it that way: the New Testament and the creeds speak of the resurrection of the *body*. It has always been orthodox Christian belief that the resurrection of Jesus was a historical event, observed by the witnesses reported in the gospels. But the claim is not that Jesus was resuscitated, that is, brought back to ordinary human life, only to die in a normal way later. The stories imply that his resurrected body was of a quite different metaphysical kind, able to appear and disappear and pass through locked doors (John 20:26), though also material enough to speak, and to hand around bread and fish (John 21:13). (But in Matthew 22:30 Jesus is reported as saying that in the resurrection men and women do not marry, which is another exclusion of sexuality from the divine.) In 1 Corinthians 15 Paul wrote in more detail about the resurrection, saying that we die as physical bodies but are raised as "spiritual bodies"; it is not clear what a spiritual body is supposed to be, but Paul did use the Greek word *soma*, which means "body."

Jesus's resurrection is supposed to show the possibility of a similar resurrection for everybody. So will there be a moment in the future at which the general resurrection will take place (as artists such as Stanley Spencer have delighted in depicting)? Paul says, "We shall not all die, we shall all be changed, in a flash, in the twinkling of an eye, at the last trumpet-call" (1 Corinthians 15:51–52, see also 2 Peter 3:10). Jesus himself is reported as predicting the imminent end of the world (Matthew 24). Paul tells his flock that the time is short, and in one of his earliest epistles (1 Thessalonians 4:16–17) he gives his most vivid description: "When God's trumpet sounds, then the Lord himself will descend from heaven; first the Christian dead will rise, then we who are still alive shall join them, caught up in clouds to meet the Lord in the air. Thus we shall always be with the Lord."

The book of Revelation is full of vivid descriptions of eschatological events, including strange beasts, battles, and tortures, and displaying a peculiar obsession with numbers. (It is like the script for a science fiction movie, with special effects in questionable taste; even the famous description of the New Jerusalem in Chapter 21 seems more interested in its jewelry and dimensions than in its spiritual qualities. Yet some people find Revelation strangely fascinating.) It is clear that the early Christians had a definite expectation of an imminent end to human history, a taking up of humanity into a metaphysically different kind of existence. It would be nice to think that all will be saved, but many passages foresee a last judgment and a final division between saved and damned; Revelation destines some for "the second death" at 21:8.

How are we to understand this eschatological vision? (Are we meant to *understand* it at all? But unless we understand it, how can we believe it?) If we are resurrected as *bodies* of some kind, those bodies have to occupy space and endure through time. Is it meant that somewhere in our universe there already exist the resurrected bodies of St. Paul, Napoleon, and Great-Aunt Agatha? That would make the belief a scientific theory, to be tested empirically. But perhaps the idea is rather that everyone (or everyone who *qualifies*) will be resurrected at the same time at the end of history. (In view of the huge number of past generations that suggests overcrowding, but if no food is required for spiritual bodies and no reproduction is possible, maybe that will not be a problem.) Is the resurrection world supposed to be timeless? If so, what sense can be made of the idea of resurrected *life*, for as we understand it life is a process in time in which people act and change, interact and communicate? If we think rather of a resurrected life that literally goes on forever, is that even an *attractive* prospect? The answer is not obvious: could life remain meaningful if we knew there could be no end to it?

Many thinking Christians may acknowledge such intellectual problems in theology but remain practicing members of a Christian community, in some sense "going along with" the orthodox doctrines because of what they find in the life and worship of the Church—a certain growth in the spiritual life. They may well say that Christianity is not just a theory but a way of life. Perhaps we can reach some degree of agreement on what counts as "spiritual growth," in terms of the "fruits of the spirit" mentioned in Galatians 5, James, and 1 John. But the claim that it can be achieved only by accepting the metaphysical, supernatural, and eschatological claims found in the New Testament is a matter for ongoing debate.

FOR FURTHER READING

There are many different English translations of the Bible. One excellent version for present purposes is the Oxford Study Bible: Revised English Bible with the Apocrypha, edited by M. J. Suggs et al. (Oxford: Oxford University Press, 1992). This contains explanatory footnotes and helpful essays on the historical, sociological, literary, and religious background of the biblical texts.

In the Very Short Introduction series published by Oxford University Press, see the titles on the Bible by J. Riches, on Judaism by N. Solomon, on theology by D. F. Ford, on Paul by E. P. Sanders, and on atheism by J. Baggini. There is also a title on Jesus, by H. Carpenter, in Oxford University Press's Past Masters series.

Nicolas de Lange, *Judaism* (Oxford: Oxford University Press, 1986), is a concise guide to Judaism down the centuries to the present day.

For classic works on Christian understandings of human nature, see Reinhold Niebuhr, *The Nature and Destiny of Man* (New York: Charles Scribner's & Sons, 1964); E. L. Mascall, *The Importance of Being Human* (New York: Columbia University Press, 1958), which presents a neo-Thomist view; E. W. Kemp, ed., *Man: Fallen and Free* (London: Hodder & Stoughton, 1969), which contains an interesting variety of essays including a notable summary by J. A. Baker of the Old Testament view; and J. Macquarrie, *In Search of Humanity* (London: SCM Press, 1982; New York: Crossroad, 1983), which offers a more existentialist view.

For a feminist critique of Christianity while retaining theism, see Daphne Hampson, *After Christianity* (London: SCM Press, 1996).

Books on philosophy of religion are countless. One comprehensive set of readings is M. Peterson et al., eds., *Philosophy of Religion: Selected Readings* (Oxford: Oxford University Press, 1996).

In *Open to New Light* (Exeter, UK, and Charlottesville, VA: Imprint Academic, 2012) Leslie Stevenson offers an introduction to Quaker spirituality in historical and philosophical context; he also has a recent paper "Atonement in Theology and Literature" in *Philosophy and Literature*, 2015.

KEY TERMS

agape	incarnation
atonement	metaphysics
covenant	pantheism
empirical statement	person
eschatological	redemption
falsifiability	resurrection
flesh	salvation
forgiveness	sin
grace	spirit

QUESTIONS FOR DISCUSSION

1. Which Biblical descriptions of God are metaphorical, and which should be taken literally?
2. If God has "chosen" a particular people, what is His will for the rest of humanity?
3. How should we understand the New Testament distinction between spirit and flesh?
4. What is the relation between sin, God's grace, and human free will?
5. What metaphysics, if any, is implicit in Christianity?

7

Islam: The *Khalifa* Ideal

HISTORICAL BACKGROUND

Many readers of this chapter may know little about Islam except what they have seen in the contemporary media. In the wake of 9/11 and the 7/7 London bombings, recent attention has focused on the immediate, the sensational, and the threatening. Despite the fact that very few Muslims have engaged in terrorism and many terrorists have not been Muslim, there is a tendency in Europe and North America to associate Islam with terrorism. A brief historical overview of the growth of Islam may help establish a more balanced view.

With strong historical roots in Judaism and Christianity, Islam is the third great monotheistic world religion of Semitic origin. It arose in Arabia in the seventh century C.E., when the prophet Muhammad had a series of visions. According to Islamic tradition, these visions are direct revelations from God (Allah) and compose what is today the text of the **Qur'an**.

Disputes arose in the wake of the Prophet's death (632 C.E.) as to who should succeed him as leader of the nascent Muslim community. A lengthy period of social and political unrest followed. In the latter decades of the seventh century, a series of civil wars split the community into a majority party (known today as "**Sunnis**," or followers of the

Prophet's practice) and a minority party (known today as "**Shi'a**," or followers of 'Ali ibn Abi Talib, a close companion and blood relative of the Prophet). The names of these parties are somewhat misleading because the minority party also considers itself to be following the practices of the Prophet. What originally distinguished the two groups was a philosophical disagreement: Who is best qualified to succeed the Prophet as leader of the Muslim community? The Shi'a held that the leader, or *imam*, should come from Muhammad's family line; and they still look to an imam from that line to continue the prophetic tradition. The Sunnis followed a practice that prevailed among many Arab tribes of the time and invested leadership in an individual chosen after consultation among tribal elders.

Despite (or, perhaps, because of) this intracommunal turmoil, the seventh century also witnessed Muslims acquiring unprecedented wealth through territorial expansion. Within a century of the death of Muhammad, Muslims had conquered the Near East, North Africa, and much of Spain and had established themselves at the gates of India and China. By the late eighth century, a Muslim Empire (ruled from Baghdad, in modern-day Iraq) rivaled the Roman Empire in extent, though it did not include Turkey, Greece, or Italy.

From the eighth to the twelfth centuries, there was a great flowering of Islamic civilization. Many Muslims interpreted their material success as vindication of the rise of Islam, and perhaps it is not surprising that this same period saw startling creativity in the religious realm. Indeed, much of what is regarded today as Islamic tradition was established during this time. Remarkably, Muslim intellectuals and pietists produced this cultural achievement without the aid of centralized institutions to guarantee uniformity of belief and practice among the faithful. Instead, Islamic traditions rely upon a broad degree of consensus among scholars (*ulama*) trained, to a large extent, in the arcane particularities of canon law. Muslim jurisprudence resembles Christian theology in that neither questions the authority of a claimed divine revelation. It resembles British common law insofar as it is case-based, but Muslim jurists do not recognize legal precedent in the same way as their common law counterparts. Like British common law, Muslim jurisprudence evolved into a highly specialized profession dominated (though never exclusively) by male elites. It is also interesting to note that, from the eighth century until the present, the majority of Muslim jurists have belonged to mystical brotherhoods.

In addition to their accomplishments in religious thought and practice, Muslim thinkers developed intellectual systems that combined the inheritance of Greek, Egyptian, Indian, and Iranian philosophies with the Islamic faith. In this age of great confidence, Muslims made advances in the fields of science, medicine, philosophy, and theology. These advances were later passed on to intellectuals in western Europe. Indeed, a persuasive case can be made that Europe's emergence from the so-called Dark Ages was facilitated by exchanges that took place among Muslim intellectuals and their Jewish and Christian counterparts in Spain during the twelfth and thirteenth centuries.

Starting in the late fifteenth century, Europeans began to explore and colonize much of the world outside of Europe. Over the course of five centuries, their great strides in military and economic development permitted them to dominate Muslim-majority countries—including those associated with the early modern empires of south Asia (the Moghuls), central Asia (the Safavids), and western Asia (the Ottomans). Since then, Muslims have debated how best to react to Western empire building and culture. Some have favored a degree of assimilation, but others have reacted by strongly affirming separate Muslim religious and cultural identity. At various times and in particular locations, the backlash has been violent (for instance, British troops put down a Muslim rebellion in the Indian mutiny of 1857 and in the Sudan at the end of that century). In recent years the continuing tragedy of the Palestinians and the invasions of Iraq and Afghanistan have also led to violent clashes.

Islam is the second largest world religion, and after recent waves of immigration, we find substantial Muslim sections of the population in Europe and North America. It is to be hoped that this chapter may assist mutual understanding.

A THIRD TESTAMENT? THE QUR'AN'S RELATION TO BIBLICAL LITERATURES

No discussion of "biblical" views of human nature or their impact upon human cultures is adequate unless it takes into consideration the challenge that the Qur'an poses to those views. Since its first, piecemeal recitations in the early decades of the seventh century C.E., the Qur'an has been in conversation with what we should term "biblical literatures." This latter term is preferable to "the Bible" because, despite its presentation as a single text, the Bible is a library of books produced by a variety of hands over a period of about a thousand years. Moreover, it is not a complete compendium of books produced during that period, nor is it by any means entirely representative of the literatures that its own authors and readership produced or held sacred. The Bible is a selection of sacred texts that provides the modern reader with a window from which to observe a particular vista of literary history and, hopefully, come to an appreciation of the Near Eastern religious genius associated with the people of Israel. The identity of that people—as with the identity of every "people"—is socially constructed: it is what has been termed an "imagined community." Biblical literatures (both within and without the biblical canon) and the literary responses to them (the Qur'an included) are crucial components of the construction of the identity of the people of Israel and of its successor communities: today's Jews, Christians, and Muslims.

The historical origins of the Qur'an are shrouded in mystery. This is because the manuscript traditions that are available for the biblical books and much ancient literature are lacking in the case of the Qur'an. Islamic tradition informs us that within a decade or two of the death of the Prophet Muhammad, the then-reigning caliph (or successor to the Prophet as leader of his community) decided that a standard edition of the Qur'an should be produced. This decision is indirect evidence that manuscript variants existed, and the tradition itself has preserved examples of small variations within a handful of Qur'anic passages. Nevertheless, nothing has come down to us that would suggest that the earliest Qur'ans differed in any significant respect from the Qur'an we possess today. This circumstance is certainly consistent with the traditional account of the caliph's decision to produce a standardized text. Historians of the Qur'an, however, remain hopeful that the early caliphate was at least as susceptible to bureaucratic inefficiency as are the governments of modern states, for such inefficiency allows the possibility that there is somewhere preserved (and forgotten) a cache of manuscripts that will eventually prove to be as illuminating for the history of Islam as the twentieth-century Qumran and Nag Hammadi discoveries have proved to be for the histories of Judaism and Christianity.

Until such a momentous discovery occurs, however, scholars of the Qur'an have no viable alternative to the Islamic tradition's account of the processes of its revelation and collection and, of course, their own historical instincts and skepticism. While no historian can regard such circumstances as ideal, they do not undermine all competent historical inquiry. In the first three centuries following the death of the Prophet Muhammad, Muslims produced a large body of literature that reflects, albeit indirectly, the social situation into which the primitive Islamic community was born. A judicious use of this material, in combination with archaeological evidence and even some texts produced by non-Muslim contemporaries, sheds fascinating light on the Qur'an and its relation to biblical literatures.

For the purposes of the present chapter, one piece of documentary evidence preserved in Muslim sources will have to suffice to illustrate the point. In the past half-century, a document known as "the compact of Medina" has come to be accepted as authentic by virtually all historians of early Islam, Muslims and non-Muslims alike. It is thus deemed to be an accurate reflection of the social and political conditions that prevailed in the Arabian oasis of Yathrib (later named Medina) that Muhammad and his followers colonized after fleeing persecution in Mecca around the year 622 C.E.

It is a remarkable document. First, it is contemporary with the Qur'an—or at least parts of the holy book. Second, it names the Arab tribes that populated the oasis when Muhammad and his beleaguered followers arrived there; it also records their religious affiliations. They were mostly Jews. Third, it enunciates the principles according to which Muhammad's followers and the Arab-Jewish residents of the village were to cohabit the town. Two main principles emerge from the text: one governing the day-to-day affairs of the people and another governing the community's response to external threats. As for daily life, each religious community was free to conduct its affairs without interference from the others. Nevertheless, they all together formed a single *umma*, or community. In the event that the town should come under attack—a circumstance that the compact of Medina appears to anticipate as imminent—all distinctions within the community would be put aside and the people of the town would band together in common defense.

The significance of this document for the interpretation of the Qur'an, the view of human nature one finds within it, and an understanding of the Prophet Muhammad's vision of a just community cannot be overestimated. It is, in fact, a key to understanding the place of the Qur'an in the literary history of the ancient Near East. When the Qur'an is read in light of the compact of Medina, and vice versa, the two documents suggest how it represents a particular response to the conditions under which it was likely to have been produced. What the Qur'an purports to disclose under these circumstances is nothing less than the divine plan that underlies human history and, with it, humanity's true nature. The division of humanity into sects and tribes that had been a perennial source of conflict prior to the arrival of the Prophet Muhammad is revealed, *sub specie aeternitatis*, as a piece of divine wisdom: "Oh Humanity! Know that We have created you from male and female and made you races and tribes in order that you may gain insight through mutual acquaintance; for truly the most noble among you in the sight of God are those who stay conscious of the divine; indeed, God knows all and is all-aware" (Qur'an 49:13). Here the Qur'an implies that the biblical story of the Tower of Babel tragically misreads human differences: the true effect of those differences (starting with differences in gender) is a particular kind of knowledge (translated above as "insight") acquired through intimate and reciprocal relations.

This celebration of difference and the underlying human equality that it implies is a theme that runs throughout the Qur'an. Indeed, the revision (re-vision) of biblical motifs and themes is one of the most characteristic means by which the Qur'an tells its story. In at least a dozen places, the

Qur'an proclaims that it is a "confirmation of the truth" of the biblical revelation (see Qur'an 2:42, 2:89, 2:91, 2:97, 2:101, 3:3, 3:81, 4:47, 5:48, 6:92, 35:31, 46:12), but it confirms that truth through the allusive retelling of vignettes familiar to its audience from biblical literatures. In the process of retelling such vignettes, the Qur'an selectively interprets many of them anew. It is on this account that many Muslims began to regard the Qur'an as a replacement for biblical literatures and to speak of the latter as having been "corrupted" by their custodians. But this does not appear to be the Qur'an's position at all. Instead, the Qur'an presumes a thorough knowledge of biblical literatures on the part of its audience; without that thorough knowledge, its original audience would have no way of knowing the transformation it was attempting to bring about in their understanding of biblical motifs and themes.

In the sections to follow, we shall revisit a number of those motifs and themes and elucidate how the Qur'an appropriates them for its own purposes. We hope to make clear the distinct alternative that the Qur'an and its interpretive traditions pose to the theories of human nature that have been inferred from biblical literatures.

METAPHYSICAL BACKGROUND: THE ISLAMIC CONCEPTION OF GOD

The Qur'an and its interpretive traditions do not argue for monotheism; they simply assume it. There is only one divine being, Allah. "Allah" is not a proper name for God (as, for example, "Zeus"); it is, rather, the elision of two Arabic words: the definite article *al-* (in English, "the") and a noun, *ilah*, which is cognate with the ancient Semitic form *el*, meaning "a god." The combination of these two words produces "Allah" or, in English, "the god." Arabic-speaking Christians, Jews, and Muslims all refer to their god as Allah. Muslims understand Allah to be the god of all monotheists regardless of religious affiliation.

Like his counterpart in biblical literatures, Allah is the Creator of the universe who communicates with humankind by means of prophets and messengers. Such figures are chosen by God at various times in history and tasked with reminding the communities to which they belong that God has expectations of them. The form that the prophetic reminder takes depends upon the community in question and its particular needs (as God sees them). The Qur'an and Islamic traditions assert the prophetic vocation of a variety of saintly figures found in biblical literatures, as well as other figures whose stories were handed down, presumably through oral traditions. So, for example, Moses brought his community a system of laws; Jesus and his mother, on the other hand, worked miracles (Mary's miracle was to conceive Jesus while yet chaste) and taught their community through their sagacity and the purity of their personal example. Muslims revere all of the figures that their traditions deem to be prophets. But the Qur'an and its interpretive traditions are adamant that such reverence must never transgress the line that is said to distinguish reverence from worship. For Muslims, worship is due to God alone.

In its insistence upon God's "unity" or "oneness" (*tawhid*), the Islamic conception of monotheism is uncompromising. For the Qur'an, the Christian doctrine of the Trinity is an ontological impossibility. Insisting that there is a distinction to be made between reverence for the prophets and worship of God, Islamic traditions implicitly criticize the Christian doctrine of the Incarnation of Christ. Today, many Christians regard Muslim intransigence on this point as a definitive barrier to interreligious dialogue, but this was not always the case. Lacking historical perspective on the development of their own dogma, many contemporary Christians are not aware of the internal politics, of the Church and the Roman Imperium, which ultimately decided the question of Christ's unique status as both human and divine. For several centuries, church authorities wrangled over what such statements as "Jesus is the Son of God" could possibly mean; and even when a negotiated settlement was eventually reached in western Europe, the churches on the eastern shores of the Mediterranean and in central Asia continued to espouse views on the nature of Christ that had been declared heretical in the Roman west.

The Qur'an's treatment of Jesus retains some of the flavor of these church polemics. Indeed, it appears, at some level, to participate in them: "Truly, in God's sight, Jesus was like Adam whom God created from dust and then said to him: 'Be!' And so he was. The truth of the matter comes from your Lord, so do not be found among those who argue about this" (Qur'an 3:59–60).

By employing the logic of the biblical tale of the creation of Adam, the Qur'an is able to affirm both the "virgin birth" of Christ and his unadulterated humanity. After all, according to Jewish and Christian tradition, Adam, though he lacked human parents, was not a god but fully human. If one accepts the biblical tale as authoritative, it is plausible to conclude that Christ, who lacked one human parent, was also not a god but fully human.

After the Council of Chalcedon (451 C.E.) definitively pronounced Christ "truly God and truly man," Christian tradition in western Europe has tended to regard the Muslim view that Jesus was neither more nor less a man than Adam as a kind of "demotion" of Christ. But from the Islamic perspective, Christ is not demoted by comparison to Adam; instead, an uncompromising monotheism is embraced and the dignity of humankind is given its due. Muslims regard both Adam and Christ as prophetic figures;

therefore, both are considered to be exemplars of humanity at its finest and worthy of emulation. We shall return to the Qur'an's treatment of Adam in the next section; but before we leave this discussion of metaphysics, it is important to acknowledge a difficulty that Islamic monotheism creates for itself and to review how Muslims have attempted to address that difficulty.

For Muslims, Allah's uniqueness implies incomparability. Not only do they insist that God cannot be compared to anyone or anything found in creation, but they also have made this insistence an article of faith. Unlike the Christian church, however, Muslims have expended very little effort on the production of catechisms, confessions, and creeds. One enters the Islamic community (the *umma*) by means of a public profession that there is "only one God and Muhammad is God's messenger." Such a bare-bones affirmation of monotheism and Muhammad's prophethood—combined with a historic aversion to centralized authority in matters of belief and practice—has left Muslims free to hold a wide variety of opinions about all manner of questions, both secular and religious. Consequently, Muslim intellectual traditions have allowed rich veins of speculation. However, on the question of divine uniqueness, traditional formulas (derived from the Qur'an) emphasize that not only is God "one" but there is nothing to which God may be compared and no one who may be regarded as God's equal. As unproblematic as this may appear on the surface, it leaves one with the question "Who or what is God?" If comparison to anything found in creation is impossible, this question is unanswerable except by a tautology: God is God.

Despite this conundrum, the Qur'an itself assures its audience that God is just and compassionate, all-knowing, all-wise, and so forth. Indeed, the Qur'an and the oral traditions believed by Muslims to have been handed down from the Prophet Muhammad himself (**hadith**) offer anthropomorphic descriptions of Allah that have puzzled Muslim intellectuals from the earliest days of the faith. One particularly enigmatic example from the Qur'an will illustrate the point: "Everything comes to ruin except God's face" (Qur'an 28:88). The mystical implications of this statement are certainly intriguing, and Muslim pietists have taken this verse to mean that, ultimately, only God is real. If that is the case, then everything one experiences in the natural world—everything subject to destruction or decay—may be compared to the passing shadows in Plato's cave. But why does the Qur'an talk of the "face" of God? Traditional commentary on this passage has encompassed a broad spectrum of interpretations from literalistic anthropomorphism (God, like human beings, has a face) to the metaphorical (God's "face" is an expression indicating the divine "essence"). Since there is no central authority responsible for endorsing an "orthodox" or correct interpretation of the sacred texts of Islam, there is no final answer to this puzzle.

Such indeterminacy in a matter as central to a theistic tradition as "who or what is God" is an obvious source of anxiety for adherents of that tradition. It should come as no surprise then that the problem of anthropomorphic descriptions of Allah has played a role in the development of Islamic traditions that is roughly analogous to the problems faced by Jews and Christians when attempting to describe God and that Christians have struggled with in understanding what it means to say that Christ is "truly God and truly man." There are deep differences between literal and metaphorical understandings of religious statements, as we saw in Chapter 6.

THEORY OF HUMAN NATURE

A key to understanding the Islamic view of human nature can be found in the Muslim reverence for Adam as a prophet, for his elevated status in Islamic traditions contrasts with his treatment in Christian dogma after the second century C.E. In that century Irenaeus, the influential bishop of Lyons, entered into a fierce controversy with Gnostic Christians. In disputing their remarkably pessimistic attitude toward human nature in general and bodily existence in particular, the bishop opened up a line of argument that would eventually find dogmatic expression as the doctrine of original sin. Biblical literatures are innocent of this notion, but the church fathers developed it from an observation of human fallibility into an imputation of universal guilt that human beings inherit as a consequence of Adam and Eve's disobedience to God in the Garden of Eden. In what appears to be a conscious refutation of this Christian view (which Jews have never adopted), the Qur'an qualifies its repeated warnings that God punishes sin with the added assurance that divine wrath will be meted out only for the sins that each individual has committed himself or herself (see, e.g., Qur'an 37:38–39).

The Qur'an also revisits the biblical tale of Adam and Eve and, in the course of retelling the story, characteristically revises it. Where the Genesis version features a wily serpent that confuses Eve as to God's precise instructions about what fruit is forbidden—and she, in turn, convinces her husband to transgress the divine command—the Qur'an identifies Satan (not a serpent) as the *couple's* tempter (the Arabic utilizes the grammatical dual, indicating that both husband and wife transgress together). Then Adam receives a revelation "from his Lord," marking him as a prophet, and the text indicates that he "turns" to God (or God to him), a term that, in Qur'anic usage, indicates forgiveness of sin (Qur'an 2:35–38; see also 7:19–25 and 20:117–124). In other words, instead of sin becoming part of the inheritance of humankind due to Adam's "fall," forgiveness is offered to a repentant Adam, for Allah is "the One who turns, the Merciful."

The Qur'an's version of this tale raises at least two issues that require further consideration. First, we are told explicitly that Adam repented his transgression and achieved the rank of prophet. But what became of Eve? Second, does the Qur'an (or its interpretive traditions) offer an explanation as to why our fabled first parents were unable to resist Satan's suggestions?

When addressing the first question, it is fair to acknowledge that the grammar of Qur'anic Arabic relieves Eve of the burden that she has carried in traditional Jewish and Christian renderings of this tale: that of the temptress and/or Satan's dupe. But the question of what becomes of Eve once the two have transgressed God's commandment is left unanswered. The grammar of the passages in question shifts abruptly from the dual ("both of you") to the second-person plural ("you all"). It is as if the divine voice turns to address persons not present in the story. When it does so, it tells them to leave paradise, some as enemies to others. Does God address all of humanity with these words? Is the Qur'an implicitly addressing its audience?

As for the second question, the Qur'an tells us that God made an agreement with Adam but that Adam forgot his obligation and did not intend to break their covenant (Qur'an 20:115). Eve's state of mind, on the other hand, is not mentioned in the text. It is difficult to know what to make of the Qur'an's relative silence as to Eve. Is there gender bias at work? This is not a question to dismiss lightly. That said, other women (such as Mary, mother of Jesus) do receive more extensive coverage in the Qur'an and its interpretive traditions. Therefore, when considering the Qur'an's references to this archetypal tale of the history of sin, the most that one can say with confidence is that Eve's role in that history is understated when compared to her role in both Jewish and Christian legend.

Adam's prominent role in the Qur'anic version of this story is picked up by later Islamic traditions that pair him with Muhammad: the two become the "alpha and omega" of a different history—the history of prophecy. For Muslims, the significance of prophecy lies in the belief not only that God communicates with humankind through selected representatives but also that those representatives are themselves emblematic of a belief in human perfectibility. In the next section we shall consider how the Qur'an and its interpretive traditions offer human nature itself as a foundation for that belief.

DIAGNOSIS

A distinguished Pakistani-American professor of Islamic studies at the University of Chicago, Fazlur Rahman, once noted that, while the Qur'an mentions Allah more than 2,500 times, its great and persistent theme is not God but humankind. The Qur'an offers itself as "guidance" for humanity but guidance presented in the form of "reminders." Indeed, one of the Qur'an's own epithets for itself is "the Reminder" (16:44). This implies that the holy book should not be understood as a source for new information about God or about humankind: its mission, and that of the Prophet who brought it, is to jog the memory of its audience, to refresh its recollection about matters it already knows but has forgotten.

Such a claim may strike the reader as remarkable given the Muslim view that the Qur'an constitutes a divine "revelation." But, as we have seen, the Qur'an's relationship to biblical literatures is revisionary. This is analogous to the relationship that the New Testament bears to Jewish scripture. It is therefore useful to think of the Qur'an as presenting its readers with a "third testament" rather than an entirely new system of religious thought and practice.

For Muslims, a "third testament" became necessary when, in their view, readers of the second, or "new," testament began to conflate the messenger (i.e., Jesus of Nazareth) with the message (his teachings about Mosaic law and his pious example) in such a way that the messenger *became* the message. The Qur'an clearly regards Christian deification of Jesus as a serious mistake (see, e.g., Qur'an 5:72), but the source of this error is ultimately like that of many human errors: the tendency to forget. As we have seen, the Qur'an's illustration of this very human tendency is Adam; and in what may be a subtle echo of St. Paul's archetypal use of Adam ("the figure of him that was to come," Romans 5:14), subsequent tradition connects Adam to Muhammad and all the prophets (including Jesus) who came between. In Islamic terms, "salvation" is achieved through individual emulation of prophetic example: conforming one's behavior to the *sunnah*, or practice of the prophets. Even prophets can be forgetful and make mistakes, but, like Adam, they never *intend* to break their covenant with God.

What all of humanity inherits from Adam, then, is not "original sin" but, rather, this covenant, according to which Allah offers guidance to Adam and his progeny. In addition, the Qur'an indicates that God's covenant invests Adam and his progeny with a unique role in creation: that of **khalifa**, God's designated representative on Earth (see, e.g., Qur'an 2:30). We shall examine both of these aspects of the divine covenant with humankind.

As we have seen, Muslims believe that Allah guides humankind by means of prophetic reminders; yet not everyone chooses to follow the guidance offered. Many who fail to follow Allah's guidance do so, like Adam, out of forgetfulness. In addition, Muslims apportion some of the blame for evil to the wiles of Satan (as in the Garden); but the Qur'an also indicates that some individuals intentionally fail to follow divine guidance, whether or not they are tempted to do so by Satan. Consequently, Muslim legal and ethical reflection emphasizes the role of intention (*niyah*) when assigning praise or blame to a given act. The discernment of intention, however, raises new questions. If Muslims are unwilling to adopt a doctrine of original sin, how are they to account for bad intent? Turning back to the Qur'an, one discovers that the origins of evil are not systematically explored there. The existence of evil (like the existence of God) is merely assumed; where it originates is unclear. Speculation on this matter—including God's potential complicity in the origins of evil— occupied some of the brightest minds of early Islam over the course of several centuries. That said, our present concern is with the part played by humanity in this cosmic drama, for the ways in which the Qur'an and its interpreters discussed human motivation in this context shed light on the Muslim view of human nature.

The Qur'an's approach to human nature relies upon a vocabulary it shares with both biblical literatures and early Arabic poetry. Two key terms dominate the discussion: *nafs*, typically translated into English as "self" or "soul," and *ruh*, literally "breath" or "wind" but also used to indicate an angelic figure or divine quality. In the Qur'an itself, these two terms are used separately; over time, however, Muslims began to use them interchangeably and fleshed out their meanings with Christian, Neoplatonic, and Aristotelian conceptions.

Generally speaking, the Qur'anic *nafs* functions like Plato's "appetitive soul." It has a tendency to desire the beautiful things that this world has to offer, preferring them to God's pleasure (Qur'an 18:28). It is thus liable to command an individual to do evil (Qur'an 12:53). "Evil" is not a quality that inheres in human beings; it is the consequence of actions taken in pursuit of particular desires. In themselves, those desires are perfectly natural, and their moral quality depends, again, on an individual's intentions and whether their satisfaction is consistent with one's role as *khalifa*. It is important to note, moreover, that the Qur'an does not consider human beings helpless in the face of their desires: they are not obliged to heed their *nafs*. Instead, they are called upon to restrain them (Qur'an 79:40–41). We shall elaborate upon this theme in our discussion of the term *khalifa*.

Non-Muslims typically associate the term *khalifa* with the political history of postprophetic Muslim society. In that context, it is a title conferred upon the successor to Muhammad as temporal leader of the community ("caliph"). But the word appears in several passages of the Qur'an itself. At Qur'an 2:30–34, God informs the angels at creation that he will place upon the earth a *khalifa*, and the context clearly indicates Adam. God then teaches Adam the names of all things in creation, and Adam, in turn, instructs the angelic host with the knowledge that he has obtained from God. When he completes the lesson, God orders the angels to bow down before Adam—something that they would ordinarily be expected to do before God alone. Presumably, this gesture is designed to demonstrate to the heavenly host in dramatic fashion that Adam has received a powerful appointment by God: he effectively stands in the divine "shoes," as it were. Human beings are God's deputies on Earth. This notion differs from the grant of "dominion" to Adam in the biblical book of Genesis insofar as Muslims hold that dominion belongs to Allah alone. He is *rabb*, or lord and sustainer of the universe, while the human being is his *'abd*, or vassal, who may exercise authority on Earth only by proxy. This view suggests that human beings must be mindful of their actions since, in theory, they have not been given free reign to do as they wish. When a human being acts, divine honor or dignity is at stake, and God is anxious that his honor not be tarnished by the misdeeds of his servants.

At Qur'an 38:26, King David is also addressed by God as *khalifa* and is told, as a consequence, that he must judge between people with truth "and not follow your desires lest they lead you astray from the path of Allah." In this passage we observe an explicit connection made between the role of *khalifa* and the restraint of desires that, if followed, would lead to unjust results. The *khalifa*, like anyone else, must learn to cope with *nafs* in order to remain on the path of godliness.

In a third passage (6:165), the Qur'an indicates that the term *khalifa* is not limited to prophetic figures like Adam and David. Instead, the narrative voice of the Qur'an addresses its audience and describes God as "the One who has made all of you the *khala'if* [plural of *khalifa*] of the earth, and has elevated some of you above others by a degree, in order that He might test you by what you have received. Truly your Lord is swift to requite and truly He is a forgiving and merciful God." Here one is reminded of the words that Luke's Gospel places on the lips of Jesus: "for of those to whom much has been given, much shall be required" (Luke 12:48).

In the Muslim religious imagination, the role of *khalifa* is not limited to prophets or to Muhammad's political successors: it is the high office to which God appointed Adam and, through him, all humankind. Some of Adam's progeny appear to have been gifted with a more favored station in this regard than others—but unfortunately, the Qur'an does not elaborate on this rather cryptic remark. It does make clear, however, that God intends such gifts to test the mettle of their recipients. One cannot help but wonder if the "degree of elevation" enjoyed compensates for the measure of advantage—if advantage is what is contemplated here: for "truly your Lord is swift to requite."

It is interesting to note that the Qur'an employs similar terminology when discussing the relationship between divorced husbands and wives. At 2:228, newly divorced women are advised to avoid sexual intercourse for a period of three menstrual cycles. One obvious reason for this waiting period is that, in the case of pregnancy, paternity would be assigned to the former spouse; the passage also suggests that the parties may become reconciled at this time. The Qur'an then states, "And to the women belongs equitable treatment like that which belongs to the men [literally, those who are against them in the divorce], and men have a degree over women, and God is mighty and wise."

Contrary to what one might expect, this passage has generated very little commentary over the past fifteen centuries. Muslim exegetes find its meaning clear and uncontroversial: women and men are entitled to equitable treatment under the law, and what constitutes equitable treatment under the law for women mirrors what constitutes equitable treatment for men—with this seemingly enigmatic caveat: that "men have a degree over women." The obvious question is, "A degree of what?" Employing the traditional rule that one part of the Qur'an interprets another, the caveat arguably indicates a "degree of elevation" intended by God to test the fairness of the man who would divorce his wife, rather than a general superiority of men over women. The Qur'an elsewhere proclaims that God assigns degrees "to everyone according to what they have done in order that He may repay them for their actions" (46:19; see also 6:132).

As with any passage of the Qur'an, we can never be certain what it meant to its original audience. From the commentary tradition, we can acquire insight into what a given passage meant to subsequent generations. Generally speaking, the statement that "men have a degree over women" has been narrowly construed: it is not a declaration of innate male superiority, for if it were, the prior statement that women are entitled to equitable treatment mirroring that of men would contradict the order of nature. Instead, reference is frequently made to the fact that, at the time of marriage, a man pays his wife a dowry and, during their married life, he is expected to support his wife financially. At the time of divorce, these expenditures merit consideration. Such concerns probably reflect the development of Muslim jurisprudence in the postprophetic period.

PRESCRIPTION

Notions concerning a divinely ordained "natural order" abound in the Qur'an, but like monotheism and the existence of evil, they are presumed rather than argued. Taking their cue from a rather obscure passage (Qur'an 30:30), Muslim thinkers have posited the existence of an "inner nature" (*fitra*) inclined toward God. As we have seen, human beings also possess an appetitive dimension (*nafs*) that may lead an individual astray from the path of God. But neither the Qur'an nor its interpretive traditions regard any human being as helpless in the face of his or her desires. We are enjoined to use our best efforts to restrain desire in the pursuit of God's pleasure.

In addition, the *hadith* literature recognizes the formative role of environment in the shaping of personality: "Every infant is born according to the *fitra*; then his parents make him a Jew or a Christian or a Magian." According to this prophetic saying, one's religious tradition is best understood as an accident of upbringing. Presumably, this principle should apply as well to those who are brought up as Sunni or Shi'a Muslims, but this author has encountered translations of the *hadith* in which Muhammad is quoted as saying "Every infant is born Muslim." Such an interpretation conflates Islamic traditions with human nature and introduces a subtle change into the apparent meaning of the *hadith*. Thus transformed, it provides a handy proof text for Muslims hoping to encourage non-Muslims to convert (or "revert") to Islam, but it is unfaithful to the wording of the Arabic text.

Conversionary applications aside, Islamic traditions contemplate human nature as a complex amalgam of intentions and desires, some of which lead one toward the divine and others which lead one astray. By themselves, none of these intentions or desires necessarily determines how a given individual will conduct her or his life. Moreover, circumstance plays an important role in every human life, but this factor, too, does not necessarily determine the final outcome. Ultimately, that outcome would appear to depend on God's inscrutable will (see, e.g., Qur'an 2:213).

Like many Christians, Muslims believe that God loves them and has a plan for their lives. The particulars of that plan, however, are unknown. The Qur'an and its interpretive traditions provide Muslims with what the New Testament memorably terms a great "cloud of witnesses" (Hebrews 12:1): prophetic exemplars beginning with Adam and ending with Muhammad. **Sharia**, misunderstood by many in the West as a kind of legal code, is an ideal of life lived according to prophetic example. Devout Muslims meditate upon the examples set by Muhammad and other prophetic figures (including Abraham, Joseph, Moses, and Jesus) as those examples have been preserved for them in a vast body of devotional literature (which includes the Qur'an and *hadith*). **Fiqh** (confused with sharia by many in the West) is not a legal code either but, instead, a highly specialized discipline of interpretation in which Muslim scholars attempt to apply rules derived from stories of the prophets (and rules derived from rules derived from those stories, etc.) in particular cases. Such scholarship has produced another vast layer of literature, which we may call "legal," although the Islamic conception of law is an expansive one and covers not only questions of legality per se (what constitutes a crime, what constitutes fair business practices, how one may inherit property from a deceased family member, etc.) but also questions of etiquette, ritual practice, personal hygiene, and much else. One could say that devout Muslims attempt to fill in the blanks of the divine plan as it applies to them in their individual lives by attending, as best they can, to particular lessons drawn from these complex literary sources. But that is not all: traditions of Muslim piety (including **Sufism**) offer further examples to emulate. Such examples are typically conveyed by means of stories in the "lives of the saints" genre: traditions concerning holy men and women (imams, master dervishes, shaykhs, and shaykhahs) whose exemplary characters demonstrate that the ideal of human perfectibility is a worthy goal and may be pursued by any person regardless of race, gender, tribe, or sect. Muslims who choose to emulate these individuals presumably desire to discipline their *nafs* and discover their "inner *khalifa*."

Rooted as it is in the Qur'anic tale of Adam, the *khalifa* ideal is regarded by Muslims as universal: "Humankind is a single community (*umma*), so God has raised up prophets: bearers of glad tidings and bearers of warning. Moreover, God has equipped the prophets with true scripture in order that it might judge between the people concerning the matters over which they differ" (Qur'an 2:213). Here, as throughout the Qur'an, we encounter the twin themes of human solidarity and difference, held in tension, with the prophets and their revelations providing criteria by which human differences may be sorted out. This would appear to be the theory of human relations and prophetic intervention implicit in the compact of Medina. Furthermore, the remainder of this passage contends (not without irony) that the prophets have delivered their messages with clear arguments designed to settle such disagreements, but those who received the scripture, driven by selfish desires, have differed among themselves as to its meaning. Therefore, God intervenes to guide those who trust him (by his will) to the truth.

CONCLUDING REMARKS

The Qur'an and its interpretive traditions present the reader with a broadly biblical yet fairly straightforward and comprehensive theory of human nature. This theory is characterized by competing elements that exist in tension: individual and environment (or society), unity and diversity within human society itself, ungodly desires and inclination to follow the divine will. Into this world of competing tensions, God has sent prophets and saints to guide those who would lead a life worthy of the high calling for which the human being was created: the *khalifa* ideal. But despite this divine intervention, human history shows how the vast majority of people on the planet have failed to live up to God's best hopes for them. In the end, it is God who guides those whom he chooses to his path.

In one respect, the story that Muslims tell one another about the human species is optimistic: men and women are not "fallen" by nature, and they are not predisposed to displease their Creator. On the other hand, "fallen" or not, men and women do displease God with remarkable consistency and are ultimately dependent upon his mercy for salvation. The biblical overtones of this message are unmistakable, and those who reject the God of biblical literatures will not find much comfort in the message of the Muslim's "third testament." That said, the world contains billions of individuals who claim to embrace, in some fashion, a biblical deity; and for them the Qur'an and its interpretive traditions present an opportunity to revisit, if not rethink, what it is that they believe about God and humankind and why they find those beliefs compelling. If this chapter has succeeded in provoking such thoughtfulness, it will have fulfilled its author's objective in writing it. Moreover, it will have permitted the Qur'an itself to live up to its claim to be an aid for reflection (Qur'an 16:44).

FURTHER READING

M. A. S. Abdel Haleem, trans., The Qur'an (Oxford: Oxford University Press, 2004).

In Oxford University Press's Very Short Introduction series, Jonathan A. C. Brown, *Muhammad* (2011), Michael Cook, *The Koran* (2000), Malise Ruthven, *Islam* (2000), and Adam J. Silverstein, *Islamic History* (2010).

L. Carl Brown, *Religion and State: The Muslim Approach to Politics* (New York: Columbia University Press, 2001), reviews both the premodern and modern history of Muslim political ideas and state formation and, in the process, exposes their rich diversity. The slogan that there can be no separation of "church and state" in Islam receives little support from the historical record of Muslim societies.

Fred McGraw Donner, *Muhammad and the Believers: At the Origins of Islam*, (Cambridge, MA: Harvard University Press, 2010). A measured but critical investigation of the rise of the early Muslim community in light of the best historical evidence presently available.

John L. Esposito, *Islam: The Straight Path* (Oxford: Oxford University Press, 2010). Now in its fourth edition, this is a very popular and competent treatment of the subject.

Wael B. Hallaq, *The Origins and Evolution of Islamic Law* (Cambridge: Cambridge University Press, 2005). Concise and readable introduction to the development of Muslim jurisprudence.

Marshall G. S. Hodgson, *The Venture of Islam*, 3 vols. (Chicago: University of Chicago Press, 1977). A comprehensive and scholarly approach to the subject that remains the gold standard in the field. Published prior to the Iranian revolution of 1978–1979, the third volume is in need of an update.

Charles Kurzman, *Liberal Islam: A Sourcebook* (Oxford: Oxford University Press, 1998). A collection of primary source materials documenting Muslim engagement with questions of democracy and pluralism throughout the twentieth century. For a more current perspective, regularly consult http://english.aljazeera.net/.

Fazlur Rahman, *Major Themes of the Qur'an* (Minneapolis: Bibliotheca Islamica, 1994). An accessible study of the Qur'an by an important modernist scholar of the late twentieth century.

Annemarie Schimmel, *Mystical Dimensions of Islam* (Chapel Hill: University of North Carolina Press, 1975). See especially Chapter 4, "Man and His Perfection."

KEY TERMS

fiqh	**sharia**
fitra	**Shi'a**
hadith	**Sufism**
khalifa	**Sunnis**
niyah	*tawhid*
Qur'an	*umma*

QUESTIONS FOR DISCUSSION

1. How does the "*khalifa* ideal" relate to the Islamic notion of prophethood?
2. How does the "*khalifa* ideal" relate to the Islamic notion of *fitra*?
3. Compare and contrast the "*khalifa* ideal" to some of the other approaches to human nature that you have encountered in this book. How, for example, is that ideal similar to the way of the Confucian sages or to the path of the Buddha? How is it different?
4. Are you persuaded that the Qur'an's approach to the problem of evil is adequate? If so, in what ways is it adequate? If not, how is it inadequate?
5. Do you think that the Islamic community's historic inability to create a centralized authority responsible for determining an "orthodox" interpretation of the Qur'an helps or hinders the articulation and maintenance of the "*khalifa* ideal"?

Historical Interlude

In our selection of theories of human nature we are jumping over a long historical gap from the ancient worlds of China, India, Palestine, Greece, and Rome to eighteenth-century Europe. In this introductory book concentrating on human nature we cannot offer comprehensive coverage of intellectual history, but it should aid readers' understanding of Kant and subsequent theories if we provide some thumbnail sketches of major intellectual developments in the intervening centuries.

THE MIDDLE AGES: WHAT PART DOES REASON PLAY IN FAITH?

Augustine (354–430)

In the fourth century Emperor Constantine adopted Christianity as the state religion; and thus, it made the transition from persecuted minority into the power structure of the Roman Empire and subsequently of medieval Europe.

St. Augustine formed the most crucial connecting link between the thought of the ancient world and the Christian worldview that was to dominate the next millennium in Europe. He came from North Africa, then part of the Roman Empire; he had a Christian mother but did not start out as a Christian himself. He was trained in the Roman tradition of rhetoric (public speaking), and he avidly studied the writings of the Manicheans, who held that there are twin powers of good and evil, and the Neoplatonists, who extended Plato's ideas in a mystical religious direction. After contact with influential Christians in Milan and studying the Bible for himself, Augustine converted to Christianity after a prolonged intellectual and moral struggle that he famously describes in his *Confessions*. He was ordained as a priest and was soon pressed into service as a bishop.

Augustine's deep and extensive writings made a synthesis of Christianity and Platonic ideas (he had little knowledge of Aristotle). He was strongly influenced by the Neoplatonist philosopher Plotinus, who saw a quasi-Platonic God as the source of everything that exists, and human beings as capable of inner spiritual illumination. These conceptions could readily be integrated with Judaic belief in God as Creator, and the Christian gospel of salvation. Augustine, when converted, saw reason as subservient to faith. In a famous phrase he said, "I believe in order to understand," by which he meant that reason alone cannot reach the most important truths; he saw the will, the disposition of the whole person, as crucial.

Augustine had a strong belief in human free will, but an even stronger sense of human sinfulness. He held that nothing we can do by ourselves can reconcile us to God. Mired in original sin, we cannot free ourselves from it by our own efforts. Only God's free action, his unmerited **grace**, can save us; moreover Augustine tended to the extreme view that if some are saved (indeed "predestined" by God's choice or "election") while others are not, this is not because of any individual merit. Augustine defended these views in a famous controversy with Pelagius (the first thinker from the British Isles to appear in history), who maintained that basically we save ourselves by our free choice and right action. A church council condemned Pelagius' view as heretical, but the relation between human freedom and divine grace remains a crucial problem for theology. According to a compromise known as "semi-Pelagianism," our free choice is a necessary, but not a sufficient, condition of salvation, God's grace being the other condition. (But if we make the right choice, why would His grace be withheld?)

Augustine's sense of human sin as manifest in our bodily desires had a baneful influence on much subsequent Christian thought, which tended to see our sexuality as the primary exemplification of sin. There was a tendency to devalue women as (supposedly) more involved with unspiritual bodily matters than men, and to regard marriage as inferior to celibacy. Augustine himself had had a concubine and a son before conversion, but afterwards he maintained the austere view that sexual intercourse, even in marriage, is legitimate only for the purpose of procreation.

He had a strong sense of history and divine providence, and made a famous distinction between "the City of Man"—the temporal order of human society and power, represented in his time by the Roman Empire in its unstable last years—and "the City of God"—the ideal destiny in which God's will is eventually fulfilled. (The Romanized Christian Church has occupied an ambiguous position between these two as an imperfect human institution, developing along with secular history and exercising power for better or for worse, yet believed by its devotees to embody God's purpose.) Augustine had a very strong belief in the authority of the Church and the importance of its unity: when a division emerged with the "Donatist" Christians in North Africa, he was prepared to use the civil powers to enforce conformity.

The Islamic Philosophers

After the rapid Muslim conquest of the Middle East and North Africa, a great flowering of Islamic civilization took place in the ninth to thirteenth centuries. In this period Islamic theology, philosophy, science, and medicine were more advanced than in medieval Europe. Islamic scholars developed intellectual systems that tried to combine Greek philosophy with religious faith (as did their Jewish and Christian contemporaries). An influential tradition of Islamic **mystical** spirituality developed in the Sufi movement (which still survives). For a while there was some fruitful contact between the rival civilizations, and the writings of Aristotle that had been lost to the West were rediscovered from Muslim scholars via the translators at Toledo in central Spain, then on the border between the Christian and Muslim worlds.

Islamic thought resembles ancient Judaism and medieval Christianity in assuming as an unquestionable premise the authority of a religious tradition based on a claimed divine revelation. But there emerged some hotly debated differences (comparable to those in the Jewish and Christian worlds) about the relation of reason to faith, and of individual religious experience to religious authority. Al-Hallaj was executed in the tenth century for proclaiming his Sufi belief in his attainment of mystical union with God, which was seen as blasphemous. Ibn Sina (Latin name Avicenna, 980–1037) used Aristotle's subtle distinction between active and passive elements within the human soul to give a two-level theory of "prophecy" or revelation. According to this, God spoke through the divine "active" intellect in the mind of Muhammad, whereas the more passive, imaginative side of the Prophet's mind expressed religious truths in terms of images or metaphors. Thus, for ibn Sina, imagery and metaphor are needed to persuade most human beings of religious truth, but philosophers can interpret the images in terms of higher spiritual truths. He expressed doubts about the literal truth of bodily resurrection, and his orthodoxy was questioned.

(There are parallels with some radical Christian thinking in recent times, including some of our comments in Chapter 6.)

Al-Ghazali (1058–1111) was a brilliant scholar who gave up his professorship in Baghdad for the life of a wandering ascetic and Sufi. In a book aggressively entitled *The Incoherence of the Philosophers* he criticized previous Islamic thinkers for being too influenced by Greek ideas and departing from Qur'anic orthodoxy. He made a striking anticipation of Hume's denial of the necessity of the cause–effect relation, and he used this to question metaphysical theories of God. He defended the Sufi appeal to religious experience rather than philosophical argument.

In Andalusia in Muslim Spain there was a redefense of philosophy by ibn Rushd (Latin name Averroes, 1126–1198). He argued that Muslims cannot avoid the use of reason because the text of the Qur'an needs rational interpretation and jurists tend to disagree on questions of law and ethics. He wrote a reply to al-Ghazali entitled *The Incoherence of "The Incoherence,"* arguing that it was inconsistent to use reason to subvert reliance on reason: he thus subordinated theology to philosophy again.

Ibn Sina and ibn Rushd had considerable influence on medieval Western thought. In the twelfth and thirteenth centuries, there developed a three-way debate between Islamic, Jewish, and Christian thinkers. The Jewish philosopher Maimonides (1135–1204) wrote a famous theological work entitled *Guide for the Perplexed*, and Aquinas read Maimonides. But this multiculturalism did not last: intolerance and conflict took over, and after the Reconquista of Spain by the Catholic monarchy in the fifteenth century, Jews and Muslims were forcibly expelled.

Aquinas (1224–1274)

As we have seen, most of the works of Aristotle did not become available to Christian Europe until the twelfth century. This produced a revolution within late medieval thought, even though some conservative Church authorities tried to suppress the new study of Aristotle. St. Thomas Aquinas's magnificent Christian systematization in his *Summa Theologica* was based on Aristotle's philosophy as well as the Bible and the church fathers. The *Summa* is like a medieval cathedral—an enormous, impressive structure of high religious aspiration, full of intricate detail that makes one marvel at the faith and the workmanship that produced it. Though controversial in its time, it has become Roman Catholic orthodoxy.

Aquinas allowed that the natural powers of human reason have a legitimate, if limited, place in the defense of Christian faith (something that Augustine and his late medieval followers like St. Bonaventure tended to deny). He held the Aristotelian, broadly **empiricist**, view that all human knowledge starts with sense perception; but he acknowledged that we have to use our intellect to recognize the types or "forms" of things and build up systematic knowledge of the world (like Kant—see Chapter 8). Crucially he distinguished between **rational theology** and **revealed theology**: in the former we can use unaided human reason to prove the *existence* of God (by his famous "Five Ways"); in the latter we receive, by **faith**, God's revelation of his *nature* through the Bible and the Church. But faith is not under the control of our will; it is infused in us by the grace of God.

On human nature Aquinas follows the Aristotelian analysis of our rational soul as consisting in our capacities for perception, intellectual conception, theoretical reasoning, and practical reasoning, resulting in exercise of our free will in action. He Christianizes Aristotle's conception of happiness by identifying our ultimate fulfillment as consisting in the knowledge and love of God. And he supplements the four classical Greek virtues of courage, temperance, prudence, and justice with the three theological virtues of faith, hope, and divine love (or "charity" in older translations), for which we need to receive divine illumination or grace.

On the question of immortality Aquinas retained, with dubious consistency, an element of Platonism along with his Aristotelian conception of the human soul, saying that although the resurrection involves the re-creation of the human being as a *union* of body and soul, the soul has a separate disembodied existence in the period between death and resurrection. This theory tries to maintain personal identity over the interim period, but it invites the question of how a disembodied soul can retain its identity.

Aquinas's *Summa* is a tour de force of intellectual organization, knowledge of sources, clarity of language and rational argument. His appeal to reason was nevertheless limited, for the authority of the Catholic Church remained paramount for him in all matters. Like Augustine, he was prepared to sanction the use of force against dissent: he wrote that those heretics who use their reason to produce perversions of the Christian faith may be "banished from the world by death" (*Summa Theologica*, II–II, Q.11, art. 3). His intellectual cathedral was built for the glory of God but also to buttress the Church, and in some of its darker corners a whiff of burning can still be detected. He did not quite finish his great construction, for in the last year of his life he experienced a mystical vision and said that all he had written now "seemed to him as straw."

THE REFORMATION: WHERE LIES THE AUTHORITY FOR FAITH?

Christianity was the dominant system of belief in Europe for some fifteen hundred years after Constantine's conversion, through the fall of Rome, the "Dark Ages" and the high medieval period, and into the modern world. Despite secular trends, it is still embedded in twenty-first-century Europe, America, and elsewhere round the globe. The popes of the Catholic Church inherited their center of power in Rome and retain it to this day. Eastern Orthodox Christianity developed separately in the Byzantine Empire, centered in Constantinople until the fall of that city to the Muslim Turks in 1453.

Four successive cultural movements of enormous historical importance developed in early modern Europe: the **Renaissance**, the **Reformation**, the rise of science, and the **Enlightenment**. In the Renaissance of the fifteenth and sixteenth centuries new attention was devoted to the pre-Christian literature, arts, and philosophy of the ancient world. The wisdom of the ancients was now read more directly, rather than through the prism of medieval Christianity, and it exerted a newly invigorating influence on Western thought. There arose a humanist style of philosophy concentrating more on human nature than on metaphysics or theology, in Pico della Mirandola in Italy and Erasmus of Rotterdam.

The religious Reformation is commonly reckoned to have started when Martin Luther (1483–1546) nailed ninety-five controversial theological propositions on a church door in Wittenberg, Germany, on November 1, 1517. But there had already been reforming voices in late medieval Europe, such as John Wycliffe in fourteenth-century England. Power was at stake, and dissent was sometimes violently suppressed: Wycliffe's follower John Huss was burned in Bohemia. Luther himself was a highly educated theologian in the Catholic tradition, but he began to question some of the ideas and practices of the Italian papacy. He vehemently opposed the Church's sale of "indulgences," by which people were led to think that they could *buy* divine forgiveness and a place in heaven by contributing to the papacy's lavish projects. The main theme of Luther's theology was the doctrine of **justification** by faith, by God's freely given grace, without the mediation of Church authority—and without appeal to reason, either (Luther notoriously condemned reason as a "whore.")

Luther was also something of a German nationalist, reacting against the power of Rome. He translated the Bible into German and wrote his controversial works in a witty and pithy language that many people could readily understand, and the new technology of printing enabled their wide distribution. The movement of religious reform spread rapidly across northern Europe, and the unity of the Western Church was shattered. A variety of different Protestant churches and sects developed, appealing to the Bible and to individual religious experience rather than the tradition of the Catholic Church. Translations of the Bible into the languages of the people became a crucial element in this new kind of spirituality. Until the Reformation the Bible had been available only to priests and theologians who could read Latin or Greek. Some of the early translators, such as William Tyndale, were burned by church authorities, who felt the threat to their own ecclesiastical power if everyone could read and interpret the sacred texts for themselves.

Appeal to scripture became the fundamental source of authority for Protestants, especially the Calvinist churches led by John Calvin (1509–1564), who summed up his theology in his *Institutes of the Christian Religion*. A theocratic Calvinist state (ruled by religious authority) was established in Geneva in Switzerland. Calvinism spread to Scotland, to the Puritan movement in England, and to America with the first settlers. There developed a doctrine of the infallibility of the Bible as the revealed word of God, but the question of who has the correct *interpretation* arises whenever readers disagree. Some of the more radical Protestant sects such as the Anabaptists on the Continent and the Quakers in England, though still strongly influenced by the New Testament, appealed to "the inner Light" of God's revelation in the individual mind or heart, thus placing most emphasis on individual religious experience.

Religious disagreements often spilled over into violent conflict. There were wars of religion in early modern Europe, often between Catholics and Protestants but also between rival Protestant sects. Luther appealed to the German rulers to suppress the Anabaptists by cruel force. The Huguenots (French Protestants) were seen as traitors to the French Catholic state and massacred or expelled. After the British civil war of the mid-seventeenth century the monarchy and the Anglican Church were restored, and religious "nonconformists" were persecuted for a while. Only gradually, after such painful experiences, did the European peoples begin to accept that different religions could be tolerated in the same country. A separation between church and state was enshrined in the new American Constitution in 1776.

THE RISE OF SCIENCE: HOW DOES SCIENTIFIC METHOD APPLY TO HUMAN BEINGS?

Modern physical science arose in the seventeenth century. The combination of experimental method with systematic mathematical theory was triumphantly demonstrated in the work of Galileo and Newton. The conspicuous explanatory success of the Newtonian system of mechanics showed how new knowledge about the universe, both in the heavens and on Earth, could be firmly established on the basis of mathematical laws of nature and carefully measured observations. Appeal could no longer be made to the authority of Aristotle, Bible or Church on matters of empirical fact about the workings of the physical world. The Catholic Church's brief attempt to retain a pre-Copernican Earth-centered cosmology in the face of the discoveries of Galileo was a last-ditch defense of the indefensible.

A more difficult problem (which still faces us today) was how far can scientific method be applied to *human beings*? To this question there often seem to be two starkly opposed answers, associated with the rival metaphysics of **materialism** and **dualism**. Are human beings entirely composed of the same kind of matter that makes up the rest of the universe and subject to the same laws of nature? (The laws were assumed to be deterministic until the advent of quantum mechanics in the twentieth century.) Or are we combinations of body and soul, where the latter is thought of as something immaterial, not subject to the laws of physical science, and supposedly leaving room for rationality and free will? These two metaphysical views were defended by Hobbes and Descartes, respectively. They still tend to dominate our own intellectual landscape, but we will see that Spinoza suggested a third way.

Hobbes (1588–1679)

The Englishman Thomas Hobbes published his most famous work *Leviathan* in 1651, in the period of the British civil war. It is one of the great classics of political philosophy, but his conclusions are derived from premises about individual human nature. Hobbes vehemently rejected dualism and medieval Aristotelianism and argued that the very notion of soul as incorporeal substance is self-contradictory. He espoused an uncompromising materialism about human nature, treating life as a motion of the limbs, sensations as motion within the bodily organs, and desires as the states of the body and brain that cause bodily movement. Hobbes's philosophy is one of the first to espouse a systematic **naturalism**, proposing to use the methods of the physical sciences to explain human nature and human society.

Hobbes had a bleak view of individual human nature as intrinsically selfish, each person's desires being for his or her own survival and reproduction. We look after our immediate family as part of human reproduction, but we have little or no concern for others. (This is a crude anticipation of Darwinian approaches that we consider in Chapter 12.) Humans are inevitably in competition with each other for food, land, and all other resources. So if there is no overarching power to keep order, people tend to resort to robbery and violence, and there is no security of property or life. In Hobbes's most quoted phrase, human life in "the state of nature" is "solitary, poor, nasty, brutish, and short." So he argued that there is a fundamental need for a state authority with effective monopoly of the use of force. Thus, it is in each person's self-interest to give up some individual freedom for the sake of security and to acknowledge the authority of whatever power is strong enough to enforce the rule of law (the law of the ruling power).

Hobbes's account of human nature is implicitly atheist. He could not openly say so in the seventeenth century, so we still find talk of God in his writings; but it seems inessential to his main argument, in which there is no appeal to divine creation, purpose, redemption, or judgment. For the sake of peace, he wanted to subordinate all churches to the authority of the state.

This is a good place to remind ourselves that the phrases "state of nature" and "human nature" are extremely ambiguous, as noted in our Introduction. Some early modern thinkers such as Thomas Hobbes, John Locke, and Jean-Jacques Rousseau tended to mean by "nature" the supposed nature of human beings before the advent of organized society. But there is every reason to believe that human beings (and our prehuman ancestors) have always been highly social creatures, and that the idea of individuals coming together to form society by a social contract is a myth, or an intellectual device to justify political authority.

Descartes (1596–1650)

The Frenchman René Descartes was a central figure in the scientific revolution of the seventeenth century, contributing crucially to the development of mathematics, physics, physiology, and philosophy. His scientific work has long been superseded, but his philosophical writings remain firmly on the syllabus, for they express fundamental conceptions and arguments that any philosopher needs to address.

What most concerns us here is Descartes's dualist account of human nature as consisting of body and soul—two distinct but interacting substances, each of which can exist without the other. In this he followed a long tradition including Plato, but he put a new gloss on the distinction and gave new arguments for it from the nature of consciousness. According to Descartes, the body occupies space and is subject to the laws of physical nature, but it has no mental properties. It is the mind or soul that thinks, feels, perceives, and decides (thereby exercising free will); it is not made of matter, does not occupy space (though it changes in time), and cannot be studied by the methods of physical science. Moreover, the soul can survive the death of the body, carrying the identity of a person into the afterlife. Descartes was thus led to make a sharp distinction between humans as possessing immaterial souls and animals as supposedly lacking consciousness.

In his *Discourse on Method* Descartes wrote a preliminary exposition of his ideas in semiautobiographical form. Expressed more carefully in the *Meditations*, his main argument for dualism starts from the reflection that whatever else one can doubt (at the initial stage of his argument he was prepared to cast doubt on all his former beliefs) one cannot doubt one's own existence as a conscious being, but one *can* (so he claimed) doubt whether one has a body. Descartes thus used his reason in a reflective, introspective way to try to prove the incorporeality of the soul, and he then argued (rather dubiously) from the nature of our ideas to the existence of God.

In Part V of the *Discourse* he offered a more empirical argument for dualism as the hypothesis that best explains the behavior of people and animals. He maintained a distinction of kind between the mental faculties of humans and other animals, focusing on language as a distinctive component of human rationality. It is this empirically based sort of rationalism, namely the assertion of certain innate mental capacities as peculiar to the human species, that Noam Chomsky renewed in the twentieth century (see Chapter 12). Having bifurcated human nature into two different metaphysical realms, Descartes (like many others) thought he could apply scientific method to study our bodies in anatomy and physiology, while remaining an orthodox Catholic believer in an infinite, immaterial God and a finite, immaterial, immortal soul with free will.

Spinoza (1632–1677)

Benedict de Spinoza lived in Amsterdam in Holland, descended from Jews expelled from Portugal after the fifteenth-century Christian Reconquista of the Iberian peninsula. He offered a possible compromise between the stark alternatives of dualism and materialism. In his main work, the *Ethics* (which actually contains more metaphysics than ethics), he identified God with the whole of nature. He retained some reverential talk of "God or Nature" but not the biblical conception of God as transcendent personal Creator of the whole of nature. This is **pantheism** rather than orthodox theism, and for it Spinoza was derided as a hideous atheist. He presented his arguments in quasi-mathematical form, with numbered theorems, proofs, and corollaries, but the content is philosophical. His technical apparatus of substances, attributes, and essences is difficult to understand; but it has an interesting intellectual descendant in twentieth-century philosophy of mind.

On the metaphysics of human nature, Spinoza developed an original theory that matter and mind are not two separate substances as Descartes argued. but two aspects of one underlying reality (indeed for Spinoza there is ultimately only one substance in his sense of the term, namely the whole of nature, which he calls "God"). This **dualism of attributes** rather than substances is also known as the "double-aspect theory of mind." According to a modern version, mental events can be identified with brain events: there are two different sets of concepts or properties (mental, in terms of the propositional contents of thoughts, and physical, in terms of neurophysiology), but they apply to the same set of events. This can be connected with the Aristotelian conception (Chapter 5) that the mind is what the functioning brain *does*.

Spinoza offered a more personal philosophy of life toward the end of the *Ethics*, distinguishing three stages of mental progress: from mere sense perception, through scientific knowledge, to the mystical state he called "blessedness" or "the intellectual love of God" in which one sees all things in the light of eternity. However, his views on biblical interpretation, on which he was a forerunner of modern historical approaches, were deemed heretical by his Jewish community, and he was expelled from his synagogue. There is a pattern down the ages of philosophers getting into trouble with religious authorities, from Socrates in ancient Greece through ibn Sina in medieval Islam to Spinoza, Rousseau, and Kant, as we will see.

THE ENLIGHTENMENT: CAN SCIENCE BE OUR GUIDE TO LIFE?

From the mid-seventeenth century onward, as science (exemplified above all by Newton) became widely accepted as the only way to gain knowledge of the material world, it was repeatedly suggested that we should apply the methods of science to human beings, to understand ourselves. In a widespread European intellectual movement centered in the eighteenth century the hope emerged that this might help us solve the problems of humanity. This **Enlightenment** can be briefly summed up as belief in the power of human reason to improve the human condition. (Proponents would say such a belief is justified by the success of science so far, but critics would say it is an unproved—or unprovable—*faith* in the power of science to explain everything.) It was widely thought that rationality, applied to the benefit of human individuals in medicine and education and to the reform of human society in economics and politics, could lead to hitherto undreamed-of progress. In its more extreme versions this became the claim that science can replace *all* other guides to life, such as religion, morality, social tradition, and the authority of monarchs.

The Enlightenment took somewhat different forms in the rival nation states of Europe. In Britain, which had been through the searing experience of civil war, there was a gradual evolution and piecemeal reform of society, and democracy was introduced in fits and starts. John Locke gave an empiricist account of the origin of all our ideas in experience in his *Essay Concerning Human Understanding* (1690). Though retaining dualism and theism, Locke appealed to reason and experience rather than to revealed religion. His political philosophy derived the need for government (and for limitations on its power) from individual human needs and rights, especially property rights. Locke's thought influenced the drafting of the American Constitution.

Hume (1711–1776)

One of the most seminal figures of the Enlightenment was the Scotsman David Hume. His magnum opus is the three-volume *Treatise of Human Nature* (1739–40), written when he was still in his twenties; later he wrote more popular expositions of his main ideas in his two *Enquiries* concerning human understanding and morals. He went on to treat many other topics, including religion, politics, and history.

Hume applied empiricism more rigorously than ever before: he held that all concepts are derived from experience, and that all knowledge about the world must be based on experience. Pure reason can prove results about "relations of ideas" in logic and mathematics (in what are now called "analytic statements"), but it cannot yield any substantive truth about the world. His *Treatise* is significantly subtitled *An Attempt to Introduce the Experimental Method of Reasoning into Moral Subjects* (where "experimental" meant experiential, and "moral" meant human). It was one of the first serious attempts at a scientific theory of human nature, but it remains more a work of philosophy than psychology.

Hume's version of empiricism asserted that all ideas are derived from impressions, either of the senses or of "reflection" (i.e., introspective awareness of one's own states of mind). He argued that we have no idea of matter except as a bundle of perceptible qualities (in that he followed the lead of Berkeley, the Irish philosopher and Anglican bishop, who even denied the very existence of matter). Hume went further than Berkeley when he argued that we have no coherent notion of *soul* or mental substance, since we are aware of nothing but a succession of mental states in ourselves and therefore have no idea of a continuing soul or self. He also famously argued that we have no idea of causation ("necessary connection") except as a repeated temporal succession of types of event. In Hume's view there is no good reason to expect correlations we have so far observed to be continued in new cases; it is only our nonrational, instinctive human nature (which in this respect resembles animal mentality) to expect the future to resemble the past.

There is thus a skeptical tendency at the foundation of Hume's theoretical philosophy, for he concluded that our most fundamental beliefs cannot be proved by reason but are due only to our innate dispositions. However, on practical matters he was more humane, cautious, and even somewhat conservative, appealing to (what he took to be) the well-known empirical facts about human beings, as evidenced by common sense, history, and anthropology. He gave an essentially humanist account of ethics and politics in terms of our tendencies to benevolence as well as selfishness, our liability to emotions, and our ability to moderate them by thought. He supported a gradual reform and development of human society.

In all this Hume made no use of theological concepts. He was one of the first thinkers to attempt a social scientific account of religious belief and practice in his *Natural History of Religion*. He critically examined traditional arguments for the existence of God, especially the argument from apparent design, in his *Dialogues Concerning Natural Religion*— but such thoughts were too controversial to be published in his own lifetime. In maturity Hume enjoyed fame as a central figure of the Scottish Enlightenment, along with Adam Smith and Thomas Reid. Yet his reputation as an atheist excluded him from appointment to a chair of philosophy in Edinburgh University, which he so richly deserved. He died in philosophic calm, with no expectation of an afterlife.

Rousseau (1712–1778)

In eighteenth-century France there emerged a group of radical Enlightenment thinkers who put their faith in the application of reason to human affairs. These so-called *philosophes* included Voltaire, Diderot, d'Alembert, Rousseau, and Condorcet. Under the prevailing French regime of absolute monarchy, aristocratic privilege, and the Catholic Church, such thinking was highly subversive. Voltaire was a **deist** (i.e., he believed in a God who created the universe but does not intervene thereafter), but others were outright atheists, a new thing in European thought. Some were also materialists, notably Baron D'Holbach and de la Mettrie, who argued in *L'Homme Machine* that human beings are biological machines, made of nothing but matter. The *philosophes* had what we might in retrospect call a naive faith in the power of human reason to reform human affairs, which was severely tested by the violent aftermath of the French Revolution.

Jean-Jacques Rousseau, born in the city state of Geneva, was one of the most influential thinkers of the Enlightenment; but he was an eccentric and atypical figure in many ways, especially in his appeal to instinctual feeling rather than pure reason. In his *Discourse on Inequality* (1755) he argued for the basic goodness of human nature, offering a speculative history of the emergence of human society from primitive origins. He claimed to show how the growth of what is called "civilization" has corrupted people's natural happiness, freedom, and morality and allowed unnatural unjust inequalities to develop.

In his elaborate treatise on education entitled *Emile* (1762), Rousseau presented his idealistic vision of the essential goodness of human nature in the form of a detailed plan for how a boy could be brought up by a superbly wise and all-controlling tutor, from infancy to marriage. Despite the impracticality of this scheme (coming from a man who consigned his own illegitimate children to orphanages), Rousseau displayed insights into child development that have been influential. He insisted that children are not miniature adults and should not be treated as such: their upbringing and education should be tailored to their particular mental stage. His prescription was that each should be allowed to develop his or her own innate nature, uncorrupted by society—especially by the wealthy, urban, fashionable society, which Rousseau so strongly felt was thoroughly corrupt. In one of his typically exaggerated sentences he wrote that "human institutions are one mass of folly and contradiction."

Rousseau's writing has a kind of eloquence that many have found persuasive, and his influence is still with us in the questionable assumption that whatever is "natural" must be good. "Oh man!" he wrote, "live your own life and you will no longer be wretched. Keep to your appointed place in the order of nature and nothing can tear you from it." This may sound attractive; but what *counts* as "one's own life," and what *is* "man's appointed place in the order of nature"? Rousseau did not reckon with our fallen nature: the fact that selfishness, rivalry, bitchiness, aggression, and bullying seem to be natural to human beings (even very young ones). And for all his progressiveness, he still treated girls and women as subordinate to the male sex (as emerges at the end of *Emile*).

In the section of *Emile* entitled "Profession of Faith of a Savoyard Priest," Rousseau expressed his attitude to religion. He defended belief in a deist conception of God and in an immaterial soul endowed with free will. But he was skeptical about the claims of revealed religion put forward by religious authorities, and preferred a naive faith in the infallibility of each person's conscience as a guide to good and evil. For this he was condemned by both French Catholicism and Genevan Calvinism; he narrowly escaped arrest and had to live in exile for the rest of his life. He may have hoped to find a middle way between the irreligious French *philosophes* and authoritarian Christianity, but he did not satisfy either. However, his insistence on the natural equality of all human beings and that "true worship is of the heart" was to influence many, including Kant as we will see in the next chapter. And his emphasis on the importance of human feeling was a precursor to the Romantic movement that took over from the Enlightenment in the nineteenth century.

KEY TERMS

deism	materialism
dualism	mysticism
dualism of attribute	naturalism
empiricism	pantheism
Enlightenment	rational theology
faith	Reformation
grace	Renaissance
justification	revealed theology

C H A P T E R

8

Kant: Reasons and Causes, Morality and Religion

LIFE AND WORK

Immanuel Kant (1724–1804) is generally recognized, along with Plato and Aristotle, as one of the three greatest philosophers of all time. He spent his whole life and his career as a professor of philosophy in the small Prussian city of Königsberg (in 1946 renamed Kaliningrad, a Russian enclave on the Baltic Sea).

Kant's philosophy is typical of most early modern Western thought in inheriting the twin influences of Christianity and science and trying to combine the two. His Christian inheritance included the usual conception of God as omniscient, omnipotent and benevolent, an immortal human soul endowed with free will, and a strong sense of morality. His family influence came from Pietism, a radical movement within Lutheranism that emphasized personal devotion and right living above dogmas, creeds, and ritual. Although Kant rejected the exclusiveness and evangelical fervor of Pietism, some of its ethos is expressed in his approach to ethics and religion.

On the scientific side, Kant lived a century after the scientific revolution started by Galileo. He understood the fundamentals of Newton's mathematical physics and regarded it as the paradigm of natural science.

He himself made a significant contribution to science as a young man when he developed the first account of the formation of the solar system by accretion of the planets from clouds of dust. In the late eighteenth century the chemical revolution—the second stage of scientific development—was under way, and Kant used some chemical examples in his philosophy. He predated the Darwinian revolution in biology, so his theorizing about **teleology** (purposiveness) in nature needs rethinking in light of the theory of evolution by natural selection.

Kant also had a thorough humanistic education, including Greek and Latin philosophy and literature, European philosophy, theology, and political theory. He started out in the German **rationalist** tradition stemming mainly from Gottfried Wilhelm Leibniz (1646–1716), who believed that our pure reason could prove **metaphysical** claims, for example, that God exists and orders the world for the best, and (idiosyncratically) that everything in the world is made up of elementary minds called "monads." Kant's early ("precritical") publications wavered between the competing influences of natural science and rationalist metaphysics, but he later became aware of the radical empiricism of Hume, and in his mature work from 1781 he achieved a strikingly original synthesis of rationalism and empiricism.

Kant was surely the deepest thinker of the Enlightenment. Though aware of the dark side of human nature, he believed in the potential for reason to improve the human condition—applying "reason" in a wide sense to science, philosophy, ethics, politics, and religion. A philosopher who made a special impression on the development of Kant's social thought was Rousseau, the maverick of the French Enlightenment (see the preceding Historical Interlude). Some of Rousseau's ideas on human nature, culture, education, history, the importance of morality and the lesser importance of theology were absorbed and transformed by Kant.

The works of Kant's "critical" philosophy appeared late in his career, in the two closing decades of the eighteenth century: the *Critique of Pure Reason* (1781), *Groundwork* (or *Foundations*) *of the Metaphysics of Morals* (1785), *Critique of Practical Reason* (1788), *Critique of Judgment* (1790), *Religion within the Bounds of Bare Reason* (1793), and *The Metaphysics of Morals* (1797). (References to the first *Critique* use the A and B page numbers of its first and second editions; references to other works are to volume and page number of the German Academy edition of the complete works.) Kant's writing is formidably abstract and bristles with technical terms often of his own coinage, but one gets the sense that he is dealing with deep issues very systematically. However, he also wrote some shorter, more stylish essays for the educated public on topics including "What Is Enlightenment?," "Idea for a Universal History with

Cosmopolitan Intent," and "Perpetual Peace." He wanted to be an influential progressive thinker as well as an academic philosopher, but in some of his popular writings he voiced regrettably racist and sexist views that were characteristic of his time.

Kant repeatedly expressed his belief in the free, democratic use of reason to examine everything, however traditional, authoritative, or sacred: human reasoning should appeal only to the uncompelled assent of anyone capable of rational judgment. He argued that the only limits on human reason are those that we discover when we scrutinize the pretensions and limitations of reason itself; thus, human reason can provide its own self-discipline by philosophical reflection. The word **critique** meant for Kant this self-conscious inquiry into the powers and limitations of the human mind. He applied his critique to science and metaphysics, to ethics, to judgments of beauty and of purpose, and to religion.

In his old age, when his international reputation was assured, Kant got into trouble with the Prussian government. For most of his life he had benefited from the comparatively enlightened rule of Frederick the Great, but after that monarch's death a more reactionary regime took over, whose censors detected unorthodox tendencies in Kant's work on religion and forbade him to publish any more on the subject. There was no question of drinking hemlock like Socrates (see Chapter 4), yet it was their alleged subversion of state-approved religion that got both philosophers into conflict with authority. (There are still places where such things can happen.) Kant's response was wily, if not conspicuously courageous: he gave a promise to obey, but worded it so that he felt bound only for the lifetime of the new king, whom he managed to outlive, so he then resumed publication.

METAPHYSICS, EPISTEMOLOGY, AND THE LIMITS OF HUMAN KNOWLEDGE

We need to begin by explaining some of Kant's technical terminology. Some statements are true merely by virtue of the meaning of the terms they contain. Kant called them **analytic**, and all other statements **synthetic**. Examples of analytic truths are "Vixens are female foxes" and "If everyone is mortal, then no one is immortal." (Not all analytic statements are *obviously* true, e.g., a lengthy sentence on which we may have to exercise some attention before we can "see" its analyticity.) To know something **a priori** is to know it without appeal to perceptual experience (which Kant called *Anschauung*, traditionally translated as **intuition**; he also counted introspective awareness of one's own states of mind as "inner intuition"). To know something **a posteriori** is to know it on the basis of experience, and an **empirical statement** is one that needs to be justified in this way.

Our knowledge of an analytic truth is a priori when we just "see" (with our minds, not our eyes) that it must be true. But Kant also claimed, crucially, that we have a priori knowledge of some synthetic (non-analytic) truths (see below). He also applied the a priori/a posteriori distinction to concepts. Empiricists such as Locke, Berkeley and Hume denied that that there are any a priori concepts (what they called "innate ideas"); rationalists such as Plato, Descartes, Spinoza, Leibniz and Kant claimed that there are (in various senses that need further elucidation).

The first half (the Aesthetic and Analytic) of the *Critique of Pure Reason* sets out Kant's elaborate theory of (1) the two "forms of our intuition" (i.e., our way of perceiving everything in space and time, whether outwardly in perception or inwardly in introspection), (2) the twelve "categories" (i.e., a priori concepts, including substance and causation), and (3) certain synthetic a priori principles involving the application of the categories. So we have three different kinds of knowledge: the vast majority of it is a posteriori, justified by experience, including geography, history, and the sciences. A small amount of knowledge (in logic and language) is analytic, provable by pure reasoning and definitions. But controversially, Kant claimed that we also have some synthetic a priori knowledge.

In his view mathematical truths (most plausibly in Euclidean geometry, where we appeal to diagrams) have this synthetic a priori status. Many philosophers have agreed with Hume in regarding mathematics as analytic. But Kant also argued that certain claims about the general structure of our experience of the world have synthetic a priori status. One fundamental theme of his philosophy is to explain how empirical knowledge (including science) is possible, and he applied his theory of human cognitive faculties to argue that perception and science depend on certain fundamental presuppositions, notably that every event has a cause and that something ("substance" in a rather elusive sense) is conserved through every change. Such principles cannot be proved by observation, so they are not a posteriori, but neither are they analytic, yet Kant argues that they are necessary conditions of our self-conscious, conceptualized perceptual experience.

Kant had a strong sense of the reality of the material world and of the objectivity of the knowledge provided by science, so he rejected Berkeley's subjective idealism according to which matter cannot exist unperceived. For Kant material things and all the objects of physical science, even those not directly perceivable by our senses, exist independently of being perceived or conceived of by anyone (see his talk of "magnetic matter" at A226/B273). But it has to be admitted that he often writes in a way that seems to deny this. He offered a double-barreled thesis combining **empirical realism** with **transcendental idealism**, the latter being an elusive doctrine that has puzzled his interpreters ever since.

One persuasive insight behind Kant's transcendental idealism is the realization that although material objects exist independently of us, the *way* we perceive them and conceptualize them depends not only on what there is out there to affect our sense organs but also on how those inputs are processed through our minds. (We need not presuppose dualism here, we can think of mental processes as instantiated in the brain.) There are some individual differences in perceptual processing, for example, some people are color-blind, and some are unable to recognize people due to malfunction in their face-recognition module. There are ranges of perception common to all *normal* humans that are nevertheless peculiar to the human *species*: we see colors and hear sounds, but this is due to the way our brains process light and sound only within certain wavelengths. Dogs have a wider range of hearing, and they have a much keener sense of smell.

Kant took a more radical and mind-boggling step when he suggested that our "a priori forms of intuition" (i.e., our innate ways of perceiving things in space and time) systematically distort our representation of what really exists outside us, so that we can only know **appearances**. Perhaps **things in themselves** may not even be in space or in time. Maybe only God, endowed with "intellectual (i.e., non-sensory) intuition," can perceive things as they really are. Another way Kant expressed his transcendental idealism was in his proposal for a "Copernican revolution" in philosophy, by which "objects must conform to our cognition" (Bxviff.). That may suggest a kind of magical effect of mind on world, but more soberly it can be interpreted as saying that anything we perceive and describe must conform to the necessary conditions for our perception and description. Some incautious phrases of Kant's even suggest that the world is produced by our mental processes, or that we never perceive anything other our own mental states. These themes are eternally debated by his interpreters, but we will see below that he made a rather different application of the appearance/thing-in-itself distinction in his theory of human nature and human action.

In the second half of the first *Critique* (the Dialectic) Kant diagnosed how human reason tries to go beyond the limits of its legitimate use by asserting illusory knowledge of things as they are in themselves (souls, the universe as a whole, uncaused events, and God). Such **metaphysical** claims have long been central to theology and to Western philosophy, but they are outside the bounds of human knowledge as set by Kant. His view is that although we can understand such metaphysical assertions, we can neither prove nor disprove them by reason nor even acquire empirical evidence for or against them.

This made a decisive break with the tradition of natural theology (by no means dead even now), which has offered either rational proofs or supposedly scientific evidence for the existence (or nature) of God. But there has long been a vital strand in religious thinking—exemplified in such different thinkers as Augustine, al-Ghazali, Pascal, and Kierkegaard—that faith goes beyond reason from the very beginning. Kant seems to fit, rather surprisingly, into that tradition when he declared that theological claims are a matter for faith rather than knowledge (Bxxx).

THEORY OF HUMAN NATURE:
REASONS, CAUSES, AND FREE WILL

The overarching agenda of Kant's philosophy was to reconcile the claims of morality and religion (as he understood them) with scientific knowledge. He hoped to paint one big complicated picture, giving human nature its appropriate place within physical nature. Let us go back to his account of human cognitive faculties as expressed at the beginning of the first *Critique*:

> Our knowledge springs from two fundamental sources of the mind; the first is the capacity for receiving representations (receptivity for impressions), the second is the power of knowing an object through these representations (spontaneity in the production of concepts). Through the first an object is *given* to us, through the second the object is *thought*. . . . To neither of these powers may a preference be given over the other. Without sensibility no object would be given to us, without understanding no object would be thought. Thoughts without content are empty, intuitions without concepts are blind. (A50–51/B74–75)

Kant was here developing a theory of human knowledge that reconciles the one-sided views of his rationalist and empiricist predecessors (especially Leibniz and Hume). He declares that our perceptual knowledge depends on the interaction of two factors: sensory states caused by physical objects, and the mind's activity in organizing these data under concepts and making judgments expressed in statements. Animals have the first capacity (**sensibility***)* but lack the second (**understanding**), for they do not use anything like human language. They perceive prey, predators, mates, and offspring; but they do not have concepts: they cannot *say* that anything is edible or dangerous, a partner or a child. Animals can feel pain and can be in states of arousal such as lust, fear, or aggression; but they cannot say (or think) that they are in pain, randy, angry, or afraid.

Kant can be seen as building on Aristotle's distinctions between plants, animals, and humans (see Chapter 5). But in the light of recent evidence about animal mentality we may have to allow that the gulf between ourselves and primates or dolphins may be less absolute than we used to think. (Infants and people suffering from dementia lack the mental powers of normal adults.) But the existence of shades of gray does not eliminate the difference between black and white: there remains a big distinction between the conceptual, linguistically expressible capacities of normal humans and anything that other animals can do (so far as we know).

There is a further depth in Kant's account of our cognition, in his stress on **reason**. This sometimes seems to be another word for "understanding," but a special role for reason emerges when he points out that we do not just make lots of particular judgments about the world, we try to integrate all those bits of knowledge into a unified system. We often want to know *why* something happens, so we try to explain one fact, or one observed regularity, in terms of others. At the beginning and end of the "Dialectic" (A299/B355ff. and A642/B670ff.) Kant gave an elaborate account of how our faculty of reason leads us toward ever-increasing systematization of our knowledge under general laws, that is, the scientific search for a unified theory of all natural phenomena ("a theory of everything").

There is a vital *practical* dimension to Kant's conception of reason (echoing Aristotle again). We are not merely perceiving, judging, and theorizing beings; we are *agents*—we do things, we affect the world and each other (and even ourselves) by our actions. In this respect too we resemble yet transcend the animals. They "act" very effectively in hunting, fleeing, mating, constructing nests, and caring for offspring. But they cannot *say* what they are doing, so we can hardly credit them with intentions to bring about linguistically specified states of affairs. We say that the cat is trying to catch a mouse, but nothing in her behavior justifies attributing to her the concept of "mouse" rather than food, prey, rodent, or something exciting. There are *causes* of animal behavior in their internal drives and external perceptions, but they cannot say what they are doing, let alone discuss reasons for and against doing it.

Kant sketched the general conceptual framework of human actions in the *Groundwork* at 4:413 and in the opening sections of the *Critique of Practical Reason* at 5:19ff. He made a crucial distinction between **hypothetical imperatives** and **categorical imperatives**. Some of our reasons for action involve only our own desires and relevant beliefs: such reasons can be expressed in the form "I want B, and I believe that A is the best way to achieve B (i.e., in these circumstances that *if* I do A, then B will probably result); therefore, I should do A" (i.e., it is rational for me to do A—this "should" is not moral, merely rational). That is what Kant in his ponderous way labels a "hypothetical imperative" (Aristotle wrote of "practical syllogisms").

But he insists that not all reasons for action take this form, involving only the selection of a means to satisfy a desire, for we sometimes accept an obligation, a moral "ought" or "should," a reason for action that we conceive of as holding irrespective of our own desires, and may even go against them. Examples include any context in which lying would be to one's advantage but where one thinks one ought to tell the truth nevertheless; any "good Samaritan" situation in which one encounters someone in need of urgent help, though one finds it inconvenient to do the necessary; and any case in which one admits the claims of justice (e.g., fair shares in cutting the available cake). In all such cases Kant says that we recognize the validity of what he calls a "categorical imperative" of the form "In this situation I ought to do C, whatever my own desires may be."

Such categorical imperatives involve what Kant calls "pure" or "a priori" practical reason. His claim is that morality is fundamentally a function of our reason, not just our feelings as empiricist moral philosophers like Hume suggested. In the *Groundwork* Kant gave some very abstract formulations of his fundamental principle of morality (over which philosophers continue to argue), but at bottom his appeal is to our experience of moral obligation, our uncomfortable awareness of tension between our individual desires and the requirements of morality. Kant had learned from Rousseau a deep respect for ordinary moral feeling, and at the end of the first *Critique*, which contains some of the most abstruse philosophizing ever, he added, "in regard to the essential ends of human nature even the highest philosophy cannot advance further than the guidance that nature has also conferred on the most common understanding" (A831/B859).

Kant's analysis of human cognitive faculties seems basically correct. But the large question that arises is what metaphysics of human nature makes these mental capacities possible? Here the going gets difficult and controversial. His official line on the issue of **dualism** against **materialism** was that we cannot know either of them, because we cannot know what we are "in ourselves." In the Paralogisms section of the first *Critique* he argues that the traditional arguments of "rational psychology" cannot prove the existence of an incorporeal soul, for even in introspection ("inner intuition") we know ourselves only as we appear to ourselves. But we cannot prove that we are merely material beings either (A379, B420): in characteristic fashion, Kant leaves the metaphysical question open. However, his own preference comes out when he rejects "a soulless materialism" (presumably he had in mind Hobbes or de la Mettrie) and suggests—though as a matter of *faith* rather than knowledge—that we survive death and live on into an infinite future (B424–26).

Kant was a rock-solid believer in human freedom and moral responsibility. He saw us as free rational beings who can make choices that are not predetermined, above all when we act on moral reasons. He dismissed as "a wretched subterfuge" the **compatibilist** account of free will offered by empiricists such as Hobbes and Hume, according to which an action counts "free" if it is caused by the agent's own desires and beliefs rather than anything outside the agent (second *Critique* 5:96). Kant held that human actions cannot be explained by physical causation, for they involve choices that are not caused *by anything*.

His solution to his Third Antinomy in the Dialectic of the first *Critique* (the apparent contradiction between free will and determinism) is that insofar as we are perceptible biological bodies we are just as causally determined as everything else in the physical world, but insofar as we are rational beings who act for reasons we are free (A549/B577ff.). He backs this up with a new application of the distinction between appearances and things in themselves, in terms of our empirical and **intelligible characters**:

> for a subject of the world of sense we would have first an empirical character, through which its actions as appearances would stand through and through in connection with other appearances in accordance with constant natural laws . . . second, one would also have to allow this subject an intelligible character, through which it is indeed the cause of those actions as appearances, but which does not stand under any condition of sensibility and is not itself appearance. The first one could call the character of such a thing in appearance, the second its character as a thing in itself. (A539/B567)

It sounds as if Kant meant that all the physical states of our bodies—the movements of our limbs and lips, the circulation of the blood, the firing of neurons in the brain, the flow of hormones—count as our empirical character. And presumably it is our beliefs, desires, hopes, fears, intentions, and emotions that count as our intelligible character, for the subject can usually state these in words. The former may be determined by the mechanisms investigated by physiology and neuroscience, whereas the latter involve intelligible, non-causal relations between beliefs, desires, and actions. For example, if someone wants a beer and believes there is beer in the fridge, that gives him or her an obvious reason to go there (we can all see the rationality of that, without knowing anything about brain functioning). But this rational relation is only to a *possible* action, for that belief and desire constitute only *one* reason for going to the fridge: there may be some *other* reasons against doing so, such as laziness, dieting, or morality (if it's someone else's beer).

The distinction between reasons and causes, rational explanation and causal explanation, is surely an essential part of any adequate account of human action; and we are all in Kant's debt for opening up this topic. If materialism or "physicalism" implies that there is only one kind of explanation—in terms of physical causes—we should reject that reductive thesis. But it remains open for us to say that human beings are *made* entirely of matter, and that there is a dualism of attributes (reasons and causes) rather than of substances. Kant can be seen as closer to Spinoza than to Descartes—though he might not welcome the comparison.

At A534/B562 Kant declares that "freedom in the practical sense is the independence of the power of choice from necessitation by impulses of sensibility," i.e., bodily-based desires. He believes that human decisions have a significant degree of freedom: although we feel the *influence* of our desires, our choices are not determined by them. We can distinguish two senses of "reasons." In one sense, two people can have the same belief and desire if they believe the same proposition and desire the same thing. In another sense, only *my* present state of believing and desiring can motivate my action. (How could someone else's mental states motivate *me*?) Mental states can be amongst the causes of actions; but propositional contents are not the sort of thing that can be causes at all, they are not events in time—which might help us interpret Kant's puzzling statement that "this acting subject, in its intelligible character, would not stand under any conditions of time" (A539/B567).

Does Kant solve the free will problem, then? We cannot pursue this question further, except to note that in the *Groundwork* at 4:446 he offered a distinctively practical defense of freedom. When one is making up one's mind what to do, one cannot at the same time think of one's decision as already determined. Even if one is impressed by theoretical arguments for determinism, there is no escaping the necessity to come to a decision here and now. As Kant put it, we have to act "under the idea of freedom," so "from the practical point of view" we are already free.

DIAGNOSIS: SELFISHNESS AND SOCIALITY

As we have seen, Kant strongly emphasizes the distinction between self-interested inclinations and moral duty. He contrasts our human nature with the animals, on the one side, and with the conception of a "holy will," on the other. Animals feel no tension between desires and duty, for they have no concept of duty. A rational being with no self-interested desires (an angel?) would not experience any tension either, but for the opposite reason: not being subject to temptation, he or she (or it?) would always do the right thing. But we humans are mixed beings, midway between animals and angels. We are embodied creatures with our individual needs, including not only physical desires for food and sex but emotional needs or drives for love, approval, status, and power. Yet we are also rational beings (some of the time!), and that involves what Kant calls "pure practical reason," the recognition of moral obligations. The tension between these two sides of our nature is an inescapable feature of the human condition, so we never achieve complete virtue or holiness.

Some philosophers have asked how anyone can ever be motivated to fulfill a moral obligation that goes against his or her own desires. "Why be moral?" moral skeptics ask, and seem to expect a justification in self-interested terms. But Kant does not see such skepticism as a real issue; he just presupposes what he calls the "fact of reason," that we all accept the validity of some moral obligations (though we may disagree about what they are in particular cases).

It is relevant here to point out a distinction *within* the class of self-interested reasons, between desires for immediate satisfaction and prudential considerations of longer-term self-interest. One can resist the allure of a third glass of wine, an expensive item of fashion, or a seductive tempter, for the sake of one's longer-term health, wealth, or happiness. Our mixed, partly rational nature is shown in our ability to recognize prudential reasons and to act on them. We all need to be able to give up satisfactions in the interest of our longer-term goals; to be unable to do this, for example, in addictions, is to be reduced to an almost animal level. Every child needs to learn how to postpone gratification, and we each have to negotiate a balance between living for the moment and planning for the future.

In his moral theory Kant tends to present his view in a very severe guise that suggests that the only motivation he really approves of is a grim determination to do one's duty irrespective of one's own inclinations. He may seem to imply that if one finds oneself quite naturally inclined to look after one's children, to tell the truth, or to help someone in distress, that does not make those actions admirable and might even *detract* from their moral value (*Groundwork* 4:398). But more careful reading, especially of his late work *The Metaphysics of Morals*, dispels this impression. Kant *is* concerned to encourage virtues as traits of character: the more that people develop mental dispositions to do the right things, the better. His point is that we are more than bundles of inclinations (like the animals): because we are rational beings, we can and should make explicit the general principles or **maxims** behind our actions, and assess them from the points of view of prudence and especially of morality. The ethical life is not just a matter of bringing about good states of affairs, for virtue depends on inner motivation: we must act for the right reasons. Kant's ethics is thus described as **deontological** as opposed to **utilitarianism**, which makes the rightness of actions depend entirely on their results. As he put it at the beginning of the *Groundwork*, the only thing that is unconditionally good is a good *will*.

But how can we measure up to the high demands of Kantian morality? In his late work *Religion within the Boundaries of Mere Reason* he wrestled with the most profound problems of human nature and suggests revised versions of old theological insights. He talks of the "radical evil" in human nature, acknowledging our "frailty"—our difficulty in doing what we know we ought to do, and our "impurity"—our tendency to confuse moral motives with others. But for Kant what is radically evil in us is not our natural desires or the tension between these and duty; it is what he calls the "depravity" of human nature—the freely chosen *subordination* of duty to inclination, the deliberate preference for one's own happiness (as one conceives of it) over one's obligations to other people (*Religion* 6:19ff.).

Here Kant along with so many other thinkers such as Augustine and Pelagius (see the Historical Interlude) is pulled in two directions. On the one hand, he insists that the evil in us is a result of our own choice, our wrong use of our freedom. On the other hand (in his version of the Christian doctrine of original sin), he wants to say that evil is "radical" or innate in us; it is a universal and unavoidable feature of our condition as needy but rational beings:

> There is in the human being a natural propensity to evil; and this propensity itself is morally evil, since it must ultimately be sought in a free power of choice, and hence is imputable. This evil is *radical*, since it corrupts the ground of all maxims; as natural propensity, it is also not to be *extirpated* through human forces. . . . Yet it must equally be possible to *overcome* this evil, for it is found in the human being as acting freely. (*Religion* 6:37)

Kant's position is *not* that radical evil attaches to our animal nature, which is innocent in itself. Nor does he attribute it to our rational nature, which would make us demonic beings. Rather, he thinks that radical evil arises from our predisposition to *prioritize* our self-love, as a result of development under social conditions. This is a theme from Rousseau: the "unsocial sociability" of human beings, our need and inclination to be members of a human society, combined with our tendency to be selfish and competitive. Paradoxically, Kant's thesis that we are by nature evil amounts to much the same thing as Rousseau's assertion that we are by nature good (there was a rather similar debate within the Confucian tradition—see the end of Chapter 1). The phrase "by nature" was used by the two philosophers in different ways: Rousseau meant *before* the advent of society, thinking that social development has corrupted original human nature, whereas Kant thought that our human nature can be expressed only in society; he didn't believe there was such a thing as a presocial *human* condition.

PRESCRIPTION: PURE RELIGION
AND CULTURAL PROGRESS

How are right intentions and virtuous dispositions to be achieved and encouraged? It is not enough to formulate a *theory* of what pure practical reason requires, universalizing the maxims that should guide our actions, and treating each person as an end "in him- or herself" (as Kant does in *Groundwork* Chapter II and in the second *Critique*). Nor is it enough to state more specific moral rules, and apply them to particular cases (as he does in *The Metaphysics of Morals*), for it is one thing to recognize an obligation and another thing to do it (as St.Paul saw). Philosophy and moralizing notoriously have limited effects on human conduct.

There are very practical problems here for parents, teachers, social workers and legislators, about how people can be taught and encouraged to develop virtue. (Here we echo Plato's and Aristotle's recognition of the need for ethics to be located in a wider conception of society.) Kant has things to say about these questions; not all of his writing is at the level of abstruse theory. The most obvious response is to offer rewards or threaten punishments, but that does not produce Kantian virtue, it only puts new self-interested reasons in place. It may induce outward conformity to rules, but it cannot create the virtuous inner attitude, the will to do the right action *just because it is right*. Kant does not regard blame and praise as mere external incentives like a slap or a sweet. Rather, they are ways of "sharing in the reason of one another," that is, of seeing other people as (partly) rational beings with needs and interests of their own. Praise and blame become part of distinctively *moral* discourse; they can *convince* or *remind* someone about what is right or wrong.

Kant's answer to the problems of human nature shares the ambiguity of his diagnosis. The above quotation from the *Religion* suggests that only a religious answer will suffice: for if the evil in us cannot be "extirpated through human forces" yet needs to be "overcome," believers will be quick to say that only God's salvation (in their recommended version) can do the trick. Much of Kant's mature work, including the later sections of all three *Critiques*, touches on theological themes. A first glance might suggest that this is mere conventional piety, artificially tacked on to his philosophical work. But more careful reading shows his understanding of religion to be serious, even if it departs from Christian orthodoxy.

In Chapter III of the "Dialectic" of the first *Critique* Kant classified all theoretical arguments for the existence of God into three kinds: the **ontological** (from the very concept of God), the **cosmological** (from the supposed necessity of a creator), and the "**physicotheological**" (from what seems to be intelligent design in the world). He examines each argument in detail, and his criticisms of them are vigorously expressed. Hume had already criticized the third in his *Dialogues Concerning Natural Religion*, but an original aspect of Kant's treatment is his claim that the design argument presupposes the cosmological, which in turn depends on the ontological. If so, demolition of the latter (realizing that real existence cannot be proved by mere reason) brings down the whole house of metaphysical cards.

But Kant destroys only to try to rebuild on a different, practical basis. Although claims about God, immortality, and free will cannot be proved or disproved by theoretical reason, he suggests that they can be justified from a moral point of view. When we are thinking how to *act* rather than what to believe, different sorts of consideration are relevant. As we have noted, the idea of our own freedom is presupposed in deliberating about what to do. But what about God and immortality—where do they come in? Kant offers "moral theology" in the Method section of the first *Critique*, the Dialectic of the second, sections 86–91 of the third, and in the *Religion*.

At A805/B833 he distinguished three questions that he says sum up "all the interests of reason, speculative as well as practical":

1. What can I know?
2. What ought I to do?
3. What may I hope?

The first question is discussed in depth in the first *Critique*. The second is treated in the *Groundwork*, the second *Critique* and other ethical works. The third (glossed as "If I do what I ought to do, what may I then hope?") introduces a new topic which is both theoretical and practical. Kant's philosophy of history and philosophy of religion come under this heading of hope.

In the Dialectic of the second *Critique* Kant gave his fullest exposition of his practical argument for belief or faith in God and immortality. He was deeply concerned about the relation between virtue and happiness. Ancient **Stoicism** maintained that virtue is the highest good, whereas **Epicureanism** said that it is happiness. Typically Kant offers a synthesis of two one-sided views. We should not be concerned *merely* for our own happiness; yet he is unwilling to disconnect virtue from happiness completely, so he argues that the "highest good," the ultimate end of all human striving, is a *combination* of virtue and happiness (like Aristotle's *eudaimonia*).

It is painfully obvious, however, that virtue is not always rewarded with happiness in the world as we know it. All too often good people suffer, and evildoers seem to flourish. It is an obvious step—which millions have taken—to say that justice requires there to be a God who knows the secrets of all human hearts and will justly reward and punish in a future life. It may seem that in invoking God and immortality Kant is doing no more than repeating this common human hope for justice and reward in a life after death. But it is fundamental to his moral philosophy that our motive for doing our duty should *not* be to reap benefit thereby, so it would be quite inconsistent for him to postulate rewards beyond death in order to motivate right action.

Yet he claims we need to be able to *hope* that virtue will eventually be rewarded. His case seems to be that our very motivation for moral action would be undermined unless we can at least believe that the combination of virtue and happiness is possible. We are not to aim directly at happiness for ourselves, but we need to have some *hope* for happiness: we have to assume that doing the right thing is not ultimately pointless.

But does this need belief in the traditional metaphysical assertions of God and immortality? In the second *Critique* Kant offered some rather shaky arguments for this, but in the *Religion* he tended to back off from such claims, at least in their traditional interpretations. For example, he said of the notions of heaven and hell that they are "representations powerful enough . . . without any necessity to presuppose dogmatically, as an item of doctrine, that an eternity of good or evil is the human lot also objectively" (6:69). He wrote that "religion is (subjectively considered) the recognition of all our duties as divine commands" (6:153-4) and that "faith needs only the *idea of God* . . . without pretending to be able to secure objective reality for it through theoretical cognition" (6:154 footnote). It looks as if we can interpret "recognition of our duties as divine commands" as the entertaining of an image or picture, rather than literal belief in the existence of a supernatural commander.

Speaking of the struggle between "the good and the evil principles" (by which Kant meant personifications of good and evil in Christ and Satan), he said,

> It is easy to see, once we divest of its mystical cover this vivid mode of representing things, apparently also the only one at the time *suited to the common people*, why it (its spirit and rational meaning) has been valid and binding practically, for the whole world and at all times: because it lies near enough to every human being for each to recognize his duty in it. Its meaning is that there is absolutely no salvation for human beings except in the innermost adoption of genuine moral principles in their disposition. (*Religion* 6:83)

Such "demythologizing" language disturbed the Prussian censors, and it challenges Christian orthodoxy even today. And we may be less inclined than Kant (and Plato) to distinguish what is believable by an educated elite and by "the common people." Kant's approach is to reinterpret theology in terms of morality, and he suggests that the scriptures should be interpreted in that way, even when it is not their literal meaning. In his view there is no need for miracles, priests, rituals, or sacraments. Yet he sees a need for a radically reformed universal church, a human institution that will set forth ethical ideals and help its members to live up to them. He hoped that what is rationally and morally acceptable in the various Christian and non-Christian religions could be gradually separated from what is unnecessary and formed into a "pure religious faith" (see *Religion* Parts III and IV).

Kant expressed more this-worldly hopes in his essays on history, which paved the way for the explicitly historicist philosophies of Hegel and Marx in the nineteenth century. He envisaged progress in human culture, despite setbacks, through education, economic development and political reform, and gradual emancipation from poverty, war, ignorance, and subjection to traditional authorities (*Critique of Judgment*, section 83). He applauded the egalitarian and democratic ideals of the French Revolution, despite its excesses. In his essay *On Perpetual Peace*, he sketched a world order of peaceful cooperation between nations with democratic constitutions. (He would perhaps be delighted with the achievements of the European Union, for all its faults.)

The status of Kant's historical hope is unclear, however. In his essay "Idea for a Universal History with a Cosmopolitan Purpose" (1784) he appealed to a conception of what "Nature" intends for human progress. He thinks there is an overall trend in history that theorists can discern, for people are "unconsciously promoting an end which even if they knew what it was, would scarcely arouse their interest." Thus, our "unsocial sociability," our social yet competitive nature, is "the means employed by Nature" to produce a law-governed social order in which human talents and powers can be fully developed.

But this concept of "Nature's design or will" is unstably poised between belief in God's providence and an obscure teleological belief in a mysterious "Nature" as having purposes that are not the conscious intentions of any rational being (divine or human). At any rate, Kant set out the idea of progress toward ever-greater fulfillment of human potential as an ideal to aspire to. It can encourage our hopes and inspire a sort of social faith. Kant was an Enlightenment philosopher, but unlike many other thinkers of his time, he had a realistic sense of the dark side of human nature, our potentiality for evil, which has been all too vividly confirmed since his time.

His practical philosophy leaves us with a combination of secular hope with a religious hope for divine grace in the transformation of our fallen, selfish human nature.

FOR FURTHER READING

A short, clear introduction to Kant is Roger Scruton, *Kant* (Oxford: Oxford University Press, 2001). A fuller introduction is Otfried Hoeffe, *Kant* (Albany: State University of New York Press, 1994). A still more comprehensive introduction, combined with some judicious critical appraisal, is Paul Guyer, *Kant* (London: Routledge, 2006). For a clear introduction to his ethics, see Roger J. Sullivan, *An Introduction to Kant's Ethics* (Cambridge: Cambridge University Press, 1994).

For those brave enough to start reading Kant for themselves, the usual starting points are his two formidably titled shorter works, *Groundwork for the Metaphysics of Morals* and *Prolegomena to Any Future Metaphysics*. Some may like to look at Kant's *Religion within the Boundaries of Mere Reason, and Other Writings*, trans. George di Giovanni (with an introduction by Robert M. Adams) (Cambridge: Cambridge University Press, 1998).

Easier reading for those more interested in the social aspects of Kant's thought can be found in L. W. Beck, ed., *Kant on History* (Indianapolis, IN: Bobbs-Merrill, 1963), or H. Reiss, ed., *Kant's Political Writings*, 2nd ed. (Cambridge: Cambridge University Press, 1991).

Allen Wood, *Kant's Moral Religion* (Ithaca, NY: Cornell University Press, 1970), defends Kant's account of religion. Wood has also contributed a chapter on this topic in *The Cambridge Companion to Kant*, ed. Paul Guyer (Cambridge: Cambridge University Press, 1992). Leslie Stevenson compares Kant's approach to religion with the Quakers in his contribution to *Kant and the New Philosophy of Religion*, ed. Chris. L. Firestone and Stephen R. Palmquist (Bloomington: Indiana University Press, 2006); a revised version forms one chapter in his *Open to New Light* (Exeter, UK, and Charlottesville, VA: Imprint Academic, 2012).

In the *Moral Gap: Kantian Ethics, Human Limits, and God's Assistance* (Oxford: Oxford University Press, 1996), John E. Hare argues that Kant's ethics needs supplementation from the Christian doctrines of grace and atonement.

Leslie Stevenson offers a Kantian solution to the problem of free will and determinism in "Who's Afraid of Determinism?" *Philosophy* 89, no. 3 (2014): 431–50; an assessment of Kant's treatment of divine grace in "Kant on Grace," in G. Michalson, ed., *Kant's Religion within the Boundaries of Mere Reason* (Cambridge: Cambridge University Press, 2014); and an overview "Kant versus Christianity?" in C.L. Firestone, ed., *Kant and the Question of Theology* (Cambridge: Cambridge University Press, 2016).

KEY TERMS

analytic statement

appearances

a posteriori

a priori

categorical imperative

compatibilism

cosmological

critique

deontology

dualism

empirical realism

empirical statement

Epicureanism

hypothetical imperative

intelligible character

intuition

materialism

maxim

metaphysics

ontological

physico-theological argument

rationalism

reason

sensibility

Stoicism

synthetic statement

teleology

things in themselves

transcendental idealism

understanding

utilitarianism

QUESTIONS FOR DISCUSSION

1. Does Kant succeed in reconciling science and religion?
2. Is Kant's theory of knowledge better than Plato's?
3. Does the distinction between reasons and causes solve the problem of free will and determinism?
4. Are you convinced by Kant's analysis of the radical evil in human nature, and by his solution for it?

9

Marx: The Economic Basis of Human Societies

Our image of Marxism is strongly colored by our knowledge of the rise and fall of communism in Russia and Eastern Europe in the twentieth century. We are also influenced by what we hear about China (though Marx's influence there has now dwindled to almost zero) and North Korea. However, this chapter is about the theories that Karl Marx himself developed in the mid-nineteenth century, not about Leninist, Stalinist, or Maoist practice. Marx can hardly be held responsible for the failings and atrocities of the communist regimes that came to power after his death.

If Kant was the deepest philosopher of the Enlightenment, Marx was the greatest theorist of the Industrial Revolution and nineteenth-century **capitalism**. Though hostile to religion, Marx inherited an ideal of human equality and freedom from Christianity, and he shared the Enlightenment faith that scientific method could diagnose and resolve the problems of human society. Behind his elaborate social and economic theorizing was a prophetic zeal to show the way toward a secular form of human salvation.

LIFE AND WORK

Marx (1818-1883) was born in the German Rhineland, of a Jewish father who, under the discriminatory laws of the time, had to convert to Christianity to practice as a lawyer. The young Karl displayed his intellectual ability early, and in 1836 he enrolled in the Law Faculty of the University of Berlin. There was a ferment of philosophical, aesthetic, and social ideas in the Romantic movement of that time, into which Marx eagerly plunged. He learned languages, composed poetry, and wrote a dissertation on ancient Greek metaphysics, while becoming deeply concerned about social reform.

The dominant influence in German thought then was the philosophy of Hegel, and Marx became so immersed in it that he abandoned his legal studies. The inspiring idea of so many thinkers at that time was progress in human history. Hegel interpreted mental and cultural progress in terms of his conception of *Geist* (i.e., **spirit** or mind in the world as a whole), so his unorthodox version of Christian theology tended toward pantheism. The whole sweep of human history was explained as the progressive self-realization of *Geist,* with increasing consciousness or self-awareness. Successive eras of human life achieve increasingly adequate ideas of reality; each stage contains conflicting tendencies, but lays the basis for a fuller development of rationality, consciousness and freedom at the next stage.

Hegel also developed an influential conception of **alienation**, in which the knowing subject is confronted with objects other than, and "alien to," himself or herself. Mysteriously, the distinction or opposition between subject and object is supposed to be overcome as the subject gets to know and understand its objects. (This sounds like a distorted version of Kant's transcendental idealism.) According to Hegel, the world-historical process of mental and cultural development will eventually arrive at a stage in which there is "absolute" perfected knowledge—and he seems to have thought that he himself had more or less achieved it. (If so, he differed from the epistemic and ethical humility of Kant, who said we cannot know things in themselves, and can never achieve moral perfection.)

The followers of Hegel split into two camps over how his ideas applied to society, politics, and religion. The "right" Hegelians held that the processes of history had already led to the full development of human potential, they saw the contemporary Prussian state as pretty near the ideal, so were conservative in politics. The "left" or "young" Hegelians believed that the highest form of human freedom had yet to be realized, that European society of the time was far from ideal, and that it was up to people to help change the old order and bring about the next stage of human development. Accordingly, they looked for radical reform, or revolution.

Marx was also influenced by Ludwig Feuerbach, an important thinker among the left Hegelians, whose book *The Essence of Christianity* was published in 1841. Feuerbach argued that Hegel had gotten things upside down, that rather than God or "Spirit" progressively realizing Himself in history, religious ideas and beliefs are produced by human beings as a pale reflection or idealization of life in this world, which is the fundamental reality. People become alienated when they project their own human ideals and potential into theological fantasies, and undervalue their actual lives. Feuerbach diagnosed theology as "esoteric psychology" (i.e., the expression or projection of our own feelings in *disguised* form as obscure **metaphysical** claims about the universe). Thus, he saw religion as a symptom of human alienation, from which we must free ourselves by realizing our real destiny in this world. This was a forerunner of the sociological or psychological explanations of religion offered by Marx, Durkheim, and Freud.

Marx's reading of Feuerbach broke the spell that Hegel had cast on him, but he retained the idea that Hegelian philosophy contained truth in an inverted form. He saw it as his mission to "put Hegel right way up" by expressing the real *material* truth about human nature and history. He wrote a critique of Hegel's *Philosophy of Right* in 1842–43 and edited a radical journal that was soon suppressed by the Prussian government, so he fled to Paris. In 1845 he was expelled from France, too, and moved to Brussels. In these formative years he encountered the other great intellectual influences of his life, including the French socialist Saint-Simon and the Scottish philosopher-economist Adam Smith, who had analyzed the workings of capital, wages, and trade in his classic book *The Wealth of Nations*, just as the Industrial Revolution was gathering momentum in late eighteenth-century Britain. Marx debated with other pioneering socialist thinkers such as Proudhon and Bakunin and began his lifelong collaboration with Friedrich Engels.

In the 1840s Marx and Engels began to formulate their **materialist theory of history**, which saw the driving force of social change as economic rather than mental. The key to human history, they claimed, did not lie in mere *ideas*—and certainly not in God or cosmic Spirit—but in the changing ways in which the material necessities of life are produced. Alienation is at root neither metaphysical nor religious but social and economic. Under the capitalist system labor is something alien to the laborer in that he or she does not work for himself or herself but for the capitalist who controls the means of production, directs its process, and owns the product as private property. The capitalist aims to maximize profits and tends to exploit employees by paying them only the minimum wage necessary for their survival. This conception of human alienation under capitalism is most vividly expressed in the *Economic and Philosophical*

Manuscripts that Marx wrote in Paris in 1844, but which remained unpublished for a century. The materialist conception of history was further developed in *The German Ideology* of 1846 (coauthored with Engels) and in *The Poverty of Philosophy* of 1847.

Marx became involved with the international **communist** movement, for he saw the purpose of his work as "not just to interpret the world, but to change it." He was primarily a social philosopher, but tried to be a political leader, too. Convinced that history was moving toward the revolution in which capitalism would give way to communism, Marx worked to educate and organize the **proletariat**—the class of industrial workers who had to sell their labor in order to survive, and to whom he thought victory in the class struggle must eventually go. Together with Engels he wrote the *Manifesto of the Communist Party* in 1848, deploying his rhetorical skills to famous effect. In that year there were abortive revolutions in several European countries, but they were soon defeated; and Marx had to find exile in Britain, where he remained for the rest of his life.

In London Marx lived a life of comparative poverty, existing on journalism and financial support from Engels (who ironically came from a factory-owning family himself). He pursued systematic research in the Reading Room of the British Museum, where he made use of the documentation about conditions in British industry. In 1857–58 he wrote another extensive set of manuscripts known as the *Grundrisse*, sketching his ambitious theory of history and society, the complete text of which was not available in English until the 1970s. In 1859 he published the *Critique of Political Economy* and in 1867 the first volume of his magnum opus *Capital*. These books contain a mass of detail on economic and social history, deployed to support the materialist interpretation of history and the inevitability of communism.

It is these later works that became best known until recently. In them we find German philosophy, French socialism, and British political economy welded into an all-embracing theory of history, economics, sociology, and politics, what Engels called "scientific socialism." Marx and Engels claimed to have found the correct *scientific* method for the study of human society and, thus, to establish the objective truth about its present workings and future development.

Marx's *Economic and Philosophical Manuscripts* from 1844 show the origins of his thinking in Hegel and the early German reactions to Hegel. Some interpreters have proposed two distinct periods in Marx—an early phase that has been called "humanist" or "existentialist," giving way later to "scientific socialism." However, the themes of alienation under capitalism and hope for overcoming it in communism are there throughout, so we shall treat his thought as a unity.

THE MATERIALIST THEORY OF HISTORY

Marx was an atheist, and the general trend of his thought is materialist and determinist. He presented himself as a social scientist, aiming to treat all human phenomena by the methods of science as he understood them. But the same applies to other thinkers of the Enlightenment such as de la Mettrie and Hume; what is distinctive of Marx is his claim to have found the truly *scientific* method for studying the *economic* history of human societies.

In his early theorizing he looked forward speculatively to the day when there would be a single science incorporating the study of humanity along with the rest of natural science. But any such unified science would have to include many levels, such as physics, chemistry, biology, psychology, and sociology. Marx implicitly compared his theory to physics when he said (in the preface to the first edition of *Capital*) that "the ultimate aim of this work is to lay bare the economic law of motion of modern society"; he wrote elsewhere of the natural laws of capitalist production "working with iron necessity towards inevitable results." But these are verbal flourishes (Marx was a great rhetorician), the detail of his theorizing does not show him to be a **reductionist** materialist or strict determinist. He did not expect every single fact about human individuals or societies to be explained in terms of physics (or brain science); rather, he looked for general socio-economic laws. The most fundamental feature of Marx's worldview is this materialist explanation both of social structure and of social change.

Synchronically, the economic base is supposed to determine the ideo-logical superstructure. Marx dismisses what rich and powerful people say in defense of capitalism as mere **ideology**, consciously or unconsciously motivated by their own economic interests. He would say that "liberal" or capitalist economic philosophy, with its rhetoric of "freedom" of en-terprise and trade, is merely an expression of the self-interest of those fortunate enough to possess land, property, and **capital**. But even if we think there is something in this suspicion of capitalist ideology, we should not let Marx have things all his own way. As we saw in the Introduction to this book, we should not allow a theorist to assume the truth of his own theory in diagnosing irrational motives in those who criticize that theory. A liberal economic philosophy (often ascribed to Adam Smith, though he was a *moral* philosopher as well) deserves a proper hearing—and critique. Ideas and opinions may well be biased by economic interests, but they need not be totally determined by them.

Marx said that in industrial societies the legal and political systems are in the hands of the capitalists, who control the processes of production. Yet governments have limited the worst excesses of early capitalism, by banning child labor, and enforcing laws about the health and safety of workers. In the developed countries there are laws and regulations governing business activity, though political battles continue about whether regulation should be increased or decreased. Marx would have to retreat to saying that law and politics are *affected*, but not totally controlled, by the capitalist class. This weakened claim is still very plausible, in view of the influence of industrial lobbyists on governments.

Diachronically, there are long-term processes of technological and economic development that result in large-scale social, political, and ideological change. Marx divided history into epochs identified by their different economic bases. First there were primitive tribes, then the "Asiatic" system of absolute monarchy, the ancient world of Greece and Rome (based on slavery), the feudal system of the Middle Ages (with peasants tied to their feudal lord), and most recently the bourgeois or capitalist phase (in which workers have to sell their labor to those who control production). Marx, echoing Hegel, holds that each stage gives way to the next when the technical and economic conditions are ripe. (Adam Smith imilarly distinguished four main economic stages: hunters, shepherds, farmers, and manufacturers.)

The best-known summary of the materialist theory of history is in the preface to Marx's *Critique of Political Economy* (1859):

> In the social production of their life, men enter into definite relations that are indispensable and independent of their will, relations of production which correspond to a definite stage of development of their material productive forces. The sum total of these relations of production constitutes the economic structure of society—the real basis, on which rises a legal and political superstructure, and to which correspond definite forms of social consciousness. The mode of production of material life conditions the social, political, and intellectual life process in general. It is not the consciousness of men that determines their being, but, on the contrary, their social being that determines their consciousness.

In some interpretations this has been taken as meaning that the economic basis of a society determines *everything* else about it. But Marx writes here only of the foundation "conditioning" social life, which could mean determining its *general* character, not every detail. He can admit the influences of nationalism, religion, wars, and charismatic individuals such as Julius Caesar, Napoleon, and Lenin. Historiography is not an exact quantitative science like physics or chemistry; and Marx, when he thought clearly, was surely under no such illusion.

Everyone now recognizes that economic factors are hugely important, no serious study of history or social science can ignore them: Marx can take much of the credit for that. But the above quotation is difficult to interpret, for there is an important ambiguity about where to draw the dividing line between "foundation" and "superstructure." Careful attention to the whole passage suggests that Marx means to distinguish three levels rather than two. He talks (a) of "the material powers of production," which would include natural resources (land, climate, plants, animals, minerals), technology (tools, machinery, communication systems), and human resources (labor power and skills). He talks (b) of the "economic structure" as including "relations of production," which presumably means the way in which work is organized, for example, the division of labor, hierarchies of authority in the workplace, the legal powers of ownership, and the systems of rewards and payments. The description of these relations of production, at least in modern societies, involves both the legal concept of property and economic concepts like money, capital, and wages. And Marx talks (c) of the ideological superstructure of a society: its beliefs, morality, laws, politics, religion, and philosophy.

What, then, did Marx mean by "the real basis" or "foundation"? Is it (a) alone, or (a) plus (b)? Is he saying that (a) determines (b) and thereby determines (c)? Or that (b) alone determines (c)? If he meant that the determining basis is only (a), the strictly material powers of production, this is implausible since similar resources and technologies can be used in societies with different ideologies or legal systems (e.g., Christian, Islamic, secular, capitalist, socialist, or communist). If the basis is (a) plus (b), does the legal concept of property belong in (b) or in (c)?

An answer to the latter objection may be that Marx can give an account of (b), the social relationships involved in economic production, in terms of actual relations of physical power and effective control, without yet using legal concepts of property and contracts. After all, he wants to apply his theory to primitive societies that lack the formalities of law but where it may be brutally clear who has control over resources and people. There are still times and places where personal power, backed up with force or the threat of force, is stronger than legal niceties.

It is open to Marx to maintain a double-barreled "conditioning" thesis: first, that (a) the material powers of production condition or limit (b) the relations of production (e.g., hand-operated mills fit into the feudal structure, but larger machinery such as steam mills requires capital investment—Marx's own example) and, second, that (a) and (b) together ("the economic structure") condition or limit (c) the ideological superstructure. If "conditioning" or 'limiting" does not mean determining every detail, Marx can avoid the objection that the same technology is used in different societies; he can say that those societies must have some relevant features in common. A modern example would be that the widespread use of computers requires a certain standard of education for most members of society, with all the social implications of that.

But all this raises the question of what Marx's talk of "conditioning" or "corresponding to" really amounts to. Just how much **determinism** did he mean to assert, synchronically or diachronically? Obviously, any society has to produce the necessities of life for individual survival and reproduction. We have to eat if we are to act or think, but it does not follow that how we produce our food determines everything that we do or think. The more plausible thing to say—and it seems to be what Marx does say when careful—is that the economic basis has a very significant influence on everything else: it sets limits within which the other factors play their part. The way a society produces the necessities of its life influences how its people tend to think. But this is vague, for it is left open what counts as "significant" influence. In the end, we have only a recommendation to seek out the economic factors in each case and examine how far they influence the rest. However, that has proved an immensely fruitful method in historiography, anthropology, and sociology.

Historiography is a systematic empirical study (what the Germans call a *Wissenschaft*) in that its propositions, however sweeping some historical claims may be, must be tested by evidence of what actually happened. But it does not follow that it is a science in the sense of involving **laws of nature** (i.e., general statements with unrestricted universality), for economic and social history is the study of what has happened in various human societies on this particular planet, in finite periods of past time. We know of no such histories elsewhere in the universe, and neither can we do experimental reruns of history.

For any particular event or series of events—even the fall of an apple from a tree—many different laws and contingent facts may be involved in its causation: for example, the laws of gravity and mechanics, the weather and gusts of wind, the decay of wood and the elasticity of twigs, shakings of the tree by animals or birds, or tweaking by human fingers. If there is no closed set of influences, and so perhaps no determinism, governing even the fall of a single apple, how much more implausible it is to say that the course of human history is predetermined. To be sure, there are some long-term and large-scale trends, such as the increase of human population and the development of ever more complex technology. But such trends are not laws of nature: their continuation is not inevitable, for they depend on conditions that can change. Population growth and technological development may be halted or reversed by war, disease, famine, or environmental catastrophe.

From his general understanding of history, Marx thought that capitalism would become more and more unstable, that the class struggle between the owners of capital and the proletariat (those who live by selling their labor) would increase, with the latter getting poorer (but larger in number) until they would take power in a revolution. But he did not make any definite predictions of communist revolution in the countries where industrial capitalism was most developed in his time, namely Britain, France, and the United States. In the *Communist Manifesto* of 1848 he pointed to Germany, still semifeudal, as a society where he expected a **bourgeois** revolution (by the middle classes, replacing feudalism—as arguably was the case in the French Revolution), to be followed only at some later stage by a proletarian one. And he saw that communist ideas could be imported into countries where a relatively small proletariat allied with impoverished peasantry could seize power from the traditional aristocratic ruling class. In war-weakened tsarist Russia, the Bolsheviks under the leadership of Lenin did just that. But the imposition of communism on Eastern Europe by the Red Army in 1945 was imperialist expansion rather than proletarian revolution. Neither Russia nor China had much capitalism at the time of their communist revolutions in 1917 and 1949; their major industrialization came later, with top-down five-year plans brutally imposed.

It can be suggested that in the past colonies (now called "developing" countries) formed the proletariat vis-à-vis the industrialized countries and that in today's globalized market we are still benefiting from the agricultural labor and sweatshops of the Third World. In the *Communist Manifesto* Marx mentioned the bourgeoisie's exploitation of the world market, noting the economic importance of slavery ("the hunting of black skins") to Britain and America. (It was not only slave owners who profited, the system of slavery contributed to general economic development, and we still benefit from that.)

History has not worked out as Marx expected. There have been no communist revolutions in the advanced capitalist countries. The capitalist economic system has become more stable than in the nineteenth century, though with notable exceptions such as the Great Depression of the 1930s and the banking crisis recently. With the globalization of trade and finance, it is hard to be confident of future stability when huge amounts of money can be switched around the world instantaneously.

Conditions of life for most people have improved vastly from what they were in Marx's time, and class divisions have in many ways been blurred. Unrestrained nineteenth-century capitalism with its dreadful conditions for the working class, including child labor, epidemic diseases and shortened life, has been considerably ameliorated in the West by employment legislation and systems of welfare. (In a *purely* free market system, those who cannot find jobs would be left "free to starve".) There are now large numbers of workers such as office staff, government employees, nurses, teachers, and lawyers who are neither manual laborers nor industrial owners. But they have no say over the globalized economic forces that affect their working conditions and whether they can find or keep a job. Marx's description of a small number of super-rich owners of capital controlling the lives of millions of workers around the world seems more accurate than ever.

THEORY OF HUMAN NATURE: ECONOMICS, SOCIETY, AND CONSCIOUSNESS

Except in his early study of Hegel and the ancient Greeks, Marx was not interested in questions of academic philosophy, which he would later dismiss as idle speculation compared to the vital task of changing the world. So when he is labeled a "materialist," this refers to his materialist understanding of history rather than a theory of the relation of mind to brain. Even if he holds that all states of consciousness are determined by economic conditions, this could be an **epiphenomenalist** position, that our mental states, though not themselves physical, have their contents determined by our brain states. This need not be a metaphysically materialist view that consciousness is identical with brain processes.

What is distinctive of Marx's concept of humanity is his view of our essentially social nature (like Plato and Aristotle). In one place he even wrote that "the real nature of man is the totality of social relations." There are obvious biological facts about all of us, such as our anatomy, our need for certain kinds of food, and our urge to reproduce; but almost everything we do presupposes the existence of other people. Marx realized that much of what is true of people in one society or period may not apply in another place or time. He remarked, with typical verve and exaggeration, that "all history is nothing but a continuous transformation of human nature." Economic production typically requires cooperation: even the ways in which we produce our food and bring up our children are socially affected. This does not mean that "society" is an abstract entity that mysteriously affects individuals: rather, what one does is affected by one's social interactions. So what seems "natural" in one society or epoch—for example, a certain role for monarchs, for priests, or for women—may be very different in another.

We can summarize this crucial point by saying that sociology is not reducible to psychology. Not everything about human beings can be explained in terms of facts about individuals: the kind of society they live in must be considered too. This methodological point is one of Marx's most distinctive contributions, and one of the most widely accepted. For this reason, he is recognized as one of the founding fathers of sociology. And this *method* can be accepted whether or not one agrees with the particular conclusions he came to.

But there is at least one substantive generalization that Marx offers about human nature: that we are *active* beings; we are different by nature from the other animals because we *produce* our means of subsistence. And this is not like bees producing honey or birds making nests, for we make conscious decisions about how to produce our livelihood in new situations: it is natural for human beings to plan ahead and work for their living, in hunting, in the agricultural cycle—sowing, weeding, harvesting, and baking—and in organized manufacture. There is a factual truth here, but as with so many assertions about what is "natural" (see the Introduction), Marx associated with it a **value judgment** that the life that is appropriate for humans involves purposive productive activity. This is connected with his diagnosis of alienation in industrial labor and his prescription for a future society in which everyone can cultivate his or her own talents. It contrasts with Aristotle's view that the highest human activity is theoretical contemplation (Chapter 5) and with the Biblical view that our highest good is the love of God (Chapter 6).

What does Marx's theory imply about the female sex? If there is a point in his concentration on production, there is also obvious truth about the necessity for *reproduction*. No society can survive unless it can produce new members to carry it on. That includes not just sexual intercourse, pregnancy, childbirth, and breastfeeding, but the longer processes of childcare, education and socialization, which are laborious in their own way—and involve men. In *The Origin of the Family, Private Property and the State*, Engels (writing without Marx) argued that economic production determines both labor and the family. But on the whole Marx was a man of his time, assuming that the traditional division of family roles has a purely physiological foundation, with women being almost totally responsible for childcare. He did not realize that what he thought of as biologically determined differences between the sexes are themselves affected by socioeconomic factors. Technical developments like reliable contraception, formula milk for babies, and economic changes that require mental skills more than manual labor have transformed the question of male and female "nature" in ways that Marx himself did not foresee but which his theory has resources to deal with.

DIAGNOSIS: ALIENATION AND EXPLOITATION UNDER CAPITALISM

Marx's diagnosis of what is wrong with society is vividly expressed in his early writings in his concept of alienation or estrangement, derived from Hegel and Feuerbach. This involved both a description of certain features of capitalist society and a value judgment that they are wrong. But Marx does not make it clear exactly which features he is criticizing. He was not, after all, totally condemnatory of capitalism: he acknowledged that it has led to a great increase in productivity and thus makes the transition to communism economically possible. It is a stage through which society has to go, but Marx thinks that it ought to be (and will be) surpassed.

Logically, alienation is a relation—it must be *from* somebody or something, one cannot be just "alienated," any more than one can be married without being married to someone. Marx wrote somewhat obscurely about human alienation in the *Economic and Philosophical Manuscripts*. In one place he says that alienation is "from man himself and from Nature": where "Nature" seems to mean for him the humanly-modified world (the opposite of its usual meaning). Workers are not what they could be and should be, because they are alienated from the products they create and alienated in the social relations involved in their work: they do not *care* about either, except as a means to earn a living. They have to sell their labor in order to survive and can be exploited by the capitalists, who can dictate the terms and conditions of their employment.

Sometimes it sounds as if it is private property that Marx primarily condemns, when he writes "the abolition of private property is the abolition of alienation." But elsewhere he says, "Although private property appears to be the basis and cause of alienated labor, it is rather a consequence of the latter." He describes this alienation of labor as consisting in the fact that the work is "not part of the worker's nature"; the worker is not fulfilled in his or her work but feels miserable, physically exhausted, and mentally debased. The work is forced on him as a means for satisfying basic needs, so at work he does not "belong to himself." Even the materials used and the objects produced are alien to the worker because they are owned by someone else.

Sometimes Marx seems to be blaming alienation on the use of money as a means of exchange that reduces all social relationships to a common commercial denominator—"callous cash payment," as he put in the *Manifesto*. In that context he was making a contrast with feudal society with its nonmonetary economic relationships (but no doubt those could be "callous" in their own way). Elsewhere he suggests that it is the division of labor that makes work an alien power, requiring people to specialize rather than switching activities at will within the course of a day (as he implausibly suggested will be possible in future communist society).

In his later work Marx offered a more direct diagnosis of the evil of capitalism (though the concept of alienation did not entirely disappear from his writing). He developed a "labor theory of value" and a concept of "surplus-value" appropriated by the owners of industry. These more technical concepts have been much discussed in economic theory, but we will not go into them here.

Marx's main diagnosis was always a moral one, about the *injustice* of the economic structure of capitalism. Surprisingly, there is some agreement here between Marx and Adam Smith. The pioneering Scottish economist has been hailed as the first apostle of capitalism and economic liberalism, advocating unfettered competition as not merely the most efficient but also the most moral foundation for modern society. But Smith was a moral philosopher as well as an economist, and he too was alarmed about the tendency for the developing capitalist economy to impoverish or alienate its working class:

> No society can surely be flourishing and happy, of which the far greater part of the members are poor and miserable. It is but equity, besides, that they who feed, clothe and lodge the whole body of the people, should have such a share of the whole produce of their own labor as to be themselves tolerably well fed, clothed and lodged. (*The Wealth of Nations* 96)

And even when material needs were met, mental or spiritual needs were not. Human potential remained sadly unrealized:

> We find that in the commercial parts of England, the tradesmen are for the most part in this despicable condition: their work through half the week is sufficient to maintain them, and through want of education they have no amusement for the other but riot and debauchery. (*Lectures on Jurisprudence* 540)

So Smith was concerned about that kind of alienation (though not under that name). And we are not free of these worries even now (*plus ça change, plus c'est la même chose*).

There is a fundamental diagnosis here which should command universal assent: that it is wrong to treat any person as only a means to an economic end (remember Kant's formulation of the moral law: always treat rational beings as ends in themselves—Chapter 8). Human beings were treated as mere means of production in the unrestrained capitalism of the early nineteenth century, when adults and children worked long hours in filthy conditions and died early deaths after miserably unfulfilled lives. This still happens in some countries; and even in nations where capitalism is trumpeted as a stunning success, there is a constant tendency for managers to try to extract the greatest possible profit from the labor of their employees, driving down wages, cutting the workforce, or extending working hours. A recent trend is to relocate business to a country where labor is much cheaper and legal regulations are weaker.

Marx's most significant idea is arguably that capitalist society restricts the full development of human potential, and encourages the exploitation of the masses by those who own or control capital. These days he could well say that alienation affects not merely manual laborers but all those who have to work under competitive economic pressures. The average employee, whether in small businesses, large corporations or government agencies, whether cleaner, machine minder, pen pusher, keyboard clicker, software programmer, salesperson or middle manager, may feel alienate" from his or her human potential by the conditions of the workplace. Even the self-employed businessperson and those at the top of the economic system, the executives, bankers and government administrators, may feel constrained by forces outside their control. Sometimes the most worrying thought is not so much that the wrong people are in control, but that nobody is in control.

We might express Marx's main point in a paraphrase of Jesus's saying about the Sabbath: human beings do not exist for the purpose of production; rather, production is supposed to be for human benefit. And this should apply to *all* the people involved—employers, employees, consumers, and anyone affected by side effects such as pollution. The huge practical difficulty is, of course, how to give social effect to this ideal.

PRESCRIPTION: REVOLUTION AND UTOPIA

"If man is formed by circumstances, these circumstances must be humanly formed." If alienation and exploitation are social problems caused by the nature of the capitalist economic system, then Marx holds that the solution is to abolish that system and replace it by a better one. He thought that this was bound to happen anyway: capitalism would burst asunder because of its inner contradictions, and the communist revolution would usher in the new social order. The resolution of the problems of capitalism was supposed to be already on the way in the forward movement of history, and our responsibility is to align ourselves with it.

Marx's materialist theory of history often sounds determinist, yet there is an element of human freedom left, for he appealed to people to realize the direction in which history is moving and to *act* accordingly. Within the communist movements there were controversies between those who emphasized the need to wait for the appropriate stage of economic development before expecting the revolution, and those like Lenin who acted to seize the moment and bring it about. But there is no contradiction here, for while Marx maintains that while the revolution is bound to occur sooner or later, it is possible for prescient individuals and organized groups to hasten its coming and "ease its birth pangs."

How can alienation be overcome? It is hard to believe that anyone can seriously advocate the abolition of money (a return to a system of barter?), the end of all specialization, or the communal control of everything (even toothbrushes, clothes, and food?). It is the private ownership of *industry*— the means of production and exchange—that is usually taken as the defining feature of capitalism. The program of the *Communist Manifesto* included the nationalization of land, factories, transport, and banks. But can state control cure the alienation of labor that Marx describes in his early work? Were not people just as alienated under communist rule in the Soviet Union? Might nationalization make things worse by increasing the power of the state and state-owned corporations over individuals?

Marx held that only a complete revolution of the capitalist economic system could solve its problems; piecemeal reforms such as higher wages, shorter hours, and pension schemes may be welcome ameliorations of the harshness of capitalism, but they do not alter its basic nature—hence the difference between communist and democratic socialist parties. But communist parties themselves disagreed about political strategy. Some thought that working to reform the system would distract attention from the class struggle and the need to *overthrow* the existing order. Others said the process of arousing workers to combine together to fight for reform would "raise their consciousness," create class solidarity, and thus hasten revolutionary change.

In fact, a long series of reforms *have* modified capitalism very considerably, beginning with the British Factory Acts in the nineteenth century which limited the worst exploitation of workers and children, and continuing with national insurance schemes, unemployment benefits, and national health services. Trade unions have made considerable progress in increasing wages and improving working conditions, though conflicts of interest remain between the two sides of industry. Many of the specific measures proposed in the *Communist Manifesto* have long since come into effect in the so-called capitalist countries—graduated income tax, free education in state schools, centralization of considerable economic control in the hands of the state, and nationalization or state control of some industries—especially defense. The unregulated capitalist system as Marx knew it in the mid-nineteenth century has largely disappeared in the developed countries, and not by revolution. This is not to say that what we have now is perfect, but it does imply that contempt for gradual reform is mistaken; and reflection on the instability, violence and suffering involved in real revolutions elsewhere may confirm this.

However, the competitiveness of life under capitalism conflicts with the ideal of solidarity. So we might understand Marx as saying that alienation consists in a lack of *community*, in that most workers cannot see their work as contributing to a group of which they are members: the factory owner is not "one of them". Most corporations are too large to be a real community, even if workers own a few shares in it. Perhaps there is more hope in business models that give employees a significant stake in the success of the business, and some say in how it is to be conducted.

Marx prophetically envisages a regeneration of humanity, within *this* world. He once described communism, with wild enthusiasm, as "the solution to the riddle of history": the abolition of private property is supposed to ensure the disappearance of alienation and exploitation and the coming of a genuinely classless society. He is extremely vague on how all this would be achieved, but he envisages an intermediate period called "the dictatorship of the proletariat" before the transition can be made to a truly communist society. In a phrase that sounds ominous in the light of twentieth-century history, he declared that "the alteration of men on a mass scale is necessary"—but in his defense it may be suggested that he had in mind an alteration of consciousness, not the forcible methods of Stalinist Russia, Maoist China, or North Korea. In the higher phase of communist society Marx supposed that the state will "wither away" and the realm of true human freedom will begin. Then human potentiality can develop for its own sake, and the guiding principle can be "from each according to his ability, to each according to his needs."

Much of this utopian vision must surely be judged unrealistic. Marx gives us no good reason to believe that communist society will be genuinely classless, that those who *exercise* the dictatorship of the proletariat will not form a new governing class, with opportunities to abuse their power and develop new forms of exploitation. No set of economic changes can be expected to eliminate *all* conflicts of interest and all feelings of boredom or "alienation" at work. States show no sign of withering away, but have become more powerful, though these days we must also recognize the power of the big corporations and the increasingly global nature of the market, which restricts the power of any one government.

Yet with other elements in Marx's vision, we may well agree. The application of science and technology to produce the necessities of life for everybody, the shortening of the working day, the provision of universal education so that all human beings can develop their potential, the vision of a more decentralized society in which people cooperate in communities for the common good, and of a society in balance with nature—these are ideals that most people now share, though it is no easy matter how they can be compatibly realized.

Probably it is because Marxism has offered this hopeful vision of a human future that it was able to win the allegiance of so many people. It has been a secular faith, a prophetic vision of social salvation. So even now, despite the disputability of some of Marx's theoretical assertions and the failures and atrocities of communist regimes, his ideas are far from dead. But his diagnosis is a good deal more convincing than his prescription. Social reforms and technical developments have altered the face of the capitalist system for the better in many ways, but many people still see the need for some limitation or transformation of global capitalism, to make it serve widespread human needs and not just enrich the already rich.

Marx's exclusive emphasis on economic factors directs our attention to only one of the obstacles in the way of human fulfillment. Sexuality and family relationships are obviously vital, as are our existential/religious attitudes to the inevitable but non-economic problems of life such as moral failings, illness, old age, and mortality. And human conflict—from tribalism to nationalism, nuclear confrontation, and terrorism—seems to involve something darker in human nature than mere economic competition. We must look elsewhere—to psychology, existentialism, evolutionary theory, and perhaps even religious conceptions—for deeper insights into the problems of human individuals and societies.

FOR FURTHER READING

There is no one main text to recommend as basic. The *Communist Manifesto* is an obvious starting point, but it is stronger on polemics than on theory, and its third section is dated; the *German Ideology* is deeper and longer but fairly readable.

There are several useful selections from Marx's works: *Karl Marx: Selected Writings in Sociology and Social Philosophy*, trans. T. B. Bottomore, ed. T. B. Bottomore and Maximilien Rubel (London: Penguin, 1963; New York: McGraw-Hill, 1964), which is helpfully organized under themes; also *Marx and Engels: Basic Writings on Politics and Philosophy*, ed. Lewis S. Feuer (New York: Anchor Books, 1959), and *Karl Marx: Selected Writings*, 2nd ed., ed. David McLellan (Oxford: Oxford University Press, 2000).

Peter Singer has a "Very Short Introduction" to Marx (Oxford: Oxford University Press, 2000). There is a readable re-evaluation by Jonathan Wolff, *Why Read Marx Today?* (Oxford: Oxford University Press, 2002) which addresses the labor theory of value, not discussed in this chapter.

There are biographies of Marx by Francis Wheen, *Karl Marx* (London: Fourth Estate, 1999), and by Isaiah Berlin and Alan Ryan, *Karl Marx: His Life and Environment*, 3rd ed. (New York: Oxford University Press, 2002).

A classic criticism of Marxism was presented by Karl Popper in *The Open Society and Its Enemies*, vol. 1 (London: Routledge, 2011). There is an in-depth discussion of Marx on human nature in John Plamenatz, *Karl Marx's Philosophy of Man* (Oxford: Oxford University Press, 1975), and a brief elucidation in Norman Geras, *Marx and Human Nature: Refutation of a Legend* (London: Verso, 1983).

The religious dimension of Marx's thought is considered by Robert Tucker in *Philosophy and Myth in Karl Marx*, 2nd ed. (Cambridge: Cambridge University Press, 1982). For a sophisticated defense of Marx using the methods of analytical philosophy, see G. A. Cohen, *Karl Marx's Theory of History: A Defense* (Princeton, NJ: Princeton University Press, 2001). On the relation of Marxism to feminism, see Friedrich Engels, *Origin of the Family, Private Property and the State* (London: Penguin, 2010), and Alison Jaggar, *Feminist Politics and Human Nature* (Totowa, NJ: Rowman & Littlefield, 1983), chapter 4. A postcommunist defense of Marx's ideas is Keith Graham, *Karl Marx Our Contemporary: Social Theory for a Post-Leninist World* (Toronto: University of Toronto Press, 1992).

For the thought of Adam Smith, see D. D. Raphael, *Adam Smith* (Oxford: Oxford University Press, 1985), and Athol Fitzgibbons, *Adam Smith's System of Liberty, Wealth and Virtue* (Oxford: Oxford University Press, 1995).

KEY TERMS

alienation	laws of nature
bourgeois	materialist theory of history
capital	metaphysics
capitalism	pantheism
communism	proletariat
determinism	reductionism
epiphenomenalism	Spirit
ideology	value judgment

QUESTIONS FOR DISCUSSION

1. Does Marx persuade you that economic factors are the main determinants of social structure and social change?
2. Is alienation inevitable under capitalism, or under any economic system?
3. Does contemporary capitalism require radical reform?
4. Can we have community without communism?

10

Freud: The Unconscious Basis of Mind

Freud's psychoanalytic approach to the mind revolutionized our understanding of human nature in the first half of the twentieth century. He spent a long career developing and modifying his theories, touching on a vast range of subjects relating to human nature, including biology, neuroscience, medicine, psychiatry, psychology, sexuality, child development, anthropology, sociology, art, and religion. Moreover, he founded and led the worldwide psychoanalytic movement. In this chapter we concentrate on Freud himself, not later developments in psychoanalytic theory and practice, and our critical points come up in two sections at the end.

LIFE AND WORK

Sigmund Freud (1865-1939) was born in Moravia, but at the age of four his family moved to Vienna, where he lived and worked until the Nazis forced him into exile in 1938. As a schoolboy his precocious interests ranged over the whole of human life, including the sciences and the Greek and Roman classics; and when he entered the University of Vienna as a medical student he attended lectures on other subjects, including those by the distinguished Austrian philosopher Franz Brentano. Freud became deeply interested in biology and spent six years doing research in the laboratory of the famous physiologist Brücke, writing papers on technical topics such as the nervous systems of fishes. But in order to marry his beloved fiancée he needed more secure employment than scientific research offered, so somewhat reluctantly he began work as a physician at Vienna General Hospital. In 1886 he set up a private practice in "nervous diseases" (i.e., psychological problems), which he maintained for the rest of his life.

Freud's subsequent intellectual career can be divided into three main sections. In a preliminary phase he put forward some original hypotheses about the nature of neurotic problems and began to develop his distinctive method of treatment which came to be known as **psychoanalysis**. His interest in human psychology had been fired by a visit to Paris in 1885–86 to study under Charcot, a French neurologist who performed striking demonstrations of the influence of mental suggestion and hypnotism on physical symptoms and behavior. Many of Freud's early patients were Viennese women suffering from what was then called "hysteria." Often they had mysterious paralyses, muteness, or loss of sensation in bodily regions that bore no relation to neurology, only to ordinary conceptions of body parts such as hand or arm. Etymologically the word "hysteria" comes from ancient attributions of such symptoms to disturbances of the womb, and nowadays the word tends to mean a state of extreme emotion; but in Freud's time it referred to these puzzling symptoms that orthodox medicine found almost impossible to treat. It seems very likely that "hysteria" in turn-of-the-century bourgeois Viennese women had much to do with their restricted social situation and repressed sexuality.

Freud had been impressed by how Charcot's purely psychological methods seemed to induce dramatic cures of "nervous" problems. Faced with similar symptoms in his own patients, he first used electrotherapy and hypnotic suggestion, but finding neither very effective, he tried a method that had been developed by Breuer, a senior Viennese consultant. Breuer's approach was based on the hypothesis that hysterical symptoms had been initiated by some intense emotional experience (a "trauma") that the patient had apparently forgotten, and his treatment was to induce recall of the experience and a "discharge" of the corresponding emotion. This theory that people could suffer from an unconscious idea, an emotion-charged memory that they were not aware of, but from which they could be relieved by bringing it into consciousness, is the germ from which psychoanalysis developed.

Freud found that the traumatic ideas in his patients' minds typically had some sexual content, and (ever ready to hazard a theoretical generalization) he speculated that neuroses *always* have a sexual origin. Indeed, in many cases his patients came up with reports of "infantile seduction"—what we now call child sexual abuse. At first he believed them, but then—in a dramatic change of tack that he regarded as a crucial discovery, but for which he has been criticized in recent years—he came to think that these reports were usually fantasies rather than memories of what had actually occurred. He was under no illusion that sexual abuse of children did happen and caused mental trauma, but he could not believe that it applied to so many of his patients. In 1895 Freud and Breuer published *Studies on Hysteria* jointly, but Breuer was unable to agree on the causal importance of sexuality: in fact, he fled Vienna when one of his own patients fell in love with him, in a clear case of what Freud came to recognize as transference, namely, the emotions that patients may feel for their therapist. Freud was not discouraged by such experiences, however, and continued on his own theoretical way.

In this early exploratory period Freud drafted his *Project for a Scientific Psychology*, in which he ambitiously tried to relate his developing psychological theory to a physical basis in the nerve cells in the brain. Though initially excited by these interdisciplinary speculations, he came to think of them as too far ahead of their time and did not submit the work for publication (the manuscript was lost, rediscovered, and eventually published in 1950). Yet the ghost of the *Project* haunts of all Freud's later works, in the form of a background assumption that the mental processes postulated in **psychoanalytic theory** could eventually be identified with movements of electrical energy in the neurons in the brain.

Around the turn of the century Freud began to formulate his distinctive theories about infantile sexuality and the interpretation of dreams, and introduced his crucial theoretical concepts of **resistance**, **repression**, and **transference**. The second phase of his work can conveniently be dated from the publication of *The Interpretation of Dreams* (1900), in which he reported his attempts to psychoanalyze himself, including virtuosic (but questionable) interpretations of his own dreams. That was followed by *The Psychopathology of Everyday Life* (1901), in which he analyzed the unconscious causation of everyday errors such as slips of the tongue, and *Three Essays on the Theory of Sexuality* (1905). These three works apply psychoanalytic theory to *normal* mental life (or what passes for normal, non-neurotic life), thus it was becoming a new kind of general psychological theory. Freud soon attracted a following, and institutes and journals of psychoanalysis sprang up. In 1909 he was invited to the United States, where he gave a popular exposition of his ideas, the *Five Lectures on*

Psycho-Analysis, at Clark University. In 1915–17 he delivered the much longer *Introductory Lectures on Psycho-Analysis* at the University of Vienna, in which he expounded the complete theory as he had developed it up until then.

The third phase of Freud's work saw some important modifications to his theories and some wide-ranging speculative attempts to apply them to social questions. In *Beyond the Pleasure Principle* (1920) he introduces his controversial concept of the **death instinct** to try to explain aggression and self-destruction, as well as the "life instincts" (self-preservation, sexuality, survival, and reproduction) which he had postulated up until then. Another late development was the famous tripartite division of the mind— **id, ego,** and **superego**—that he presents in *The Ego and the Id* (1923). In a second popular exposition *The Question of Lay Analysis* (1926), he expounded his general theory in terms of his new three-part structure.

Many of Freud's later years were devoted to social theorizing. Already in 1913 he had speculated about anthropology and human prehistory in *Totem and Taboo*. After the First World War, and with the rise of fascism in Europe, his thought took on a more pessimistic tone. In *The Future of an Illusion* (1927) he treated religion as a system of false beliefs whose deep infantile roots in our minds can be explained psychoanalytically. In *Civilization and Its Discontents* (1930) he discussed the alleged conflict between individual human drives and the morality of civilized society, and in *Moses and Monotheism* (1939) he offered a controversial psychoanalytic interpretation of Jewish history. In 1938 Hitler annexed Austria (the *Anschluss*), and Jews were in danger. Though not a believer, Freud was ethnically Jewish and he had experienced Austrian anti-Semitism throughout his life. But because of his huge international fame the Nazis allowed him (for a large fee) to escape to London, "to die in freedom" as he put it, where he spent his last year writing a brief final *Outline of Psycho-Analysis*.

METAPHYSICAL BACKGROUND: NEUROSCIENCE, DETERMINISM, AND MATERIALISM

What is distinctive in Freud's thought is, of course, his theory of the human mind, but we first should take note of his metaphysical and methodological assumptions. From the start he rejected theology and **metaphysics**. He started his research career as a physiologist, and though he entered into the depths of individual psychology and theorized boldly about human culture and society, he claimed to remain a scientist throughout; his aim was to explain all the phenomena of human life scientifically. He was not a Marxist but he shared the common belief in progress and the Enlightenment faith that the application of science could improve the human condition.

Thoroughly trained in post-Darwinian biology, Freud accepted that human beings are a species of animal, albeit of a special sort. With his knowledge of biological science and his experience of physiological research, he assumed that everything that happens in our *bodies* is **determined** by the laws of physics, chemistry, and biology. He has been well described as a "biologist of the mind," who assumed that our *mental* events and processes are also determined by preceding causes.

Freud was a philosophical materialist as well as a determinist. He acknowledged a distinction of some sort between mental states and brain states, but this was for him only a dualism of attributes (akin to Spinoza), not of two substances or two parallel sets of events. Materialist philosophers say that in talking of mental states such as sensations, thoughts, wishes, and emotions we are not committed to Cartesian dualism, for they can be understood as the mental aspects of our complex brain states. Freud held the same about the **unconscious** mental states that he postulated, believing that they too must be based in the brain, as he said in his *Scientific Project*. It is significant, however, that he sometimes uses the German word *Seele* ("soul"), thereby suggesting that he saw his work as part of the humanities as much as the sciences, dealing with the problems of life as we experience them. Psychoanalysis depends on the analyst presenting his or her interpretations in ordinary, non-scientific language that the patient can understand. After his early attempt to relate his developing psychological theory to neuroscience, Freud was content to leave the neurological basis of psychology to be discovered in future research. Enormous progress has been made in this in recent years; Freud's speculations look primitive but by no means silly.

THEORY OF HUMAN NATURE: MENTAL DETERMINISM, THE UNCONSCIOUS, DRIVES, AND CHILD DEVELOPMENT

Freud's approach can be summarized under four main headings. The first is his strict application of determinism—the principle that every event has preceding causes—to the realm of the mental. Thoughts and behavior that had been assumed to be accidental and of no great significance for understanding a person, such as slips of the tongue, failures of memory, faulty actions, dreams, and neurotic symptoms, Freud assumed must have hidden mental causes, which can reveal themselves in disguised form: hence the well-known concept of the "Freudian slip." In this he remains close to our everyday explanations of human failings ("How could he forget her birthday?" "Why did she spill his drink?"), and to the understanding of human nature deployed by novelists and dramatists. Freud presented his psychoanalytic theory as applying to all human behavior, not just neurotic patients. In his understanding, nothing that a person thinks or does or says is truly haphazard or accidental; everything can in principle be traced to some cause, often unconsciously processed through the mind.

This seems to imply a denial of free will, for even when we think we are choosing perfectly freely, Freud tends to claim that there are unknown causes determining our choice. There is an interesting parallel with Marx here, in that both suggest that the contents of our consciousness, far from being uniquely "free" and "rational," are determined by causes of which we are not normally aware. But whereas Marx says that the causes are social and economic, Freud claims they are individual and psychological, rooted in our biological drives. However, both thinkers presuppose that some of us some of the time (especially would-be scientific thinkers like themselves!) make rational judgments and decisions based on objective evidence. Can those judgments, based on the *right kind* of causes, count as "free"? There is much more to be said about freedom on a philosophical level, but Freud had no time for what he saw as the philosophical trivialities of his day.

The second and most distinctive feature of Freud's theorizing—the postulation of *unconscious* mental states—arises out of the first. But we must be careful to understand his concept of the unconscious correctly. There are lots of mental states, such as memories, of which we are not continually conscious, but which can readily be recalled to mind when they become relevant. These Freud calls **preconscious**, reserving the term "unconscious" for states that *cannot* become conscious under normal circumstances. His crucial assertion is that our minds are not coextensive with what is available to our attention (the conscious plus preconscious) but include elements of which we have no ordinary awareness. To extend a familiar analogy, the mind is like an iceberg, with some of it above the surface of the sea, some of it occasionally visible as the waves rise and fall, and the vast bulk of it hidden below the surface, influencing the rest.

So far, this gives us a *descriptive* account of the unconscious, but Freud's concept is also *dynamic*. To explain puzzling human phenomena such as hysterical paralyses, neurotic behavior, obsessive thoughts, and dreams, Freud postulated the existence of emotionally charged ideas in the unconscious part of the mind, which actively yet mysteriously exert causal influences on what a person thinks, feels, and does. Unconscious wishes or emotions can make a person do things that he or she cannot explain rationally, for example, obsessive behavior such as repeated washing. Traumatic emotional experiences were conscious at the time, but were then repressed because they were too painful to remember. Repression is thus postulated as a mental process or force pushing ideas into the unconscious and keeping them there. But the rest of the unconscious contains the innate driving forces of our mental life which operate from infancy and have always been unconscious.

Freud introduced a new *structural* concept of the mind in the 1920s, which does not exactly coincide with his earlier distinction between conscious, preconscious, and unconscious. In this late phase he distinguished three systems within the mental apparatus. In the standard English translations these have been called "id," "ego," and "superego"; but Freud himself used the ordinary German words *es*, *ich*, and *uberich*, which translate literally as "it," "I," and "higher I," and relate more closely to our everyday self-understanding. The *id* contains the instinctual drives that seek immediate satisfaction like a small child, and Freud says it operates according to the "pleasure principle." The *ego*, or "I" is nearest to our ordinary conception of self, with our conscious mental states that we can articulate as "I think . . . ," "I feel . . . ," "I want . . . ," including perceptions of the real world and decisions about how to act; Freud says the ego is governed by the "reality principle." Whatever *can* become conscious is in the ego (though Freud says mysteriously that it also contains elements that remain unconscious), whereas everything in the id is unconscious. The third character in this internal drama, the *superego*, contains the person's conscience derived from the moral norms learned in childhood; it can confront the ego with rules and prohibitions like a strict parent or tyrant, inducing feelings of guilt or anxiety. The forces of repression are located in the ego and superego, and they typically operate unconsciously. The poor old ego (self or person) has the difficult job of trying to reconcile the conflicting demands of the id and superego, given the often unhelpful facts of the real world. This is Freud's dramatic picture of the human condition, beset by external problems and internal conflict.

There are interesting parallels with Plato's tripartite theory of mental structure (see Chapter 4). The id obviously corresponds to Appetite, but it is not so clear how well the ego and superego correspond to Reason and Spirit. In its knowledge of reality, the ego would seem akin to Reason, but for Plato Reason has also a moral function that Freud allocates to the superego; this reflects Plato's belief in the objectivity of value judgments, about which Freud was not so sure. And Plato's Spirit also seems to have a moral function in passing judgment on some desires.

The **instincts** or drives are the third main feature of Freud's theory. In postulating the existence of motivating factors of which the person may not be aware, his thought links with Schopenhauer and Nietzsche, two nineteenth-century German philosophers who theorized about the will as the driving force in human life. Freud's word *Trieb* is sometimes translated as "instinct," but the term "drive" is more appropriate because instincts in animals are usually thought of as innate impulsions to specific behaviors, such as fly eating by spiders, nest building by birds, and rutting by stags in the mating season, whereas it is a feature of Freud's theorizing that the same underlying drive can be the motivating force or energy behind a variety of *different* behaviors. For example, the human sexual drive can motivate sending flowers, writing poetry, and the pledging of marriage vows in church; and it can be manifest in homosexuality or a foot fetish as well as in heterosexual intercourse.

The drives are the motive forces within our minds; they generate the mental energy that seeks "discharge." Freud used this mechanical or electrical language in an almost literal way, influenced by his scientific training and his early *Project* in which he presciently wrote about flows of electrical charge through the neurons in the brain. His description of mental drives makes them sound like electrical charges or hydraulic pressures, but his theorizing about the variety of behaviors that they can motivate extends to the whole of human life.

Freud's classification of drives was one of the most speculative and variable parts of his theory. Of course, one main kind of drive is sexual (who could deny it?), and Freud notoriously traces a great deal of human behavior, especially in his neurotic patients, back to sexual desires and thoughts experienced in childhood and sometimes repressed into the unconscious. But it is a gross misinterpretation to say that he tried to explain *all* human phenomena in terms of sex. It is true that he gives sexuality a much wider scope in human life than had formerly been recognized, claiming that it begins in infancy, that it plays a crucial role in adult neuroses, and that sexual energy (**libido**) can be "sublimated" or diverted into other activity, such as art.

But Freud always held that there was at least one *other* basic drive besides sex. In his early period he distinguished the "self-preservative" instincts (nourishment and self-protection) from the reproductive drive. But after 1920 he changed his classification, lumping together hunger, sex, and self-preservation into one "life" instinct called *eros* (echoing Plato's idea of a spiritual kind of love that includes more than sexuality). Freud then attributed sadism, aggression, and self-destruction to what he calls the "death instinct" or destructive drive (*thanatos*). To put it in popular language, the duality of love and hunger was replaced by love and hatred. But he acknowledged the tentative nature of this theorizing, and in his last work he humbly admitted that human drives are insufficiently understood.

The fourth main aspect of Freud's theory is his *developmental* account of individual human character. This is more than the obvious truism that personality depends on experience as well as on heredity. Freud started from Breuer's discovery that particular traumatic experiences, though apparently forgotten, could exercise a baneful influence on a person's mental health. His full-fledged theory of psychoanalysis generalizes from this and asserts the crucial importance for adult character of the experiences of infancy and early childhood. The first five years are the time in which the basis of each personality is laid down, so one cannot fully understand a person until one comes to know the psychologically crucial facts about his or her early childhood. Freud produces detailed theories about the psychosexual stages of development, extending the concept of sexuality to include any kind of bodily pleasure. He claims that infants obtain pleasure first from the mouth (the oral stage), then from the other end of the alimentary tract (the anal stage); boys and girls then become interested in the penis (the phallic stage), and girls are alleged to lament its absence. From age five until puberty (the latency period) sexuality is less manifest. It then reappears, and if all goes well it attains its full genital expression in adulthood.

Freud was vilified for his conception of the **Oedipus complex**, in which the little boy is alleged to feel sexual desire for his mom and rivalry with his dad (as foreshadowed in Sophocles's classic Greek drama in which Oedipus unknowingly kills his father and marries his mother). But perhaps Freud's understanding of child psychology need not be taken quite so literally. or in such a male-oriented way. We need not suppose that boys and girls feel anything like adult sexual desire for their mothers or fathers, but rather that the dependent attachment that they undoubtedly feel for their parents contains an element that is sexual in the broader sense, for it contains the seed from which adult love and sexuality can grow. Moreover, this infantile dependence is ambivalent, for it typically involves some resentment, jealousy or aggression, as well as love. And as children grow up and enter into social relations they will have to learn what is acceptable behavior and what is not, so acting on their feelings will be limited by parental and social prohibitions. Everyone needs to pass this crucial stage in psychological development, and if it is not managed successfully, perhaps only psychoanalysis can reverse the damage by taking the patient mentally back to the childhood stage and renegotiating the transition.

DIAGNOSIS: MENTAL DISHARMONY, REPRESSION, AND NEUROSIS

Like Plato, Freud holds that individual well-being, happiness, or mental health depends on a harmonious relationship between the various parts of the mind, and between the whole person and society. The ego or ordinary self has to reconcile the id, the superego, and the external world, finding opportunities to satisfy instinctual demands without transgressing the standards set by society. If the world does not supply enough opportunity for fulfillment, the result will be pain or frustration; but even when the external environment is favorable, there can be mental disturbance if there is too much inner conflict between the parts of the mind or soul. In cases of obsessive action or neurotic guilt the superego has somehow come to set impossible standards, beyond what most people would accept as reasonable.

Freud believed that repression is crucial in the causation of neurotic illnesses. In a situation of mental conflict, where someone experiences an impulse sharply incompatible with the standards he or she feels must be adhered to, it will be repressed out of consciousness. Repression is the basic **defense mechanism** by which people attempt to avoid inner conflict. But it is essentially a pretense, a withdrawal from reality, and is doomed to failure. What is repressed does not really cease to exist; it remains in the unconscious portion of the mind with all its emotional energy, and it "returns" by sending into consciousness a disguised substitute for itself in the form of a dream, a neurotic symptom, a faulty action or a slip of tongue. Thus, people can find themselves behaving in ways that they may admit are irrational yet which they feel compelled to continue. By repressing an idea, they have given up effective control over it: they can neither get rid of the symptoms it causes, nor lift the repression and recall it to consciousness.

Freud located the decisive repressions in early childhood: it is essential for future mental health that the child successfully passes through the normal stages of sexual development. But this does not always proceed smoothly; any hitch leaves a predisposition to future problems, and sexual **perversions** can be traced to such a cause. One typical kind of neurosis consists in what Freud calls **regression**, the return to a stage at which childish satisfaction was obtained. He even described certain adult character types as "oral" and "anal" by reference to the stages from which he thought they originated.

There is elaborate detail in Freud's theories of the neuroses into which we cannot enter here; but he put *some* of the blame on the social world, and we should note this aspect of his diagnosis. The standards to which a person feels obliged to conform are one of the crucial factors in mental problems, but they are a product of the social environment—first the parents, then anyone else who has exerted influence on the growing child. The instilling of ethical standards is an essential part of education, for as Freud sees it civilization requires some self-control of instincts to make human society possible. However, the standards imposed by a particular family or society may not be conducive to general happiness or sociability: maladjusted parents are notoriously likely to produce maladjusted children. Freud entertained wider speculations that the relationship between society and individuals has gotten out of balance so that our whole civilized life might be described as neurotic. This theme came to the fore in his late work *Civilization and Its Discontents*, but as early as the *Five Lectures* of 1909 he had suggested that our civilized standards tend to make life too difficult for most people and that we should not deny a certain amount of satisfaction to our instinctual impulses. So there is a basis for those neo-Freudians who diagnose our troubles as lying as much in society as in individuals.

PRESCRIPTION: PSYCHOANALYTIC THERAPY

Freud's great hope was that our human problems can be diagnosed and ameliorated by the methods of science. His project was to restore a harmonious balance between the parts of the mind and, if possible, to suggest a better adjustment between individuals and the social world. The latter might involve political programs, but Freud's profession was the treatment of neurotic patients: he was not a politician or social reformer. Moreover, he was realistic about the limits of therapeutic influence, famously describing the aim of psychoanalysis as "to replace neurotic unhappiness by ordinary unhappiness." It is this peculiar kind of therapy that we must now examine.

Freud's method developed gradually out of Breuer's discovery that a hysterical woman could be helped by being encouraged to *talk* about the thoughts and fantasies that had been filling her mind, and seemed to be cured when she was able to remember the traumatic experiences that had induced her problems. Freud tried this "talking cure," assuming that the pathogenic memories were still in his patients' unconscious minds, so he asked them to talk to him quite uninhibitedly, hoping that he could interpret the unconscious mental forces behind what was said. The fundamental rule of his treatment was that patients were to say whatever came into their mind, however disconnected, absurd, or embarrassing it might be (the method of **free association**). But he often found that the flow of words would dry up; the patient would have nothing more to say and might object to further inquiry. When such resistance happened Freud took it as a sign that the conversation was getting near the repressed complex and that the patient's unconscious was trying to prevent the painful idea from coming to the surface. He believed that if it could be brought back into consciousness despite resistance, the patient's rational mind could be given back power over the noxious ideas and his or her neurosis would be cured.

But to achieve this result could require a long process, involving weekly sessions even over a period of years. Freud's case studies (which read like stylish works of fiction) show him exercising enormous patience and persistence in unraveling the many layers of repressed and traumatic ideas in the mind of a deeply troubled patient. The analyst must try to arrive at the correct interpretations of the patient's unconscious mental states and to present them at such a time and in such a way that the patient may accept them, not just intellectually as bits of theory but as new ways in which he or she can see the world, and live and act accordingly. Freud was in the business of *psycho*therapy, akin to what used to be called "the cure of souls" though he tried to express it in scientific rather than theological terms. The patient's dreams can provide fruitful material for psychoanalytic interpretation, for according to Freud's theory the consciously reported **manifest content** of a dream is the disguised fulfillment of unconscious wishes that are its real or **latent content**. Errors and faulty actions can also be interpreted to reveal their unconscious causation. There will typically be discussion of the patient's sexual life, childhood experiences, and relationships to parents and others.

Clearly, all this demands a relationship of peculiar confidence between patient and analyst, but Freud often found that his patients manifested strong emotions toward him that could amount to love or hatred. He called this "transference," on the assumption that the emotion was projected onto the analyst from the life situations in which it had formerly been experienced, or from the unconscious fantasies of the patient. The handling of transference is crucially important for the analysis because it provides a crucial opportunity for it itself to be analyzed and traced back to its sources in the unconscious, so that the patient can come to understand what lies behind his or her feelings and why they need not be continued.

The goal of psychoanalytic treatment can be summarized as self-knowledge (echoing Socrates—see Chapter 4). What the "cured" neurotic does with this new self-understanding is up to him or her, and various outcomes are possible. The person may replace the unhealthy repression of instinctual wishes by a rational, conscious control of them (**suppression** rather than repression); the person may be able to divert his or her instincts into acceptable channels (**sublimation**); or the person may decide to satisfy them after all. But according to Freud there is no need to fear that primitive passions will "take over" the person, for their power is *reduced* by being brought into consciousness. Despite everything, he retained some faith in rational, conscious choice.

Freud never thought of psychoanalysis as the answer to *every* human problem. When considering the problems of "civilized" modern society he was realistic enough to accept their extreme complexity and to abstain from offering any social or political program. But he did suggest that psychoanalysis has wider applications than the treatment of neurotics. He wrote, "our civilization imposes an almost intolerable pressure on us," meaning primarily the conventional moral restriction of sex to marriage; and he speculated that psychoanalysis might help prepare a corrective—presumably some loosening of sexual morality, though he did not say what he had in mind. In fact, much of the restriction on both heterosexual and homosexual expression that was characteristic of Freud's time has been lifted (making some of his writing about "civilization" sound old-fashioned), but whether this has made us any happier overall is a moot point.

CRITICAL DISCUSSION: (A) FREUD AS WOULD-BE SCIENTIST

The validity of psychoanalysis has been a matter of dispute ever since its inception. There were early "schismatics" from the Freudian fold such as Adler, Jung, and Rank, who took his ideas in different directions; and there have since been influential developments in psychoanalytic theory and therapy by Melanie Klein, W. R. Bion, Freud's daughter Anna Freud, and others. But we cannot consider these here.

Many academic psychologists have condemned psychoanalytic theories as unscientific—either too vague to be testable (falsifiable), or not supported by the evidence where the claims *are* testable. We should distinguish two questions here: the truth of the theories and the effectiveness of treatment based on them.

Let us take the latter question first. Since psychoanalytic therapy has been widely applied for over a century, one might expect that we could by now make a good estimate of its effectiveness. But these matters are far from straightforward. First, understanding the causes of a condition does not necessarily give us the power to change it (climate change is a contemporary example; another is the effect of a traumatic childhood on personality, which may be difficult or impossible to undo, however well understood). Second, a true theory might be inadequately applied in clinical practice: all sorts of thing can go wrong in medicine, psychiatry, and psychotherapy. Third, there is considerable vagueness about what constitutes *cure* from neurosis: who is to make such a judgment—the patient, the therapist, or society generally? Should we require the disappearance of neurotic symptoms, or just a reduction of them—and by how much? We need to compare with a control group of similar neurotics who are not given any treatment, to see if psychoanalysis does any better than "normal" life in relieving neurosis. But fourth, since psychoanalysis is such a very individual therapy, going into the emotional history of a patient in intimate detail, it is very hard to establish relevant comparisons between different people, and to set up the kind of control groups that objective testing requires. Besides, it is a very lengthy and expensive therapy, so only the wealthy can afford it. All in all, there are considerable difficulties with objective testing of its effectiveness, so we tend to be reduced to anecdotal evidence of patients saying that psychoanalysis has helped them.

On the question of the truth of the theories, the fundamental question is whether they are empirically testable at all, for as we saw in the Introduction **falsifiability** by observation is a necessary condition for scientific status. Freud put forward his theories as scientific hypotheses to explain the evidence that patients revealed to him in his therapeutic sessions; but some of his theorizing seems to go way beyond such evidence, and it is not clear how it is testable. We can illustrate this problem in various parts of Freudian theorizing.

By applying his postulate of psychic determinism Freud arrived at some general theoretical claims, for example, that all dreams are wish fulfillments, usually in disguised form. But even if we accept that the content of every dream must have a cause of *some* sort, it does not follow that the cause must be mental rather than physical. Couldn't it be something one has eaten, or a need for "cleaning out" of surplus information in the brain? And if the cause *is* mental, it does not follow that it is unconscious or deeply significant—couldn't it involve banal memories of the previous day, or ordinary concerns about the morrow? So how can Freud's bold generalization that the cause of every dream is a wish be tested? When an interpretation in terms of an independently established wish of the dreamer is made plausible, that is good so far. But what if no such interpretation is found? A convinced Freudian may insist that there *must* be a wish whose disguise has not yet been seen through. But how could we show that a certain dream is *not* a disguised wish fulfillment? It is difficult to prove such a negative statement. This threatens to evacuate any empirical content from Freud's general claim, leaving only the practical suggestion that we should always *look* for a disguised wish. It is hard to see the kind of linguistic virtuosity that Freud deployed in *The Interpretation of Dreams* as an exercise in science. Similar doubts can be raised about the postulation of an unconscious cause for *every* slip of the tongue or mistaken action. What we seem to be left with is not a scientific theory but practical guidance that in trying to understand people we should consider possible hidden meanings in what they do and say.

Consider next the basic postulate of unconscious mental states. Freud quite reasonably dismissed the a priori claim of some philosophers that being mental logically implies being conscious, for there are no such absolute rules governing the elastic term "mental." Descartes influenced many philosophers to identify the mental with consciousness, and the behaviorists rejected any conception of mental states not definable in terms of observable behavior (see Chapter 12); but psychologists these days theorize freely about information-processing states at various levels of the mind. The constraint is only that such claims need to be testable by observable evidence, and must explain it well in order to be accepted. So the question we must ask is whether Freud's postulation of unconscious mental states offers any good explanation of what we observe about human beings and their behavior.

After all, in explaining human action and behavior in everyday terms we appeal to *conscious* perceptions, sensations, desires, and intentions—and none of these are literally observable by the senses, though we are introspectively aware of them in ourselves and can observe other people's relevant behavior and speech. Some of Freud's theorizing goes only a little way beyond this everyday sort of mental explanation. Under hypnotic suggestion a subject may deliberately perform unusual actions that the hypnotist has previously told him or her to do (e.g., opening an umbrella indoors); if asked why he or she is doing it, the subject does not seem to remember the hypnotist's instructions but offers rather lame reasons for the action (such as saying there might be drips from the ceiling). It is very plausible to explain such behavior in terms of an unconscious memory of the hypnotist's instructions. Some of the symptoms of Freud's hysterical patients invite similar explanations (e.g., the lady who went through a ritual of calling her maid to look at a stain on the tablecloth, which Freud was able to link with a traumatic memory of putting red ink on the bedsheet to try to disguise a failure in the marriage bed). Sometimes such explanations can be confirmed by independent evidence about what the person has previously experienced or done.

However, Freud's theorizing about unconscious mental states or agencies goes a long way beyond our everyday explanations. In particular he appeals to repression as a postulated process of pushing mental ideas into the unconscious and keeping them there. Repression is described as purposeful; it functions to keep a disagreeable idea or memory out of consciousness and "exerts itself" to do that, producing resistance to the analyst's interpretations. Here Freud is in danger of talking of persons within the person, internal "homunculi" with knowledge and desires of their own. So what exactly is it that "does" the repressing, and how does it "know" which items to select for repression? (As we shall see in Chapter 11, Sartre poses this challenge.) Similar questions arise for Freud's theory of three internal "agencies"—id, ego, and superego. There is unfinished work here, to understand what the postulation of unconscious yet purposeful states can legitimately do.

The suggestion emerges that psychoanalytic theory is not so much a set of scientific hypotheses to be tested empirically but rather a **hermeneutic** method: a way of understanding people, of seeing a *meaning* in their actions, mishaps and errors, jokes, dreams, and neurotic symptoms. Since conscious, supposedly rational beings are so different from the entities studied in physics and chemistry, why should we criticize psychoanalysis for failing to meet criteria for scientific status that have been taken from the physical sciences? Perhaps the psychoanalytic interpretation of a dream or a symptom, or of a person, is more akin to the interpretation of a poem or painting, in which there may be reasons (of an inconclusive kind) for a variety of interpretations.

Many of Freud's theoretical conceptions are extensions of our ordinary ways of understanding one another in terms of concepts such as sexual attraction, love, hate, fear, anxiety, and rivalry. And perhaps the experienced psychoanalyst can be seen as someone who has acquired a deep intuitive understanding of the springs of human motivation and a skill in interpreting the complexities of how they work out in particular situations, regardless of how well he or she can articulate reasons for their interpretations in scientific fashion. However, there is still a reasonable demand that any particular interpretation should be backed up with evidence about the relevant person and his or her life. Even if we accept that unconscious mental states can explain hypnosis, dreams, errors, and certain kinds of neurosis, success in those special cases does not prove the whole of psychoanalytic theory. The trouble with many of the Freudian postulates is the unclarity of the criteria for inferring their presence or absence. If stamp collecting is alleged to be a sign of unconscious "anal retentiveness," how can one show that that really is, or is not, the relevant cause?

This hermeneutic view of psychoanalysis can be given philosophical backing by the distinction between reasons and causes. Typical scientific explanation in terms of causes has been contrasted with the explanation of human actions in terms of the beliefs and desires that made it rational for the agent to do what he or she did. (Compare what Kant and Sartre have to say on this—see Chapters 8 and 11.) It has been suggested that Freud misunderstood the nature of his own theories by presenting them as scientific discoveries about the causes of human behavior. However, some philosophers argue that beliefs and desires can be both reasons and causes, and that unconscious beliefs and desires can play this dual role too. There are deep philosophical issues here about how far the methods of investigation and explanation of the physical sciences are applicable to human beliefs and actions.

Freud himself acknowledged that his theorizing about drives was one of the most uncertain parts of his work. He wanted to claim only a small *number* of basic drives (or "instincts"), but how are they to be distinguished and counted? If the sexual drive is alleged to be behind behavior that we do not at first recognize as sexual, such as artistic creation, how are we to test that? Further questions arise about Freud's late theory of a biologically implausible "death instinct." We know that human beings can be aggressive in certain situations, and sometimes self-destructive or suicidal, but to postulate a general drive toward death is surely an unnecessary overdescription of this. Freud had great insights into human nature and made brave efforts to synthesize ideas from many sources into an interdisciplinary science of mind, but it does seem that he was overconfident in his own powers of theorizing.

Freud never treated female psychology as thoroughly as male. Much of his writing about sexuality seems to reflect stereotypical male experience, with more emphasis on orgasms than on long-lasting love. For someone who laid such stress on infantile experience, there seems to be remarkably little in Freud about the bond between mother and baby: but subsequent psychoanalytic work by John Bowlby and others has addressed this. In 1926 Freud made a statement that is astonishing, coming from someone whose professional practice consisted so largely in treating the psychological problems of women, when he wrote that "the sexual life of adult women is a dark continent for psychology" (SE XX, 212). Dark continent or not, Freud was not inhibited from making some dogmatic, unsupported assertions about it. In *Civilization and Its Discontents* he said that women "represent the interests of the family and of sexual life" (SE XXI, 103)—but one wonders, can't men do some of that? And in the next sentence he declared that women are hardly capable of the instinctual sublimation that men manage in "the work of civilization." It seems that Freud too was imbued with some prejudices of his time.

CRITICAL DISCUSSION: (B) FREUD AS MORALIST

Freud's theory of instincts or drives often seems unduly reductionist and physiological. In *The Question of Lay Analysis* he wrote, "What, then, do these instincts want? Satisfaction—that is, the establishment of situations in which the bodily needs can be extinguished" (SE XX, 200). Obviously, he had sexual intercourse in mind, and presumably eating and drinking. But is it plausible to say that *all* human behavior is driven, directly or indirectly, by short-term bodily needs and desires? This is not true of many animals: many creatures expend considerable energy on nest building, defense of territory, and the feeding and care of their young; and although such behavior is instinctual, it is attributable to drives other than copulation (see the discussion of ethology in Chapter 12). Humans also show parental behavior that surely has an instinctive, biological component.

In *Civilization and Its Discontents* Freud wrote that the question of the purpose of human life has never received a satisfactory answer, yet what people show by their behavior to be the purpose of their lives seems to be merely the operation of "the pleasure principle": the seeking of immediate satisfaction for their instinctual impulses (SE XXI, 75–76). He also said "in the last analysis, all suffering is nothing else than sensation" (SE XXI, 78). Both assertions express a very reductionist conception of human life, assimilating us too closely to the animals, from which Plato, Aristotle, and Kant distinguished us. Freud seems remarkably insensitive to philosophical, let alone religious, accounts of human motivation. Should not he, of all people, have made more of the fact that human beings are manifestly capable of distinctively *mental* forms of happiness and unhappiness?

He conceded that there is a "finer and higher" joy for artists in creating and for scientists in discovering. But he remarked, first, that such satisfactions are mild compared with "the sating of crude and primary instinctual impulses," for they do not "convulse our physical being" (SE XXI, 79–80) and, second, that such higher satisfactions are accessible to only a few people with rare gifts. But he did not mention other nonbodily forms of satisfaction that do not depend on special talents, such as friendship, pleasure in the growth and success of one's children and grandchildren, or the appreciation of nature or music. These quiet joys may not convulse our physical being (like orgasms or drug-induced "highs"), but they are more reliable, long-lasting, relatively independent of the body, and free of side effects—they can even be enjoyed in old age.

Freud no doubt had his reasons (or causes?) for the pessimistic account of the human condition that he offers toward the end of his life. He was in continuous pain from cancer of the jaw, and several operations could not cure it. He had lived through the First World War, knew about its horrors, and was aware of the aggressive and nationalistic feelings in the uneasy aftermath in central Europe where (in contrast to the comparatively settled condition of the United States and Britain) the dark social forces that were to bring the Nazis to power were already operating.

Freud refused to offer consolation where he thought none is to be had, and sternly requires us all to face up to unvarnished reality. In *The Future of an Illusion* he firmly rejected religious belief as a projection onto the universe of our childhood attitudes to our parents: we would like to believe that a heavenly father who brought us into being is also in benevolent control of our lives, and we see ourselves as having a duty to live up to the standards he has set. (See the final lecture, "The Question of a *Weltanschauung*," of the *New Introductory Lectures*). Freud tried to explain the immense and enduring influence of religion over people, compared with science and philosophy, as due to its having "the strongest emotions of human beings at its service" (SE XXII, 161). But the finding of infant psychological roots for something does not automatically devalue the mature project: what we find in infants is not necessarily "infantile" in a bad sense. Freud himself, in postulating the role of sexuality in our infancy, did not think that that undermines the value of mature erotic love. So the fact (if it *is* a fact) that the roots of religious belief can be found in infancy need not undermine all forms of mature religion. Freud was for his entire life a firm atheist, who thought that all or most forms of religion do more harm than good; but that view does not follow from his psychoanalytic theory.

In Chapter IV of *Civilization and Its Discontents* Freud claimed that the few saintly people who seem able to live up to the biblical injunction to "love thy neighbor as thyself" really derive the relevant mental energy from the sexual instinct. "What they bring about in themselves in this way is a state of evenly suspended, steadfast, affectionate feeling, which has little external resemblance any more to the stormy agitations of genital love, from which it is nevertheless derived" (SE XXI, 102). But this is assertion rather than argument. It would seem more plausible to say that if Christian agape is derived from some natural tendency, the instinctual love of parents for their children (and the protective and affectionate feelings that many people have for most children) would be a stronger candidate.

Similarly, Freud's assertion that the energy that some people devote to art or to science must also be "aim-inhibited libido," a sublimation of the sexual drive, is unproven. Presumably he would have to say the same about athletic and sporting achievement and many other human activities that do not involve food or sex—even his own lifelong devotion to psychological theory! Freud wanted a biological theory of human motivation, but he tended to write as if it must all reduce to nutrition and copulation, which is not true even of animal behavior. We have a need for meaning and purpose. We need to work, or to do something that serves a meaningful end; if our desires for food, drink, and sex are plentifully fulfilled (as in the grosser conceptions of paradise) but there is nothing *else* to do, we soon become bored.

Freud remarked that not everybody is worthy of love. He had scant respect for the vast mass of humanity who behave in accordance with the "pleasure principle," and little hope that human nature could be changed by the radical social experiments in Soviet Russia in the 1920s and 30s. In *Why War?* (an exchange of open letters with Einstein) he suggested a need for something like Platonic guardians of the state, when he writes that "more care should be taken than hitherto to educate an upper stratum of men with independent minds, not open to intimidation and eager in the pursuit of truth, whose business it would be to give direction to the dependent masses" (SE XXII, 212). At the end of the letter, he expressed a modicum of hope for the long-term future of humanity without war, if the evolution of culture will allow a strengthening of reason and an internalization of aggressive impulses.

No unambiguous verdict can be passed on Freud's work as a whole. His imaginative power in suggesting new psychological hypotheses is obvious, as was his bravery in venturing into highly emotive and controversial psychological territory. But his theorizing was overambitious and became too distant from the possibility of empirical testing, thus endangering the scientific status that he hoped for it. Somewhat prone to dogmatism, he did not learn from the progress of other disciplines, or from other approaches in psychology and psychiatry. He was blessed with a considerable literary gift, and many readers have been carried along by the clarity and stylishness of his prose. But however influential and persuasive someone's thought and writing may be, we should never excuse ourselves from the task of critical evaluation.

FOR FURTHER READING

References to Freud's writings are to SE, *The Standard Edition of the Complete Psychological Works of Sigmund Freud*, ed. James Strachey (London: Hogarth Press, 1953–66). A new edition is in preparation.

A good starting point for reading Freud is his *Five Lectures on Psycho-Analysis*, reprinted in *Two Short Accounts of Psycho-Analysis* (London: Penguin, 1962) and in *A General Selection from the Works of Sigmund Freud*, ed. J. Rickman (New York: Bantam Doubleday Dell, 1989). Both books also include Freud's second short account, *The Question of Lay Analysis*, which introduces his later theory of id, ego, and superego. Another good starting point is Freud's "Autobiographical Study" of 1925, reprinted in Peter Gay's comprehensive selection from Freud's writings *The Freud Reader* (New York: Vintage, 1995).

Bruno Bettelheim, in *Freud and Man's Soul* (New York: Vintage Books, 1984), argues that the English translations of Freud's works have misrepresented his thought as more technical and scientific than it really is.

Reliable introductions to Freud's thought are given by B. A. Farrell, *The Standing of Psycho-Analysis* (Oxford: Oxford University Press, 1981), Anthony Storr, *Freud* (Oxford: Oxford University Press, 2001), and Richard Wollheim, *Freud,* 2nd ed., (London: Fontana Press, 2008).

Biographies include Frank J. Sulloway, *Freud: Biologist of the Mind* (New York: Basic Books, 1979; London: Fontana, 1980), and Peter Gay, *Freud: A Life for Our Time* (New York: W. W. Norton, 1988). In *A Godless Jew: Freud, Atheism and the Making of Psychoanalysis* (New Haven, CT: Yale University Press, 1987) Gay explores the relations between Freud's science, his opposition to religion, and his Jewishness.

Jeffrey Masson, in *The Assault on Truth: Freud's Suppression of the Seduction Theory* (New York: Farrar, Straus & Giroux, 1987), questioned Freud's theorizing and even his integrity over the issue of child sexual abuse.

Patricia Kitcher, in *Freud's Dream: A Complete Interdisciplinary Science of Mind* (Cambridge, MA: MIT Press, 1992), shows how Freud's theorizing rapidly became outdated and draws lessons for our own day.

For discussion of philosophical issues arising from Freud's work, see R. Wollheim and J. Hopkins (eds.), *Philosophical Essays on Freud* (Cambridge: Cambridge University Press, 1982), Jerome Neu, ed., *The Cambridge Companion to Freud* (Cambridge: Cambridge University Press, 1991), and Jonathan Lear, *Freud* (London: Routledge, 2005).

C. Jung, *Modern Man in Search of a Soul* (London: Routledge 2001), is an introduction to Jung's more religious, less sex-centered approach to psychoanalysis.

KEY TERMS

death instinct	perversions
defense mechanism	preconscious
ego	psychoanalysis (theory)
falsifiability	psychoanalysis (therapy)
free association	regression
hermeneutic	repression
id	resistance
instincts	sublimation
latent content	superego
libido	suppression
manifest content	transference
metaphysics	unconscious
Oedipus complex	

QUESTIONS FOR DISCUSSION

1. Does the notion of an unconscious mental state make sense?
2. Does Freud's theory leave any room for free will?
3. Can a person repress something without being aware of what he or she is repressing?
4. Does sexuality lie behind as much human life as Freud thought?
5. Can Freudian theory give any adequate account of the finer things in life?

11

Sartre: Radical Freedom

Jean-Paul Sartre (1905–1980) was a philosopher in two senses. After a brilliant student career, he wrote some strikingly original books and with the publication of his magnum opus *Being and Nothingness* he was widely recognized as France's leading philosopher. But he was also a very public intellectual who expressed his ideas in novels, plays and biographical studies, and applied them to the great social and political issues of his time, taking controversially radical stances against the conventional wisdom of his day.

Let us first put Sartre in the context of **existentialist** thought over the preceding century. Three main concerns were central. The first is with *individual* human beings: existentialists think that general theories about human nature leave out precisely what is most important, namely the uniqueness of each individual and his or her life situation. Second, they are concerned with the *meaning* of human lives rather than scientific or metaphysical truths (even if the latter are about human beings). Inner or "subjective" experience is at the center of attention, rather than "objective" truth. Third, there is a very strong emphasis on *freedom*, on the ability of each individual to choose not just particular actions but attitudes, projects, purposes, values, and lifestyles. Moreover, the typical existentialist concern is not just to assert this but to persuade people to *act* on it, to exercise their freedom.

These themes can be found in a wide variety of contexts, especially in descriptions of the concrete detail of particular characters, situations, and choices, whether in biography or in fiction. But an existentialist *philosopher* must offer some general analysis of the human condition, and the most obvious division is between theist and atheist accounts.

The Danish Christian thinker Søren Kierkegaard (1813–1855) is generally recognized as the first modern existentialist, though there is an existential dimension to all religions, notably in Paul, Augustine, Luther, and Pascal in the Christian tradition. Like his contemporary Karl Marx, Kierkegaard reacted against Hegel's philosophy, but in a very different direction. He rejected the abstract Hegelian system of world-historical development, likening it to a vast mansion in which the owner does not actually live. Kierkegaard concentrated instead on what he thought supremely important, the individual person and his or her life choices. However, he did offer *some* generalizations about life, distinguishing three basic attitudes: the aesthetic (the search for pleasure), the ethical (commitment to marriage, family, work, and social responsibility), and the religious (seeing everything in terms of the eternal, the transcendent, the divine). He held that the religious (more specifically, the Christian) way is the highest, although it can be reached only by a free "leap into the arms of God." But he was scathingly critical of the conventional Christian church of his time, thinking that it diverted its adherents from making their own decisions about how to live.

The other great nineteenth-century existentialist was a crusading atheist. The German philosopher Friedrich Nietzsche (1844–1900) notoriously said "God is dead, and we have killed him." That was obviously a metaphorical statement meaning that "we" (the European culture of his time or the more influential sections of it) have ceased to find Christianity credible and ignore it in practice. So we need to rethink the meaning and purpose of our lives and use our radical, unsettling freedom to change the basis of our attitudes and values (there Kierkegaard would agree), finding meaning in human terms alone (there he would disagree). In this, Nietzsche had much in common with his earlier compatriot Feuerbach. In many existentialist thinkers there is a tension between a relativist tendency to say that there is no objective basis for choosing or valuing one way of life more than another, and a recommendation of a particular choice or values. In Nietzsche's case the latter was expressed in his vision of the **superman** (*Ubermensch*) of the future, who will reject conventional values based on Christian humility (which Nietzsche rather implausibly connected with the resentment felt by an underclass—so-called "slave morality") and replace them with ideals of human fulfillment based on creativity, and self-assertion, even the "will to power." After Nietzsche's collapse into madness, that latter incautious phrase was used by his sister in a book edited from his unpublished notes; it was taken up by the Nazis—but probably he would have been horrified.

In the twentieth century, too, existentialists included both believers and atheists. Notable existentialist theologians were Gabriel Marcel (1889–1973) in France, Rudolf Bultmann (1884–1976) in Germany, and the Jewish thinker Martin Buber (1878–1965). Existentialist philosophy developed mainly in continental Europe, and in the hands of Heidegger and Sartre it became academic, jargon-ridden and system-building. An important source was "phenomenology," the method of Edmund Husserl (1859–1938) based on giving detailed descriptions of phenomena, how things appear to human consciousness. This concern with human experience rather than scientific truth is characteristic of existentialism, but a different version developed in the "ordinary language philosophy" in the English-speaking world in the mid-twentieth century, especially in the later work of Ludwig Wittgenstein (1889–1951) which explored the subtlety of our everyday descriptions of things.

The most original twentieth-century existentialist philosopher was Martin Heidegger (1889–1976), whose *Being and Time* was published in 1927. Heidegger's language is strange and difficult: in his effort to rethink the fundamental concepts of Western philosophy he invented a system of hyphenated neologisms in the German language. Although he often seems to be doing abstract metaphysics (like Aristotle), it emerges through his ponderous prose that he has a central concern with the meaning of human existence, which he calls our relation to **Being**, and he points to the possibility of **authentic** life by facing up to one's real situation in the world, especially to the inevitability of one's own death (again, this seems to be the recommendation of a particular kind of attitude). "Being" in Heidegger often sounds like an impersonal substitute for God—the elusive ultimate reality of which we can become aware if we attend in the right sort of way. In his later work there is an emphasis on quasi-mystical kinds of experience that may be expressed in poetry or music but not in literal philosophical statements.

LIFE AND WORK

The precocious young Sartre rapidly absorbed the thought of those three formidable German *H*s—Hegel, Husserl, and Heidegger—and much of the obscurity in his writing reflects the influence of those purveyors of ponderous abstractions. Themes from Husserlian phenomenology are prominent in his early books, the remarkably philosophical novel *Nausea* (1938) and three short studies in the philosophy of mind: *The Transcendence of the Ego* (1936), *Sketch for a Theory of the Emotions* (1939), and *The Imaginary* (1940). The centerpiece of Sartre's early philosophy is his massive work *Being and Nothingness* (1943), strongly influenced by Heidegger's *Being and Time* but written with Sartre's own French flair.

At the beginning of the Second World War Sartre served as a meteorologist in the French army but was soon taken prisoner, and apparently he spent the time reading Heidegger. After release back into Nazi-occupied Paris, he was sympathetic to the French Resistance but devoted himself to writing *Being and Nothingness*. Something of the atmosphere of that time can perhaps be detected in the pessimistic conception of the human condition he presents in that work. The choice that confronted each French citizen—collaboration, risky resistance, or quiet self-preservation—was an obvious example of what Sartre saw as the ever-present necessity for individual choice. Similar themes are expressed in his trilogy of novels *Roads to Freedom* and in his plays *No Exit* and *Flies*. After the liberation he gave a stylish account of his atheistic existentialism in *Existentialism and Humanism*, a lecture delivered in 1945 to much public acclaim—but his treatment there was brief and popular and does not express the depth of his thought.

Sartre formed a famous open relationship with Simone de Beauvoir, a talented philosopher in her own right and a highly influential feminist. He rejected academic positions and became a freelance writer and a leading French intellectual for the rest of his life. As time went on he modified the very individualist approach of his early philosophy and devoted more attention to social, economic, and political realities. He asserted the need for a classless democratic society if genuine human freedom was to be possible for everyone, and he came to espouse a form of Marxism that he described as "the inescapable philosophy of our time," though needing fertilization by an existentialist account of individual freedom. He joined the Communist Party at the time of the Korean War but left it a few years later when the Soviets invaded Hungary in 1956.

The later phase of Sartre's philosophy started with *Search for a Method* (1957) and continued with the *Critique of Dialectical Reason*, the first volume of which appeared in 1960, concentrating on the French Revolution; the second volume, about the Russian Revolution, was published posthumously in 1985. Sartre developed a strong sympathy for the oppressed, both the workers under capitalism and the population of Third World countries suffering from colonialism or imperialism. He supported

Algeria's violent struggle for liberation from French rule, and he campaigned against the American war in Vietnam. He gave a notable lecture on his mature view of ethics in Rome in 1964, and toward the end of his life, unable to write because of blindness after a stroke, he gave interviews that have since been published. His funeral was attended by some fifty thousand people.

Like that of any other serious philosopher, Sartre's thought was never at rest and cannot be captured in a single system. There is a fairly clear distinction between his early philosophy which focuses on individual freedom, and the second phase which explores the social and economic limitations on freedom. The former is that for which Sartre has become most famous. We will concentrate here on his central work *Being and Nothingness* (with page references to the English translation) but will add a final section giving an outline of his later approach to ethics.

It is only fair to warn students that *Being and Nothingness* is difficult reading (the other early works mentioned above, especially the 1945 lecture, are more accessible). This is a matter not just of length and repetitiousness but of technical terms, abstract nouns, and unresolved paradoxes. Sartre seems to enjoy teasing his readers with obscure, apparently contradictory, or grossly exaggerated statements. He had an extraordinarily self-confident facility to pour out philosophical verbiage onto pages (in Parisian cafés, at the dead of night, so the story goes), but he does not seem to have been so good at self-criticism or revision (legend has it that his manuscripts were delivered straight to the printer from the café tables). There are passages of relative lucidity and psychological insight, however; and the effort to understand his system reveals a view of human nature that has a certain compelling fascination.

METAPHYSICS: CONSCIOUSNESS, OBJECTS, ATHEISM

The most basic feature of Sartre's system is his radical distinction between consciousness or "human reality" (*être-pour-soi*, **being-for-itself**) and inanimate, nonconscious reality (*être-en-soi*, **being-in-itself**). These terms derive from Hegel but are given new definitions by Sartre in his Introduction. This distinction may sound like the dualism of mind and body of Sartre's French predecessor Descartes, but it is important to see how very different it is. Sartre affirmed that a human being is a unified reality ("the concrete is man within the world," p. 3): there are not two substances or "beings," but two modes of being—the *way* that conscious beings exist is different from the way that inanimate things exist. Sartre understood human consciousness as **intentional** in the Brentano's sense: our states of consciousness are typically of something conceived as distinct from the subject (p. xxvii), but they also involve an implicit awareness of oneself (pp. xxviii–xxx). In contrast, being-in-itself (the mode of existence of rocks, oceans, and tables) involves no awareness of anything and no conception of itself (pp. xxxix–xlii). (What Sartre would say about animal perception and action is not clear.)

Sartre made a further distinction between **reflective** ("positional" or "thetic") and **prereflective** (nonpositional, nonthetic) consciousness. All consciousness is positional in the sense that it is of something distinct from the subject. But "every positional consciousness of an object is at the same time a non-positional consciousness of itself" (p. xxix). In his example, if I am counting the cigarettes in my case, I am conscious of the cigarettes and that there are a dozen of them; and I am *prereflectively* conscious that I am counting them, as is shown by the answer I immediately give when asked what I am doing; but I am not *reflectively* conscious of my activity until someone asks me (or I ask myself what I am trying to do).

Perhaps Sartre's next most important metaphysical assertion is his denial of the existence of God. (He did not take over the mystical, quasi-religious dimension of Heidegger's conception of Being, though his posthumously published manuscript *Truth and Existence* is closer to the spirit of Heidegger.) Sartre makes the remarkable claim that we all fundamentally desire to *be* God in the sense that we want to "be our own foundation"; that is, we would like to be perfectly "complete" and self-justifying: as he puts it, we aspire to become **in-itself-for-itself** (p. 566). But he thinks this ideal, which he identifies with God, is self-contradictory (pp. 90, 615); so it is a necessary truth that God does not exist.

Like Nietzsche, Sartre held that the absence of God is of the utmost significance: the atheist does not merely differ from the theist on a point of abstruse metaphysics; he holds a profoundly different attitude to human life. (In Chapter 6 we raised a doubt about this, if the concept of God is interpreted metaphorically.) In Sartre's worldview there are no transcendent objective values set for us—neither commandments of God nor a Platonic form of the Good, nor is there any intrinsic meaning or purpose in human existence (no Aristotelean *telos*). In this sense, our life can be described as **absurd**: we are "forlorn" or "abandoned" in this world. There is no heavenly father to tell us what to do, or help us do it; as grown-up people we have to decide for ourselves what is worth aiming for, and look after own destiny. Sartre repeatedly insisted that the only foundation for **value judgments** lies in our own choices; there is no external, objective justification for the projects and ways of life that people adopt (pp. 38, 443, 626–27).

THEORY OF HUMAN NATURE: EXISTENCE
AND ESSENCE, NEGATION AND FREEDOM

In one sense Sartre denied that there is any such thing as human nature for there to be theories about. This would be a typical existentialist rejection of generalizations about human beings and human lives. He expressed it in a summarizing formula, "man's existence precedes his essence" (pp. 438–39), by which he meant that we have no essential nature: we have not been created for any particular purpose, whether by God or evolution or anything else; we simply find ourselves existing by no choice of our own, and we have to *decide* what to make of ourselves; each of us must create his or her own nature or "essence". Of course, there are some true generalizations about our *bodily* nature, such as our necessity to eat, our metabolism, and our sexual impulses. But, as we noticed in Chapter 9, there is room for some dispute about what count as *purely* biological facts. Sartre certainly thought there are no general truths about what human beings want to be: the alleged universal project of "becoming God" is only the abstract form of our particular desires, which are many and various (pp. 566–67). There are no general truths about what we ought to be.

An existentialist philosopher, however, is bound to offer some generalizations about the human condition, and Sartre's central assertion is freedom. We are "condemned to be free"; there is no limit to our freedom except that we cannot cease being free as long as we are alive and conscious (p. 439). He derived this conclusion from his understanding of conscious intentionality as of something distinct from oneself. (Even if someone is mistaken in a particular case, as Macbeth was about an illusory dagger, he was thinking of something that he *believed* to exist at a position in space.) Sartre saw a connection between consciousness and the mysterious concept of **nothingness** that appears in the title of his book. The subject is aware in a prereflective way that the perceived object is *not* the subject: it has (or is believed to have) a separate existence of its own (pp. xxvii–xxix, 74–75). That is one way in which negation is involved in conscious awareness. Another way is that many of our judgments about the world are negative in their content: we can recognize what is not the case, as when I look unsuccessfully for Pierre in the café where we arranged to meet and say disappointedly, "Pierre is not here" (pp. 9–10). When we ask a question, we already understand the possibility of a negative reply (p. 5). We also perceive the world as enabling possibilities for our actions, and this involves conceiving of possible states of affairs that are not already the case ("nothingnesses" in Sartre's rebarbative language), but which we might decide to make real. Desire and intention involve recognition of the *lack* of something (p. 87, 433ff.). Thus, conscious beings, who can think and say what *is* the case, also conceive of what *is not* the case.

Sartre indulges in some verbal play with this concept of nothingness in paradoxical phrases such as "the objective existence of a non-being" (p. 5), which presumably means some negative statements are true, and in dark metaphorical sayings like "Nothingness lies coiled in the heart of being—like a worm" (p. 21), which presumably means that we can think of what is not true, as well as what is true. "Nothingness" makes a conceptual connection between consciousness and freedom, for the ability to conceive of what is not the case implies the freedom to imagine other possibilities (pp. 24–25) and to try to bring them about. As long as one is conscious one can conceive of something being otherwise than it is, and one may desire it to be otherwise. Our mental power of negation thus involves both freedom of mind (to imagine new possibilities) and freedom of action (to try to actualize them). So to be conscious is to be continually faced with choices about what to think and what to do, and we can never become the Godlike "in-itself-for-itself".

Sartre thus contradicts two fundamental Freudian claims. His view is flatly incompatible with complete psychic determinism (p. 458ff.). He also rejects the postulate of unconscious mental states, on the ground that consciousness is necessarily transparent to itself, prereflectively (p. 49ff.). However the latter point sounds like mere verbal legislation: of course, *consciousness* cannot be unconscious, but Sartre has not shown that it is illegitimate to talk of unconscious states that are *mental* in some wider sense.

Every aspect of our mental lives is, in Sartre's view, chosen in some sense and is ultimately one's own responsibility. Emotions are usually thought to be outside the control of our will, but Sartre rather heroically maintains that if I am sad, it is only because I have chosen to make myself sad (p. 61). His view, explained more fully in *Sketch for a Theory of the Emotions*, is that emotions are not just moods that "come over us," but ways in which we apprehend the world. They are "intentional" in the sense that they typically have objects—for example, one is fearful *of* some possible event, or angry *with* someone *about* something. But what distinguishes emotions from other ways of being aware of things is, in Sartre's view, that they involve an irrational attempt to transform the world by magic. When one cannot reach a tempting bunch of grapes, one may dismiss them as "too green," attributing this quality to them even though one knows that their ripeness does not depend on their reachability. We are responsible for our emotions, for they are ways in which we have chosen to react to the world (p. 445).

There is something right about this, in that emotions presuppose both beliefs and value judgments; for example, anger with someone involves belief that he or she has done something wrong. If one ceases to believe that they did it or did it intentionally, or if one ceases to judge it as wrong, one's anger disappears. (The ancient Stoic philosophers tried to cure us of emotion by telling us to stop caring about anything other than our own virtue, which they assumed is completely under our own control.) But much of what we care about—whether our own health and freedom from pain, the attractiveness of others, or the well-being of our children—does not seem to be a matter of choice but more of a biological given. On emotion and what we care about, and on moods like depression or mania that may well have neurophysiological causes, Sartre seems to overstate his case.

He held us equally responsible for longer-lasting features of our personality or character. He argued that one cannot just assert "I am shy" (or a great lover, or unable to do even simple math) as if this is an unchangeable fact about oneself like "I am female, or black, or five feet tall," for the former descriptions depend on the way we behave in certain situations—and we are always free to behave differently, or at least to *try* to do so. To say "I am ugly" (or attractive, persevering, or easily discouraged) is not to assert a determinate fact that is already in existence, but to anticipate how one will act and how other people will react in future—and one has choices about that (p. 459). However there is reason to wonder how much truth there is in this, in view of the evidence of genetic influences on personality and sexuality.

Sartre tries to extend our freedom and our responsibility to everything we think, feel, and do. He suggests there are certain situations in which this radical freedom is clearly manifested to us. In moments of temptation or indecision (e.g., when the person who has resolved to give up gambling is confronted with the gaming tables once again), one realizes, painfully, that no motive or no past resolution, however strong, determines what one does *next* (p. 33). Every moment requires a new or renewed choice. Following leads from Kant's practical defense of free will, Kierkegaard and Heidegger, Sartre uses the emotive term **anguish** to describe this consciousness of one's own freedom (pp. 29, 464). Anguish is not fear of an external object but the uneasy awareness of the unpredictability of one's own behavior. The soldier fears injury, pain or death, but feels anguish when he wonders whether he is going to be able to "hold up" courageously in the coming battle. The person walking on a clifftop fears falling, but feels anguish in realizing that there is nothing to stop them from jumping (pp. 29–32). Anguish is relatively unusual because it is "the reflective apprehension of freedom by itself" (p. 39).

DIAGNOSIS: ANGUISH AND BAD FAITH, CONFLICT WITH OTHERS

Anguish, the consciousness of freedom, is mentally painful; and we try to avoid it (pp. 40, 556). Sartre thinks we would all like to achieve a state in which there are no choices left open for us so that we would "coincide with ourselves" like inanimate objects and would not be subject to anguish. But that is illusory, for conscious beings like us are necessarily free and without external justifications for our hoices. Such is Sartre's metaphysical diagnosis of the human condition, hence his gloomy descriptions of our life as "an unhappy consciousness with no possibility of surpassing its unhappy state" (p. 90) and "a useless passion" (p. 615).

The crucial concept in Sartre's diagnosis is that of **bad faith** (*mauvaise foi*, sometimes translated as "self-deception"). Bad faith is the attempt to escape anguish by trying to represent one's attitudes and actions as determined by one's situation or character, relationship to others, employment or social role—anything other than one's own choices. Sartre believes bad faith is the characteristic mode of most human life (p. 556) and gives two famous examples of bad faith, both of them scenes from the Parisian cafés that were his favorite haunts (pp. 55–60). He pictures a young woman sitting with a man who she has every reason to suspect would like to seduce her. But when he takes her hand, she tries to avoid a decision to accept or reject him, by seeming not to notice: she carries on their intellectual conversation while leaving her hand in his as if she were not aware of what is going on. In Sartre's interpretation, she is in bad faith because she pretends—not just to her companion but *to herself*—that she is something distinct from her body, that her hand is a passive object, a mere thing, whereas she is a conscious embodied person who knows perfectly well what is happening and is responsible for her actions.

The second example is of the waiter who is doing his job a little too keenly, his movements with the trays and cups are flourished and overly dramatic: he is "acting the part" of being a waiter. If there is bad faith here at all (and there need not be), it would lie in his identifying himself completely with the role, thinking that it determines his every action and attitude, whereas the truth is that he has chosen to take on the job and is free to give it up at any time, even if he might face unemployment. He is not *essentially* a waiter, for nobody is essentially anything. As Sartre puts it, "the waiter cannot be immediately a café waiter in the sense that this inkwell *is* an inkwell"; "it is necessary that we *make ourselves* what we are" (p. 59). An employee's actions are not literally determined by company policy, for he or she can always decide to object or to resign. Even a soldier can refuse to fight, at the cost of court martial or execution.

Anything we do, any role we play, and any value we respect (pp. 38, 627) is sustained only by our own constantly remade decision.

Sartre rejects any explanation of bad faith in terms of unconscious mental states (pp. 50–54). A Freudian might try to analyze the café examples as cases of repression: the girl could be repressing the consciousness that her companion has made a sexual advance. But Sartre points out an apparent contradiction in the very idea of repression. We attribute the act or process of repressing to some element within the mind (which Sartre calls "the censor"), yet this censor must be able to distinguish between what to repress and what to retain in consciousness, so it must be aware of the repressed idea in order to become *un*aware of it. He concludes that the censor itself would have to be in bad faith, and that we cannot explain how bad faith is possible by localizing it in one putative part of the mind rather than in the person as a whole (pp. 52–53).

Sartre goes on to argue that "good faith" (or sincerity) presents just as much of a conceptual problem: for as soon as one describes one's role or character in some way ("I am a waiter," "I am shy," "I am gay"), a distinction is involved between the self doing the describing and the self described. The ideal of complete sincerity seems doomed to failure (p. 62), for we can never be mere objects to be observed and described like external matters of fact. Sartre offers the example of someone with a clear record of homosexual activity but who resists describing himself as gay (p. 63): he is in bad faith because he refuses to admit his inclinations and tries to offer some other explanation of his sexual encounters. His candid friend ("a champion of sincerity") demands that he acknowledge that he is indeed gay, but in Sartre's view nobody just *is* gay in the way that a table is made of wood or a person is red-haired. If the gay person were to admit that he is gay and imply that he *cannot* cease his homosexual activity, he would also be in bad faith—and so would any "champion of sincerity" who demanded such an admission (p. 63). But we may want to make a distinction here between sexual orientation—which may be a matter of unchosen genetics (though the point is controversial)—and sexual activity, over which it is hard to deny that we have some degree of control.

Sartre is touching here on the deep difficulties of self-knowledge which arise for all serious philosophies. But his account threatens to make these matters unnecessarily perplexing, for he displays an inordinate fondness for the paradoxical formula that "human reality must be what it is not, and not be what it is" which recurs throughout *Being and Nothingness* (e.g., pp. xli, 67, 90). But it is a self-contradiction, so we cannot literally believe it. What did Sartre mean? (Did he enjoy teasing his philosophical readers?) He leaves us some hints about how to resolve the paradox, however: we can take it as misleading shorthand for "people are not *necessarily* what they are, but must be *able* to become what they are not yet," which is a paraphrase of what he says on p. 58. The crucial point remains that we are always free to try to become different from what we are.

In Part 3 of *Being and Nothingness* entitled "Being-for-Others," Sartre gives his philosophical analysis of interpersonal relations and comes to some further pessimistic conclusions. He throws some light on the philosophical problem of other minds by arguing that in common experience we often have an immediate, non-inferential awareness of other people's mental states. When one sees a human face (or even an animal's) with two open eyes directed at oneself one immediately knows one is being *observed*, and one knows it with as much certainty as any merely physical facts in the world. Sartre emphasizes the special power the "look" of another person has over us: if we are engrossed in doing something not normally approved of such as spying through a keyhole or picking our nose, and we hear (or think we hear) a footstep approaching behind us, we suddenly feel *ashamed*, aware of someone else who will probably be critical of our actions. Conversely, when witnessed doing something admirable, like winning a race, we feel pride. Many of our emotions involve the existence of other people and their reactions to oneself.

Sartre goes on to argue for the more disputable thesis that the relationship between any two conscious beings necessarily involves conflict. Supposedly, another person represents a threat to one's freedom by their conscious existence, in that their perception "objectifies" oneself as an object in the world. According to Sartre one has only two strategies to ward off this alleged threat: one can try to treat the other person as a mere object without freedom, or one can try to "possess" their freedom and use it for one's own purposes (p. 363). He gives a persuasive version of Hegel's famous discussion of the master–slave relation in which, paradoxically, the slave ends up with more psychological power because the master needs the slave to *recognize* him as master. Sartre applies this analysis to some forms of sexual desire, especially sadism and masochism (p. 364ff.). He demonstrates that sexual relations raise philosophical issues about human nature, but he goes on to allege that genuine respect for the freedom of other people, in friendship or in erotic love, is an impossible ideal (p. 394ff.). At this stage the outlook seems bleak.

But is there not a contradiction between Sartre's insistence on our freedom and his analysis of the human condition as determined in these ways? He asserts that we all aspire to fill the "nothingness" that is the "essence" of our existence as conscious beings, and we aspire to become Godlike, the foundation of our own being, an "in-itself-for-itself" (pp. 90, 566, 615). And, as we have just seen, he claims that any personal relationship always involves conflict, an attempt to deny or to possess the freedom of the other (pp. 363, 394, 429). In these two ways he represents human life as a perpetual striving for the logically impossible. But *must* it be like that? Can't we acknowledge the impossibility of becoming objects, and choose not to treat other people as objects? Are we not free *in this respect* too?

PRESCRIPTION: REFLECTIVE CHOICE

In view of the rejection of objective values (in his early philosophy), Sartre's prescription has to be a somewhat empty one. There is no *particular* project or way of life that he can recommend. But he condemns bad faith, the attempt to think of oneself as not free. Bad faith may be the usual attitude of most people, but Sartre implies that it *is* possible reflectively to *affirm* one's own freedom. It seems that all he can praise is the making of our individual choices with fully self-conscious, "anguished" awareness that nothing determines them. We must accept our responsibility for everything about ourselves—not just our actions, but our attitudes, emotions and characters. The **spirit of seriousness**, namely the illusion that values are objectively in the world rather than sustained by human choice—which Sartre tends to ascribe especially to "the bourgeois" who are comfortable with their situation in life—must be decisively repudiated (pp. 580, 626).

In *Existentialism and Humanism* Sartre illustrates the impossibility of prescription by the case of a young Frenchman at the time of the Nazi occupation who was faced with the choice of joining the free French forces in England or staying at home to be with his mother, who lived only for him. The former course would be directed to his nation, but would make little difference to the war effort. The latter would be of immediate practical effect, but directed to only one person. Sartre suggests that no ethical doctrine can arbitrate between such incommensurable claims. Nor can strength of feeling settle the matter, for there is no measure of such feeling except in terms of what the subject actually does—which is precisely what he has to decide. To consult an adviser or supposed moral authority and to take the advice is only another sort of choice. So when Sartre was consulted by this young man, he could only say, "You are free, therefore choose."

It has to be admitted that no system of objective ethical values (whether Platonic, Aristotelian, Christian, or Kantian) can offer a determinate, unambiguous answer to every individual human dilemma in every complicated situation. Sometimes more than one course of action may be morally permissible; but this is certainly not to say that *anything* is permissible, or that no moral question ever has a right answer, which seems to be what Sartre implies.

He does commit himself to the intrinsic value of "authentic" self-conscious choice, and his descriptions of cases of bad faith are not morally neutral, but implicitly condemn any refusal to acknowledge the reality of one's freedom and one's choices. Sartre thus offers another perspective on the ancient virtue of self-knowledge put before us by Socrates, Spinoza, Freud, and many others. For all its obscurities, there is something important to learn from his analysis of how the very notion of consciousness involves freedom. His view is not a misuse of language, for we commonly reproach each other not only for our actions but for our attitudes, reactions and emotions: "How *could* you feel like that, when you know that *p*?" "I don't like your attitude to *X*," "*Must* you be so selfish?" Such reproaches (and more neutral psychotherapeutic interventions) are not without effect, for to make someone *aware* that he or she is feeling or behaving in a certain way can make a difference. The more a person becomes aware of their own anger or pride or self-centeredness, the more they may be capable of change.

Sartre's understanding of the nature and possibility of self-knowledge differs from Freud's, however. He rejects the very idea of unconscious causes of mental events; for him everything is supposed to be already available to consciousness, if we use our power of reflection (p. 571). But in view of how much has since been discovered about the operation of the brain, this is assertion rather than argument. Since Freud there is a strong empirical case (confirmed by much recent psychology) for the existence of unconscious processes not open to introspection that deserve to be called mental in view of their influence on behavior.

What Sartre calls **existential psychoanalysis** is an interpretive, hermeneutic program rather than a scientific one (compare the discussion of Freud toward the end of Chapter 10). We are to look not for the *causes* of a person's behavior but for the *meaning* of it, that is, for *reasons* involving the person's beliefs and desires (Kant's "intelligible character"—see Chapter 8). And for Sartre desires depend more on value judgments than on biological drives or instincts (pp. 568–75). (Some psychiatrists have emphasized this methodology of seeking to understand how patients see their world, rather than—or as well as—looking for unconscious drives or brain states behind their behavior.)

Sartre argues that because a person has to be a unity, not just a bundle of unrelated desires or habits, so there must be for each person a "fundamental choice," what he calls an **original project**, that gives the ultimate meaning or purpose behind every aspect of his or her life (pp. 561–65). The biographies he wrote of Baudelaire, Genet, and Flaubert are exercises in existential psychoanalysis, applied to the whole of a life. But it is not obvious that for each person there must be a *single* fundamental choice, and Sartre himself allows that people can sometimes make a sudden "conversion" of their original project (pp. 475–76). And need there be just *one* such project in each stage of life? Can't someone have several projects that are not derived from any common formula (e.g., family, career, sport, art, or politics)? And aren't some people radically disunited, even caught up in inner conflict?

If no reasons can be given for fundamental choices, they would seem to be unjustified and arbitrary. On his own premises it seems Sartre would have to commend, or at least not condemn, the man who "authentically" chooses to devote himself to exterminating Jews, attacking non-Muslims, tricking people out of their money, abusing children, or playing computer games—provided that he makes such choices with full reflective awareness. Can Sartre find within his own philosophy any reason to criticize a Nietzschean superman who resolutely and reflectively develops his own freedom at the cost of other less-than-super human beings? Conversely, if someone devotes himself or herself to bringing up children, helping the disabled, or playing the cello, but deceives himself or herself (in Sartre's view) into thinking that these are objective values, would he condemn that person as living in bad faith?

In some intriguing footnotes in *Being and Nothingness* Sartre uses quasi-religious language to suggest that it is possible to "radically escape bad faith" in "a self-recovery of being which was previously corrupted." He calls this "authenticity" (in the footnote on p. 70), and he talks of "an ethics of deliverance and salvation" and of "a radical conversion" (p. 412). And in the midst of some of his most obscure theorizing (about time in Part Two) he distinguishes "purifying" or **pure reflection** from "impure" or "accessory" reflection (pp. 155, 159ff.). He attributes a peculiarly moral power to the former, which can be attained only as the result of a "katharsis" or cleansing. However, he says these ideas cannot be developed in a work of ontology, and he ended *Being and Nothingness* with a promise to write another book on the ethical plane (p. 628). But he never published such a work, presumably because his views began to change.

AUTHENTICITY AND FREEDOM FOR EVERYONE

Sartre's *War Diaries* and *Notebooks for an Ethics* were published posthumously, so it is possible to see in what direction his ethical thought was heading. (These notes, not authorized for publication by Sartre himself, run to hundreds of pages. Clearly, the flow of words never left him, indeed he entitled his autobiography *Words!*)

Sartre came to recognize, even more explicitly than in *Being and Nothingness,* that human freedom is situated within **facticity**, the facts about oneself and one's situation that constrain the ways in which one can express one's freedom. One kind of facticity is the vulnerability of the human body; for example, one's freedom is importantly limited if one contracts a serious illness such as tuberculosis. Another kind of facticity is one's situation in a society at a certain stage in history. A slave, a manual laborer, a worker on an assembly line, a sales assistant, a cleaner or a "sex worker" may have some very limited choices about how to react in his or her situation; but it would be a cruel deception to assure such people that they are fundamentally as free as every other human being, simply because of the nature of consciousness. In the abstract philosophical terms of *Being and Nothingness* perhaps they are free, but in concrete realistic terms they are not. Thus, Sartre acknowledges the obvious: that socio-economic factors limit human freedom, even if they do not determine every choice. (Compare our discussion of Marx in Chapter 9.) So he now rejects "abstract morality" in favor of an ethics that takes account of biological, economic and social factors and places its hopes in social (perhaps revolutionary) change, as much as in individual psychological transformation.

In the *Notebooks* Sartre says some interesting things about pure reflection and the authentic human existence it is supposed to give rise to. Pure reflection enables us to give up the project of becoming Godlike beings, which he had previously represented as our inevitable but useless passion. We can come to accept the contingency of our existence, and in a creative, generous spirit we can give meaning and purpose to our lives and thereby to the world:

> authentic man never loses sight of the absolute goals of the human condition . . . to save the world (in making there be being), to make freedom the foundation of the world, to take responsibility for creation, and to make the origin of the world absolute through freedom taking hold of itself. (*Notebooks*, p. 448)

It sounds as if we are to give up the project of becoming God in one sense by becoming divine in another sense, seeing ourselves as the only source of salvation for the world—an assertion of heroic human pride that most religions would reject.

Sartre now allows that in authentic existence, relations with other people can be transformed for the better. Another person's perception of me, although "objectifying" in the obvious sense that they perceive my body as one particular physical object, is not necessarily a threat:

> It only becomes so if the Other refuses to see a freedom in me *too*. But if, on the contrary, he makes me exist as an existing freedom as well as a *Being/object* . . . he enriches the world and me, he *gives a meaning* to my existence *in addition to* the subjective meaning that I myself give it. (*Notebooks*, p. 500, italics in original)

So sympathetic comprehension of another person, and assistance in pursuing his or her goals, is possible after all. Sartre even talks of "authentic love" that "rejoices in the Other's being-in-the-world, without appropriating it" (*Notebooks,* p. 508), which is surprisingly reminiscent of Christian *agape*.

The freedom of the individual thus becomes Sartre's basic value. This has to be understood as not merely the necessary truth that every conscious being is free in the abstract sense, but the value judgment that every person should be able to *exercise* his or her freedom in concrete ways and, therefore, that human societies should make this a reality for everyone. Sartrean authenticity, the reflective assuming of responsibility for one's own free choices, now involves respecting and valuing the freedom of all other conscious, rational beings.

He had earlier made a suggestion in this Kantian direction in *Existentialism and Humanism* (p. 29), where he said that in choosing for oneself one chooses for all people, and thereby creates an image of people as one believes they ought to be. In the *Notebooks* he uses the phrase "a city of ends" to express this goal, which he now sees as "absolute". That phrase echoes two previous ideals: Augustine's "City of God" (distinct from all earthly societies) and Kant's formula of the "Kingdom of Ends" (that we should treat every rational being never merely as a means but always as an end). Sartre, however, interprets the goal in more down-to-earth terms as a socialist, classless society—invoking the same sort of utopian ideal as Marx's envisioned "truly communist" state of future society in which all human beings will be free.

The vast verbiage of Sartre's philosophy thus issues a practical challenge to us all: first, to become more truly self-aware and use our freedom to change ourselves for the better and, second, to work toward a worldwide society in which all people have equal opportunity to exercise their freedom.

FOR FURTHER READING

For thought-provoking introductions to existentialism see William Barrett, *Irrational Man: A Study in Existential Philosophy* (New York: Anchor Books/ Doubleday, 1962), and David E. Cooper, *Existentialism: A Reconstruction* (Oxford: Blackwell, 1990).

For admirable short guides to important existentialist thinkers, Patrick Gardiner, *Kierkegaard* (Oxford: Oxford University Press, 1988); Michael Tanner, *Nietzsche* (Oxford: Oxford University Press, 1994); George Steiner, *Heidegger* (London: Fontana, 1978); Arthur C. Danto, *Sartre* (London: Fontana, 1975).

Anyone wanting to get acquainted with Heidegger's though might start with his "Letter on Humanism" of 1947, translated in *Heidegger: Basic Writings*, ed. David Farrell Krell (London: Routledge, revised and expanded edition 1993).

Those who want to read Sartre for themselves could begin with his philosophical novel *Nausea* and his lecture *Existentialism and Humanism* (London: Methuen, 1948), then his short books *The Transcendence of the Ego* (New York: Farrar, Straus & Giroux, 1957) and *Sketch for a Theory of the Emotions* (London: Methuen, 1962). Rather than trying to plow straight through *Being and Nothingness*, trans. Hazel Barnes, (London: Routledge, 2002; Secaucus, NJ: Citadel Press, 2001), it might be helpful to start with Part 4, the second chapter of Part 1 ("Bad Faith"), the concluding pages ("Ethical Implications"), then Part 3, Chapter 1, section III ("The Look").

Francis Jeanson, *Sartre and the Problem of Morality* (Bloomington: Indiana University Press, 1980, first published in French in 1947), is an interpretation of the early philosophy that was endorsed by Sartre himself.

In *Sartre's Two Ethics: From Authenticity to Integral Humanity* (Peru, IL: Open Court, 1993), Thomas C. Anderson gives an account of Sartre's "first ethics" from the period immediately after *Being and Nothingness*, and his "second ethics" especially as presented in the Rome lecture of 1964. (Anderson's summary saves us from wading through hundreds of pages of jottings "of uneven clarity and significance.")

Gregory McCulloch, *Using Sartre: An Analytical Introduction to Early Sartrean Themes* (London: Routledge, 1994), offers a clear interpretation of some fundamental issues in Sartre, relating them to analytical philosophy of mind and epistemology.

Sebastian Gardner, *Sartre's Being and Nothingness: A Reader's Guide* (London: Continuum, 2009), is an excellent aid to deeper understanding of that difficult text.

Leslie Stevenson, "Kant and Sartre on Self-Knowledge," in *Comparing Kant and Sartre*, ed. S. Baiasu (New York: Palgrave-Macmillan, 2015).

KEY TERMS

absurd	in-itself-for-itself
anguish	intentionality
authentic	nothingness
bad faith	original project
Being	prereflective
being-for-itself	pure reflection
being-in-itself	reflection
existential psychoanalysis	spirit of seriousness
existentialism	superman
facticity	value judgment

QUESTIONS FOR DISCUSSION

1. What does Sartre mean by calling human life "absurd"? Is he right?
2. Can you explain and defend Sartre's concept of "nothingness"?
3. Do we choose our own emotions?
4. Is Sartre's conception of "bad faith" coherent?
5. Is there any sense in which when we choose for ourselves, we choose for everyone?

C　H　A　P　T　E　R

12

Darwinian Theories
of Human Nature

Some readers may be wondering whether it is worth giving so much attention to the religious traditions, philosophies, and speculative theories of previous centuries. Now that the scientific method has established itself as the proper way of understanding everything in the world, including living beings like ourselves, surely we should look to science for the truth about human nature?

In fact, this program is nothing new: it inspired many thinkers in the seventeenth and eighteenth centuries, notably Hobbes, Hume, and the *philosophes* of the French Enlightenment. But it has gained new momentum since Darwin propounded his theory of evolution in the mid-nineteenth century. Most educated people have since come to accept as a scientifically proved truth that humans share a common descent with all other creatures on Earth, but it is still resisted by some religious believers (Muslim as well as Christian). Since Darwin's time there has been a complex series of developments of biological theory, along with wider public controversy about its implications. In this almost double-length chapter we will examine three main waves of evolutionary thinking about human nature, and in a fourth section we will address the live issues about the relation between evolutionary science and our values, hopes, and religious aspirations.

Many biologists, psychologists, and social scientists have been chary of talking about something as vague and controversial as "human nature," tending to concentrate on advancing the field and making their professional reputations by specialized technical studies. A few of them, however, have been bold enough to offer some sort of diagnosis and prescription for human problems, that is, a "theory" of human nature in the wide sense used in this book. But, as we will see, when would-be scientists of human nature offer their secular schemes of progress or salvation, their claims involve value judgments beyond their area of scientific expertise, and become just as controversial as the older "theories" considered in previous chapters. So along with an exposition of various stages of evolutionary theorizing, we will offer some conceptual and ethical critique.

EVOLUTIONARY THEORY, STAGE I: DARWIN AND HIS CONTEMPORARIES

Metaphysical / Scientific Background

Before Darwin came on the scene scientists were beginning to realize that the world had a vastly longer history than previously thought. Most people in the Judaic and Christian traditions had assumed the biblical stories to be literally true; for example, it was widely believed that the Creation had occurred only about six thousand years ago (shortly followed by the Flood). But in 1755 the youthful Kant (then at the forefront of science) propounded the "nebular" hypothesis that the solar system had "evolved" over a much longer time, by the gradual accretion of planets from primordial dust swirling around the sun. And in the early nineteenth century geologists were coming to realize how the rock strata (vividly revealed as canals were dug) had been formed and molded by well-known processes of eruption and sedimentation, earth movement and erosion, acting over vast periods of past time. This "uniformitarian" theory was authoritatively propounded in Charles Lyell's *Principles of Geology* (1830–33), and it strongly influenced Darwin's thought. Indeed, he made his own early reputation more as geologist than biologist.

The most famous use of the word "evolution" is, of course, for the processes of formation and adaptation in biological *species*. The notion of long-term species change was already around in Darwin's time as the increasing discoveries of fossilized skeletons showed that there had once been creatures very different from those that exist now. The idea that the kinds of creatures found on Earth have been "transmuted" from their predecessors by a series of small changes was propounded by Darwin's grandfather Erasmus Darwin, and by the grandly-named French biologists Georges-Louis Leclerc de Buffon and Jean-Baptiste de Monet de Lamarck.

Darwin on Natural Selection

It is a very significant further step from the overall *fact* of the transmutation or evolution of species, evidenced by the gradations found in the fossil record, to an understanding of how such processes could actually work. The great contribution of Charles Darwin (1809–1882) was to realize the *causal mechanism* for gradual adaptive species change, the process that he came to call **natural selection**. In previous speculations about the means by which species might change Lamarck had suggested in 1809 that creatures can pass on to their offspring some physical traits they had developed during their own lifetimes. According to this theory of **inheritance of acquired characteristics**, an individual herbivore that had stretched its neck to eat leaves off tall trees might produce progeny with longer necks—and thus, over generations, giraffes might have evolved. But there was no known biological mechanism for this, and it seemed implausible that all change in species could be explained this way.

As a student, Darwin developed a passionate interest in biology and geology, neglecting his university curricula in medicine at Edinburgh, and in theology at Cambridge, but managing to impress the researchers in his unofficial studies. At the age of twenty-two he had an extremely lucky break when, with professorial backing from Cambridge, he was offered the position of naturalist on the British naval surveying ship the *Beagle* (though it took the persuasiveness of his uncle to overcome the objections of his father). During that famous voyage, which took nearly five years (1831–36), Darwin spent most of the time in and around South America and on various islands along the way. He seized opportunities to make extensive inland explorations of little-known territories. He was entranced by the biological profusion of the Amazonian rainforest, he found fossils of enormous extinct animals, and the remains of sea creatures high in the Andes Mountains, and he witnessed an earthquake in Chile that uplifted the earth. All this was clear evidence of long-term and continually-acting processes of geological and biological change. He made extensive collections of flora and fauna previously unknown to science, sending them back to London for scientific study. He was especially puzzled by the birds and animals of the Galapagos Islands in the Pacific Ocean, which resembled those of South America yet differed in intriguing detail from island to island, where the habitats were subtly different. The youthful Darwin was thus blessed with a unique opportunity to gather vast quantities of new evidence. But what was it evidence *for*?

After his return from this epic voyage, Darwin settled down to marriage (to his cousin Emma Wedgwood), a large Victorian family, and life as an independent scientist (supported by Emma's inherited capitalist wealth). The basic idea of natural selection came to him quite soon, and he wrote down a first sketch of his theory in 1844. But he did not publish it for the next fifteen years, for he was painfully aware of just how controversial it would be. It was incompatible with the biblical story of God's creation of animals and humans in Genesis, if read literally—not that that worried Darwin himself, but he was reluctant to get embroiled in religious controversy, or to distress his pious wife. There had already been some amateurish books about species change that had aroused intense public interest, but he wanted to document his ideas in proper scientific fashion, patiently clarifying his arguments and assembling all the varied evidence he could find.

Publication of Darwin's long-gestated theory was provoked by the sudden arrival in 1858 of a paper from Alfred Wallace, a young English naturalist then researching in the East Indies, who had independently hit on the idea of natural selection. Not wanting to be anticipated, Darwin hurriedly wrote up the fruits of his years of research in his epoch-making book *The Origin of Species*, published in 1859. Wallace shared the initial scientific credit at a meeting of the Royal Society, but he did not have nearly as much evidence as Darwin, and could not match him in detailed argument. (He later compromised his biological insights when he became a convert to spiritualism and tried to exempt the human mind from evolution.)

The heart of the Darwinian argument for natural selection is an elegant logical deduction from four large empirical generalizations. The first two are as follows:

1. There is variation in the traits of individuals of a given species.
2. Traits of parents tend to be passed on to their offspring.

These two general trends emerge from a wide variety of plants and animals, and they had long been put to very practical use in the selective breeding of new varieties of plants, farm animals, dogs, and pigeons. That was one main source of evidence for Darwin, and it justifies his talk of "natural *selection*" as a process that, analogously to human selection, modifies species—but unintentionally, of course. The other premises of his argument are as follows:

3. Species are intrinsically capable of a geometric rate of increase of population.
4. The resources of the environment typically cannot support such an increase.

The truth of (3) consists in the fact that any pair can produce considerably more than two offspring—in many plants and fishes, thousands of seeds or eggs are produced. It follows from (3) and (4) that only a small proportion of seeds, eggs, and young reach maturity. In effect, there is competition for survival and reproduction between members of the *same* species, even more than between different species. This need not mean bodily confrontation, as when individuals scrabble with each other for food or males fight for females: in Darwin's sense plants "compete" for light and nutrients, and many creatures "compete" to avoid being detected by predators.

From the inevitability of such competition and from the variability in (1), we can deduce that at any stage there will be some individuals in the population that because of their innate differences from others will have better chances of surviving long enough to reproduce. They can be described as the **fittest** in their environment or ecological "niche," which includes all the factors relevant to their life. Given (2), those with "fitter" traits will tend to pass them on to their offspring, but those with less advantageous traits will not survive and reproduce so well.

Thus, over many generations the typical characteristics of a population can change significantly. And given the immense periods of past time proved by geology, and the geographical distribution and separation of plants and animals into the wide variety of ecological niches around the world, different species can evolve from common ancestors. All that is needed is the constant pressure of natural selection acting on the variations within the populations in various environments. There is no need to postulate any Lamarckian inheritance of acquired characteristics, although Darwin himself did some backsliding on this point, partly because he did not know the *genetic basis* of the patterns of inheritance summed up in (1) and (2).

Besides natural selection—or rather as a special case of it—Darwin recognized the operation of what he called "sexual selection," treated at length in his double-barreled work of 1871, *The Descent of Man, and Selection in Relation to Sex*. The heavy antlers of the stag and the elaborate tail of the peacock would seem to be encumbrances to the ordinary business of their lives such as getting around in search of food and fleeing from predators. Surely natural selection would give the advantage to deer with more manageable antlers and to peacocks with more modest tails. But that would be to ignore the biologically crucial business of sexual reproduction. Stags use their antlers in the "rut" when they fight with each other to get access to the hinds, while male peacocks display their gloriously colored fashion accessory to prospective mates, who exercise their privilege of female choice of the most impressive partner. So there is competition not just to survive but to breed. Individuals with traits that lead to sexual success are more likely to pass them on to offspring, and that presumably outweighs any disadvantages outside the mating season.

The Origin of Species was that rare thing, an original work of science written in a vivid style that was intelligible to most educated readers.

Darwin was able to document his case with a virtuoso display of evidence from selective breeding, worldwide natural history, and paleontology. The book was an immediate bestseller and was translated into many languages. It aroused controversy straight away, and in some quarters it still does.

Darwin on Human Evolution

With characteristic caution, Darwin did not at first make explicit his view that humans are descended from apelike ancestors. In the closing words of the *Origin* he allowed himself only a classic English understatement—that "light will be thrown on the origin of man and his history." But to his readers the cat—or should we say *the apeman?*—was already out of the bag, and Thomas H. Huxley, his most forthright supporter, produced a book on the evolutionary origins of humans only four years later. In 1871 Darwin at last published his own thoughts on human evolution in *The Descent of Man.* (Page references below are to the modern edition.) With his usual scientific thoroughness he reviewed the anatomical, medical, embryological, and behavioral evidence for our kindred with other animals, calling attention to telltale "rudiments" such as the little feature in our outer ears that he argued is the result of the infolding of the pointed ears of our distant simian ancestors.

The evolution of all species including ourselves from simpler forms of life is now acknowledged by biologists to be not just a theory but a *fact.* There is plenty of empirical evidence for our common ancestry with other animals. The human body has the same plan as other vertebrates: four limbs with five digits on each. Our much closer similarity to monkeys, and especially to the great apes, in heads and hands is obvious. The human embryo goes through stages of development in which it resembles the embryos of lower forms of life. In our bodies there are remnants of ancestral forms, for example, a vestigial tail. The biochemistry of our bodies—cells, proteins, blood, DNA—is very similar to that of other creatures. And in recent years many thousands of fossil remains of a variety of hominoid species intermediate between apes and humans have been unearthed. That we have evolved from more primitive creatures is by now as well-established a fact as anything in science. No doubt some details remain to be sorted out (science is never complete). With the ongoing discoveries of more hominoid fossils (including the remarkably small "Hobbit" on an Indonesian island), the pathways of subhuman evolution are proving to be much more complex than Darwin or his successors imagined.

Social Darwinism

Contemporary readers may be keen to debate the ethical or political or religious implications of evolutionary theory. But we should first ask ourselves whether and how a scientific theory can have implications for what we ought to do. Science is supposed, by definition, to find out truths about the physical world; it is described as "dealing only with *facts*." How then can a scientific theory imply anything about **value judgments**? As David Hume put it, how can we deduce an "ought" from an "is"? The answer is surely that we can do so only if we include at least one value judgment in the premises, explicitly or implicitly. For example, medical science tells what we "ought" to do, by showing us what treatments and policies we need to use to cure or prevent various diseases. We take for granted that it is a Good Thing to reduce human suffering whenever we can—that is the relevant value judgment (uncontroversial in this case). Science has also made possible new kinds of weapons—chemical, biological, and nuclear—but it does not tell us whether and when to deploy them. Science and technology do not change our basic values, they may give us new means of promoting them, but they can also pose new value questions (such as the possibilities of manipulating genes) which they cannot themselves answer.

So the theory that humans are evolved creatures does not in itself tell us how we ought to live. Yet there has been a tendency to go beyond this purely scientific view and to suggest that evolution in some sense creates its own values. After all, the basic point of Darwinian theory is that the biologically fittest individuals are those that survive longest and leave the most progeny; and the successful species in a given environment are those that survive over many generations, perhaps increasing their numbers. And, it may be asked, isn't biological *success* the ultimate value? Among humans the strongest, the cleverest, the sexiest seem to be the most successful—so aren't *they* the most valuable, to be most admired and emulated? Some may jump to the conclusion that the ethical message of Darwinian evolution is that it is every man (and woman) for himself (or herself), perhaps even that "greed is good" after all. But if there were to be any such Darwinian ethic, it would recommend those with the biggest families or, more precisely, those who *bring the most offspring to maturity*—which is not always the same thing as being strong or clever or sexy, though those traits obviously help at certain situations in life.

The much-used and -abused phrase "survival of the fittest" suggests that those who survive and reproduce best are the *best in some wider sense*. The phrase and the associated outlook were around before the publication of Darwin's *Origin*, in the writings of the influential Victorian social philosopher Herbert Spencer (1820–1903). Like Darwin, he had been strongly influenced by Thomas Malthus's 1798 *Essay on the Principle of Population*, which argued that population has a natural tendency to outstrip resources, with the result that the weakest get weeded out. The questionable implication was drawn that charitable aid to the starving is pointless (a principle notoriously followed by the British government during the Irish potato famine in the 1840s). Spencer was a philosopher of social progress, the general idea of which had taken root in European and American thought since the Enlightenment. In the footsteps of Hegel, he developed an elaborate theory about the "evolution" of human society, seeing the "civilized" society of nineteenth-century capitalism as the inevitable—and *best!*—outcome of all preceding human history.

Many thinkers in the second half of the nineteenth century, including E. L. Youmans and W. G. Sumner in the United States, eagerly took up this theme. It seemed to them that there was a straightforward inference from the fact of biological evolution by natural selection to the need for severe competition within human society. In this they thought they saw a justification for unrestrained laissez-faire capitalism, with its extreme disparities between rich and poor. There was an easy transition to racist attitudes, even trying to excuse the near-extermination of the aboriginal populations of the Americas and Australia as the inevitable victory of the supposedly advanced peoples over the primitive races. At both the individual and the social levels, might was pretty well identified with right.

But surely an "ought" has been smuggled in somewhere, in trying to derive such dramatic ethical and political consequences from the theory of evolution. It surely does *not* follow that people who are the fittest in the biological terms of survival and reproduction are the *best* in any other sense (they may not be morally, artistically, intellectually, or spiritually distinguished at all). And conversely the richest (or those most admirable in higher ways) are not necessarily the most fecund at reproduction. As we will see, Darwin himself did not endorse what has been called **social Darwinism**. The label has stuck, but it would be more historically accurate to call it "social Spencerism," for Darwinism is a strictly scientific theory about the origin of species, whereas Spencerism was a speculative, value-laden interpretation of history, set in a background metaphysics of "cosmic" evolution.

Marx was a contemporaneous social theorist at the opposite extreme of politics. Whereas Spencer glorified those who did well out of capitalism, Marx saw them as an exploiting class who would be dispossessed in the coming communist revolution. As we saw in Chapter 9, he had his own speculative theory of the historical development of human societies through economic stages; and he too hailed Darwinian evolution in his own support. The fact that such opposing social thinkers could both try to hitch their bandwagons to evolutionary theory should alert us to the logical gulf between scientific theories and political ideologies.

Darwin's Own Values

In *The Descent of Man*, after reviewing the physical evidence for our common ancestry with the apes, Darwin went on to offer some interesting suggestions about how our intellectual and moral faculties might have evolved from more primitive antecedents. Against the common objection that our human language, intelligence, emotions, morality, and religion make us different in kind from even the most advanced ape, Darwin insisted that there was no barrier in principle to a gradual mental as well as physical evolution over huge periods of time. He had acquired an encyclopedic knowledge of animal behavior (for his time), and he found primitive analogues and possible antecedents for much human behavior. Percipiently, he picked out our social nature and language as crucial to human mentality.

Darwin was aware that many of his ideas in *The Descent of Man* were speculations rather than proven facts, as he took natural selection to be proven. He was suggesting how human evolution *might* have proceeded, not demonstrating the path it must have taken (some later evolutionary theorizers have done the same, without always being aware of it). In two respects he argued in ways that later biologists questioned (though very recently there has been some reopening of both issues). He sometimes appealed to inheritance of acquired characteristics, and he postulated a time when natural selection operated by competition between *groups*, as well as between individuals. For instance, a tribe in which some members were willing to sacrifice their lives in warfare might perhaps be expected to survive better than more peace-loving tribes. But it is unclear how such "group selection" could operate: aggressive warriors may not survive battles to propagate their genes, whereas the "draft dodger" presumably has more opportunity of doing so, so surely selection would favor the latter?

As for value judgments in aesthetics, morality, or religion, Darwin offered various suggestions about how our capacity for them may have evolved. But he did *not* take the reductionist line typical of social Darwinism. He confidently made his own judgments about beauty and morality, and was inclined to attribute the origin of our sense of beauty to sexual selection. And he remarked how standards of beauty differed between societies, patronizingly contrasting the "hideous" ornaments and music of "savages" with the "refined" tastes of the "civilized races."

In *The Descent of Man* Darwin described our conscience or "moral sense" as "the most noble of the attributes of man," and he paid homage to Kant's concept of duty as the highest human motivation of all, quite distinct from biologically based "appetite." He did not see any incompatibility between this philosophical endorsement of morality and his evolutionary account of it as emerging from a combination of social instincts and intellectual powers. While speculating about evolutionary struggles between tribes or races, he also talked of the "great sin" of slavery and of the treatment of wives like slaves (p. 94). Insofar as he expressed views on history and politics, Darwin was on the liberal or progressive side. He wrote that "man has risen, though by slow and interrupted steps, from a lowly condition to the highest standard as yet attained by him in knowledge, morals, and religion." Admittedly he did in one place offer a prescription tending toward social Spencerism:

> The advancement of the welfare of mankind is a most intricate problem: all ought to refrain from marriage who cannot avoid abject poverty for their children . . . . Man, like every other animal, has no doubt advanced to his present high condition through a struggle for existence consequent on his rapid multiplication; and if he is to advance still higher he must remain subject to a severe struggle . . . . There should be open competition for all men; and the most able should not be prevented by laws or customs from succeeding best and rearing the largest number of offspring. (p. 403)

But he was wise enough to recognize the limits of natural selection and the crucial importance of human culture and ethics:

> Important as the struggle for existence has been and even still is, yet as far as the highest part of man's nature is concerned there are other agencies more important. For the moral qualities are advanced . . . much more through the effects of habit, the reasoning powers, instruction, religion, etc., than through natural selection. (p. 404)

He voiced some worry about the multiplication of inferior types of people being "injurious to society," but he immediately went on so to say that we could not check our sympathy for the weaker members of our society "without deterioration in the noblest part of our nature" (pp. 168–69). So the ethic of universal compassion and respect or "love thy neighbor as thyself" should take precedence over any hardheaded biological calculations about benefits to society as a whole. Such arguments would be based on scientific hypotheses that are far from certain; as Darwin put it, they "could only be for a contingent benefit," whereas there would be "a certain and great present evil" if we intentionally neglect the weak and helpless.

These humane remarks encourage us to reply to the social Spencerist tendency as follows: since our human evolution has given us both the sympathy to care for our fellow humans and the intelligence to institute laws and social programs to help them, shouldn't we use those mental capacities to try to steer human society in the direction of greater equality? Isn't that more "natural" to us than unflinching adherence to "the survival of the fittest"?

It would be dangerous, however, to rest our case on the extremely ambiguous concept of what is "natural" (remember the warning in our Introduction). It would be better to appeal to explicit ethical principles about human dignity, equality, needs, and rights (as in Kant or Marx and in the New Testament) that cannot be derived from any factual statements about evolution.

About religion Darwin was more circumspect. He talked of the "ennobling" belief in an omnipotent God but noted that it is not present in all human cultures, though the belief in unseen spiritual agencies of some sort seems to be universal. He said that the existence of a Creator and ruler of the universe has been affirmed by "the highest intellects that have ever lived," but he refrained from directly endorsing it himself (presumably not just from modesty). He described the feeling of religious devotion as a complex mixture of "love, complete submission to an exalted and mysterious superior, dependence, fear, reverence, gratitude, and hope," yet he suggested a distant antecedent for it in the love of a dog for its master. Privately he admitted that his early belief in Christianity had faded away, without pain. But he shied away from controversy; his wife was a believer, and their children were brought up in the Church of England. Charles Darwin was a rather typical specimen of the Victorian age—an ethically serious, politically liberal, closet atheist.

EVOLUTIONARY THEORY, STAGE II: THE REACTION AGAINST BIOLOGICAL ACCOUNTS OF HUMAN NATURE

The Genetic Basis of Heredity

Darwin could not himself explain the facts about heredity expressed in generalizations (1) and (2) set out above. It was sufficient for his basic argument that they were true, even though he did not have any explanation of *why* they were true. But the source of variations within a species and the mechanism of inheritance were obvious fundamental questions for biology, and Darwin later offered his own speculative theory, which he called "pangenesis." His hypothesis was that inside the organs of every plant and animal were small particles he called "gemmules" that developed through the life of the organism and somehow represented the nature of those organs. For example, a strong muscle would produce gemmules for strong muscles, and a clever brain might generate corresponding particles for intelligence. Darwin suggested that gemmules circulate around the body and collect in the reproductive organs, from where they would be passed on to the offspring. This would have provided a mechanism for the inheritance of acquired characteristics.

It was not a bad guess for its time, but soon after Darwin's death it was shown to be completely wrong. There is a useful lesson here, that even the most distinguished scientists are fallible. (Einstein never accepted quantum mechanics.) Fallibility is all the more likely when a scientist ventures outside his or her special field. (Newton dabbled in alchemy.) Publicly verifiable evidence is the final test of scientific theories. But let us hasten to add that the falsity of Darwin's hypothesis of gemmules does nothing to disprove evolution by natural selection, which does not depend on his hypothesis about the *mechanism* of inheritance.

In the 1880s the German biologist August Weismann argued that the **germ plasm** of an organism—the parts of the reproductive system that carry the hereditary information such as the eggs and sperm—remain quite independent of all the other organs in the body, contrary to Darwin's idea of migrating gemmules. So no matter what changes occur in an animal *in its own lifetime*, those changes cannot be passed on to its offspring. In classic experiments the descendants of generations of mice whose tails had been systematically docked were born with tails just as long as ever.

The correct theoretical explanation of the patterns of biological inheritance had been offered by the Austrian monk Gregor Mendel in Darwin's own lifetime, but the crucial importance of that work was not recognized until after 1900. Mendel postulated distinct, indivisible, causal factors, now called **genes**, that are passed on from parents to offspring in a process of random mixing of the genes from two parents in sexual reproduction. Mendel produced evidence for this theory by systematically breeding peas in the garden of his monastery. As Weismann said, the genes carried in the reproductive organs remain unaffected by changes over the lifetime of the individual. The distinction between **dominant** and **recessive genes** explains how traits of parents that do *not* appear in their offspring can reappear in the third generation if two recessive genes for the relevant trait are inherited.

A certain mystery remained about the sources of the *variation* between genes within populations of organisms. It was concluded that genes occasionally change or "mutate" for no known biological reason, so these **mutations** were described as "random." (Natural or artificial radiation is now known to be one cause of mutations.) In the 1920s and 30s it was realized that a precise account of how natural selection operating over time on large populations required considerable use of statistics. Mathematical biologists such as Sewell Wright and R. A. Fisher transformed the theory of evolution into a sophisticated "modern synthesis." (Darwin's original theory involved informal argument about probabilities, but his mathematical abilities were modest, so he would not have understood these mathematicized versions of his own theory.)

The biochemical basis of inheritance through the unwinding of the elegant double-helix structure of the molecules of DNA (deoxyribonucleic acid) that are present in every living cell was revealed by Watson and Crick's Nobel Prize–winning discovery in 1953. Genes could now be identified as bits of information encoded in words of the four-letter "alphabet" consisting of the chemical bases labeled A, C, G, and T. The copying mechanism in reproduction depends on the fact that these four bases can combine only in the pairs A-T and C-G, so that the same encoded information is passed on into the next generation, with occasional errors in copying providing variations for natural selection to work on. This was a remarkable discovery of the biochemical basis of all life. But the biochemical process of "reading" the code to produce the variety of proteins that make up our bodies has turned out to be very complicated. The fact that our life *depends* on biochemistry does not imply that everything about us can be *explained* in terms of biochemistry.

Eugenics, Racism, and Sexism

While that post-Darwinian synthesis was being worked out, its apparent social implications were also eagerly discussed. Some people were quick to jump to the very contentious conclusion that if there is no inheritance of acquired characteristics, then there must be innate differences between individuals, races, and the sexes, which make some of them innately inferior; and (predictably) the "gold standard" for humanity was often assumed to be set by intelligent, white, "civilized" males.

Darwin's cousin Francis Galton, a statistician well versed in his relative's biology, picked up on worries that Darwin himself had expressed about civilized societies being undermined because they allowed the physically and mentally weak to breed. Legal rights, charity, vaccination, health care, and governmental welfare programs seemed to mean that natural selection operating by the elimination of the unfit, or at least the restriction of their reproduction, no longer applied to human society. That, it was feared, was a very Bad Thing. Galton coined the word **eugenics** for the study of how to produce fine offspring, with the practical implication that society ought to take care of its genetic future. The antidote to "the multiplication of the reckless and the improvident" (Darwin's incautious phrase) seemed to be a program of selective breeding. So in a chilling echo of Plato's *Republic*, the state should prevent "inferior" humans being born (negative eugenics), and encourage the production of "superior" types of people (positive eugenics).

The eugenics movement gathered widespread support across the political spectrum, from both reformers and conservatives—though significantly opposed by the Roman Catholic Church. In the early decades of the twentieth century, many US states and some Scandinavian countries passed laws for the compulsory sterilization of confirmed criminals and those labeled "feeble-minded." Germany joined in before Hitler's accession to power, but under the Nazis the production of "pure-blood Aryan" children was encouraged, and "defectives" of various kinds were not just sterilized but exterminated.

The basic ethical objection to positive or negative eugenic programs is that they involve the state intruding on one of the most basic human rights, to form sexual relationships and produce children. There is also an important practical difficulty in trying to eradicate defects or diseases that are carried by recessive genes, since many of the population may carry one such gene yet the problem will show up only in those who inherit two. To prevent reproduction by *all* those who carry the gene would be impossible, even if it were ethically acceptable; and its effects on the overall population would be very unpredictable.

Eugenics depended on making discriminatory value judgments about who counts as inferior, so it was easily associated with racism. Racial prejudice was deeply entrenched in European culture, even in some of the foremost philosophers of the Enlightenment such as Hume and Kant. Black slaves were brutally imported into the Americas (North, South, and Caribbean) by the early European colonists, and the social and economic aftereffects of that system of slavery persist, so that race has remained an emotionally charged issue to the present day.

Darwin wrote a chapter about "the races of man," trying to take an objective biological point of view. He remarked that he had once been friends with "a full-blooded Negro" at some point on his epic voyage. Physical differences between races are obvious to the eye, but Darwin pointed out that *within* each racial type there is a great deal of variety. And despite the differences in skin color and physiognomy, we all have enormous similarities in biochemistry, anatomy, and psychology. All human beings can interbreed, and the offspring tend to display a graduating blend of characteristics; so there is often no sharp distinction between black and white, brown, and yellow. The fact that some people with light brown skin are labeled "black" and that many different people count as "white" shows that our everyday classifications are social rather than biological. Darwin concluded that the so-called races of man were "varieties" that had arisen under long periods of geographical separation, perhaps by sexual selection as much as natural selection. He was quite clear that races are not separate species.

However, Darwin was not entirely free of the prejudices of his time. He talked of "civilized" and "barbarous" races. He was struck by the differences between himself and the impoverished natives he encountered in Tierra del Fuego, but he hoped that individuals such as Jeremy Button (who was transported from there to Britain, and back) could be "improved" by English education (the effect did not last). He thought of such "savages" as examples of how our own distant ancestors must have been. Archaeology showed that many ancient cultures had become extinct, and he predicted that the remaining primitive peoples would die out in the worldwide competition for resources.

Darwin's speculative suggestion about natural selection in human prehistory operating on *tribes* as much as on individuals encouraged the conclusion that the now-dominant races, cultures, or nations had been successful because they were innately superior. Many people wanted to believe this, and eagerly latched on to what looked like scientific backing for their prejudice. Weismann's refutation of the inheritance of acquired characteristics seemed to them to leave little hope for the advancement of "innately inferior" races by education and social programs. In the United States the Harvard psychologist William McDougall declared in 1921 that the races differ in intellectual stature as they do in physical stature. Social and political thinkers who were inclined to racism found a ready "justification" for continued discrimination and exploitation. In the early twentieth century there was considerable worry about an alleged weakening of the American population through the immigration of "inferior" peoples from southern and eastern Europe, including many Jews. Psychologists such as Carl Brigham of Princeton claimed that the evidence showed "Nordics" to be superior to all other groups. The US Immigration Act of 1924 showed racial bias against Chinese, Japanese, and non-Nordic Europeans.

Another conspicuous form of discrimination was by gender. On this topic too, Darwin's legacy was somewhat ambiguous. No naturalist could fail to notice differences in physique, coloration, and behavior between the sexes in many species, and Darwin had argued that sexual selection was an important factor in natural selection. About women, some of his remarks concerning alleged mental differences raise hackles now. He said that "man is more courageous, pugnacious, and energetic than woman, and has a more inventive genius" (p. 316); and worse, he wrote,

> The chief distinction in the intellectual powers of the two sexes is shewn by man attaining to a higher eminence, in whatever he takes up, than woman can attain—whether requiring deep thought, reason, or imagination, or merely the use of the senses and hands. . . . We may also infer . . . the average standard of mental power in man must be above that of woman. (p. 327)

However, he went on to say,

> In order that woman should reach the same standard as man, she ought, when nearly adult, to be trained to energy and perseverance, and to have her reason and imagination exercised to the highest point. (p. 329)

So Darwin could not be numbered among the opponents of higher education for women, who tried to argue that women's place was in the home and that they were innately incapable of benefiting from advanced education.

The Reaction in Favor of Culture and Education: Intelligence Tests, Sociology, and Anthropology

By what criteria were these invidious distinctions between the races and the sexes drawn? That there are bodily differences in both cases is obvious. The controversial point is whether these correlate, on average, with mental differences, especially with intelligence. We have just seen Darwin himself asserting this—but where was his evidence? It fell below his usual high scientific standard, being nothing more than an impressionistic survey of the characteristics of the races and the sexes in history so far. But the inference from actual to potential achievement, from difference in mental performance to difference in innate mental power, is not valid unless the conditions are equal for the individuals or groups being compared. So it is perfectly reasonable to object that the social conditions and educational opportunities for nonwhites and for women had been far from equal to those for white men up to 1900 and beyond.

In comparing the intelligence of different groups, psychologists and social scientists in the first half of the twentieth century tended to assume that in each individual there is some fixed, innate factor that they called "intelligence," which could be measured by intelligence tests resulting in an **intelligence quotient (IQ)**. Such tests were introduced in the First World War to assign US Army recruits to different roles, and were also used to diagnose "mental deficiency" or "feeblemindedness" and thus identify candidates for sterilization under eugenic laws. And they were applied to compare men and women. Some of the early IQ tests actually showed women in the lead; but the testers could not believe that was correct, so they changed the content of the tests to include more spatial reasoning, which "corrected" the presumed "imbalance."

The significance of intelligence tests has been hotly debated by psychologists. Of course there are various mental differences between individuals, but it does not follow that there is a single thing called "intelligence." Some people are good at mathematics, some at carpentry, music, languages, cooking, business, childcare, psychotherapy, politics, and so on. It is not clear that all these different kinds of mental ability can be amalgamated onto a common scale, with each person labeled with a number representing their IQ. Some psychologists have talked of "social intelligence" and "emotional intelligence," usefully widening the debate.

About any individual's performance, we can always ask how much of it is due to innate "intelligence" (or, better, to innate abilities *for specific activities*), and how much is due to opportunities, need, encouragement, and training. It is often difficult to say. There are *individual* differences, but it does not follow that they are correlated with distinctions of race, ethnicity, or gender. If someone is categorized as "mentally deficient" as a result of certain tests, how much of the explanation should we put down to innate factors. and how much to lack of developmental opportunity, especially because of early experience in a dysfunctional family? The whole business of intelligence testing and the supposed scientific basis of intergroup mental comparisons is thoroughly controversial.

Around this same period (roughly 1875–1925) what we now call the "social sciences" were emerging as the academic disciplines of anthropology, sociology, social psychology, economics, and the oddly named "political science" (which may have merits but is hardly what we normally count as a science). There are ongoing philosophical questions about whether these studies are really sciences, and even about what counts as "science." The founding fathers of social science, Marx, Weber, and Durkheim. held that apart from biological universals like eating, defecating, sleeping, copulating, giving birth, and breastfeeding, human behavior depends more on culture than on biology. The claim for a distinctive subject matter for social science was based on a threefold division of facts about human beings:

1. the physical facts—studied by anatomy, physiology, and evolutionary theory

2. the (individual) psychological facts—studied by individual psychology

3. the social/cultural facts—studied by the social sciences

The pioneering French sociologist Émile Durkheim (1858–1917) argued strongly for the irreducibility of social facts (about what is legal or moral) to any ensemble of individual psychological facts. He insisted that social facts are "things" in the sense that their existence is just as independent of human will as anything in the physical world. Disobey a moral or legal rule, and you may find yourself faced with very real sanctions or penalties. Such social facts are **emergent**, in the way that many facts about wholes cannot be derived from their parts—for example, the wetness of water cannot be deduced from the properties of hydrogen and oxygen.

Society is not a mysterious abstract entity, operating by some sort of magic: social rules can affect people only via other people's actions, such as law enforcement by police officers and magistrates, or reminders about etiquette or dress code from mothers or mothers-in-law. But police officers have to be appointed by social institutions, and they are supposed to have some understanding of the legal powers they are given. Mothers and other family authorities stand in specific social relationships to their family members, and their ideas typically have a distinctively social content (revealed in comments like "What will the neighbors say?"). So there seems to be no reduction of social facts to purely psychological facts.

Durkheim was an evolutionary theorist only in a very general, nonbiological sense, in that he believed in law-governed processes of change and development in human societies. He saw some analogy between the evolution of species and the social trend toward increasing division of labor, and hence he talked of the differentiation of "species" of economic and social roles. But he was under no illusion that this was Darwinian natural selection, for he held that it is subject to distinctively sociological laws.

In the United States Alfred Kroeber (1876–1960) of the University of California arrived at a similar conception with his concept of the "superorganic," by which he meant the variable element of culture that is superimposed on common biological human nature and is irreducible to it. "Civilization and heredity," he wrote, "are two things that operate in separate ways." Kroeber was a pupil of Franz Boas (1858–1942), the founding father of anthropology in the United States. From the very beginning of his career, Boas relentlessly opposed the idea that cultural differences were based on innate racial differences. He almost single-handedly persuaded social scientists that culture is irreducible to biology, thus introducing the modern conception of **cultures** in the plural.

Boas's influence was due not only to a priori arguments but also to a striking empirical study, whose results surprised him. At the time, the most widely accepted measure of innate biological differences between peoples was the "cephalic index," the ratio of length to width of the human head. Boas's 1911 study showed that the cephalic index of the children of immigrants to the United States had changed significantly within ten years of arrival. This must have been caused by some kind of environmental change, for there was obviously no change in genes. In a quite different study, of auditory perception, Boas showed that our inability to hear certain crucial differences in sounds in foreign languages is a result not of innate differences but of our early training in our native language. Such evidence provided a direct counter to claims that different races had innately different mental capacities. Boas was happy about that, for he was a resolute opponent of the prevailing racism in American society and academia. He had been born into a liberal Jewish family in Germany but emigrated to the United States because of rising anti-Semitism. His liberal convictions fitted with his theoretical claims, but there is no evidence that they distorted them.

Value judgments of equality of opportunity, equality before the law, and equal respect for human dignity in every person, were deeply involved in the reaction of so many twentieth-century social thinkers against what they saw as the insidious influence of evolutionary biology toward racism and sexism. The concept of culture as independent of biology in explaining human nature was the linchpin of this whole generation of thought. Culture was not merely a theoretical concept but was strongly associated with an ethical/political outlook that proposed to treat all people (in the singular) and all peoples (in the plural) as equal.

But there is an important distinction here. It is one thing to insist that all human *individuals* should be given equal respect and opportunities, but quite another to say that all human *cultures* are of equal value. Boas himself thought that the best future for Afro-Americans and Amerindians was to assimilate to the dominant American culture of European origin. Talk of individual human rights has a clear meaning and authority in many contexts, but it is not so obvious that talk of the rights of *cultures* makes similar sense. After all, some cultural practices—for example, suttee (or sati, the practice of a widow throwing herself on her husband's funeral pyre), foot-binding, or female genital mutilation—come into blatant conflict with individual rights (especially of women, or homosexuals). Anthropologists have tried to describe the variety of human cultures all around the world. Indeed, there was a rush to catalog the remaining "primitive" societies before they died out or became homogenized into the global economy. Whether such extinction or assimilation is a good or bad (or indifferent) thing is a value judgment.

Difference between the sexes was a different issue, which affected people closer to home, quite literally. There have been several generations and varieties of feminist thought. "Equality feminists" argue that apart from the physical differences, the human sexes are innately very much the same in mental endowment, so that any average differences in performance are due to the different expectations, education, and social roles that societies impose. The policy implication was usually drawn that all such differential treatment should be eliminated, with the aim of strict equality. On the other hand, "difference feminists" have argued that there are, on average, innate mental differences between men and women, and that society should treat them differently in some ways (to be much debated). Some difference feminists have been prepared to claim that women are morally superior to men because they are more caring, sympathetic, and cooperative. (See Chapter 13 for a full discussion).

The Reaction against Instinct Theory: Behaviorist Psychology

Within psychology there was a similar pattern of early influence of Darwinian (or supposedly Darwinian) ideas, followed by a strong reaction against them. The thought of Sigmund Freud was an attempt to put psychology on a biological basis. As we saw in Chapter 10, he postulated instincts as the fundamental driving forces in the human mind, but was frustratingly vague in his account of them. In the United States the concept of instinct was deployed in the psychologies of William James (1842–1910) and William McDougall (1871–1938). James defined "instinct" as "the faculty of acting in such a way as to produce certain ends, without foresight . . . or without previous education in the performance," and he talked of instincts for standing, walking, rivalry, anger, resentment, hunting, and fear—a notably longer and more diverse list than Freud's. James was an interesting philosopher and a founding father of scientific psychology, but there was a reaction against the vagueness of this conception. If we are to recognize instincts *in the plural*, there ought to be a determinate way of counting just how many there are (in a given species).

The behaviorist movement initiated by John B. Watson (1878–1958) proposed to put psychology on a newly rigorous methodological basis by defining it as the study of the observable behavior of animals and humans and forbidding it to invoke any suspiciously "mentalistic" notions such as instinct, intention, or consciousness in the explanation of behavior. Watson proclaimed a rather naive faith in the power of environmental influences over individual differences, as when he claimed that any healthy child could be trained or "conditioned" to become a world-class athlete, a physicist, a captain of industry, or a thief. (Perhaps it is no surprise that he ended up in the advertising industry.)

The behaviorist program was carried further at Harvard by B. F. Skinner (1904–1990), one of the most influential experimental psychologists of his time. Skinner liked to draw an analogy between his theory of behavioral conditioning and Darwinian natural selection, saying that the environment "shapes" or "selects" behavior, rewarding or "reinforcing" some behaviors so that they tend to be repeated. He hoped to find "laws of behavior" and "schedules of reinforcement" that would hold good across all, or many, different species. To that end he conducted carefully-controlled laboratory experiments, mainly on rats and pigeons; and he tried—very contentiously—to extrapolate his findings to human beings in popular books such as *Science and Human Behavior* (1953).

Skinner tended to assume that animal and human behavior can be explained in terms of *environmental* causes. He could not deny the differences between species, but he assumed there are no significant innate differences between individuals of the same species. However, the fact that identical twins brought up apart usually turn out remarkably similar in personality and mental ability is clear evidence for inherited *individual* differences. Human behavior manifestly depends on innate factors as well as environmental input. Much of what is innate in us is our common biological, gene-based nature, which is distinct from our nearest relatives the great apes. But there are also innate individual differences, as parents know.

Because of the strength of this mid-twentieth-century political/cultural and environmental/behavioral reaction against *supposedly* Darwinian ideas and their perversions in social Darwinism and Nazi ideology, these facts were somewhat obscured from view for a generation or more. *Both* the racist and sexist prejudices and the equality-of-opportunity rejection of them were based on social values more than biology. We may continue to applaud and endorse the value judgments about equal rights for all, but we should not confuse them with scientific facts.

EVOLUTIONARY THEORY, STAGE III: THE RETURN TO INNATENESS IN HUMAN NATURE

Genes and Memes

After the modern synthesis of evolutionary theory in the 1930s and 40s, further depth of biological understanding was reached by a new generation in the 1960s and 70s. George Williams, Robert Trivers, William Hamilton, and John Maynard Smith offered new mathematically-based applications of game theory to evolving populations, to explain adaptation, kin selection, and reciprocal altruism.

It now became possible to reformulate Darwin's insights in terms of genes, as Richard Dawkins did in his famous book *The Selfish Gene* (1976). That title is a well-chosen metaphor, inviting us to take a "gene's-eye view" of evolution. Philosophers diagnosed a conceptual mistake here, since genes cannot literally be selfish, only whole people (or perhaps animals). But Dawkins's point was to see biological evolution not just as *species* changing because of competition between individuals, but as a vast population of *genes* competing with each other to be copied into the genes of the next generation. Animals are born and die, but genes are passed on through the copying mechanism of DNA: compared to individual organisms, genes are immortal (though they are occasionally modified in mutation, and they are lost when a species goes extinct).

In a more speculative chapter at the end of his book, Dawkins suggested that human culture could be seen as a field of analogous but much faster evolution. This would require identifying fundamental items of human culture (ideas? beliefs? practices? fashions?) for which Dawkins proposed the neologism **memes**. His idea was that memes, like genes, can be transferred from person to person; some ideas "catch on" and survive (with modifications) over many generations, but others die out rather quickly. (There was an anticipation of this by the far-seeing Darwin, when he compared the survival of words in human languages to that of organisms in environments.) However, it is very unclear what should count as a "unit of culture" or meme (how are we to distinguish one meme from another?), so the concept has not found a firm scientific footing. Discussion continues among biologists over exactly what should be seen as the units of selection: genes, packages of genes, individual organisms, memes, or perhaps (after all) groups such as human tribes. Maybe there are *multiple* levels of simultaneous selection—things are getting very complicated in evolutionary theorizing.

The Rise of Ethology

In the mid-twentieth century a new discipline emerged that came to be called **ethology**, the scientific study of animal behavior in its natural environment. This had roots in the work of earlier naturalists, including Darwin himself who argued in *The Expression of the Emotions in Animals and Man* that much animal behavior is just as innate as their physiological features. Niko Tinbergen, a Dutchman who became a professor at Oxford, was one of the founding fathers of ethology; other pioneers (and Nobel Prize winners) were the Austrian Konrad Lorenz, who wrote popular books as well as technical papers, and Karl von Frisch, famous for his studies of the communicative dances of bees.

The ethologists argued that many patterns of animal behavior (mainly those that we colloquially describe as "instinctive") could not be explained in the behaviorist way since they appear spontaneously in all individuals of the species (or at least in all males, or all females) almost independently of previous experience or learning. In many birds the typical patterns of feeding, courtship, nest building, and care of the young answer to this description. During the rut, male deer fight with each other and pursue the females. Seagull chicks peck at the red spot on the beak of their parent to stimulate the disgorging of food. Male stickleback fish react aggressively to the distinctive coloration of another male on their territory. Such behaviors seemed to Lorenz to be "fixed," in that they cannot be eliminated however much the environment is varied (though it was soon realized that the story was not quite so simple). To explain such apparently instinctive behavior, ethologists appealed not to the past experience of the *individual* animal but to the process of evolution that has given rise to the *species*.

Tinbergen distinguished four questions about behavior, or four senses of the question "Why did that creature perform that behavior in that situation?"

1. What was the *internal physiological cause* of the behavior? To this an answer may be given in terms of muscle contractions, nervous impulses, hormone secretions, and so on.

2. What in the *development* or *experience* of the individual prepared the way for that behavior? Here, the answer may appeal to the development of the fetus in the womb and to the normal growth pattern in the species (e.g., the hormonal changes involved in reaching sexual

maturity). But there is also room for particular experiences of the individual to make a difference to later behavior (e.g., the detail of adult birdsong may depend on what songs the individual has heard; different bands of chimpanzees have developed different kinds of tool use, passed on by imitation).

3. What is the *function* of the behavior? That is, what is it *for*; what goal does it typically achieve for the individual? Here, the answer is sometimes obvious, in the case of feeding, predator avoidance, mating, or care of the young. But in other cases it is not so clear what the function of a peculiar behavior is, although it may be quite distinctive in terms of bodily movements—is it threat, courtship, defense against predators, or reinforcement of a bond between a "married" pair? Prolonged observation of a behavior pattern in various contexts may enable ethologists to interpret it as contributing in some indirect way to survival and reproduction.

4. What is the *evolutionary history* of this pattern of behavior? Sometimes this seems hardly distinguishable from (3); for example, the bodily movements involved in feeding have surely always had the same function. In other cases, however, a distinctive behavior pattern in a species may not have had the same function in the ancestors. For example, the "signaling" postures of birds, which now function as threats or courtship, have been argued to result from a "ritualization" of what were once merely "intention movements" preparatory to flight. The evolution of *bodily* features sometimes involves "jerrybuilding," the adaptation of inherited items to new uses in changing conditions, and the same may be true of behavior patterns. We cannot press rewind buttons and observe the past, but in some cases ethologists can make reasonable inferences about a pathway of evolution and thus distinguish (4) from (3).

Explanations of these four kinds are perfectly compatible with each other; they are all part of the overall complicated truth about animal behavior. If there is such a thing as a complete explanation of any single action, it would have to include the relevant facts at all four levels. (There is an analogy between Tinbergen's four questions and Aristotle's Four Causes that we encountered in Chapter 5.)

Konrad Lorenz (1903–1989) made his reputation with his studies of animal behavior, notably the "imprinting" of ducklings on the first moving thing they see (usually their mother), which they follow thereafter. He wrote engagingly for the general public and tried to apply his biological understanding to human problems, though his reputation was sullied by revelations of his collaboration with the Nazis. In *On Aggression* in 1963 he offered a diagnosis of human problems based on our allegedly innate aggressive tendencies. He suggested that humans have an innate drive to aggressive behavior toward members of their own species, and he sought an evolutionary explanation, speculating that at a certain stage of ancestral evolution, the main threat to life may have come from other hominoid groups, so those groups that banded together best to fight other groups would tend to survive longest.

But Lorenz tended to fall into a trap that awaits such attempts at popular evolutionary explanation of human traits—namely, to assume too readily that a certain pattern of observed human behavior is innate rather than culturally learned or encouraged, and then to imagine (without testing) a hypothesis about what selection pressures were at work in some long-distant era of our ancestors' evolution. There is then a strong temptation to infer that since a given sort of behavior is (supposedly) innate in humans, it is *inevitable*—or at least very difficult to eradicate or discourage. This pattern of argument has been applied, extremely dubiously, to aggression, warfare, and rape. Biologists also criticized Lorenz for appealing to **group selection**, which was invoked by Darwin himself but rejected by his successors. Debate continues about the possibility of group selection in certain conditions, so perhaps we can say that the jury is still out on the hypothesis of an *innate* human tendency to group aggression (though the tendency tragically and indisputably exists).

Chomsky and Cognitive Psychology

One especially distinctive (indeed defining) feature of human behavior is the use of language. In his 1957 book *Verbal Behavior* B. F. Skinner proposed to show that all human speech can be explained in terms of the conditioning of children in their early social environment, namely the speech of surrounding humans and their reactions to babbling by the infant. Thus, a baby in a Spanish-speaking family is subjected to many samples of the Spanish language in use, and when its responses are reasonably accurate reproductions of what it has heard, they are reinforced by approval and reward; thus, the child learns to speak Spanish.

The crucial defects in Skinner's account of language were pointed out by Noam Chomsky, a professor of linguistics at MIT whose research has been fundamental to the cognitive revolution in psychology since the 1960s. Chomsky argued that Skinner's account of *how* language is learned pays no attention to the question of *what* it is that we learn. The *creative* and *structural* features of human language—the way in which we can all speak and understand sentences we have never heard before—make it quite different from any other kind of animal behavior. There is also the matter of innate learning capacities. Obviously the linguistic environment determines which language is learned. But all normal children learn at least one language, whereas no other animal learns anything resembling a human language, with the formation of indefinitely many complex sentences according to rules of grammar. Experiments on teaching chimpanzees signing systems have claimed to show some approximations to human language, but it still seems that the capacity to use a full range of language is peculiar to the human species. Chomsky argued that the amazing speed with which children learn their native language from exposure to a very limited and imperfect sample can be explained only by the assumption that there is in the human species an *innate* capacity to process language according to grammatical rules of the special kind common to all human languages. So underlying the variety of human languages there must be a systematic structure in common, and the evidence is that children do not learn this structure from their society but process whatever linguistic input they receive in terms of it.

Given that we are an evolved species, this peculiar linguistic ability that we have—this "mental organ"—must presumably be an **adaptation**, a feature that has been bred into our genes by natural selection operating on hominoid populations in the distant past. That is what recent evolutionary psychologists have argued, though Chomsky himself has expressed skepticism about such evolutionary speculations concerning language. Further research continues at three levels: in linguistics, into more detailed specification of just what is characteristic of human languages; in brain science, how language is processed and how the brain of the infant develops; and in hominid evolution, how our language ability may have evolved.

Speech is not the only human activity, but it is crucially important for all the higher human mental abilities. This opens up the possibility that *other* important determinants of human behavior are not learned from the environment but are innate. Much recent research in psychology has concerned innate mechanisms in perception, an influential paradigm being the work of David Marr on vision. We must reckon with the thought that the evolution of our ancestors may have produced other genetically based "modules" in humans.

Wilson and Sociobiology

Can Darwinian evolution, the biochemical understanding of genes, and the study of innate capacities and behavior patterns be brought together and applied to the study of human nature? The Harvard biologist Edward O. Wilson boldly claimed to do just that in his 1975 book *Sociobiology: The New Synthesis*. He outlined a newly unified approach to biology that would apply the rigorous methods of population biology and genetics to complex social systems. Building on his earlier studies of social insects such as ants, Wilson applied a similar method to other social creatures; and in his final chapter he sketched how it might be extended to humans. Here is the first paragraph of that controversial chapter:

> Let us now consider man in the free spirit of natural history, as though we were zoologists from another planet completing a catalog of social species on Earth. In this macroscopic view the humanities and social sciences shrink to specialized branches of biology; history, biography, and fiction are the protocols of human ethology; and anthropology and sociology together constitute the sociobiology of a single primate species.

Wilson was thus suggesting that the humanities and social sciences should become sub-departments of biology, and that other areas of biology would be absorbed into his envisioned super-science of **sociobiology**. One reason for the vivid controversies that arose was academic turf wars: the various specialists in the humanities and the sciences defending their professional territories against this takeover bid. But the main reason was the boldness of Wilson's claims about human nature. The section headings of his chapter on humans indicate the tremendous range of material that he hoped to bring within his explanatory ambitions: Plasticity of Social Organization; Barter and Reciprocal Altruism; Bonding, Sex, and Division of Labor; Role Playing and Polytheism; Communication; Culture, Ritual, and Religion: Ethics; Esthetics; Territoriality and Tribalism; Early Social Evolution; Later Social Evolution—and even The Future. It seems nothing was to be beyond the bounds of sociobiology!

In his next book, *On Human Nature* (1978), Wilson argued in more detail that the only way toward understanding human nature is to study it as part of the natural sciences. Disarmingly, he said this book was not a work of science but *about* science, "a speculative essay about the profound consequences that will follow as social theory at long last meets that part of the natural sciences most relevant to it." The central chapters are more empirical, however, making claims about innate factors in human aggression, sexuality, altruism, and religion. But the beginning and end of the book are about the alleged "spiritual dilemmas" consequent on the truth of evolution. This biological scientist was turning philosopher or prophet.

Wilson went on to write several other wide-ranging, popular-level, philosophizing books. Clearly he is a man of tireless energy, with an omnivorous intellectual appetite in both the sciences and the arts, an eloquent flow of words, and a certain missionary zeal. In *The Diversity of Life* and *Biophilia* he campaigned to try to stop the human-caused extinction of so many species on this planet that is still continuing apace. In *Naturalist* he gave us his autobiography, including his own account of the controversies over sociobiology. And in *Consilience* (1998) he argued again for the unification of all legitimate knowledge—social sciences and humanities included—under the scientific banner. The unity he envisages sometimes sounds very extreme, namely, the reduction of all other scientific principles to the laws of physics. But in other places he admits that there may be a genuine emergence of new properties irreducible to those of lower levels (philosophical clarity is somewhat lacking). He announces that the Enlightenment belief in the possibility of unlimited human progress is being confirmed by scientific evidence, which suggests an element of naive secular faith and confusion between facts and values underneath the scientific sophistication. Wilson has been a man with a mission: to apply the theories of evolution, population biology, genetics, and neuroscience to *all* aspects of human existence—and perhaps to save the world.

This explains the scientific and moral/political objections that were brought against sociobiology, some of them from Wilson's distinguished colleagues in the Harvard Biology Department, Richard Lewontin and Stephen Jay Gould. There was a strong feeling that in emphasizing the biological factors in human life and apparently neglecting the role of culture, Wilson was giving (presumably unintentional) aid and comfort to reactionary tendencies in American society. If nature is more influential than nurture in forming human individuals and societies, it seemed there would be much less possibility than many social theorists had liked to think of improving individuals and society by education, social programs, and political change. Moralists and politicians of conservative tendency might thus be encouraged to reaffirm the old prejudice that if the differences between individuals, the races, and the sexes are innate there is no point in trying to reduce them. Socialists, antiracists, and feminists therefore responded that the only correct position was that, apart from our bodily physiology and a few general-purpose learning devices, human nature is basically a "blank slate" to be written on by society.

Hot though the controversy was, it looks to have been the last big throw of the antibiological, procultural movement that dominated academic social thought in the middle years of the twentieth century. Careful reading of Wilson's work, particularly his later writings, shows that far from denying the influence of culture, he sees biology and culture as *both* contributing to the development of individuals and of human societies, but his main point remains that our biology *limits the range* of variety of human cultures: as he put it, "genes hold culture on a leash." When the blur of ideological prejudice and journalistic oversimplification has cleared away, it should be obvious that there is no binary choice to be made between nature and nurture, for both are crucial to the formation of each individual. The only sensible question about human behavior is *how much* of it is due to nature and how much to nurture—which is often difficult to answer.

The relevant value judgment is how far we should treat people differently when they manifest different innate abilities.

Chomsky's approach to language remains a paradigm here: the common grammatical form of human languages is due to our biology, hardwired in the brain, whereas the enormous variety of human languages is due to culture. Similarly, the human propensity for athletic sports is universal across cultures, but the popularity of different kinds of games is culturally specific (e.g., baseball in the United States, cricket in England—and if the Mayan ball games involved human sacrifice, that was going a bit beyond sport as we understand it). And the whole business of being a successful parent—from courtship and sexual union, through baby care and childrearing, up to the stage when one's offspring leave home and perhaps become parents in turn—is the most complex of life's challenges, involving both our most deeply biological behaviors and the helps and hazards of the culture we inhabit.

Very roughly, we can see the dialectic of stages of post-Darwinian evolutionary thinking as follows:

Part I: emphasis on biology, on what is in our nature, innate, "in the genes"
Part II: emphasis on culture, on what is due to nurture, education, and society
Part III: recognition that genes and culture, nature and nurture, are both crucial

Away from the oversimplifications of popular thought, the cutting edge of biological theory has now become highly mathematical. This trend started with the statistical treatment of genetics and population biology, and it has proceeded apace. Physicists have long been used to the fact that the only way they can try to explain their highly technical mathematical theories to the public is to talk in metaphors that are easily misunderstood (e.g., space being curved, time starting with a big bang). Biologists now have to get used to a similar situation in their own discipline. In *Genes, Mind and Culture* (1981) Wilson and his physicist collaborator Charles Lumsden offered a mathematical theory of how genes and culture co-evolve, but it was too technical to affect the controversies of the time. Others, like Robert Boyd and Peter Richerson in *Culture and the Evolutionary Process* (1985), have followed up this line of research.

Cosmides and Tooby and the Integrated Causal Model
Because of the controversy that Wilson's program aroused, his term "sociobiology" has fallen out of favor, and "evolutionary psychology" has become the preferred label for most of those who persist in applying a Darwinian

approach to the human mind. In 1992 an influential collection of research papers was published entitled *The Adapted Mind: Evolutionary Psychology and the Generation of Culture*. The first 150 pages or so consist of a densely-argued programmatic statement of the approach favored by Leda Cosmides and John Tooby, backed up by Donald Symons and Jerome Barkow. (The first three were at the University of California at Santa Barbara, so they have been labeled "the Santa Barbara school.")

The basic premise of this school of thought is that there is indeed a universal human nature, but more at the level of evolved *psychological mechanisms* than of specific patterns of behavior. To be sure, there are some bodily movements that are distinctively and universally human, such as walking, talking, and face-to-face sexual intercourse. But culture produces marked variations in most of what we do—it affects what language we use; what we use it to say on all sorts of occasions; what music we sing, play, or listen to; and all that goes before and after copulation (perhaps even the postures of sexual congress itself).

The second main premise is that our evolved psychological mechanisms are adaptations that have been selected for over many generations of our ancestors. It is important here to make a distinction between what is an adaptation and what is merely **adaptive**. Adaptive behavior is what leads to better survival and reproduction in *present* circumstances. For example, going to college is supposed to lead to an economically better life and hence (perhaps?) to more descendants; if so, it is adaptive in present circumstances. But it has obviously not been selected for in the prehistory of hominids (there were no colleges on the primeval African savannah). Conversely, if something is an adaptation that does not imply it is still adaptive now. Possibly a male predisposition to anger and aggression in frustrating circumstances has been selected for (*perhaps!*—it is very controversial), but it does not follow that such a character is conducive to survival and reproduction in present-day societies in which knives and guns are readily available.

A third premise of the Santa Barbara school is that the evolved human mind as we know it contains a number of adaptations to the way of life of our distant ancestors—the hunter–gatherers of the Stone Age, the Pleistocene era over the last 1.7 million years or so (cumbrously labeled "the Environment of Evolutionary Adaptedness"). If that is the case, we should not be surprised if our psychological inheritance is not well adapted to contemporary cultures in the skyscrapers of New York, the suburbs of Glasgow, or the shantytowns of Rio. Cosmides and Tooby assume it is unlikely that there have been any significant changes in the human gene pool since the beginning of agriculture, let alone industrial or postindustrial economies. But other evolutionists have pointed out that they are on very shaky empirical ground there, for example since the spread of dairy farming over only a few thousand years—a short period in evolutionary terms—many (though not all) humans have evolved digestive systems to be able to cope with the lactose in cows' milk. Is it possible that certain aspects of our *psychology* have also evolved in response to major economic/social/cultural developments? The question appears to be interestingly open, and data from the Human Genome Project are said to support the argument for rapid recent evolution of the genes expressed in the human brain.

Cosmides and Tooby give a very thorough exposition and critique of what they call "the standard social science model" of cultural influence which typified the social sciences for most of the twentieth century (see Stage II of this chapter). They argue that because of the intensity of its antiracist and antisexist ideology, this approach has ignored the evidence for many innate evolutionarily produced cognitive mechanisms in the human mind and has mistakenly concentrated on culture as the major influence on each individual. Like Wilson, they propose instead that the biological, the psychological, and the cultural should be seen as interlocking parts of a complex causal web behind human nature:

> The rich complexity of each individual is produced by a cognitive architecture, embodied in a physiological system, which interacts with the social and nonsocial world that surrounds it. Thus humans, like every other natural system, are embedded in the contingencies of a larger principled history, and explaining any particular fact about them requires the joint analysis of all the principles and contingencies involved. To break this seamless matrix of causation—to attempt to dismember the individual into "biological" versus "non-biological" aspects—is to embrace and perpetuate an ancient dualism endemic to the Western cultural tradition: material/spiritual, body/mind, physical/mental, natural/human, animal/human, biological/social, biological/cultural. This dualist view expresses only a pre-modern version of biology, whose intellectual warrant has vanished.

According to this "integrated causal model," behind any human phenomenon—even a single action—there is a complex set of chains of causation, involving

1. natural selection operating on our ancestors over many thousands or millions of years to produce a variety of innate mental modules in the human species

2. the historical development of a variety of human economies and cultures over many centuries

3. the random mixing of genes in sexual reproduction that gives every human being his or her own unique set (except in the case of identical twins)

4. the effects of the physical and social/cultural environment on bodily and mental development over the lifetime of each individual

5. the information processing involved in perception and speech recognition, the results of which ("beliefs") join with motivational factors ("desires") to be the immediate causes of particular actions

The picture is of "a seamless matrix of causation," and the only kind of explanation that is here recognized is scientific, *causal* explanation. But where that leaves our giving of *reasons* for our actions and for our beliefs (touched on in Chapter 7 on Kant) is an issue that remains at the center of philosophy.

All this, according to the Santa Barbara school, makes it very likely that there are a number of innate human **mental modules** produced by the natural selection that operated on our hominid ancestors. And that these modules have to do with matters that were relevant to the reproductive fitness of our ancestors—such as perception, social communication and language use, cooperation and trade, mate selection, pregnancy, and parental care—is no surprise. The human mind has thus been compared to a Swiss army knife, a compendium of specialized tools rather than a single, all-purpose device (which intelligence tests were supposed to measure).

The issues here are empirical, and in many cases open. The role of culture may be dangerously underemphasized in (4). The cultural influence is dynamic, constantly changing, and socially transmitted. As well as mental modules designed by evolution to perform specific tasks, we humans have a flexible kind of general intelligence that enables us to solve new unpredictable problems encountered in experience. Detailed argument and elusive empirical evidence are needed to establish just what our mental modules are, and what selection pressures produced them. It is not sufficient to invent plausible evolutionary speculations, "just-so stories," that say "That is how it must have been back in the Pleistocene when our distant ancestors were evolving, so that is why it is now" (and must evermore be so, as long as our genes don't change). Much empirical work is being done, and evolutionary psychology (in general, not just the Santa Barbara school) promises to enter on the secure path of an empirical science.

Yet a word of caution still seems appropriate, for it is extremely difficult to know how the postulated selective processes may have panned out in the long-vanished Pleistocene era or even in the last ten thousand years. And though today's evolutionary psychologists are committed to putting a good deal of the causation down to culture, their conception of culture might be rejected as inadequate by social anthropologists. The Santa Barbara brand of evolutionary psychology is not the only game in scientific town. There are ongoing research programs in human behavioral ecology and in gene/culture coevolution, outlined by Laland and Brown in *Sense and Nonsense: Evolutionary Perspectives on Human Behaviour.*

EVOLUTIONARY THEORIZING PART IV: WHAT HOPE FOR HUMANITY?

The claim that we humans have evolved from apelike creatures (and indeed share a common biological descent with all other life on earth) is still rejected by some religious believers (Muslim as well as Christian), though most mainstream denominations have accommodated to it. What lies behind this resistance? The general question of what is the attraction of "fundamentalist" forms of religion can hardly be addressed in this book. Probably the maintenance of group identity, in opposition to other forms of culture and social change, has a lot to do with it. What we can review here are some of the intellectual issues around the relation between evolutionary theory, ethics, social hope, and religion.

Tree- or Bush-Shaped Evolution?

"Evolution" is a word with multiple ambiguities. In its most general sense it can refer to any extended process with an identifiable end product: thus, we can talk of the evolution of the solar system, of constitutions and amendments, and of machines such as the automobile. Chemists also talk of substances "evolving" (i.e., emitting) gases. There is often a connotation that evolutionary processes are progressive, in the sense that the latest product is better than those that have gone before. But progress is not involved in the emission of gas; and in political and technical developments the latest version is not always an improvement.

Among Darwinian theorists an interesting distinction can be drawn between those who think the evolution of species is inherently progressive and those who deny it. The evolution of manifold life forms on Earth seems to show some definite progress, for over vast geological time there has been a noticeable increase of the complexity of some animals, especially in brain size and power (the human brain is said to be the most complex object in the universe), although there also are plenty of very ancient primitive forms still around (e.g., the horseshoe crab). And, of course, we humans like to see ourselves as "higher" than all the rest, the culminating stage of the whole complex process.

In the nineteenth century the idea of progress was part of the prevailing climate of thought, and popular philosophers like Herbert Spencer interpreted both biological evolution and human history as leading the whole world onward and upward. Darwin himself sometimes went with this intellectual flow, writing at one point of "man" being "the wonder and glory of the Universe." In the mid-twentieth century the Catholic priest and paleontologist Teilhard de Chardin interpreted the whole process of evolution as guided by God toward a spiritual destiny (and got roundly criticized for it by biologists and some fellow-religionists).

The very word "evolution" tends to suggest progress, but in the *Origin of Species* Darwin preferred the phrase "descent with modification," which does not carry the same connotation. Some Darwinians have questioned whether species change is necessarily progressive: indeed, natural selection does not imply that new forms are *better* as judged by some human criterion, only that they are *better adapted* to the prevailing set of environmental conditions. And a species does not have to be *ideally* adapted to its ecological niche, only well enough adapted to survive and reproduce. Ecosystems can be finely balanced and upset by apparently small changes: notoriously, a plant or animal introduced from another part of the world may flourish better than a native species and may even drive the natives to extinction. If climatic conditions change suddenly, more complex or "higher" species can get wiped out, as apparently happened to the dinosaurs when a large asteroid hit the Earth, and ash and smoke obscured the sunlight. (If we humans mess up our environment sufficiently, we might become extinct too, and insects might inherit the earth.)

The difference between progressive and non-progressive understandings of evolution can be pictured by different shapes of the overall pattern of descent (or "ascent"?) It has usually been presented as like a tall *tree* growing steadily upward, with many diverging branches, but some definitely higher than others, and a topmost twig on which sit—guess who?—human beings. Richard Dawkins and E. O. Wilson are prominent evolutionists who think of it in that way. But Stephen Jay Gould has offered instead the picture of a *bush,* which grows sideways and outward in all directions according to opportunity, with no standard shape and no topmost branch. On this view there was no predetermined necessity about the evolution of mammals, apes, and humans with their impressive brains. If it had not been for that asteroid impact and other contingencies such as dramatic climate changes, the dinosaurs or their reptilian descendants might still reign supreme. We had better admit that there is no necessary connection between the biological story of life on earth and the values that we favor now. This is a lesson we have already encountered many times, that scientific theories do not imply value judgments.

Progress in Human History?

In Chapters 8 and 9 we saw how Kant, Hegel, and Marx developed philosophies of history. Each claimed to discern an overall pattern in human history and made predictions and expressed hopes on that basis.

This historicizing mode of thought was something rather new in Western culture. (It was partially anticipated by the eighteenth-century Italian thinker Giambattista Vico, who had a cyclical theory of history, unlike the linear progressive understanding of the later Enlightenment.)

The Judeo–Christian and Islamic traditions have always offered an interpretation of history in terms of God's creative and redemptive purposes. The Jews still define their identity as a people in terms of events dating back some four millennia—God's deliverance of the people of Israel from their captivity in Egypt and their entrance into the "promised land"—and their prophets interpreted their subsequent vicissitudes in terms of God's will for them. Christianity claims that in the person of Jesus God has entered uniquely into history with universal redemptive effect. Islam recognizes Muhammad as the last of the prophets, who received the final divine revelation. All three religions have maintained a faith in God's "providence" (though sorely tested by events) that the events of history work toward His purpose.

The belief in human progress that is so characteristic of the Enlightenment philosophies of Kant and Hegel, the revolutionary program of Marx, and much humanist social and political thought ever since can be seen as a secular echo of the religious belief in God's providence. These days hope is more often put in our human intelligence, technical ingenuity, education, political sophistication or military prowess, rather than in divine guidance. But if hope in God is fragile in the face of the manifest evils of the world, how much more fragile is hope in human powers? There have been some times and places in which it seemed that things were moving in the right direction, and that there were grounds to hope that most of humanity might be happier in the future. The century of peace in Europe between 1815 and 1914 was one such period; indeed, it was the great high-water mark of belief in secular progress. The descent of the nations into mutual slaughter in the First World War shook that faith, and arguably it has never fully recovered. Perhaps the two decades after the Second World War allowed a briefer period of confidence amongst the victors, but much of the news has turned grimmer since.

Will there be progress in human history? Of course, there can be scientific discoveries and technological innovations, maybe even new sources of energy, if we are lucky. And there *might* be wiser political leadership than much of what we have had; there could develop cultures with higher levels of education, greater tolerance of harmless diversity, and (dare one say it?) deeper spiritual values. But this is only to say that the *potential* is there. Will it be realized? A long view of history does not support any very confident answer.

Theism or Darwinism—or Both?

We still need hope for the future, individually and collectively. Without it we tend toward cynicism, depression, or despair. Presumably this need for hope lies behind the clash between biological science and some fundamentalist forms of religious belief, for how else are we to find meaning and purpose in life?

As we have seen in this chapter, there is overwhelming evidence that human beings have evolved from simpler forms of life. Whether the first life on earth somehow emerged from inanimate matter remains unknown, though it is thought probable by many scientists. Yet some believers still feel constrained to exempt humans from Darwinian evolution, and to insist that we have been specially created by God. (A literal reading of Genesis 1:11–12, 20–25, and 2:19 would suggest the same for every species of plant and animal.) Some Muslims may similarly insist on a literal reading of the accounts of God's creation in the Qur'an.

In recent years it has been argued in some American courtrooms that evolution is "only a theory" and that another theory labelled "special creation" or "intelligent design" is at least equally worthy of belief, and should be given equal time in schools. But that, we suggest, is mixing science with religion, to the detriment of both. Scientific theories, and the evidence for and against them, develop over time. What at one point was only a speculative hypothesis may become so well confirmed by all available evidence that it becomes legitimate to say it is not just a theory but a fact. We do not say it is "only a theory" that the Earth is round, even though people once believed it was flat. The Catholic Church in Galileo's time tried to retain the pre-Copernican cosmology in which the sun was believed to go round the Earth, but we do not now say it is "only a theory" that the Earth revolves around the sun; the papacy has long since changed its mind on that issue and does not see anything in astronomy as a threat to Christian faith. Most mainstream Christian denominations now take a similar attitude to biological evolution.

In fact, ever since Darwin there have been theists who say that the talk of God creating or forming creatures "out of the dust of the ground" does not have to be understood as saying that at some particular time in past history God quite literally got his hands dirty, and miraculously and instantaneously fashioned living things out of dust and mud. Those passages can instead be interpreted as saying that living beings are made of the same matter as the rest of the universe, though combined in distinctive ways, with the emergent properties of nutrition and reproduction. God's creativity can be seen as a continuous process rather than a one-off event. The six "days" of creation do not have to be taken literally:

scientifically-informed theists can say that God's creative activity extends from the Big Bang through stellar evolution, planetary formation, and all the eras of geology, paleontology, and human history down to the present day, and beyond. Thus believers in God can say that evolution by natural selection is *the way* He has brought us into being, the process He always intended to lead up to creatures made in His own image, endowed with consciousness, reason and free will.

We would therefore invite anyone who comes from a religious tradition that teaches its followers to reject the theory of evolution (as applied to human beings) to consider whether what is spiritually valuable in that tradition really requires that rejection. We can address the fear that accepting Darwinian evolution would bring us down to a merely animal level and deny our "higher" nature. Admittedly, there are people around, both in bars and in seminars, who delight in taking a reductionist line that offers a semiplausible way of diagnosing selfish, biologically-based motivations behind whatever people do, thus appearing to deflate all human pretensions to aspire to anything beyond the biological imperatives of survival and reproduction. But rather than reacting to such reductionism by relapsing into antiscientific dogma, *both* kinds of attitudes need to have their intellectual credentials carefully scrutinized.

It is worth noting that Darwin himself, though in no doubt whatsoever that evolution applies to ourselves, did not see this as "reducing" us to a merely animal level. As we saw in Stage I of this chapter, he did not cease to apply ethical and aesthetic standards to human activities, and to make political judgments about society. He himself was agnostic or atheist, but he was never tempted to think that people are *just* like other animals and have no uniquely human abilities and aspirations. A cynic may snort that this was just Darwin's mental hangover as an upper-class English gentleman of the Victorian age who was unwilling to face up to the truly bleak implications of his own theory. And, of course, nothing can be proved by appeal to the authority of one person, however distinguished.

The Biblical talk of men and women as made "in the image of God" and as being given "dominion" over the rest of creation (Genesis 1:27–28) implies some vitally important difference between us and all other animals. But it remains to be elucidated what exactly that is. There has been a tendency among some theists to postulate a particular time in human embryonic growth, and in evolution, when some absolute change takes place. For those who conceive of the soul as a separable substance there is an obvious difficulty in locating a sharp metaphysical break—the coming into existence of a human soul—in those two empirical continua: the evolution of the human species, and the development of the human fetus in the womb. We have important faculties that our hominid ancestors lacked, and similarly for the human adult compared to the fetus; but it does not follow that there must be some definite point in development where the new features first appear. There are plenty of concepts that we now apply (e.g., marriage, crime, war, scientist, novel, symphony) for which we should not expect there to have been some exact point in history when they became applicable for the first time (given the gradual nature of evolution, there will have been no first oak tree or elephant either). These concepts have vague borderlines. We cannot say precisely when concepts such as consciousness, free will, sin, classical music, democracy, or supermodel came into play in the often messy development of human mentality and culture; but that does not prevent us from applying such terms quite determinately in many cases now. A gradual account of the genesis of a human capacity or practice is consistent with saying that it has now become different in kind *and in value* from its predecessors.

The supposed threat to the reality or value of persons from evolution is no greater than that already posed by materialist and determinist accounts of human nature in the seventeenth and eighteenth centuries, before Darwin. Perhaps evolution just makes the issues more vivid. To see how the threat can be seen off without appeal to metaphysical dualism, an Aristotelian approach to personhood can help. If we identify the mind or soul with whatever the brain enables us to do (the "software" of the brain), we are still left with a dualism of attributes. The mental vocabulary figures essentially in the reasons we give for our actions, beliefs, desires, hopes, and fears. Neuron firings, neurotransmitters, and hormones figure in scientific explanations of muscle movements, vocalizations, and other physically described bodily events. These two levels of language are irreducible to each other, for there is no necessity that the same belief or desire, identified in terms of its content (i.e., *what* is believed or desired), is embodied in exactly the same physiological kind of brain state in two individuals or even in the same person at different times. (If there are extraterrestrial beings, they might have some of the same beliefs as us, at least about science and math, but the chemistry of their brains could be very different.)

Since everyone has beliefs, nobody—least of all the biological scientist, who wants to be rationally responsible to the evidence—can opt out of giving reasons for his or her beliefs. The fact that our mental faculties are products of evolution need not threaten the rationality or the truth of (many of) the beliefs that we arrive at by using those faculties. Our reasons for our beliefs (including mathematical theorems and ethical principles) are not undermined by the fact that our mental capacities for forming such reasons and such beliefs have evolved from more primitive levels of mentality by a long process of natural selection.

Ethical Values and Evolution

Darwinian evolution may still seem to threaten a radical challenge to our values. If humans are descended from animals, some may say that we are "nothing more than" apes, and conclude that none of our values have any objective validity. Human life may be seen as *merely* a struggle for survival and reproduction. Fear of this bleak conclusion, this apparent lack of meaning in life, is surely part of what underlies the religious resistance to evolution. There is an understandable worry about the reductionist thesis that any nonbiological reasons offered for human actions—for example, the pursuit of artistic or scientific excellence, charitable giving, or religious vocation—are not the "real" reasons. As we saw in Chapter 10, Freud tended to argue that all human striving is ultimately motivated by hunger and sexual desire; but we also saw how questionable that is. Recent research in biology has shown that "altruistic" behavior in ants and some higher creatures is in proportion to genetic relatedness (thus one might make a sacrifice for a sibling, who shares half our genes, that one would not make for others less closely related to us); but that does not amount to a genetic reduction of all *human* altruism, for it is a fact that we are (sometimes) kind to people we are not related to at all.

Why should our *ethical* values be undermined by evolutionary reflections, any more than our scientific or mathematical or historical beliefs? Why shouldn't we hold that we do have some objective values to guide our lives by—whether we express them in terms of Platonic harmony of soul, Aristotelian flourishing, Kantian respect for persons, Marxist social justice, Judeo–Christian love of God and love of neighbor, Muslim *khalifa*, Confucian benevolence, or Buddhist compassion? Human evolution does not prove that we have no goal external to our biological nature. There are other reasons for doubting the objectivity of ethics, aesthetic judgments or religious claims—such as the notorious absence of consensus on such matters—but the mere fact of human evolution is not one of them.

Some evolutionary explanations of the origin of human ethical beliefs and feelings may make us more aware of their social function and more skeptical of the unreflective deliverances of ethical prejudice or "intuition," including our own. There is nothing new in *that* kind of thought: it has been put before us in Feuerbach's account of religion, Marx's theory of ideology, Nietzsche's genealogy of morals, Freud's account of the development of moral feelings, and Durkheim's sociology of religion. But no one can opt out of valuing some kinds of behavior and character as better than others. No scientific theory, even one as wide-ranging as the Darwinian theory of evolution, can give the guidance for life that religions have traditionally offered. Future human societies may pursue factual knowledge, yet could vary widely in their values: some might promote the dominance of a master race, a powerful nation or a fundamentalist religion, while others may value everyone as an end in himself or herself. That we need more than science as a source of our value judgments is surely a conceptual truth.

In conclusion, we dare to suggest that there is still such a thing as individual choice, even a certain degree of free will. To be sure, our brain states and our hormones can affect our behavior, but it is conversely true that our behavior can affect our brains or hormones—by taking pills, taking exercise, or taking part in meditation or religious practices. We may hope for scientific guidance on how to solve our personal or social problems, but solid scientific knowledge is an elusive commodity, above all on topics as complicated as individual human nature and the variety of human societies. And as we have seen at several junctures in this book, science is applicable to social problems only in conjunction with value judgments, which we must make on some basis other than science. Useful scientific knowledge is welcome when it comes—especially in medicine—but often we have to get on with our lives without it, and even when it comes, it cannot answer all the questions of life.

FOR FURTHER READING

Darwin's classic *The Origin of Species* is reprinted in Pelican classics and in a Mentor paperback (New York: New American Library). The full title of the book is *The Origin of Species by Means of Natural Selection: Or the Preservation of Favored Races in the Struggle of Life*. The geneticist Steve Jones has updated the *Origin* for today in *Almost Like a Whale* (New York: Doubleday, 1999). Darwin's second major book, *The Descent of Man and Selection in Relation to Sex*, is now available with a useful introduction by John Tyler Bonner and Robert M. May (Princeton, NJ: Princeton University Press, 1981). What is in effect the third part of that work has been republished separately as *The Expression of the Emotions in Man and Animals* (Chicago: University of Chicago Press, 1965).

There is an excellent critical discussion of the many sides of Darwin's thought by Tim Lewens in *Darwin* (London: Routledge, 2007) with chapters on mind, ethics, knowledge, politics, and philosophy.

Philip Kitcher, *Living with Darwin: Evolution, Design, and the Future of Faith* (New York: Oxford University Press, 2007).

Philosophical issues about evolutionary psychology are discussed by Anthony O'Hear in *Beyond Evolution: Human Nature and the Limits of Evolutionary Explanation* (Oxford: Oxford University Press, 1997); Janet R. Richards, *Human Nature after Darwin: A Philosophical Introduction* (London: Routledge, 2000); and John Dupre, *Human Nature and the Limits of Science* (Oxford: Oxford University Press, 2001) and *Humans and Other Animals* (Oxford: Oxford University Press, 2002).

In the Very Short Introduction series published by Oxford University Press, there are relevant titles on Darwin, evolution, evolutionary psychology, psychology, and social and cultural anthropology.

Our structuring of the post-Darwinian debates was influenced by Carl N. Degler's book *In Search of Human Nature: The Decline and Revival of Darwinism in American Social Thought* (Oxford: Oxford University Press, 1991).

An insightful brief survey of Darwinian thought and its wider implications is given by the philosopher John Dupre in *Darwin's Legacy: What Evolution Means Today* (Oxford: Oxford University Press, 2003).

Two thought-provoking histories of psychology are George A. Millar and R. Buckout, *Psychology: The Science of Mental Life*, 2nd ed. (New York: Harper & Row, 1973), and L. S. Hearnshaw, *The Shaping of Modern Psychology: An Historical Introduction* (London: Routledge, 1987) which covers the story since ancient times. In *Acts of Meaning* (Cambridge, MA: Harvard University Press, 1990), Jerome Bruner reviews the progress of psychology and recommends "cultural psychology."

Stephen Jay Gould, *The Mismeasure of Man* (New York: W. W. Norton, 1981), provides a detailed critique of biological determinism and intelligence testing.

Edward O. Wilson's ideas are to be found in *Sociobiology: The New Synthesis* (Cambridge, MA: Harvard University Press, 2000), *On Human Nature* (Cambridge, MA: Harvard University Press, 1978), and *Consilience: The Unity of Knowledge* (Boston: Little, Brown, 1998).

Opposition to sociobiology was vigorously expressed by Steven Rose, R. C. Lewontin, and Leon J. Kamin in *Not in Our Genes: Biology, Ideology and Human and Nature* (New York: Penguin, 1984), and the controversy is examined in detail by the sociologist Ullica Segerstrale in *Defenders of the Truth: The Sociobiology Debate* (Oxford: Oxford University Press, 2000). Philosophical critiques include Michael Ruse, *Sociobiology: Sense or Nonsense?* (Dordrecht, The Netherlands: Reidel, 1985), Mary Midgeley, *Beast and Man: The Roots of Human Nature* (London: Methuen, 1980), and Philip Kitcher, *Vaulting Ambition: Sociobiology and the Quest for Human Nature* (Cambridge, MA: MIT Press, 1985). Kitcher's book is technically demanding; he gave a useful précis in *Behavioral and Brain Sciences* 10 (1987): 61–100.

Robert Wright, *The Moral Animal: Evolutionary Psychology and Everyday Life* (New York: Random House 1994), interweaves Darwin's theories, his life, and modern evolutionary psychology. Steven Pinker has readable accounts of evolutionary psychology in *How the Mind Works* (New York: W. W. Norton, 1997) and *The Blank Slate: The Modern Denial of Human Nature* (New York: Viking, 2002). The Santa Barbara school's manifesto is in *The Adapted Mind: Evolutionary Psychology and the Generation of Culture*, ed. J. H. Barkow, L. Cosmides, and J. Tooby (New York: Oxford University Press, 1996).

Textbooks of evolutionary psychology include David M. Buss, *Evolutionary Psychology: The New Science of the Mind* (New York: Pearson, 2011); Louise Barrett, Robin Dunbar, and John Lycett, *Human Evolutionary Psychology* (Princeton, NJ: Princeton University Press, 2002); K. L. Laland and G. R. Brown, *Sense and Nonsense: Evolutionary Perspectives on Human Behaviour* (Oxford: Oxford University Press, 2002); and *The Oxford Handbook of Evolutionary Psychology*, ed. Robin Dunbar and Louise Barrett (Oxford: Oxford University Press, 2007).

Denis Noble, *The Music of Life: Biology beyond the Genome* (Oxford: Oxford University Press, 2006), presents a critique of biochemical reductionism and an elegant defense of "systems biology," in which many levels of causation are recognized.

Roger Scruton's *Intelligent Person's Guide to Philosophy* (London: Duckworth, 1996) is fired by his conviction that "scientific truth has human illusion as its regular by-product, and that philosophy is our surest weapon in the attempt to rescue truth from this predicament." See also Scruton's *Intelligent Person's Guide to Modern Culture* (London: Duckworth, 1998).

Mary E. Clark, retired from a chair in conflict resolution, has written a wide-ranging interdisciplinary book, *In Search of Human Nature* (London: Routledge, 2002), in which she offers hope for the future, despite our manifold problems.

John Cottingham *On the Meaning of Life* (London: Routledge, 2003) is a clear, concise, and balanced discussion that ends up recommending some form of non=doctrinal spiritual practice to develop our responses to objective truth, goodness and beauty, and our faith, hope and love. More recently he has added, to beautiful effect, *How to Believe* (London: Bloomsbury, 2015).

KEY TERMS

adaptation	**genes**
adaptive	**germ plasm**
cultures	**group selection**
dominant gene	**inheritance of acquired**
emergent	**characteristics**
ethology	**intelligence quotient (IQ)**
eugenics	**memes**
fitness	**mental modules**

mutation   **social Darwinism (or Spencerism)**
natural selection   **sociobiology**
recessive gene   **value judgment**

QUESTIONS FOR DISCUSSION

1. Is natural selection the only factor in the evolution of species?
2. Is there any truth at all in social Darwinism ("Spencerism")?
3. Can the concept of culture figure in scientific explanation?
4. Is the concept of mental modules any clearer than that of instincts?
5. Is the fact of evolution any real threat to religious belief and practice?

13

Human Nature and Feminist Theory

In the Western philosophical tradition theories of human nature frequently run aground upon the fact of sexual difference. Feminist historians of philosophy have documented the ways in which sexual difference (and hence women) pose challenges to philosophical theories from Plato to Sartre. The basic difficulty is that so many philosophers have tended, either implicitly or explicitly, to equate human nature with male nature. But then where do women fit in?

Traditionally, this problem receives one of two solutions: either women and men are different kinds of beings with different excellences and possibilities or women are incomplete men, that is to say, imperfect human beings, approximating but not attaining the relevant excellences. Rousseau exemplifies the first approach in his treatise on education: "It being once demonstrated . . . that man and woman are not, nor ought to be, constituted alike in temperament and character, it follows of course that they should not be educated in the same manner" (*Emilius and Sophia*, H. Baldwin 3:5.8, 1783). Aristotle, in contrast, views the female animal as being "like a deformed male" (*Generation of Animals*, 737a27–28). Males and females, men and women, share a single *telos* (or end), which is the full realization of their natural human capacities—but females cannot fully attain that end. Female animals, unlike male animals, "lack the appropriate heat to fully concoct their residues into seed that can convey soul to their offspring." In Aristotle's biology concoction is like cooking, and he thought that only the bodily substances (or residues) that become male semen are fully "cooked." It is not (entirely) clear how Aristotle's biological view of females as "deformed" males relates to his claims in the *Politics* about the failure of women's rational faculty to be "authoritative" (see Chapter 5). But it is clear that, according to Aristotle, women are neither biologically nor politically fully developed; they cannot fully realize what it is to be human. Although they offer different explanations of the situation of women in relation to human nature, both Rousseau and Aristotle think that women's education, place in society, and place in the household are rightly subordinate to those of men. Either women are different from men, and hence not correctly measured by the standard set by male human nature, or they partake of the same human nature as men but never fully achieve it. Given this history, it is reasonable to wonder whether the concept of human nature has anything to offer feminist theory.

However, **humanist feminists** believe that the notion of human nature, although historically unable to accommodate sexual difference (or women) coherently, is nonetheless an indispensable notion for feminists to interpret and to use in their arguments against sexism. Moreover, humanist feminists point out that, like any social or political theory, feminist theory relies (either tacitly or explicitly) on a view of human nature. And, unlike **difference feminists**, who emphasize the ethical and psychological differences between men and women as exemplified and reinforced by the centrality of maternal and care practices in women's ethical lives, humanist feminists believe that there is a core human nature common to women and to men. Where philosophical humanism has gone wrong in the past is in believing either that men and women do not share a single nature or that women can only approximate its achievement.

Historically, one strand of humanist feminism originates in the liberal political thought of Mary Wollstonecraft (1759–1797), a philosopher of the Enlightenment, who argued vehemently in *A Vindication of the Rights of Woman* (1792) against Rousseau's view that men and women have two, complementary human natures. She argued for the rational nature of women despite their inadequate education, socialized interest in appearance, and trivial pursuits like reading romance novels. Wollstonecraft argued for equality in education and political rights for women. "Strengthen the female mind by enlarging it, and there will be an end to blind obedience."(Chapter II, section 21)

A second strand of humanist feminism originates in Simone de Beauvoir's (1908–1986) feminist classic *The Second Sex* (1949), which combines an extensive description of the social meaning of being gendered a woman with an ontology that draws a fundamental distinction between self and other. Beauvoir is often cited as the originator of **social constructionist** views of gender in her detailed account of the social conditioning of girls and women. Social constructionism is the view that gender is a social, rather than a biological, category. In Beauvoir's famous words, "One is not born, but rather becomes, a woman" (p. 301). Beauvoir's ontology of self and other draws on the ideas of Sartre (see Chapter 11) but uses them in an original description of the lived experience of women. For Beauvoir we humans are all intricate combinations of self and other, of subject and object, of agent and patient; but women do not realize their full humanity because of oppressive social structures and because they tend to abdicate their full selfhood, subjectivity, and agency. Beauvoir thought that both marriage and maternity were institutions in which women lose (or relinquish) their freedom and agency by immersing themselves in the needs and demands of others.

Despite their philosophical differences, Wollstonecraft and Beauvoir share the assumption that there is a common human nature and that political and social change is needed in order for women to be able to fully achieve it. For Wollstonecraft, the core of being human is being rational, so her emphasis is on education for women. Beauvoir's emphasis is on human freedom and the social and political changes that would make full subjectivity and freedom a reality for women. Although their views of what is ethically important about being human differ, they agree that realizing women's full human potential requires significant social and political change.

FEMINIST PHILOSOPHY AND FEMINISM

It will be useful to draw a distinction between feminist *philosophy* and feminism as a *political* movement, although in practice there is much interplay between the two. Feminist philosophy or theory refers to writing or arguments that support the equality of women and men or that argue against the oppression of women by men. Surprisingly, one of the earliest philosophical arguments for sexual equality is found in Plato's *Republic* (see Chapter 4). Socrates and his interlocutors discuss the education and roles of men and women of the guardian or ruling class in the ideal state or *polis*. What kind of education and which roles are appropriate for women? Socrates argues that if women are to play the same roles as men, then they must receive the same education (music, gymnastics, and the art of war). But, it is objected, all agree that men and women have different natures, so how can they play the same roles as men? Socrates replies, "Suppose that by way of illustration we were to ask the question whether there is not an opposition in nature between bald men and hairy men; and if this is admitted by us, then, if bald men are cobblers, we should forbid the hairy men to be cobblers, and conversely?" (*Republic*, 454c–d). His point is that the differences must be relevant to the role in question. So simply pointing to differences between men and women does not settle the question of whether or not women can perform the same roles as men and hence require the same rigorous education and may take part in ruling society. Despite its limitations, this argument might well be the first identifiable piece of feminist argument in the Western philosophical tradition.

After Plato, we find sporadic episodes of feminist thinking like the argument for the superiority of women made on Aristotelian grounds by the Renaissance philosopher Lucrezia Marinella (1571–1653). Beginning in the eighteenth century, Enlightenment philosophers like Mary Wollstonecraft argued for the equality of women. In the nineteenth and twentieth centuries philosophers like John Stuart Mill (1806–1873) and Harriet Taylor (1807–1858) developed complex and detailed arguments for the social, political, and legal equality of women and men. The notion of human nature played a key role in all of their arguments, which could be summed up by saying that since the normatively important features of human nature are equally present in women and in men, both are deserving of equal education, equal political rights, and social benefits. As we will see, humanist feminist theory was interwoven with feminism as a political movement in Britain and in the United States.

Modern Western feminism as a political movement grew up nourished by the ideas and ideals of the eighteenth-century Enlightenment and the French Revolution. The appearance of the women's movement in the United States is usually dated to the Seneca Falls Convention of 1848. In the United States feminists were also abolitionists, working to end slavery. Later they worked to get women the vote and were also allied with antiwar and disarmament groups. During the same period British and French suffragettes also pursued the vote for women. The feminist movement of the nineteenth and early twentieth centuries is sometimes called "first-wave" feminism. Second-wave feminism is often dated to the mid-twentieth century and connected to other political liberation movements in the United States and the West like the civil rights movement and the protests against the Vietnam War. Finally, third-wave feminism dates from the 1990s when women of color protested against their exclusion from both the theory and the practice of feminism. In Kimberlé Crenshaw's words, "I am suggesting that Black women can experience discrimination in ways that are both similar to and different from those experienced by white women and Black men" (see "Demarginalizing the Intersection of

Race and Sex: A Black Feminist Critique of Antidiscrimination Doctrine, Feminist Theory and Antiracist Politics," p. 149). Crenshaw and other feminists of color developed the concept of **intersectionality**, to express the idea that our social identities are complex blends of social positions like race, class, and gender and that feminist theories and political actions should reflect that fact.

There is much more to be said about the history of feminism, including the development of feminism in the Middle East, in Africa, and in other parts of the globe. Humanist feminism, however, is a distinctively Western phenomenon both historically and theoretically, so that is our focus here. (For an introduction to feminism theory from a non-Western perspective, see Uma Narayan's *Dislocating Cultures: Identities, Traditions, and Third World Feminism*. For more on women in non-Western philosophy, see Chapters 1–3 and 7 in this volume.)

Feminism as a political movement is directed toward action and political change rather than merely toward ideas and understanding the situation of women. Feminist philosophy, in contrast, seeks to understand the structure of inequality or oppression in order to suggest avenues for change. While feminist philosophy has sometimes directly influenced feminist politics (and vice versa), it is useful to distinguish the two because they have different, though sometimes overlapping, histories and purposes.

CONTEMPORARY HUMANIST FEMINISM

Contemporary humanist feminists argue that men and women share those properties or capacities that are relevant to living a flourishing human life and that they should have equal opportunity to exercise these shared human capacities. Because of their emphasis on equality between men and women, humanist feminists are also sometimes call "sameness" or "equality" feminists. Humanist feminists appeal to the notion of a common human nature, either tacitly or explicitly, in order to ground their demands for equal treatment for women.

In *Justice, Gender and the Family* political philosopher Susan Moller Okin (1946–2004) focused a critical eye on the family and the private realm as the site of serious injustice for women. Okin criticized political philosopher John Rawls's (1921–2002) very influential theory of justice as fairness for reserving the notion of justice for the public realm, which left the family as a sphere in which there could be, in principle, no injustice. Since, Okin argued, the family is one of the most important contexts of inequality and oppression for women, Rawls's account of justice is seriously flawed and limited. Okin clearly had in mind a patriarchal, heteronormative family in which the wife engages in unpaid housework and maternal labor and is under the authority of the husband. Okin thinks that the state should do more than simply increase the voluntariness of women's choices and compensate for whatever disadvantage they incur. She argues in addition that the state should promote an egalitarian ideal of family life. The state should "encourage and facilitate the equal sharing by men and women of paid and unpaid work, or productive and reproductive labor" (p. 171). Okin's emphasis on state intervention to secure the *equality* of men and women in both public and private spheres places her groundbreaking work in political philosophy in the category of feminist humanism.

Martha Nussbaum, drawing on the ideas of Aristotle, has developed the **capabilities approach** toward social justice, which includes equal opportunity for women. The capabilities approach bases the concept of justice on a neo-Aristotelian idea of human flourishing, or living well and doing well. Nussbaum's idea of human flourishing parts ways with Aristotle, however, who thought that the best life for a human being is one of virtuous activity (see Chapter 5). In contrast, Nussbaum proposes a list of ten basic capabilities that just societies should provide their citizens:

1. *Life.* Being able to live to the end of a human life of normal length; not dying prematurely, or before one's life is so reduced as to be not worth living.
2. *Bodily Health.* Being able to have good health, including reproductive health; to be adequately nourished; to have adequate shelter.
3. *Bodily Integrity.* Being able to move freely from place to place; to be secure against violent assault, including sexual assault and domestic violence; having opportunities for sexual satisfaction and for choice in matters of reproduction.
4. *Senses, Imagination, and Thought.* Being able to use the senses, to imagine, think, and to reason and to do these things in a "truly human" way, a way informed and cultivated by an adequate education, including, but by no means limited to, literacy and basic mathematical and scientific training. Being able to use imagination and thought in connection with experiencing and producing works and events of one's own choice, religious, literary, musical, and so forth. Being able to use one's mind in ways protected by guarantees of freedom of expression with respect to both political and artistic speech, and freedom of religious exercise. Being able to have pleasurable experiences and to avoid non-beneficial pain.
5. *Emotions.* Being able to have attachments to things and people outside ourselves; to love those who love and care for us, to grieve at their absence; in general, to love, to grieve, to experience longing, gratitude, and justified anger. Not having one's emotional development blighted by fear and anxiety. (Supporting this capability means

supporting forms of human association that can be shown to be crucial in their development.)

6. *Practical Reason.* Being able to form a conception of the good and to engage in critical reflection about the planning of one's life. (This entails protection for the liberty of conscience and religious observance.)

7. *Affiliation.*

    A. Being able to live with and toward others, to recognize and show concern for other human beings, to engage in various forms of social interaction; to be able to imagine the situation of another. (Protecting this capability means protecting institutions that constitute and nourish such forms of affiliation, and also protecting the freedom of assembly and political speech.)

    B. Having the social bases of self-respect and non-humiliation; being able to be treated as a dignified being whose worth is equal to that of others. This entails provisions of non-discrimination on the basis of race, sex, sexual orientation, ethnicity, caste, religion, national origin.

8. *Other Species.* Being able to live with concern for and in relation to animals, plants, and the world of nature.

9. *Play.* Being able to laugh, to play, to enjoy recreational activities.

10. *Control over One's Environment.*

    A. Political. Being able to participate effectively in political choices that govern one's life; having the right of political participation and protections of free speech and association.

    B. Material. Being able to hold property (both land and movable goods), and having property rights on an equal basis with others; having the right to seek employment on an equal basis with others; having the freedom from unwarranted search and seizure. In work, being able to work as a human being, exercising practical reason and entering into meaningful relationships of mutual recognition with other workers. (*Harvard Human Rights Journal* 20:22–24)

Nussbaum's list provides a rich and complex picture of human nature that encompasses those capabilities that are distinctively human. A just society will support the development of these capabilities in *all* its citizens. And Nussbaum's capabilities pertain to both women and men equally so that the list can be read as, among other things, a call for gender equality as a component of social justice. It is important to note that though societies are required to provide for the development of these central human capabilities, they are not mandated to enforce their activation. (A just society will provide playgrounds, but it will not make a bookish child play on them.)

Nussbaum compiled her list of human capabilities dialectically, in conversation with other philosophers, social theorists, and ordinary people in the United States and abroad. The list remains open to revision as required through dialectical exchange. She argued that the dialectical method allows for inclusion of non-Western views and the claims of excluded groups. Nonetheless, her list is criticized as **essentialist** (by those who deny there is a universal human nature), as Western (by those who think it only recognizes, or favors, Western values), as prejudiced against various groups (for example, disabled people who might not be able to play and hence would be lacking in an essential human capacity), and as androcentric (for example, by not recognizing sufficiently women's capacity for reproduction and the gender-specific needs it entails).

In addition to these specific criticisms of Nussbaum's theory, Louise Antony in "Nature and Norms" (*Ethics* 111, no. 1 [2000]:8–36) develops a systematic critique of the capabilities view of human nature. Antony focuses on Nussbaum's use of philosopher Bernard Williams's (1929–2003) distinction between **internal and external accounts** of human nature, which raises the issue of what *kind* of concept of human nature Nussbaum presupposes. Is our notion of human nature primarily biological or scientific, what Williams and Nussbaum call an external account, referring to the characteristics that are used to demarcate members of the human species like our DNA or a distinctive capacity like speech, the ability to reason, or the ability to use tools? External accounts of human nature do not have any normative content; they may tell us what human beings as a species are like, but they do not tell us how they ought to be.

Or is our notion of human nature intrinsically normative, referring to human characteristics that have ethical significance, like rationality, autonomy, or free will? Internal accounts of human nature record our individual or communal self-understandings and commitments; what we think is descriptively and normatively constitutive of being human. Nussbaum identifies her notion of human nature as internalist. But, according to Antony, that entirely defeats the purpose of appealing to human nature in the first place. "What I want to point out is that the appeal to the audience's own values—the move that made the account internalist rather than externalist—completely obviates the reference to human nature" (p. 23). Once we clarify which sense of human nature Nussbaum uses, we find that it cannot serve as an external justification for normative claims because it just *is* a normative concept of human nature. And, rather than provide a grounding for normative claims, it will not be persuasive to anyone who does not already accept it. After all, there is quite a bit of disagreement over what is valuable about human lives both across cultures and even within a single culture.

We seem to have reached an impasse. There seems to be an unbridgeable gap between human nature understood in biological terms as defining membership in the human species, which is a conception devoid of norms and values, and the normative notion of human nature (for example, as a being with rationality, autonomy, or free will) needed to ground political and ethical argument (see Chapter 12 on Darwinian theories). Although Nussbaum is explicit that her theory is internal and does not rely upon (or need) external grounding, the very notion of a human capability appears to appeal to facts about human nature rather than to make a normative claim about human lives. Human nature is either too little (biological species notion) or too much (ethical notion) to do the job of grounding an ethical theory.

The discussion so far touches on a difficult and complex philosophical question. Does an ethical theory require grounding? Or can we proceed by working with common-sense morality or our shared moral commitments? And, if we do think that some kind of grounding is required, does the grounding have to be external, to come from outside the realm of ethics itself? These are important issues, which we can only touch upon here because a discussion of them would take us far from the topic of humanist feminism.

NEOHUMANIST FEMINISM AND DEHUMANIZATION

Another approach to formulating a normative theory of human nature is to think about its opposite, **dehumanization**. What do we mean when we say that an act or policy is dehumanizing? How do we come to dehumanize others? And does this line of thought about human nature supply a concept that is useful for feminist political and ethical theorizing?

Mari Mikkola thinks it does. In *The Wrong of Injustice: Dehumanization and Its Role in Feminist Philosophy* Mikkola makes the notion of dehumanization the centerpiece of her neohumanist feminism. Unlike Nussbaum, whose notion of human nature relies upon our internal, normative views of what it is to be human, Mikkola uses the external, biological notion of the human species to fix the population under consideration. Where does the normativity in Mikkola's story come from? She suggests that we look at a paradigm case of dehumanization—wartime rape—and develop an account of dehumanization by considering what the fundamental wrong is in the paradigm case. Mikkola proposes a definition of dehumanization "that can be used as a humanist feminist tool when discerning which modes of treating women (*qua* human beings) are inappropriate and why." (p. 164) As a humanist feminist Mikkola focuses on the wrongful treatment of women *qua human beings*, which means that her definition will apply to men as well as women. Indeed, it will apply to members of the human species of any gender (e.g., men, women, genderqueer). From her reflections on the wrongness of rape in wartime Mikkola distilled the following definition of dehumanization: "Dehumanization: An act or treatment is dehumanizing if and only if it is an indefensible setback to some of our legitimate human interests, where this setback constitutes a moral injury" (p. 229). Mikkola uses the notion of dehumanization to explain what is wrong with the "core" forms of injustice: discrimination, domination, and oppression. These forms of social injustice clearly overlap with issues of concern for feminists in both the public and the private realms. For example, consider a society where women are discriminated against and not granted educational opportunities. The exclusion of women is indefensible because it lacks a rational basis, and it is a setback to their legitimate interests. Moreover, this educational discrimination constitutes a moral (and not merely a pragmatic) injury, which means a failure of respect for these individuals' inherent value.

For Mikkola the external, biological notion of the human species sets the boundaries on who falls under the definition of dehumanization; it determines *whose* interests are relevant in considering cases of dehumanization. Recall that according to the terms of the external/internal distinction, the biological notion of the human species does not include any normative or ethical content. Mikkola thinks, however, that biological science *can* tell us more about ourselves than just who the members of the human species are. "Externalism provides the foundation for thinking about the legitimate human interests set back by dehumanizing acts" (p. 164). However, the phrases "legitimate human interests" and "dehumanizing acts" bring considerable normative content to what was supposed to be a non-normative or "thin" description. So, whatever its other attractive features, Mikkola's neohumanist feminism runs the risk of blurring the dichotomy between external and internal descriptions of human nature.

Feminist humanism responds to feminist demands for equality and justice by understanding them as human demands. Okin works within the framework of a theory of justice as fairness to argue for its expansion from the public sphere to the private realm of the family. Nussbaum develops a complex positive view of human nature understood as a bundle of ten capacities that distinguish human life and make it worth living. And, finally, Mikkola works in the reverse direction by analyzing the notion of dehumanization to extract a definition of inhumane treatment, which is treatment that does not respect an individual's legitimate human interests and inherent value. In these theories the notion of human nature, or humanity, plays a central, regulative role.

CRITICAL PERSPECTIVES ON HUMANIST FEMINISM

Humanist feminism remains a controversial theory. In *Justice and the Politics of Difference* Iris Marion Young criticizes humanist feminism from the perspective of difference feminism. Traditional concepts of human nature, according to Young, reflect the values of a politically and economically privileged group, namely white, upper-class men, and in this way assimilate women (and other oppressed groups) to them. For example, the property of being autonomous as distinctive of human nature celebrates the typical experience of many men and ignores their differences from women, who are often deeply embedded in relationships of care. It is a form of cultural imperialism when the "male" standard is used as a basis for ethical reflection and ethical evaluation as if it were a universal. Furthermore, by defining human nature using properties like autonomy or rationality, humanist philosophers cannot recognize fully the diversity of human beings. After all, some people have physical or mental handicaps, and all of us are dependent upon the care of others at some stages of life, especially in childhood or old age. So, in addition to the concern about the gendered character of the property, we might wonder about those human beings (of any gender) who are dependent rather than autonomous or are unable to reason or lacking in one or more perceptual capacity. Are these individuals fully human, or are they lesser exemplars of human nature? Can humanist feminism fully embrace the wide range of differences among human beings?

A more systematic criticism of humanist feminism focuses on the distinction between external and internal descriptions of human nature presupposed by Nussbaum and Mikkola. Recall that this distinction leads to an impasse because the external account of human nature, the biological species concept, provides no normative content or foothold for normative prescriptions. But the internal notion of human nature simply reflects our individual or communal values, what we value in being human. If these values vary among people or cultures, then appeals to internal notions of human nature will cut no ice. Moreover, resting feminist humanism on the distinction between the external perspective on human nature and the internal perspective severs the unity of being human and leaves us with two human natures and no clear way to unite them.

There is another perspective on human nature, however, that avoids the dead end by rejecting the terms of the distinction. Borrowing another idea from Aristotle, it might be fruitful to acknowledge a continuum between biological normativity and the normativity characteristic of the social world. If what is at issue is a distinction *and* a continuity between two types of normativity, then we are not facing a huge gulf between a biological conception of human nature and a merely subjective ethical conception or trying to fudge the difference between the two. Rather, there is a continuum of normativity from the biological world of organs and organisms to the social world of social roles and social agency. Since, as Aristotle tells us, we are political animals essentially, that is, we are animals that live together in societies, feminist theorists ultimately need to focus on social normativity and the ways in which this web of rules and customs disadvantages women and promotes inequality between women and men.

Let's clarify the terms of this proposal. What is biological normativity? Think about the human heart. It has a certain function (to pump blood) in the human body, and that function brings with it a kind of normativity in that it specifies what the heart *ought* to do. Organs have a function within bodies or organisms, and organisms function to maintain themselves and to reproduce. Biological normativity is species-based; it is as a member of the human species that our biological functions are fixed. This kind of functional normativity pervades the biological world at the level of organs and organisms.

Social normativity pertains to the norms and rules (tacit and explicit) governing our social life. The terms "norm" and "normative" are very broad and include everything from what God has ordered us to do to which fork to use for the fish course at dinner to how to sit and everything in between. Although one can think of social norms as rules, and in some cases they are rules, many norms are tacit ways of doing things that are habitual. We can be responsive to a norm without being conscious that we are responding to it. Further, norms are socially established and socially enforced. Hence, social norms are not fixed by species membership alone, and they may vary widely in different cultures and in different historical periods. However, what a norm requires and whether or not an individual has satisfied a norm are not subjective matters; it is not up to the individual social agent to decide.

Let's look at an example. Human reproductive functioning can be considered from at least two perspectives. As a biological function, human reproduction has a normative component. Our organs and parts can function as they should or fail to function as they should; they can succeed, or they can fail. A man's sperm count can be adequate to its function in reproduction or too low. As a socially mediated function, however, human reproduction has a second, thick layer of normativity—social normativity, which is specified in a culture's norms and expectations. Social norms vary from culture to culture and historically. Social recognition by others in the community is an intrinsic ingredient in social normativity (but not in biological normativity) because of the role played by social recognition in the determination of what an individual should do and whether or not an individual has done what he or she should do. Should a mother have a cesarean section? Should a mother breastfeed her children? Should a father share the childcare? The answers to these questions depend upon the culture and time period. In the 1950s in middle-class America the answer to the breastfeeding question was "no." Today it is the reverse.

Rather than divide human nature into two irreconcilable halves, the biological and the normative, the neo-Aristotelian understands human nature as a unity comprising both; we are naturally social beings. The neo-Aristotelian perspective allows us to understand human agency as always embedded in a web of social relations and social normativity, and in this way it is responsive to the feminist insight that we humans are interdependent beings rather than the autonomous individuals presupposed by some versions of humanism including some humanist feminisms. Although there is a continuum of normativity from the biological, functional level to the elaborately normed social world, there are any number of possible social worlds, including ones in which women are equal to men and are no longer under the yoke of oppressive social relations.

CONCLUDING THOUGHTS ON HUMAN NATURE AND FEMINIST THEORY

As we have seen, some of the most powerful feminist theories and arguments, both in the history of philosophy and in contemporary thought, take the form of humanism and rely upon a concept of human nature. In a nutshell, feminist humanists argue that what is wrong with the inequality of women and men (or the oppression of women by men) is precisely what is wrong when any human being is treated unjustly, oppressed, or dehumanized. Humanist feminism has a universal appeal in that it appeals to our shared humanity in order to argue for equality between the sexes or to explain the wrongs of sexism. We have also considered several criticisms of humanist feminism throughout the chapter, and we invite the reader to weigh these strengths and weaknesses and then to evaluate humanist feminism as a response to sexual inequality and the oppression of women.

FOR FURTHER READING

For a discussion of feminist work on the history of philosophy, see The Stanford Encyclopedia of Philosophy entry "Feminist History of Philosophy," http://plato .stanford.edu/archives/spr2016/entries/feminism-femhist/.

Here are two suggestions for those wanting to know more about the history of feminism and the wide range of theoretical perspectives that fit under the umbrella of feminist theory: Margaret Walters, *Feminism: A Very Short Introduction* (Oxford: Oxford University Press, 2006), is a useful historical introduction to feminism as a political movement with a focus on England, although some attention is paid to the history of global feminism.

For a good introduction to feminist philosophy that emphasizes the multiplicity of feminist theoretical perspectives, we recommend *Theorizing Feminisms*, ed. Elizabeth Hackett and Sally Haslanger (Oxford: Oxford University Press, 2005).

Theorizing Feminisms contains several articles relevant to humanist feminism. We recommend particularly Iris M. Young, "Humanism, Gynocentrism, and Feminist Politics," which articulates important criticisms of humanist feminists (including Beauvoir) from the difference perspective.

For more on the critique of humanist feminism as not including women of color and a detailed case for the notion of intersectionality, see Kimberlé Crenshaw, "Demarginalizing the Intersection of Race and Sex: A Black Feminist Critique of Antidiscrimination Doctrine, Feminist Theory and Antiracist Politics," *University of Chicago Legal Forum* 140 (1989): 139–67.

In *Justice, Gender and the Family* (New York: Basic Books, 1989) Susan Moller Okin makes the case for expanding the sphere of justice to the family and familial relations. She argues for an egalitarian notion of the family.

Martha Nussbaum is a prolific writer with many articles relevant to the topic of this chapter. Here are a few suggestions for further reading: "Human Nature and the Foundations of Ethics," in *World, Mind and Ethics: Essays on the Ethical Philosophy of Bernard Williams*, ed. J. E. J. Altham and Ross Harrison (Cambridge University Press, 1995). This article discusses Williams's distinction between external and internal notions of human nature and Nussbaum's response to it. More on the capabilities view of human nature and its relation to social justice and feminism can be found in "Capabilities and Social Justice," *International Studies Review* 4, no. 2 (2002): 123–35. "Human Functioning and Social Justice: In Defense of Aristotelian Essentialism," *Political Theory* 20 (1992): 202–46, contains Nussbaum's response to the criticisms that the capabilities approach is essentialist, Western, prejudiced against various groups and androcentric. Finally, Nussbaum criticizes Rousseau's "difference" approach to human nature in "Human Capabilities, Female Human Beings" in *Women, Culture and Development*, ed. Martha C. Nussbaum and Jonathan Glover (Oxford: Clarendon, 1995, 64–104).

Louise Antony's criticism of Nussbaum is in "Nature and Norms," *Ethics* 111, no. 1 (2000): 8–36.

Mari Mikkola presents her theory of neohumanist feminism in *The Wrong of Injustice: Dehumanization and Its Role in Feminist Theory* (New York: Oxford University Press, 2016). Chapter 6.2 contains a response to the criticisms of difference feminists like Iris Marion Young.

For more reading on the notion of dehumanization, see David Livingstone Smith, *Less than Human: Why We Demean, Enslave and Exterminate Others* (New York: St. Martin's Press, 2011).

Justice and the Politics of Difference (Princeton University Press, 1990) by Iris Marion Young is a good source for learning more about the connection between difference feminism and intersectionality in thinking about justice.

In Chapter 2 of Charlotte Witt's *The Metaphysics of Gender* (New York: Oxford University Press, 2011) there is a discussion of social normativity and its centrality for understanding the gendered lives that we live.

A good place to start thinking about feminism, including humanist feminism, outside of the Western context is Uma Narayan's *Dislocating Cultures: Identities, Traditions, and Third World Feminism* (New York and London: Routledge, 1997).

KEY TERMS

capabilities approach   **humanist feminism**
dehumanization   **internal and external accounts**
difference feminism   **intersectionality**
essentialism   **social constructionism**

QUESTIONS FOR DISCUSSION

1. Humanist feminists argue that men and women are the same in all (or most) important respects and therefore should receive equal treatment and have equal opportunities. Difference feminists point to women's social role as caregivers and maternity as underlying a different (and some think superior) ethical orientation, one based on connection and care rather than autonomy and individualism. Do you think that one of these feminist orientations to ethics is right? Is it possible to combine insights from each of them?

2. Martha Nussbaum proposes a list of ten specific capabilities that, together, make up a good human life. Has she left anything out? Could a good human life lack any of the capabilities? What is the strongest criticism of her theory, and what is its greatest strength?

3. How well does the idea of dehumanization fit with the kinds of unequal and oppressive treatment of women that feminism addresses? Is unequal pay dehumanizing? Is doing unpaid work in the home dehumanizing? Is sexual assault or rape dehumanizing?

4. What can our biology tell us about how we ought to live?

GLOSSARY

absurd: for Sartre, human actions, projects, or ways of life are "absurd" in the sense that there is no objective rational foundation or purpose for them, only whatever the person chooses.

adaptation: a trait of an organism is an adaptation if it is present now because it has aided the survival and reproduction of the organism's ancestors in their environment in the past.

adaptive: a trait of an organism is adaptive if it aids survival and reproduction in the present environment.

agape (in the New Testament): divine (or divinely inspired) love.

ahamkara (in Hinduism): "ego," the (false) autonomous self.

alienation (in Hegel and Marx): being estranged from one's fellows, from one's work, from oneself, from how one could be or ought to be.

analytic statement: a statement that is necessarily true because of the laws of logic and the meanings of its terms.

anatma (in Buddhism): "no self," the recognition that there is no permanent autonomous self.

anguish (in Sartre): the full conscious awareness of one's own freedom, that nothing determines one to choose or act in any particular way.

anitya (in Buddhism): "impermanence," the understanding that all things are subject to change.

a posteriori: knowable only by appeal to experience.

appearances (in Kant): the way things appear to us in perception (and in introspection).

appetite (in Plato): the part of the soul that has desires.

a priori: knowable without appeal to experience.

Aristotelian realism: the theory that when a general term is correctly applied to many different things, that is because they share a common property or nature, which exists in each of them.

atman (in Hinduism): the true self that is nondifferent from the unified reality of *brahman*.

atonement: reconciliation ("at-one-ment") between people or between God and humanity, usually achieved by some sort of reparation or sacrifice.

authentic (in Heidegger and Sartre): an action, project, or way of life that is chosen with full conscious awareness of one's own freedom.

bad faith (in Sartre): the refusal to acknowledge, even to oneself, the real nature of the feelings and intentions one is harboring or the choices one is making.

behaviorism: the program for scientific psychology that aimed to describe and explain animal and human behavior without appeal to mental entities.

Being (in Heidegger): the ultimate but inexpressible reality behind or within everything.

being-for-itself (*être-pour-soi* in Sartre): consciousness or conscious beings.

being-in-itself (*être-en-soi* in Sartre): inanimate, nonconscious reality.

bourgeois: the middle classes in industrialized society, who have some specialized skills and who own some property not amounting to capital.

brahman (in Hinduism): the ultimate unified reality.

Buddha: "the Awakened One," the paradigmatic figure for Buddhist traditions who discovered the spiritual path to freedom and established an ideal pattern for life.

capabilities approach: the identification of a range of basic capacities that we have as human beings, hence measuring the justice of a society in terms of how well it supports these basic human capacities, for example, life, bodily health and integrity, emotions, and practical reasoning.

capital: accumulated private wealth which can be used for further investment, production, and generating profits.

capitalism: the economic system in which the investment of privately owned capital is the dominant form of production.

categorical imperative (in Kant): a moral principle that requires the performance (or omission) of a certain action, whatever one's own desires or preferences may be.

Classics (in Confucianism): a collection of six ancient texts that express the Way of the sages.

closed system: a worldview defended by (a) not allowing any evidence to count against it and (b) answering criticism by analyzing the motivations of the critic in terms of the theory itself.

communism: the economic system of common (social or state) ownership of all the major means of economic production.

compatibilism: the theory that free will is consistent with determinism since a free choice or action can be understood as one that is caused by the person's own relevant beliefs and desires.

cosmological: to do with the world as a whole; for Kant, the cosmological argument for the existence of God has as the premise simply that the world exists.

covenant: a quasi-legal agreement between a powerful conqueror and a subject state or between God and his chosen people.

critique (in Kant): the systematic application of philosophical reason to any area of inquiry, to elucidate its fundamental principles and their epistemological status.

cultures: an inevitably vague term used to distinguish the patterns of life in different societies or different periods; most clearly applicable in anthropology to monolithic societies with little internal differentiation, little change over time, and little or no interaction with others.

death instinct (in Freud): the supposed drive underlying aggression, war, and self-destruction.

Decree of Heaven (*t'ien ming* in Confucius): a heavenly moral mandate everyone is to follow; heaven is understood to be the author of virtue.

defense mechanism (in Freud): an unconscious mental process by which unpleasant ideas and realities are hidden from the conscious mind.

dehumanization: treating another human being as an object, as not fully human (as an animal), or as not respecting his or her moral value.

deism: the view that God created the world but does not intervene in it thereafter.

deontology: the view that duty is the most fundamental concept in moral philosophy.

dependent origination (in Buddhism): the teaching that everything is dependent on something else since there is no autonomous core to anything, everything is interrelated.

destiny (in Confucianism): an aspect of heaven's design that determines one's place in life.

determinism: the theory that every event that happens is caused, and necessitated, by the preceding states of affairs.

dharma: Buddhist teachings, ultimate reality for some Mahayanist Buddhists.

difference feminism: difference feminists emphasize the contrast between the lived experience and ethical lives of women and men and reject the idea of a single human nature as an adequate basis for ethics. They sometimes suggest that relationships of care should form the ethical core of our lives rather than autonomous agency.

dominant gene: when two types of gene (a dominant G, and a recessive g) combine, there are four possible combinations GG, Gg, gG, and gg; only in the case gg will the recessive gene g be expressed in the resulting organism.

dualism: the theory that persons consist of bodies and minds (or souls), with the soul understood as a nonmaterial thing (a substance) that can separate from the body at death.

dualism of attribute: the theory that persons are single, non-composite subjects of two different kinds of properties—physical and mental.

dukkha (in Buddhism): the human condition of "unsatisfactoriness," one of the marks of human existence, and the first of the Four Noble Truths.

ego (in Freud): the conscious mind, that level of mental functioning which includes conscious beliefs, desires, and emotions and makes decisions.

Eightfold Path (in Buddhism): the "Middle Way" between the ordinary pursuit of pleasure and extreme asceticism and articulated as the eight practices that lead to nirvana.

emergent: a property of a whole that cannot be deduced from the properties of its parts.

empirical realism: Kant's label for the view that material objects and the entities of scientific theory exist independently of human perception and thought.

empirical statement: a statement that can be known or justified by investigation of the relevant facts by perception through our human senses, directly or indirectly.

empiricism: the view that all our knowledge (apart from analytic truths) has to be derived from perceptual experience.

emptiness (in Buddhism): means specifically empty of "own being," it is another way of expressing the radically interconnected nature of everything.

Enlightenment: the intellectual movement centered in eighteenth-century Europe (and North America) that proposed to apply reason to all questions, especially about human affairs.

Epicureanism: the view (attributed to the ancient Greek philosopher Epicurus) that the highest good in life is happiness and that virtue is a means to happiness.

epiphenomenalism: the theory that mental events are caused by brain events but do not cause anything material.

epistemology: the theory of knowledge, a systemization of what sorts of thing we can know and how we can know them.

eschatology: to do with the end of the world and God's last judgment.

essentialism: in the context of humanist feminism, essentialism refers to the idea that there is a property or properties common to all human beings (e.g., autonomy or rationality).

ethology: the study of animal behavior in the wild, with special interest in innate patterns of behavior.

eugenics: a program to improve the gene pool of a society by selective breeding of those individuals designated as "better" (positive eugenics) or by discouraging or preventing breeding by those designated as "inferior" (negative eugenics).

excellence (*arete* in Aristotle): whatever makes something of any kind a good example of its kind.

existential psychoanalysis (in Sartre): the method of interpreting the meanings of a person's actions, projects, and way of life in terms of his or her most fundamental beliefs and values.

existentialism: the style of philosophy that puts the emphasis on human individuals, the meaning of their lives, and their freedom to choose.

facticity (in Sartre): all the facts about a person and his or her social situation that limit the expression of freedom.

faith: belief or trust that goes beyond rational argument or evidence.

falsifiability: a falsifiable statement or theory is open to test by investigation of the relevant facts involving perception and might thus be disproved; falsifiability is generally recognized as a necessary condition for being a scientific theory.

filial piety: respect for elders.

fiqh: the body of case law produced by Muslim jurists through the application of sharia to real-life situations.

fitness (in biology): the overall adaptation of an organism for survival and re-production in its environment, hence the phrase "survival of the fittest" in natural selection.

fitra: The "inner nature" of the human being that inclines the heart toward God.

flesh (in the New Testament): our worldly, unspiritual, unredeemed nature.

forgiveness: ceasing to resent a wrong and accepting reconciliation.

forms (in Plato): the ultimate, eternal realities that exist beyond the world of perceptible, changing material things, setting the standards for truth, good-ness, and beauty.

Four Causes (in Aristotle): the material, formal, efficient, and "final" (i.e., pur-posive) accounts or explanations of anything.

Four Noble Truths: the core Buddhist teachings that provide a diagnosis of the human condition, identify its cause, give expression to the goal of freedom, and lay out a pathway of achieving this end.

free association (in Freud): a therapeutic method that encourages the patient to say whatever comes into his or her mind, however disconnected, absurd, or embarrassing, especially in response to dreams.

genes: first postulated as theoretically distinct, indivisible factors responsible for passing on traits from one generation to another; later identified biochemically as "words" in the four-letter "alphabet" of bases within molecules of DNA.

gentleman (*junzi*): exemplary moral person, the Confucian ideal of human perfection.

germ plasm: the parts of the reproductive system of an organism that carry information into its offspring.

grace (in theology): what God freely gives to us, whether deserved or not.

group selection: the hypothesis that natural selection can operate on sets or groups of organisms, as well as individuals.

guardians (in Plato): the philosophically educated ruling class in the ideal republic.

hadith: a large body of originally oral traditions that purport to preserve the memory of things that the Prophet Muhammad, his wives, his companions, and other prophetic figures (e.g., Jesus) said or did.

happiness (*eudaimonia* in Aristotle): the ultimate purpose of human life at which we all aim.

hermeneutic: interpretation of the meanings of a text or the speech and actions of a person.

humanist feminism: humanist feminists believe in essentialism, holding that there is a morally significant property or properties common to all human beings; so because of their common human nature, women and men should be treated equally and have equal opportunities.

hypothetical imperative (in Kant): a rational reason for performing an action because it is seen as likely to satisfy one's own desires or preferences.

id (in Freud): the part of the mind that is totally unconscious, containing the instinctual drives and repressed material.

ideology: the beliefs and values by which a society or community lives or claims to live.

incarnation: the theological dogma that Jesus was both human and divine, the eternal Word of God made flesh.

inheritance of acquired characteristics: the hypothesis that traits an individual animal has acquired during its lifetime can be passed on to its offspring, not by teaching but through heredity (i.e., in its genes).

in-itself-for-itself (in Sartre): the impossible ideal of being like God is supposed to be, that is, conscious and rational yet not burdened by the necessity to make choices.

instincts: the biologically innate dispositions or drives that move a human or other animal to certain characteristic forms of behavior.

intelligence quotient (IQ): the postulated but much disputed numerical measure of overall intelligence.

intelligible character (in Kant): our beliefs, desires, and feelings that form the reasons for our actions.

intentionality: the fundamental feature of human mental states, identified by Brentano and elaborated on by Husserl, that they are about something, that is, directed ("intended") toward some object or state of affairs.

internal and external reasons: internal reasons for action are connected to an individual's existing set of desires or values and are directly motivating only for people with those desires or values; external reasons, such as those based on a biological account of the human species, are not directly motivating but have universal reach and might be able to convince others.

intersectionality: the view developed by black feminists that feminist theories and policies ought to recognize that our social identities consist of the intersection of multiple identities, gender, race, social class, etc.

intuition (*Anschauung* in Kant): primarily perception through the sense organs (outer sense) but also including introspective awareness of one's own mental states (inner sense).

jiva (in Hinduism): the "individual soul" that is both continuous with and differentiated from *brahman*.

justice (*dikaiosune* in Plato): the ideal harmonious working together of the three parts of the soul and the three classes in society.

justification (in theology): being made acceptable or right in the sight of God.

karma: conditioned volitional action.

khalifa: the unique role assigned by God to humanity at creation (i.e., that of being God's deputy or representative on earth).

latent content (in Freud): the unconscious truth behind a conscious idea, especially a dream.

laws of nature: completely general truths about how the universe works, with no exceptions (unless, controversially, in miracles).

libido (in Freud): the energy of the sexual drive or instinct.

manifest content (in Freud): the conscious description or meaning of any idea, especially dreams.

materialism: the view that there is no incorporeal, nonphysical mind or soul and that all our mental states are embodied in our brains and nervous systems.

materialist theory of history: the view that economic facts about the means of production are the basic explanation of social structure and the causes of social change.

maxim (in Kant): a general principle (good, bad, or indifferent) that is someone's rationale for an action.

maya (in Hinduism): that power by which the undifferentiated becomes differentiated; can be translated as either "illusion" or "creative force" depending on the philosophical context.

memes: supposed units of mentality or culture, postulated to try to explain cultural changes on the analogy of genes.

mental modules: subsystems within the mind that are directed to specific tasks (e.g., visual recognition of individual human faces); usually understood as adaptations (i.e., products of evolution).

metaphysics: a metaphysical statement or theory makes some very general and fundamental claim about the nature of everything that exists, going beyond scientific evidence.

moksha (in Hinduism): freedom or liberation from conditioned existence.

mutations: changes in genes, usually understood as "random" in the sense that they have nonbiological causes (e.g., radiation), though they may have biological effects.

mysticism: direct personal awareness of God.

natural selection: the mechanism of species change identified by Darwin, in which those individuals that are fittest for survival and reproduction in their environment are most likely to have offspring that will tend to have the same traits.

naturalism: the view that all questions, or at least all factual questions, can be answered by the methods of science.

naturalistic fallacy: a confusion between empirical statements and value judgments.

nirvana (in Buddhism): freedom from dissatisfactory conditioned existence.

niyah: in Islamic legal and ethical thought, *niyah* ("intention") is a significant factor in determining the legal or moral quality of an individual's actions.

nominalism: the view that when a general term is applied to many different things, what they have in common is only some approximate similarities.

nothingness (or non-being) (in Sartre): a fact or state of affairs that consists in the absence of something and is expressed in a true negative proposition.

Oedipus complex (in Freud): the theory that little boys at a certain stage feel sexual desire for their mother and rivalry with their father.

ontological: to do with existence; for Kant the ontological argument for the existence of God starts from the mere concept of God.

original project (in Sartre): the supposed single, fundamental project or aim that lies behind the whole of someone's life, at least for a period.

pantheism: the view that God can be identified with the whole universe.

person: a being with some degree of rationality, free will and moral responsibility.

perversion: the diversion of an instinct, usually sexual, to an object different from its standard biological object.

physico-theological argument: for Kant this form of argument for the existence of God appeals to the premise that there appears to be (nonhuman) design in the world; it is more generally called the argument from design.

Platonic realism: the theory that when a general term is correctly applied to many different things, that is because they participate in a separately existing eternal form.

postmodernism: a view according to which no cultural tradition or ideology can have any more rational justification than any other and that there are no general truths about human nature.

preconscious: a mental state or idea that can readily become conscious, when it is relevant.

prereflective (in Sartre): the common kind of consciousness in which one is not thinking explicitly of what one is doing and why, though one can say so if asked.

profit (in Confucianism): pursuit of selfish gains, the opposite of moral righteousness.

proletariat: the class of workers in industrialized society who have to subsist by selling their labor.

psychoanalysis (theory): the theory that many mental states (called "mental" because of their influence on feelings and behavior) are unconscious; that is, they cannot become conscious unless in certain special conditions.

psychoanalysis (therapy): the method of treating neurotic problems by interpreting what unconscious mental states are causing them and offering these interpretations to the patient in the hope that he or she can acknowledge them and regain some conscious control.

pure reflection (in Sartre): explicitly, honestly asking oneself what one is doing and why, thus avoiding "bad faith."

Qur'an: literally, "something that is recited"; according to Islamic tradition, the collection of prophetic declamations transmitted to the Prophet Muhammad through the angel Gabriel over a period of about twenty years.

rationalism: the view that we can have some substantial (nonanalytic) knowledge of the world that is not empirical (a posteriori) but derived from reason alone.

rational theology: part of theology that claims to prove things about God by reason alone.

reason (in Plato): the part of the soul that discerns the forms of Truth and Goodness; (in Aristotle and Kant): our faculty for judging the truth of propositions and the wisdom and ethics of actions; (*Vernunft*, a more specialized sense in Kant): our faculty for systematizing our knowledge in science and more generally engaging in any kind of rational inquiry.

recessive gene: when two types of gene (a dominant G, and a recessive g) combine, there are four possible combinations GG, Gg, gG, and gg; only in the case gg will the recessive gene g be expressed in the resulting organism.

redemption: saving from sin and its consequences.

reductionism: any theory that tries to define or explain one level of reality in terms of a lower one, especially the mental in terms of the bodily.

reflective: the introspective kind of consciousness in which one thinks about one's own mental states.

Reformation: the religious movement in sixteenth- and seventeenth-century Europe in which new Protestant churches split off from Catholicism.

regression: going back to an earlier, less mature state of mental development.

relativism: a view that no cultural belief or practice can have any more rational justification than any other.

ren: benevolence or humaneness, the zenith of human excellence for Confucius.

Renaissance: in the fourteenth to sixteenth centuries in Europe, the revival of philosophy, literature, and art under the renewed influence of the classics of ancient Greece and Rome.

renunciation: a religious move involving the abandonment of ordinary domestic life to pursue some transcendent aim, often involving a negative view of the world.

repression (in Freud): the mental process by which an unpleasant idea is pushed into the unconscious level of the mind and kept there.

resistance (in Freud): the process in which, motivated by an unconscious mental state, a person shows unwillingness to accept a new idea, especially an interpretation offered by his or her psychoanalyst.

resurrection (in the New Testament): life after death in a new spiritual body that is not subject to death.

revealed theology: theological claims accepted on the basis of putative divine revelation, in the Bible, the church, or the Qu'ran.

rites (*li* in Confucianism): correct behavior, ceremonial propriety, moral actions exemplified by the sages.

sages: the paradigmatic figures within Confucianism who establish the ideal pattern for human life.

salvation: a regeneration of individual people made possible by the mercy, forgiveness, and love of God, whether in this life or in life after death.

sensibility (*Sinnlichkeit* in Kant): the capacity to receive sense impressions in perception.

sharia: literally, "the path to the water (of life)"; the ideal of a life lived according to prophetic example.

Shi'a: one of the two main branches of the Islamic tradition; the Shi'a represent the smaller branch (roughly 20% of the Islamic community), distinguished from the larger branch (the Sunnis) by their belief that leadership of the umma rightfully belongs to individuals directly descended from the family of the Prophet Muhammad.

sin: doing wrong and being wrong in the sight of God.

skandhas (in Buddhism): the five "aggregates" or "components" that make up a person.

social constructionism: social constructionism about gender is the idea that gender is a social, rather than a biological, category; in general, social constructionism about category X is the idea that X is a socially defined category rather than a natural category.

social Darwinism: a view that the theory of natural selection can and should be applied in social and political programs.

sociobiology: the proposed program for synthesizing biology and the social sciences.

soul (in Plato and Descartes): a nonmaterial, imperceptible substance that persists through time carrying personal identity so that a person can continue to exist after death; (in Aristotle): the principle of life in any living thing— plant, animal, or human.

spirit (in Plato): the part of the soul that feels emotions; (in the New Testament): our spiritual redeemed nature; (*Geist* in Hegel): the mental or spiritual principle behind the whole of human history, gradually realized in successive stages of historical progress.

spirit of seriousness (in Sartre): the "bad faith" of assuming that the values one espouses and the projects one is engaged in are given as objective values by one's society or social situation, rather than one's own choice.

Stoicism: the view (stemming from the ancient Greek Stoic philosophers) that the highest good in life is to be virtuous rather than happy.

study: within Confucianism this means studying the classics.

sublimation (in Freud): the process by which the power of a "lower" instinct or drive, usually sex, is diverted into some "higher" activity, such as art or religion.

Sufism: Muslim pietism; the vast majority of Muslim pietists are drawn from the Sunni branch of Islam; as pietists, they seek to cultivate an intimate relation to the divine through ascetic practices; they are also notable for their poets and musicians and for engaging in esoteric speculation.

Sunnis: the larger of the two main branches of the Islamic community (roughly 80%), distinguished from the smaller branch (the Shi'a) by their belief that leadership of the Islamic community rightfully belongs to individuals designated by the general consent of the umma (without regard to descent from Muhammad's family).

superego (in Freud): the part of the mind that sets the morals or ideal standards of the person.

superman (in Nietzsche): the envisioned future person who will consciously embrace and live out his or her own values, rather than what society has suggested.

suppression: the conscious decision or process of *not* expressing or satisfying a desire.

synthetic statement: any statement that is not analytic.

tawhid: the Islamic understanding of monotheism posits a strict ontological distinction between the divine Creator and the creation; certain schools of Sufism, however, complicate this dogma.

teleology: the theory and study of purposes in the world (other than human intentions).

things in themselves: the way things really are, independently of human perception and thought.

transcendental idealism: Kant's view that we cannot know things as they are in themselves.

transference (in Freud): a stage in psychoanalytic therapy when the patient transfers emotions he or she has previously felt onto the therapist, typically either love or hate.

umma: the worldwide community composed of those who "bear witness" to the Islamic understanding of monotheism (*tawhid*) and the prophethood of Muhammad.

unconscious (in Freud): the level of the mind that contains all those drives, emotions, memories, and ideas that cannot, except in special circumstances, become available to the person's conscious awareness.

understanding (*Verstand* in Kant): our faculty for applying concepts and making judgments.

utilitarianism: the moral theory that what makes an action good or bad is its consequences for pain and pleasure, happiness or unhappiness.

value judgment: a statement or judgment about how things ought (or ought not) to be, rather than a factual assertion about what is actually the case.

Vinaya: Buddhist monastic discipline defined by a number of rules.

Way (Dao in Confucianism): the path of proper conduct set by heaven.

Index